Malthus's *Essay on Population* was seen in 1798 as a complete refutation of Godwin and all 'Jacobin' ideology. It proved that a state of equality and justice for all was unfeasible; and it demonstrated the inevitability and beneficence of private property and political institutions. But its central theme, the dominance of scarcity in human affairs, presented the theological 'problem of evil' in novel and threatening form.

For thirty-five years both the economics and the theology of the *Essay* were modified and refined: first by Paley, Sumner and Malthus himself, and later by Copleston, Whately and Chalmers. The result was 'Christian Political Economy': an ideological alliance of political economy and Christian theology, congenial to a new 'liberal-conservatism' in the early nineteenth century, which found middle ground between the ultra-tory defence of the *ancien régime* and a 'radical' repudiation of existing institutions. Thanks to Whately's demarcation of 'scientific' from 'theological' knowledge, Christian Political Economy was able to beat off the Benthamite challenge of 'Philosophic Radicalism' and to remain ideologically dominant for most of the nineteenth century. As an unintended outcome of all this ideological polemic, there emerged certain ideas now recognized as fundamental to economic science. Professor Waterman analyses this story of the 'intellectual repulse of revolution', and describes the ideological alliance of political economy and Christian theology after 1798. In doing so, he supplies the missing piece of the jigsaw puzzle of English intellectual history, and offers the first clear analysis of the axial period between the 1790s and 1832.

REVOLUTION, ECONOMICS AND RELIGION

REVOLUTION, ECONOMICS AND RELIGION

Christian Political Economy, 1798–1833

A. M. C. WATERMAN

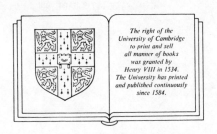

CAMBRIDGE UNIVERSITY PRESS

Cambridge
New York   Port Chester
Melbourne   Sydney

Published by the Press Syndicate of the University of Cambridge
The Pitt Building, Trumpington Street, Cambridge CB2 1RP
40 West 20th Street, New York, NY 10011, USA
10 Stamford Road, Oakleigh, Melbourne 3166, Australia

© Cambridge University Press 1991

First published 1991

Printed in Great Britain at the University Press, Cambridge

British Library cataloguing in publication data
Waterman, A. M. C.
Revolution, economics and religion: Christian Political Economy, 1798–1833
1. Economics. Theories of Malthus, T. R. (Thomas Robert), 1766–1834
1. Title
330.153

Library of Congress cataloguing in publication data
Waterman, Anthony Michael C.
Revolution, economics and religion: Christian Political Economy, 1798–1833 / A. M. C.
Waterman.
p.   cm.
Includes bibliographical references and index.
ISBN 0-521-39447-3
1. Sociology, Christian – Great Britain – History of doctrines. 2. Christianity and politics –
Protestant churches. 3. Economics – Religious aspects – Christianity – History of doctrines.
4. Malthus, T. R. (Thomas Robert), 1766–1834. An essay on the principle of population.
5. Theodicy – History of doctrines. 6. Conservatism – Great Britain – History. 7.
Conservatism – Religious aspects – Christianity – History of doctrines. 8. Revolutions –
Religious aspects – Christianity – History of doctrines. 9. Great Britain – Politics and
government – 1789–1833. 10. Great Britain – Politics and government – 1800–1833. 1.
Title. 11. Title: Christian Political Economy. 1798–1833.
BT738.W342   1991
320.5'2'094109034 – dc20   90-44207 CIP

ISBN 0 521 39447 3 hardback

UP

All apparent opposition to religion which we meet in this age should not blind us to the fact that all intellectual problems are fused with religious problems, and that the former find their constant and deepest inspiration in the latter.

Ernst von Cassirer, *Philosophy of the Enlightenment.*

Contents

Figures

Acknowledgements

An economist with a smattering of divinity who ventures to write a work of history can only hope to succeed if he gets a great deal of help. At every stage of my research for this book I have been dependent upon the generosity of real historians who have pardoned my intrusion upon their turf and have upheld me with their expert knowledge, judgement, criticism and encouragement. Because of the interdisciplinary character of the research I have in addition made heavy demands upon various philosophers, political scientists, theologians, economists and others. And because it has been costly in time and money I have needed the more material support afforded by funding bodies and academic institutions. These acknowledgements are therefore much longer than a book of such modest scope would normally require. They are not intended to implicate my benefactors in the opinions expressed or in any errors committed therein.

My first obligation is to the Christendom Trust, which provided a Maurice Reckitt fellowship in Christian social thought at the University of Sussex during the tenure of which I began this study. At a crucial stage I was invited by Istvan Hont to visit the Research Centre at King's College, Cambridge, with financial support from the British Council. In 1986–7 I was elected to a bye-fellowship at Robinson College, Cambridge where I was able to write most of the first draft in circumstances of great amenity. To the Warden and Fellows of that congenial society I owe much indeed. At various times I have been supported by research/study leave from the University of Manitoba, and by research grants from that university and from the Social Sciences and Humanities Research Council of Canada. I could never have undertaken this project at all but for the willingness of my departmental colleagues to entertain a very liberal notion of what might count as 'economics'.

At Sussex I met Donald Winch, and since that time he has been a constant source of advice, criticism and encouragement, faithfully responding to my importunities in the midst of heavy and pressing administrative duties. If books had god-fathers he should stand first at the font. Boyd Hilton has magnanimously encouraged (and written letters in support of) a project some might have shunned as a rival to their own; and has provided detailed comments on the final draft. Edward Norman gave me warm encouragement from the first; and at a later stage, when difficulties multiplied, I was much heartened by Quentin Skinner and by Jonathan Clark. The latter's shrewd criticism of the first draft has eliminated some of the more blatant nonsense from the final product. The remaining god-father – in John Stuart Mill's sense – must be Samuel Hollander. His friendly support has been invaluable; and I hope I may have begun to learn from his exact scholarship and vast learning.

In addition to these, many others have read and commented on work-in-progress. Mary Kinnear, David Levy and Salim Rashid have read the entire draft. Paul Heyne persuaded me to abandon my original draft of chapter 1 and to some extent to rethink the entire enterprise. Don Locke gave me the benefit of his expert knowledge of William Godwin, and James Crimmins did the same with respect to Jeremy Bentham. Stewart K. Brown read and criticized chapter 6 on Thomas Chalmers. And Geoffrey Brennan, Grahame Cole, Ross Emmett, John Gascoigne, Michael Hennell, Derek Hum, John Kendle, Margaret Morgan, Ronald Preston, John Pullen, Andrew Robinson, T. K. Rymes and Stephen Taylor have read and criticized chapters which encroach in various ways on their particular fields of knowledge. Most, if not all, will recognize some improvement in the final draft for which they deserve the credit.

I owe a different but hardly less important debt of gratitude to several of the above, and to some others, who allowed me to see and make use of their own work-in-progress many months, in some cases years, before its publication. It was particularly valuable for me to see pre-publication scripts of Boyd Hilton's *Age of Atonement*, Robert Hole's *Pulpits, Politics and Public Order* and the various essays on Chalmers edited by A. C. Cheyne. I was also much helped by seeing unpublished papers on Bentham and Paley by James Crimmins; on Malthus by Istvan Hont, John Pullen and Samuel Hollander; on other topics related to my concerns by Graham Cole, Margaret Morgan and Salim Rashid; and by certain chapters of John

Gascoigne's *Cambridge in the Age of the Enlightenment*, and Donald Winch's *Malthus*.

In addition to those who have read my drafts and shown me their own, I am grateful to Pietro Corsi, Biancamaria Fontana, John Hartwick, Michael Norris, H. C. Porter, D. T. Whiteside and E. A. Wrigley for helpful conversation or correspondence at various stages of my research.

Many of those I have acknowledged will find – if they do not already know – that I have bitten the hands that fed me by criticizing their works in my own. In the first chapter I have supplied an apology for this ungracious procedure which I hope will satisfy any who might otherwise convict me of ingratitude.

Like all Malthus scholars all over the world I incurred a particularly heavy obligation to the late Patricia James and the late John Harrison. Both read and commented on parts of my draft and the latter was engaged in collaboration with me at the time of his death. I deeply regret that they did not live to see the completion of an undertaking to which each gave such signal assistance.

Every book condemns its author to long hours of drudgery, and happy is he who can transfer as much of it as I did to the courteous and efficient hands of others. The staffs of many libraries have laboured cheerfully for me: at home, St John's College, the Dafoe Library, and the library of the University of Winnipeg; in Toronto, the Robarts Library and those of Trinity, Knox and Emmanuel Colleges; the Kress Library at Harvard and the Wilson Library at the University of Minnesota; in Britain, the Cambridge University Library, the Marshall library and the libraries of Robinson College and Ridley Hall, the British Library, Lambeth Palace Library and the National Library of Scotland. I am particularly grateful to those who have given me access to manuscript and archival material: the late John Harrison, keeper of the Malthus collection at Jesus College, Cambridge; Michael Halls, modern archivist at King's College, Cambridge; William Parry, senior librarian of Oriel College, Oxford; Murray Simpson, librarian of New College, Edinburgh; and R. Smart, archivist of St Andrew's University. I am also obliged to Prabir Kumar Mitra who drew the diagrams; and to my research assistants, especially Ross Emmett whose critical appreciation of my project, and perceptive comments upon it, entitle him to more than perfunctory acknowledgement. To Joyce Laird, who typed and retyped successive outlines, studies and drafts for more than ten years, I add my own tribute to that of a whole generation of St John's College fellows.

It seems almost impertinent to mention my wife in this context. For though she too has shared in the chores of preparing this book and has borne patiently the many absences of body and mind it occasioned, her contribution is incommensurable with that of any other. I can only hope she thinks it has all been worthwhile.

A. M. C. Waterman
St John's College, Winnipeg

Abbreviations

AJR	*Anti-Jacobin Review*
AJRM	*Anti-Jacobin Review and Magazine*
AR	*Annual Review*
BC	*British Critic*
BL	British Library
CHA	Collection of Chalmers papers in New College, Edinburgh
Civ. Dei	*De Civitate Dei* of St Augustine of Hippo
DNB	*Dictionary of National Biography*
DR	*Dublin Review*
EB	1824 *Supplement to Encyclopaedia Britannica*
ER	*Edinburgh Review*
GM	*Gentleman's Magazine*
MLC	*Malthus Library Catalogue*
MM	*Monthly Magazine*
MR	*Monthly Review*
NAR	*New Annual Register*
NP	*The New Palgrave: A Dictionary of Economics* (1987)
PC	*Public Characters*
QR	*Quarterly Review*
ST	*Summa Theologiae* of St Thomas Aquinas
WR	*Westminster Review*

CHAPTER I

Polemic, ideology and 'Christian Political Economy'

INTELLECTUAL HISTORY AS POLEMIC: AND VICE VERSA

To expect an historian to write with no polemical intent is not unlike expecting a privately owned business to conduct its affairs with a view to the public interest. No doubt it can be done. But to require it is unreasonable and is, moreover, to miss the point of the activity. History is served not so much by the pure intentions of the author as by the criticism of his colleagues.

The original purpose of this book, therefore, was unashamedly polemical. It was to disturb a popular view of modern intellectual history, and to challenge one of its scholarly correlatives. I have by no means lost sight of this object. But its pursuit has generated a number of secondary aims, some of which may interest historians, economists, theologians, political theorists, and others with no desire to grind my particular axe. What this means is that instead of having only one reason for existing, my book now has no fewer than five. For the evidence which supports my primary thesis bears upon two questions much canvassed by historians of eighteenth and early nineteenth-century British politics; and upon two others of importance for some, at least, among my fellow economists. Each of the five must be explained.

The popular view that I had in mind is a belief that 'Christian Social Thought' – or 'Christian Social Teaching' for the two are all too often confounded – was more or less moribund from the Reformation until the emergence of 'Christian socialism' (alternatively, the 'Social Encyclicals') in the nineteenth century. As Tawney said of the Church of England, 'The social teaching of the Church had ceased to count, because the Church itself had ceased to think' (Tawney 1947, 147). The scholarly correlative may also be found in Tawney, though it has lately been revived by E. R. Norman. 'An institution which possesses no philosophy of its own', declared Tawney, 'inevitably accepts that which happens to be fashionable'. Throughout the eighteenth century and well into the nineteenth, the church 'accepted the prevalent social philosophy and adapted its teaching to it'. Religious thought was no longer 'an imperious master' of political theory 'but a docile pupil' (Tawney 1947, 160, 161). For at least three centuries, Norman has suggested, 'the social attitudes of the church have derived from the surrounding intellectual and political culture and not...from theological learning' (Norman 1976, 10).

It was Tawney's own polemical purpose to contrast this putative quiescence unfavourably with that late-Victorian Anglican socialism to which, through the influence of Charles Gore and William Temple, he had become affected (Preston 1979, 83–110). 'Silently, but unmistakably, the conception of the scope and content of christian ethics which was generally, though not universally accepted in the nineteenth century, is undergoing a revision' (Tawney 1947, 12). Once again, after a lapse of some two or three centuries, the Christian churches are and ought to be engaged in social criticism. 'Issues which were thought to have been buried by the discretion of centuries have shown in our own day that they were not dead but sleeping' (Tawney 1947, 12).

At first glance it may seem surprising that Edward Norman should have accepted Tawney's account of the passive and accommodating nature of Christian social thought in eighteenth and nineteenth-century Britain. He did so, however, in order to make a polemical point which is almost the opposite of Tawney's. The secularization of European thought which the latter (incorrectly) identified in the seventeenth century was not reversed in Victorian times, but accelerated. What was true of the eighteenth century is true, *a fortiori*, of the present. 'The Christian religion has lost the power, and also the confidence, to define the areas of public debate, even in moral questions. Instead, it follows the definitions made by others' (Norman 1979, 4). Tawney's strictures upon the social ethics of Josiah Tucker and Paley apply with equal force to those of Maurice and Westcott, Gore, Temple *and of Tawney himself.* For at least since the English Revolution, shall we say,

The theologians have always managed to reinterpret their sources in ways which have somehow made their version of Christianity correspond almost exactly to the values of their class and generation. Thus theological scholarship justified the structural obligations of the eighteenth-century world, then it provided a Christian basis for Political Economy; later collectivist principles were hailed as the most perfect embodiment of the compassion prescribed in the New Testament; and even the contemporary doctrines of 'liberation' and 'secularization' have been given powerful theological support. (Norman 1976, 10–11).

There is no denying a large measure of plausibility to this account. It would have been strange indeed had Tawney's own views escaped the social conditioning he perceived in earlier stages of European capitalism. Norman may well hoist him with his own petard.

Like Edward Norman I wish to dispute the widely held belief that the faithful practice of Christianity, rightly understood, must create a predisposition in favour of a collectivist, or non-market social order. Yet I am easy with his strategy. For two reasons, one theoretical, the other empirical, I believe it to be vulnerable to objection. In the first place, it must be the case that all political doctrines in whatsoever period of history are socially conditioned. This tells us nothing about their truth or falsehood, nor about their logical connexion with the Christian or any other religion. Moreover, even 'theological learning' itself is and must be 'derived from the surrounding intellectual and political culture' to an extent that weakens the force of Norman's antithesis between the two. In the second place, as I have previously argued (Waterman 1983a), a close inspection of the evidence does not wholly support the claim that 'theological scholarship... provided a Christian basis for Political Economy'. 'Theology' and 'political economy' were then (and perhaps still are) less distinctly separated than Norman makes it appear, and were frequently the intellectual property of one and the same scholar. During the early decades of the nineteenth century at any rate, 'theological scholarship' played a more active rôle than he allows.

I shall therefore adopt a different strategy to make what I take to be the same point. Leaving aside the validity or otherwise of present-day attitudes, I shall exhibit a pre-Victorian tradition of Christian social thought in order to demonstrate first, that 'the Church' had by no means 'ceased to think' at that time; and secondly, that the results of such 'thinking' were drastically opposed in their political implications to that automatic hostility to capitalism which Tawney and those of like mind held to be inseparable from Christianity.

It is of the first importance that I declare my purpose in so doing. 'Christian Political Economy' was strongly favourable to private property rights, free and competitive markets, the institutions of marriage and wage-labour, and a high degree of social and economic inequality. I report and analyse its arguments in this book not in order to recommend them to the reader, nor because I believe they have any immediate or obvious relevance to the social problems of our own time. Nor do I expose the content of this tradition in order to criticize, appraise or refute it. Still less is it my object (as to some extent, and in different ways, it was both Tawney's and Norman's object), to provide an externalist 'explanation' of its intellectual history in terms of some causal social process and thus to discredit its message. My purpose – the *first purpose* of this book – is none of these, but rather to *understand* the tradition, and so to help the reader understand it. For in this way we may begin to discover, as Quentin Skinner (1969, 52) has well put it, 'the essential variety of viable moral assumptions and political comments'.

It is impossible to understand the political ideas of eighteenth-century Europeans without recognizing that the distinctions we now quite properly draw between specialized branches of 'theological', 'philosophical', 'scientific' and 'social' inquiry were then of far less importance and in many cases hardly possible. David Hume's *Essays*, for example, contain matter that he described as 'Moral, Literary and Political' and which we should now classify as 'anthropology', 'economics', 'history', 'journalism', 'philosophy', 'political science' and 'theology'. Samuel Johnson was expert in law, knowledgeable in 'chymistry' and theology, learned in classical and much other European literature, and omnicompetent as lexicographer. After seven years in the chair of Chemistry at Cambridge, during which he conducted many important researches, Richard Watson became Regius Professor of Divinity in 1771 whereupon he pursued his new studies with as much assiduity and success. There was then a unity to intellectual activity which is now forever lost. Above all is it impossible to understand the thought of pre-industrial, European society without an imaginative awareness of the extent to which that unity was determined by the presuppositions of Western Christianity. Though Hobbes and Helvetius, Hume and Voltaire, and many another 'infidel' had wholly or partially detached themselves from Christianity or even, in some cases, from religious belief of any kind, the 'secularization of the European mind' (Chadwick 1975) was a concomitant of widespread industrialization and did not occur until well into the next century. The terms of political debate, in the *ancien régime*, were set by the theological requirements of Christian orthodoxy.

I am aware that this claim may still appear controversial. As recently as 1985 Professor J. G. A. Pocock (1985a, 33), reviewing the 'state of the art' in eighteenth-century historiography, could report that 'we study the era in which English and Scottish writers for the first time engaged in fully secular discussion of their society and its destinies, from which point British intellectual history can begin to be written'. Insofar as this book supplies evidence of the centrality of theological concerns in pre-industrial political discourse, its *second purpose* may thus be seen as affording support for the position of I. R. Christie (1984, esp. 184–5, 206–14), J. C. D. Clark (1985) and others (e.g., Le Mahieu 1976; Crimmins 1983, 1986, 1989a; Hole 1989) who have called in question the prevailing 'positivism' and consequent reductionism, of eighteenth and early nineteenth-century historiography.

Ian Christie, Jonathan Clark, R. A. Soloway (1969) and Robert Hole have described the crucial part played by orthodox Anglican theology in 'The intellectual repulse of revolution' by British intellectuals in the 1790s. It is now generally agreed, moreover, that the English Jacobins were not so much muzzled as actually vanquished in fair fight. '... the radicals were defeated by the force of their opponents' arguments and by the climate of conservative opinion among the politically conscious, not simply by recourse to repressive measures and the forces of order' (Dickinson 1977, 272, cit. Christie 1984, 159). None of these accounts, however, nor any other that I am aware of, continues the story of the 'intellectual repulse of revolution' to its final and most interesting chapter, which is the classic confrontation between William Godwin and T. R. Malthus from 1798 to 1803. For Godwin had answered Burke in 1793 with such authority that for four crucial years, from the Reign of Terror to the French landing in Wales, the initiative passed back to the 'radicals'. Not until the first *Essay on Population* (1798) were the Jacobins finally routed.

The essential ingredient in Malthus's victory, and that which was entirely new in counter-revolutionary polemic of the time, was the 'new science' of political economy. The unassailable prestige of Newton's scientific method, and that method itself, first appropriated to the study of human social phenomena by David Hume in the mid-1750s (Waterman 1988), were brilliantly deployed by Malthus to show that *both* Burke *and* Godwin were wrong: and wrong for the same reason. Partly because of the requirement that anti-Jacobin doctrine should be consistent with Anglican orthodoxy, there was considerable criticism and development of Malthus's ideas – by himself and others – over the next three decades, and it is this particular programme that I have labelled 'Christian Political Economy'. Its theological aspects were crucially dependent upon a 'liberal' mutation of orthodoxy which, I shall argue, had its origins in Cambridge in the last quarter of the eighteenth century.

The 'ideological alliance of political economy and Christian theology' (Waterman 1983a) in these years was a decidedly new strain in British 'conservative' thought. Its social theory, whilst demonstrating both the inevitability and the beneficence of existing economic institutions, did so in a way that was wholly compatible with the most whiggish desire for 'reform'. Its theological aspects, though satisfying both the letter and the spirit of the Anglican formularies, did so in a way that successfully enlisted in the service of Christianity the new insights of the Enlightenment. It is therefore the *third purpose* of this book, and that for which I claim the greatest novelty, to demonstrate that Christian Political Economy discovered tenable middle ground, during the first three decades of the nineteenth century, between an ultra-tory defence of the *ancien régime* on the one hand, and 'radicalism' in any of its varieties, Jacobin, plebeian or 'Philosophic', on the other. In so doing it supplied the ideological underpinnings of the new 'liberal-conservatism' of Canning, Huskisson and Peel, thereby smoothing the transition from what was left of an *ancien régime* in the 1820s to the emerging industrial and increasingly pluralistic society of the Victorian age. Viewed from this standpoint my book may be regarded as an extended footnote, or technical appendix, to Boyd Hilton's (1988) recent work on 'Evangelical' social thought.

In the terminology of Lakatos (1970, 133–4), the social-theoretic 'hard core' of this programme was the central, organizing conception of classical political economy: Adam Smith's 'cheerful' vision of a self-regulating market economy, as modified by Malthus's 'gloomy' recognition of the dominance of scarcity in human social life. It is no accident that Christian Political Economy should be almost exactly conterminous with the evolution, at the hands of Chalmers, Malthus, West, Ricardo, Senior and others, of what Samuelson (1978) has aptly called the 'canonical classical model' of political economy. Though Ricardo deserved (and has always received) the chief credit for defining the formal structure of this 'model', his achievement would have been impossible but for the pioneering work of Malthus on population, diminishing returns and rent. And in fact there was the most fruitful friendship, collaboration and mutual criticism between the two until Ricardo's early death in 1823.

Those authors who followed Malthus in the theoretical elaboration of Christian Political Economy – Paley, J. B. Sumner, Copleston, Whately and Chalmers – criticized and improved various aspects of the arguments presented in the first and subsequent editions of the *Essay on Population*; and Malthus responded to their criticisms in five successive recensions over twenty-eight years. Of necessity therefore there is much about Malthus and his works in what I have to say. Viewed indeed from the blinkered standpoint of my own academic discipline – economics and the history of economic thought – this book may well appear, at least in part, as a microscopic examination of certain parts of the *Essay on Population*: carried out under far greater magnification than has ever yet been employed.

In view of the immense volume of ink that has been spilt over the *Essay* for nearly two hundred years, it may well be wondered what more of use remains to be said. The answer is a corollary of my *second* theme. Economists, for the most part, have been even more willing than historians to filter the literature of pre-industrial society through the conceptual apparatus of their own secularized, technical and specialist consciousness. Malthus above all seems to have created a problem for the 'economic mind'. Marx and Bagehot, Cannan, Schumpeter and many others equally eminent would seem to have missed the point of what Malthus was trying to say.

At bottom this has almost always been a consequence of the same, fundamental misperception. The *Essay* has been seen as a book 'about' economics, or demography, or politics, or even theology. It has not been seen for what I believe it is: an anti-Jacobin defence of property rights embedded in the religious world-view and theological framework of eighteenth-century Anglican Christianity. I am aware that this is a somewhat eccentric view, which I hold, at least so far as my own profession is concerned, with a small handful of others. I am also aware that Malthus himself displayed a certain ambivalence towards his adversaries in 1798. Though a clergyman he was a whig, reared by Dissenters. Cambridge of the 1780s had afforded but indifferent preparation for the unaccustomed rôle of *defensor fidei*. There is no reason to doubt his sincerity in regarding Godwin's 'system of equality' as 'beautiful and engaging'. Nevertheless it is the *fourth purpose* of this book to supply evidence in support of my opinion that the *Essay on Population* is largely unintelligible without an intimate awareness of the ideological warfare of which it was a part, and of the philosophical and theological discourse with which that warfare was carried on.

Enough has now been said to make it quite clear that this is a polemical book about polemical books. How is human knowledge enlarged by so ignoble a purpose? First I owe an explanation of two words I have so far used without apology: 'polemic' and 'ideology'.

'Polemic' is a ritualized act of war – similar in that respect to games of chess or bridge – whereby one author seeks to 'defeat' another by demonstrating to the satisfaction of informed bystanders that his opponent's arguments are ill-founded and therefore untenable. There is no reason (save human pride, vainglory and hypocrisy) why this activity need not take place with the utmost charity and mutual forbearance. Malthus and Ricardo were intimate friends. But it is of the essence that both – or all, in a multi-person game – should play to win.

'Ideology' now has many meanings, and no meaning. I shall not use the word in a Marxian sense as a form of 'false consciousness' capable in principle of being dispelled by 'correct' social analysis. Instead I shall follow Schumpeter's usage and mean by it a set of 'rationalizations', produced in any society by those groups or classes in a position to assert themselves, which serve to glorify the importance or otherwise advance the interests of those groups or classes. In this sense Marxism itself is 'ideology', but none the worse for that. For as Schumpeter insisted, 'it cannot be emphasized too strongly that, like individual rationalizations, ideologies are not lies' (Schumpeter 1954, 36).

Though polemic may arise from many different motives, one of the strongest of which is the sheer joy of competitive sport, it is obvious that much – perhaps most – of the 'polemic' engaged in by historians, economists and other students of human society, has an 'ideological' function. Malthus sought to refute the arguments of Godwin in order to show that 'the established administration of property' maximized the disposable income of landlords, thereby affording 'everything that distinguishes the civilized, from the savage state' and so making the world safe for clergymen and college fellows. Nevertheless it is often felt, especially by economists, that it is very unscientific, not to say demeaning, to descend to ideological polemic. Economics should be 'value free'; economists should refrain from offering advice or passing judgement upon social goals; and should concern themselves with establishing 'meaningful theorems' which 'predict', 'describe' or 'explain' observable (and measurable) economic phenomena.

Deeply as I approve of this orthodox view of social science, honesty compels me to admit that it often fails to describe what actually happens. For in some cases at least, if not in most, what is eventually acknowledged to have been 'scientific progress' emerged not as the fruit of disinterested inquiry but as the *unintended outcome* of ideological polemic. So long as a community exists of informed and critical colleagues, and so long as the prizes for polemical victory are awarded fairly by that community the operation of Gresham's Law will be suspended: good arguments – however unworthy their motivation – will drive out bad.

Economists, of all people, should find it no surprise that an Invisible Hand may operate in the history of their own discipline. It is at any rate the *fifth* and final *purpose* of this book to illustrate that point by showing that the eventual outcome of the ideological polemic I describe was of profound and lasting significance for economic science.

Before turning to these tasks it remains only to say rather more carefully just what will be meant in this book by 'Christian Political Economy'.

A DEFINITION OF 'CHRISTIAN POLITICAL ECONOMY'

The astute reader will already have noticed that I have committed, or seem about to commit, a serious anachronism. If it be true that the unity of pre-industrial thought was determined by the presuppositions of the Christian religion, how can there be useful work for the adjective 'Christian' in 'Christian Political Economy'? Traditional European society – Jonathan Clark's *ancien régime* – was founded upon the unity of 'church' and 'state'. In principle at least, all social theory was therefore a branch of ecclesiology. Only when a non-theological, empirical and 'scientific' study of society had emerged, owing no deference to the 'Queen of the Sciences', could there be any social theory (or 'social thought' or 'social teaching' – the three are blurred together in Troeltsch's *Soziallehren*) which was *not* 'Christian'. But in that case, of course, a formidable epistemological question arises. How might such a 'secular', or 'autonomous' social theory be called 'Christian' at all? Are we hopelessly poised between the devil of anachronism and the deep blue sea of unmeaning?

This merely formal dilemma mirrors a genuine predicament of the authors to be considered in this book. For by the end of the eighteenth century the world of ideas was in a condition somewhat like that of a great lake in early spring. To a casual glance all is as it ever has been: nothing but ice to the horizon. But on closer inspection all is in flux: cracks and fissures everywhere, patches of water, and great flows beginning to break off and drift downstream. Thus did the intellectual unity of traditional society appear when Malthus wrote his first *Essay* in 1798. Europe was evidently no longer strictly 'traditional'. But as yet there was hardly a sign of what it would look like when it became 'modern' in the second half of the next century. Those who wished to welcome and avail themselves of the new knowledge associated with the Enlightenment, whilst at the same time remaining true to the faith and practice of Christianity, were treading on thin ice indeed.

Especially was this the case with political economy, which was gradually making way, in France and Great Britain at any rate, as a legitimate and useful inquiry governed by canons owing nothing to Christian or any other theology. For precisely this reason it was reviled as godless and repudiated as 'hostile to religion' by a wide spectrum of theological opinion ranging from 'two-bottle orthodoxy' at the one end to the Lake Poets at the other. The belief that political economy and Christian theology are mutually exclusive and antipathetic was shared by a very different and politically opposed party: a small but highly influential group of radicals led by Jeremy Bentham and James Mill. In the early 1820s the 'Philosophic Radicals', as they later became known, made a determined attempt to hijack political economy to their own, unashamedly atheistic programme of 'reform'. It has lately been suggested, indeed, that political economy supplied the tools for undermining the legitimacy of the English *ancien régime* (Kanth 1986). But this is to exaggerate both the political and the intellectual potency of Bentham and his disciples. It was the single-handed achievement of Richard Whately to defeat the Philosophic Radicals by showing that a defensible demarcation is possible between 'scientific' and 'theological' knowledge, thereby insulating each from illegitimate encroachment by the other.

Whately's demarcation afforded retroactive justification of those – such as Malthus, Paley, Sumner and Copleston – who had risked the censure of their fellow Christians by defending a social theory based almost entirely upon political economy and hardly at all upon a traditional ontology of society that Troeltsch (1931) misleadingly described as 'christian sociology'. It freed political economy from attachment to any particular religious or political creed, making it equally accessible to all who would submit to its discipline. And by safeguarding the integrity of each, it validated the ideological alliance of political economy and Christian theology that Malthus and his colleagues attempted to create.

Now, a distinction between theological and scientific 'knowledge' which recognizes the proper territory of each whilst denying to either the right to invade the other is precisely characteristic – if not definitive – of modern, 'pluralistic' or 'secular' consciousness. In forging his powerful weapon for the ideological defence of the establishment, Whately surrendered the traditional justification of its intellectual monopoly: the sovereignty of Christian dogma over all human inquiry. What I have called 'Christian Political Economy' is therefore of necessity a phenomenon of the brief transition between '*ancien régime*' and the 'secular society' it helped to create. It had its origin in that moment when classical political economy was conceived through the insemination of 'Smith on the Wealth of Nations' by 'Malthus on Population'. Though cracks and fissures were apparent to a discerning eye, the ideas, attitudes and institutions of traditional society still filled the landscape. Political economy might be serviceable in repelling the adversaries of the *ancien régime*, but only if consistent with orthodox Christianity. Forty years later most of the ice had floated out of the lake and the shape of things to come was clearly visible to all – save to Keble, Newman and the other 'Tractites'. The *ancien régime* was dead, and its defence was thus a dead issue. Political economy and Christian theology had been set free to go their separate ways. Very soon it ceased to be part of the ordinary, public business of a scientist to reconcile his findings with religious doctrine.

In a formal sense, therefore, 'Christian Political Economy' is a label for the intellectual enterprise of combining classical political economy with Christian – specifically Anglican – theology in normative social theory. The term 'classical political economy' is often used loosely to embrace everything from Petty's *Political Arithmetick* (1690) to Marx's *Capital* (1867). As I have already indicated, I use if more precisely in Samuelson's 'canonical' sense. Therefore the first *Essay on Population* must be the earliest possible *terminus a quo* both of 'classical' and therefore of 'Christian' political economy. By the end of the 1830s the latter enterprise ceased to have any compelling ideological or scientific motivation. Until the Disruption of the Kirk in 1843 Thomas Chalmers continued to assert his (non-Anglican) version of the 'Christian Political Economy' case for the ancient establishment in church and state. But he produced no new ideas after his *Political Economy* (1832) and Bridgewater Treatise (1833) and even in these works the intellectual degeneration of the tradition is all too evident. I shall therefore select the appearance of the latter as the *terminus ad quem*. In between lie Paley's *Natural Theology* (1802), several revisions of the *Essay* by Malthus, and important works by John Bird Sumner, Edward Copleston and Richard Whately.

'Christian Political Economy' is not an entirely new name. It was originally coined in the 1830s to refer to a very different tradition of thought. And it has lately been reintroduced by Salim Rashid in a sense similar to mine, though less clearly specified. Rashid employed the term to label Whately's contributions to economics (Rashid 1977), and it would appear that he means it to apply to the works of any English-speaking economist in Holy Orders from Josiah Tucker (1713–99; see Shelton 1981) to Richard Jones (1790–1855). My reasons for preferring a more restrictive definition have already been given. More must be said, however, about its nineteenth-century usage.

The *Dublin Review* of July 1837 printed a lengthy article on 'Christian Political Economy' (*DR* July 1837, 165–98), being a review of the celebrated treatise of Alban de Villeneuve-Bargemont, *Economie politique chrétienne*, first published in Paris in 1834 (Villeneuve 1834). Villeneuve had read Adam Smith and Say, but 'the works of Malthus afterwards shook all his preconceived ideas'. His purpose was to discover 'the Causes of Pauperism as it exists in France and Europe, and ... the Means of Relieving and Preventing it' (*DR*, 177, 165). Yet his work, and that of the school of French catholic economists of which he was the most distinguished member, cannot be described as 'Christian Political Economy' in the sense in which I use it. For the explicit distinction between 'science' and 'theology' which became characteristic of the British tradition was unknown to him.

Au sein d'une paisible retraite, je m'attachai à recueillir mes souvenirs et mon expérience, à interroger tour à tour l'économie politique, les théories philosophiques de la civilisation, la statistique, la législation et les sciences morales qui avaient rapport aux causes de l'indigence. D'abord un horizon vague et immense s'était offert à mes regards; peu à peu, *à l'aide surtout du phare lumineux du christianisme*, il me sembla que l'on pouvait distinguer nettement les causes des désordres moraux et matériels des sociétés; les faits se classèrent naturellement... (Villeneuve 1834, I, 20; my italics)

His reviewer described the tradition as 'a new school of political economists. Catholic in its faith, and *catholic in its manner of conceiving science*' (*DR*, 175; my italics). As a result, the outcome in terms of fruitful explanation was disappointing, as even the favourably disposed *Dublin Review* acknowledged. Villeneuve maintained that 'the accumulation and concentration of commercial capital, the universal use of machinery ... would indefinitely multiply the number of the poor' (*DR*, 178–9). Schumpeter later recognized 'the depth and social significance of his convictions; the wisdom of many of his practical recommendations; the scientific value of much of his sociology': but noted 'the defects of his technical economics, which was in fact rudimentary' (Schumpeter 1954, 490, n. 1). After Villeneuve's death the term 'Christian Political Economy' passed out of mind for more than a century, its author remembered, more fittingly, as the 'Precursor of Modern Social Catholicism' (Ring 1935).

Villeneuve's unsuccessful attempt to construct a political economy that should be 'catholic in its manner of conceiving science' was evidently more consistent with the world-view of traditional society than Whately's secularized 'science'. Yet Whately only expressed more sharply and explicitly what in retrospect can be seen to have characterized British political economy from the first: the attempt to separate questions of 'fact' from questions of 'value'. According to the *Edinburgh Review*, indeed, it was precisely this point which distinguished 'the English writers, or chrysologists as M. Cherbuliez would call them, or followers of Dr Smith' from 'the foreign school (we term them so for convenience, although there are many English authors whose views assimilate to theirs)'. The latter maintained 'that it is the office of the political economist to point out in what way social happiness may best be attained through the medium of national wealth. Our own writers reply, that this is the province not of the economist, but of the politician'. Following Senior, whose *Outline of the Science of Political Economy* (1836) was the subject of his article, the reviewer contends that 'the study is purely a science', but 'a science which neither recommends to do, or to abstain from doing...which regards Man in the abstract, and, simply as a wealth-creating animal' (*ER* October 1837, 77–83 *passim*). Senior was a former pupil and life-long friend of Whately and his methodological position was defined and determined by the latter. Though the distinction between 'fact' and 'value' is less clear in earlier writers of the English-speaking classical school, it was the considered opinion of Schumpeter that

Most of the writers of standing who paid serious attention to the fundamental questions of methodology clearly saw, and strongly empha-sized, the distinction between arguments about what is and arguments about what ought to be: the distinction between the 'science' of economics and the 'art' of policy. (Schumpeter 1954, 540)

We see from this that 'Christian Political Economy' was the mainstream of Anglo-Scottish social theory in the early nineteenth century, and that 'Philosophic Radicalism' was a backwater. For the latter, by its desire to subsume questions of 'value' under questions of 'fact', was merely the formal opposite of Villeneuve's 'catholic' social science. 'Philosophic Radicalism' asserted the empire of science over religion: '*Economie politique chrétienne*' the empire of religion over science. By developing a distinction between 'fact' and 'value' latent in earlier work, Christian Political Economy' constructed a typically British compromise between absurd extremes. As I hope my remaining chapters will show, this is only one of several ways in which the tradition I shall describe revealed the English, specifically Anglican, genius for discovering a navigable *via media* through which to steer the ship of church and state.

CHAPTER 2

The first Essay on Population: *political economy*

POLEMICAL PURPOSE OF THE FIRST *ESSAY*

Any book called *An Essay on the Principle of Population, as it Affects the Future Improvement of Society, with Remarks on the Speculations of Mr Godwin, M. Condorcet, and other Writers* was bound to be polemical: especially if published in 1798. Its anonymous author 'whom we understand to be a Mr Malthas' [*sic*] (*BC* 1801, 279) claimed to have discovered 'the strongest obstacle in the way to any very great future improvement of society' (Malthus 1798, iii). Though the *Essay* owed its origin to a discussion of William Godwin's lately published *Enquirer* (1797), its chief target was his revolutionary *Political Justice* (1793, 1796, 1798), especially the putative 'Benefits Attendant on a System of Equality' which form the centre-piece of Book VIII ('Of Property') of Godwin's great work.

The system of equality which Mr Godwin proposes, is, without doubt, by far the most beautiful and engaging of any that has yet appeared...it is impossible to contemplate the whole of this fair structure, without emotions of delight and admiration, accompanied with ardent longing for the period of its accomplishment. But alas! that moment can never arrive. (1798, 174–5)

The 'true and genuine situation of man on earth' is created by 'the grinding law of necessity' and for most people, in most times and places, is characterized by 'misery and vice'. Godwin is mistaken in 'attributing almost all the vices and miseries that are seen in civil society to human institutions' (196). They proceed, rather, from 'the necessary and inevitable laws of nature, which human institutions, so far from aggravating, have tended considerably to mitigate' (194).

Godwin's ideal is acknowledged to be superior to the status quo, and there is no reason to doubt the sincerity of Malthus at this point.

But the ideal state is unstable, and its temporary establishment leads to unforeseen consequences which produce a state of affairs *inferior* to the status quo. From this condition society is – would be – fortunately rescued by the continued operation of the 'laws of nature'. Those very institutions which Godwin had denounced – private property, marriage, competitive food and labour markets – would emerge 'in a very short period' to create 'a society, constructed upon a plan not essentially different from that which prevails in every known State at present' (207).

It is thus an important part of Malthus's counter-revolutionary doctrine to show that 'human institutions', especially private property in land, do indeed 'mitigate' the most distressing effects of the 'laws of nature'. With Godwin he agrees that 'The subject of property is the key-stone that completes the fabric of political justice' (Godwin 1798a, II, 420). But Godwin is quite wrong to attribute 'The spirit of oppression, the spirit of servility and the spirit of fraud' to 'the established administration of property' (II, 463). He is wrong, moreover, to suppose that if property were equalized, 'the narrow spirit of selfishness would inevitably expire' (II, 464); or, that if this happened it would be a good thing. We may therefore distinguish a 'positive' polemic in the first *Essay* from the merely 'negative' polemic designed to demolish Godwin's system. Not only had Malthus to show that

no sufficient change, has as yet taken place in the nature of civilized man, to enable us to say, that he either is, or ever will be, in a state, when he may safely throw down the ladder by which he has risen to this eminence. (Malthus 1798, 287)

He had also to demonstrate that

It is to the established administration of property, and to the apparently narrow principle of self-love, that we are indebted for all the noblest exertions of human genius, all the finer and more delicate emotions of the soul, for everything, indeed, that distinguishes the civilized, from the savage state (286–7)

In my opinion it is this latter, 'positive' programme which forms the central polemical purpose of the first *Essay*.

A very different interpretation has lately been advanced by Gertrude Himmelfarb in her important study of *The Idea of Poverty* (1984) in early Victorian Britain.

Had Godwin or Condorcet been Malthus's main target, the *Essay* would have been an exercise in 'overkill'. The principle of population was not

necessary to refute the doctrine of perfectibility. A modicum of common sense, some good-natured ridicule, and a liberal dose of quotations would have sufficed...
What was very much alive in 1798 was the spirit of Adam Smith. And it was the refutation of Smith's theory of progress, not Godwin's theory of perfectibility, that was the significant purpose of the *Essay*. (Himmelfarb 1984, 107–8)

According to this view, Malthus threw up a smokescreen of 303 pages before 'backing into his argument...warily and respectfully' in chapter xvi (24 pages). Presumably the remaining three chapters of the *Essay* (69 pages) are also part of the smokescreen for they have nothing to do with Smith's theory of progress.

It is certainly the case that chapter xvi of the first *Essay* constitutes an attack upon Smith's belief that an increase in the wealth of the nation would result in an increase in 'the happiness and comfort of the lower orders of society'. There is, however, no evidence that either Malthus himself, or any of his contemporaries, regarded this as the 'significant purpose of the *Essay*'. Those periodicals which noticed the work – the *Analytical*, the *Monthly Magazine*, the *Monthly Review* and the *British Critic* – took it at its face value as the refutation of Godwin and Condorcet. The *Analytical* and the *British Critic* each remarked upon chapter xvi in a single line, but the latter thought its purpose was to expose a technical error in Smith's capital theory. When Dugald Stewart – himself a former student admirer, and popularizer of Adam Smith – lectured on political economy in Edinburgh in the winter of 1800–1, he discussed the *Essay* with approval, assuming like the reviewers that it was aimed at Godwin and Condorcet. It would seem, therefore, if Malthus really had intended the *Essay* as an attack upon *Wealth of Nations* he was so pusillanimously evasive that his point was missed by all save Chalmers (in 1808). And as we shall see in chapter 6, Chalmers's (valid) recognition that the *Essay* drastically modifies the analytical apparatus of Smithian political economy was largely ignored.

The conjecture that Malthus wrote the *Essay* in order to attack Smith's theory of progress rests upon two correct observations: 'perfectibility' is too small a target to justify the discharge of much literary ordnance; and chapter xvi does indeed make explicit the fact that the principle of population subverts the 'optimistic' message of *Wealth of Nations*. But the conjecture fails, I believe, because it ignores the all-important ideological issue of the later

1790s, which was the Jacobin attack upon property. Rather than supposing, therefore, that the first fifteen chapters of the *Essay* are merely a ruse by Malthus for 'smuggling in his criticism of Smith's modest vision of progress in the guise of an attack upon Godwin's outlandish theory of perfectibility' (Himmelfarb 1984, 108), it seems more plausible to regard them as an extended, carefully articulated and by no means covert attack upon Godwin's far from 'outlandish' derogation of 'the established administration of property'.

Whether or not I am correct in this, it undoubtedly afforded the starting point of Christian Political Economy: not because of any particular novelty in the programme itself, for that is at least as old as Lactantius and Theodoretus (Viner 1978, 18–21), but rather because of the unique combination of pre-Ricardian classical economics and heterodox Christian theology that Malthus brought to the task. It is of the utmost importance, therefore, to examine both elements of that combination with great care. Before doing so, however, we must consider two preliminary questions: just what was going on in 1798 which induced Malthus to issue his tract; and why did he choose this particular method of dealing with revolutionary propaganda? To answer the first question we must review the political, economic and literary scene from the storming of the Bastille to the French landings in Ireland and Wales. To answer the second, some attention must be paid, however cursory, to the language of social theory that Malthus inherited, by a tangled and incestuous pedigree, from three generations or more of whigs, radicals, latitudinarians and Dissenters.

THE INTELLECTUAL CLIMATE IN 1798

The existence of a Jacobin faction, in the bosom of our country, can no longer be denied. Its members are vigilant, persevering, indefatigable; desperate in their plans and daring in their language. The torrent of licentiousness, incessantly rushing forth from their numerous presses, exceeds, in violence and duration, all former examples. Their falsehoods have been detected, their errors exposed, their misrepresentations corrected, and their malignity pointed out and chastised. – Still they persist, callous alike to the emotions of shame, the admonitions of duty, and the effects of public indignation. The Regicides of France and the Traitors of Ireland find ready advocates in the heart of our metropolis, and in the seats of our universities. (*AJRM* 1798, 1–2)

Such, at any rate, was the belief of the *Anti-Jacobin Review* in July

1798. A heterogeneous cast of miscreants was singled out for vilification: such acknowledged firebrands as Paine and Thelwall; the radical scholars – Horne Tooke, Priestley, Erasmus Darwin, Wakefield and Godwin; an ill-assorted group of literary men – Holcroft, Coleridge, Southey and Lambe [*sic*]; the politicians, Fox and Grey and their noble abettors, the dukes of Norfolk and Bedford; and a miscellaneous category which included the brewing MP Samuel Whitbread and Joseph Johnson, publisher of the detested *Analytical Review* and also of Priestley, Darwin, Horne Tooke and Mary Wollstonecraft. All were part of the 'Grand Conspiracy against Social Order' so assiduously fostered by the 'Jacobin' publications: the *Analytical*, the *Monthly*, the *Critical* reviews and the *New Annual Register*. All were lampooned in verses which competed for the readers' attention with such other poetry as 'The Wanderings of Iapis' (*AJRM* 1798, 228–32), an Old Etonian in urgent need of a lavatory at his *alma mater*. In more serious contributions, the 'Jacobin' periodicals were scrutinized minutely for subversive intentions; *Lovers' Vows* exposed for its 'evident tendency' to 'render the upper classes of society, objects of indignation or contempt' (*AJRM* 1798, 480; Butler 1975, 92–3, 232–4); short haircuts reviled as revolutionary (*AJRM* 1798, 480); and the 'fanciful hypotheses' of 'Mr Locke' reprobated for having 'opened the way to other theories equally false, and more immediately noxious' – the 'visionary doctrines' of Price, Priestley, Rousseau, and Paine (*AJRM* 1798, 395, 528).

It is easy enough now to see both the hysteria and also the undergraduate irresponsibility and naivety in all this. The existence of a 'Grand Conspiracy' of the kind that suggested itself to Barruel's apocalyptic imagination may have found credibility with the more excitable of the English episcopate (Soloway 1969, 34–40), but was utterly out of character with the priggish, middle-class respectability of the English Dissenters. Though some members of the London Corresponding Society had indeed been foolish enough to conspire with the United Irishmen in 1798, the 'English Jacobins' were a spent force by July of that year, their leaders imprisoned, exiled or retired into private life, their organization hamstrung by the Two Acts of December 1795, and their public support dissipated by world events of the past five years (Cone 1968, 210–24). Except for Holcroft – who left England in 1799 – the other dangerous writers had repented them of their youthful radicalism: in a letter of April

1798 to his brother, Coleridge declared that he had 'snapped his squeaking baby-trumpet of sedition' (Willey 1940, 255). The Foxites in parliament had been diminished by the secession of the Portland whigs in 1794, and in any case were cut off from the main stream of revolutionary thought by the contradiction of their position, smugly advocating parliamentary reform from safe seats in rotten boroughs (Watson 1960, 325, 357).

And yet – or so at least it appeared to Canning and his coadjutors of the *Anti-Jacobin* – the war of ideas was not yet won. Richard Price and Mary Wollstonecraft were dead. Priestley migrated to America in 1794; Paine had lived abroad since 1792, and had lost credit with many former supporters by Part II of his *Age of Reason* (1795) and by his open encouragement of Buonaparte's invasion plans. But their books were still read and their ideas disseminated and popularized by a literary establishment – 'the lords paramount of literature' (*AJRM* 1798, 475) – which by 1790 had come to be almost wholly in the hands of the Rational Dissenters (Lincoln 1938, 29–37). One of the most distinguished and talented of the 'Jacobin' intellectuals, moreover, was still living unmolested in London, still publishing his insidious ideas, and still as yet unanswered. This was the philosopher and publicist, William Godwin, author of *Political Justice*, the third (1798) edition of which appeared in December 1797; and of *Caleb Williams* (1794), the *Enquirer* (1797), and the notorious *Memoirs* (1798b) of Mary Wollstonecraft, noticed with venomous derision in the first volume of the *Anti-Jacobin*. An anonymous *Examination* of *Political Justice* was also noticed in the same volume. Its reviewer commended the 'Examiner' for his refutation of Godwin's account of virtue, but went on to hope that 'he will continue his labours and expose the absurdity of the whole theory, moral, religious, and political' (*AJRM* 1798, 333). To understand why the 'exposure' of Godwin's 'whole theory' was high on the counter-revolutionary agenda in mid-1798, we first must go back nine years to the opening salvoes of the bloodiest pitched battle in English literary history. For the unheralded intervention of an obscure (but ideologically suspect) 'Mr Malthas' turns out to have been the decisive encounter of an engagement that began in November 1789 with Richard Price's *Discourse on the Love of our Country*.

Those Englishmen who noticed the storming of the Bastille and its immediate sequel were generally favourable to the idea of a French Revolution. For 'revolution' was a good word in eighteenth-century

English usage – an 'assertion of right' (Price 1790, 30), or more
neutrally 'a change in the state of a government or country'
(Johnson 1755), sharply contrasted with the bad word 'rebellion' –
an 'invasion of right' (Price 1790, 30) or an 'insurrection against
lawful authority' (Johnson 1755). Whig and tory alike were firmly
persuaded of the blessings of constitutional monarchy, and many
influential voices, including that of Edmund Burke, had been raised
in support of the American Revolution thirteen years before. There
was scant sympathy for Louis XVI, whose support of the American
insurgents was remembered against him by tories; and William Pitt
agreed with Fox that 'The present convulsions in France must
sooner or later culminate in general harmony and regular order'
(Locke 1980, 41). Sheridan 'professed, in common with most of his
friends, an enthusiastic admiration for the French Revolution, and
considered the constitution it had formed, as a glorious fabric of
human wisdom, erected for the perfection of human happiness' (*PC*
1799–1800, 45). The whig Bishop Watson of Llandaff rejoiced in the
'glorious prospect of the prevalence of general freedom and general
happiness' (Watson 1790, 105; cit. Soloway 1969, 30). As for the
youngest generation, the delirium which possessed the Cambridge
juveniles at that time was recollected in tranquility by Wordsworth
in 1804:

> ...mighty were the auxiliars which then stood
> Upon our side, we who were strong in love!
> Bliss was it in that dawn to be alive,
> But to be young was very heaven! – Oh! times,
> In which the meagre, stale, forbidding ways
> Of custom, law, and statute, took at once
> The attraction of a country in romance!
> When Reason seemed the most to assert her rights,
> When most intent on making of herself
> A prime Enchantress – to assist the work
> Which then was going forward in her name!

Many Englishmen, however, took no notice at all. Even Major
Cartwright made no mention in his correspondence of the fall of the
Bastille until a month after the news had reached England, and the
response of the Society for Constitutional Information – 'almost as
though between yawns' – was delayed until November (Cone 1968,
80). As for Fanny Burney and thousands like her, the transcendent
event of the summer of 1789 was the King's recovery, and his

triumphal progress through the South-West of England after sea-bathing at Weymouth. 'The crowds, the rejoicings, the halooing, and singing, and garlanding...such happy loyalty as beamed from all ranks and descriptions of men' were conclusive. 'The greatest conqueror could never pass through his dominions with fuller acclamations of joy from his devoted subjects than George III experienced, simply from having won their love by the even tenor of an unspotted life, which, at length, has vanquished all the hearts of all his subjects' (Burney 1940, 259). Not quite all. When it came to monarchy, the heart of Dr Richard Price was made of stone. 'In our late addresses to our King, on his recovery from the severe illness with which God had been pleased to afflict him, we have appeared more like a herd crawling at the feet of a master than like enlightened and manly citizens rejoicing with a beloved Sovereign but at the same time conscious that he derives all his consequence from themselves' (Price 1790, 22).

There was a great deal more of this sort of thing, sour, rational and sectarian, in Price's sermon to the Revolution Society of 4 November 1789. The 'principles of the Revolution' (of 1688) were 'FIRST; The right to liberty of conscience in religious matters. SECONDLY; The right to resist power when abused. And THIRDLY; The right to chuse our own governors; to cashier them for misconduct; and to frame a government for ourselves' (30). The sermon concluded with a stirring peroration addressed to the literary intelligentsia:

Be encouraged, all ye friends of freedom, and writers in its defence! The times are auspicious. Your labours have not been in vain. Behold kingdoms, admonished by you, starting from sleep, breaking their fetters, and claiming justice from their oppressors! Behold, the light you have struck out, after setting *America* free, reflected to *France*, and there kindled into a blaze that lays despotism in ashes, and warms and illuminates Europe! TREMBLE all ye oppressors of the world! Take warning all ye supporters of slavish governments, and slavish hierarchies! Call no more (absurdly and wickedly) REFORMATION, innovation... (40)

Burke rose to the bait and battle was joined.

It has been argued by Carl B. Cone that in publishing his extended rebuttal almost exactly one year later, Burke actually gave life to the 'reform movement' which, by this time, was dying for 'want of attention' (Cone 1968, 91–2). Be that as it may, the response was unprecedented. By the time of publication of Part II of the *Rights of Man* (February 1792), forty-five answers had been printed; in all some seventy replies and counter-replies were produced by 14

February 1793, when there appeared 'the book that would mark the culmination of the war of pamphlets, and raise the whole debate to a more reflective, more philosophic level' (Locke 1980, 48): Godwin's *Political Justice*.

Burke, whose initial reaction to the French Revolution had been cautious, quickly became persuaded of two startling ideas which, for the next year or two, continued to elude most of his fellow-countrymen: first, the events in France were radically unlike those which had characterized the Glorious Revolution of 1688 or the American Revolution of 1776, and would lead inevitably to bloodshed, tyranny and war; secondly, they were not 'a sequence of spontaneous happenings but a systematic plan to spread a false philosophy and to destroy the established European order' (Cone 1968, 93). The first made it urgently necessary to disabuse the tolerant and well-meaning of their mistake; the second, to expose and refute the seditious propaganda of the disingenuous. In carrying out this programme Burke was led to propound a general theory of 'revolution' in the modern, pejorative sense of that word: 'there is a law of nature which states that revolution, which is the pure practical implementation of radical political theory, leads necessarily via anarchy to tyranny' (Freeman 1980, 14).

Though many of the answers to Burke remarked, with justice, that he 'pitied the plumage but forgets the dying bird', and gleefully scarified him for his contempt of the 'swinish multitude', only three stand out for their cogency – Mary Wollstonecraft's *Vindication of the Rights of Men*, Mackintosh's *Vindiciae Gallicae* and Paine's *Rights of Man* – and none of these comes to grips in a satisfactory way with Burke's fundamental argument. The mythopoeia so evident in Price's *Discourse*, that fatal confusion between things as the Rational Dissenter would have them be and things as they actually are, surfaces again in Paine. 'It is Paine who relies on an abstract doctrine of natural rights and an optimistic faith in human nature, while Burke appeals to the hard reality of social institutions; where Burke puts his trust in precedent and experience, Paine is content to rely on a scrap of paper drawn up by the French National Assembly' (Locke 1980, 46).

It was not so much a cool appraisal of rival arguments, however, as the tragic procession of events in France which finally rallied public opinion in Britain behind Burke's view of what was going on (Schofield 1986, 602–3). France declared war on Austria in April 1792; in August the Royal Family was placed under detention; the following month the Republic was proclaimed, and in January of 1793 Louis XVI went to the guillotine. One month later, France declared war on Britain and in July 1793 began a Reign of Terror which only ended with the execution of Robespierre twelve months later. Burke was vindicated and his opponents thrown into disorder, forced into those many twists and turns of spurious justification which gave such savage delight to the *Anti-Jacobin* three or four years later.

At the moment of crisis, in the very month that war broke out, the first edition of *Political Justice* appeared. Though leading members of the Dissenting Interest were careful to distance themselves from the more extravagant of its conclusions – Horne Tooke thought it 'a bad book, and will do a great deal of harm', and the 'Jacobin' monthlies were cool – it was enthusiastically welcomed by a younger generation of literary radicals. Hazlitt wrote in retrospect: 'No work in our time gave such a blow to the philosophical mind of the country... Tom Paine was considered for a time as Tom Fool to him; Paley an old woman; Edmund Burke a flashy sophist' (Hazlitt 1881, 59; cit. Carter 1971, xi). For as Don Locke has perceptively remarked, 'Political Justice might almost be a reply to Paine, for Godwin rejects out of hand both natural rights and written constitutions, the twin planks of Paine's political platform (Locke 1980, 49). Like Burke, whom he greatly admired, Godwin was a gradualist who explicitly repudiated a violent disturbance of the social fabric (Godwin 1798a, 1, 269–74). But whereas Burke had argued that the dissolution of these institutional ties which bind society together would lead, by the inevitable operation of natural laws, first to chaotic anarchy and then to tyranny, Godwin met his arguments head-on with a large-scale, systemic, gently-reasoned rebuttal. The intellectual initiative passed once again to the revolutionists, and Godwin became an instant hero to Gerrald, Merry and Porson; Wedgewood, Thelwall; Southey, Coleridge and Wordsworth (Locke 1980, 64–90) and thousands like them who still clung, for a while, to the faith that was born in 1789.

That faith was sorely tried in the next four years, during which Godwin brought out a second, greatly strengthened (Locke 1980, 59–60) version of his argument and a third edition at the end of 1797. The more thorough-going British supporters of the French Revolution were become objects of suspicion and harassment; in 1793 the leaders of the British Convention were charged with sedition; late in 1795 Pitt and Grenville brought in the Treasonable Practices and Unlawful Assembly Acts; Paine produced a serious rift among English progressives by the second part of his *Age of Reason*; and famine conditions in 1795–6, the year in which the Speen-hamland system was introduced, raised fears of domestic insur-rection. The year 1797 was climactic: in February the French landed in Pembrokeshire; in April the fleet mutinied at Spithead followed by a more dangerous mutiny a month later at the Nore; Grey's ill-timed campaign for parliamentary reform was finally defeated and his cause set back thirty-five years; and in late autumn the *Anti-Jacobin Weekly* began its assault on Dissenting intellectuals and their publications. Godwin himself later dated the reaction against him from the spring of this year. Nevertheless his *Enquirer*, published in February, was popular with many, and the immediate cause of that 'conversation with a friend' which prompted the unknown curate of Okewood to compose the most radical, yet most profoundly counter-revolutionary contribution to the nine years' war.

For though the revolutionists were in serious disarray from 1794 to 1798 the uneasy feeling persisted, thanks in large measure to the well-earned prestige of Godwin's writings, that they were as yet undislodged from the commanding heights of intellectual and moral superiority which they had occupied at least since the death of Samuel Johnson. Though tory bishops such as Pretyman (Charge to the Clergy of Lincoln, 1794; cit. Soloway 1969, 62) continued to maintain that Christianity is fundamentally a religion of in-equality dependent upon the exercise of 'compassion, gratitude and humility' (Soloway 1969, 62; see also Schofield 1986), their arguments had been met in advance and their general position undermined by Godwin's predecessors. The propertied classes 'demanded that the poor be reassured that the inequities of rank, wealth and power were indeed part of a grand design to maximize human happiness' (Soloway, 58). Burke had spoken indeed, but much of the ideological efficacy of the *Reflections* had by now been neutralized by Godwin's massive rebuttal. The challenge thrown out in one of the numerous replies to Burke had not yet lost its power to disturb:

As I am a believer in Revelation, I, of course, live in hope of better things; a millennium (not a fifth monarchy, sir, of enthusiasts and fanatics), but a new heaven and a new earth in which dwelleth righteousness; or, to drop the eastern figure and use a more philosophic language, a state of equal liberty and justice for all. (Lincoln 1938, 3)

It was the achievement of Malthus single-handedly to demonstrate that 'a state of equal liberty and justice for all' is impossible, thereby capturing the high ground once again for conservatism and throwing 'Jacobin' thought on the defensive for more than a generation.

An important element in that achievement, as it had been in Godwin's before him, was a willingness to acknowledge a large area of common ground with the adversary and a corresponding reliance upon sweet reason rather than invective in meeting his arguments. As we shall see in the following sections of this and the next chapter, Malthus took all that he needed to refute Godwin from Godwin's own work. This was no mere debating device. Malthus had imbibed subversive ideas, if not with his mother's milk, at least by influence of his 'Two fairy godmothers, Jean-Jacques Rousseau and David Hume' (Keynes 1972, 74); and was educated at Warrington Academy under Gilbert Wakefield, who had replied in January 1798 to Watson's *Address* and was incarcerated in Dorchester gaol for seditious libel (James 1979, 54). He was exposed to the whiggish air of Cambridge (Robbins 1961, 13) at a time when latitudinarian ideas were resurgent and his tutor, William Frend, in deep trouble over the Thirtynine Articles. And – if the recently published *Catalogue* of his library (*MLC*) be any guide – an avid reader, or at least collector, of all the dangerous authors celebrated in Richard Price's *Discourse* (Price 1790, 15–16), especially of Archbishop Fénélon, who seems to have been something of a cult-figure among trendies of the 1790s. Though a priest of the established church, Malthus was writing from within a whig tradition of social theory, and it has lately been claimed that 'From a psycho-historical point of view, the [first] *Essay* represented Malthus' moment of conversion' (Hont, Ignatieff and Fontana 1980, 1). It is no accident that it appeared before the world under the imprint of the 'Jacobin' publisher, Joseph Johnson. The *Essay* was given immediate and respectful attention in the *Analytical* (of course), the *Monthly Review* and the *New Annual Register*. But the high-church *British Critic* only noticed it after very long hesitation (*BC* 1801, 278–82); and the *Anti-Jacobin*, in its fanatical detestation of all that came out of Joseph Johnson's stable, altogether ignored it.

The relation between Malthus's argument and that of his two great predecessors in the debate may be illustrated, very crudely, in

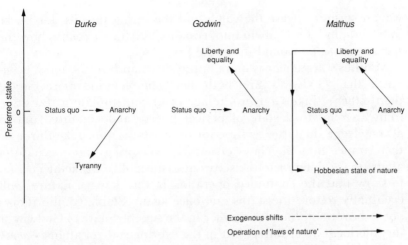

Fig. 1. Burke, Godwin and Malthus compared.

diagrammatic form. Preferred states are displayed ordinally on the vertical axis of figure 1: the horizontal axis is without significance. All three authors invite us to consider the consequences of an exogenous dissolution of the existing social fabric. Property rights, laws, customs, duties are placed – temporarily and notionally – in abeyance and a state of anarchy results. All three then consider, explicitly or implicitly, the operation of the 'laws of nature' on this new state. For Burke, as Michael Freeman has convincingly shown (Freeman 1980), society will gravitate to a stable equilibrium of 'tyranny', from which it can only be again dislodged by further exogenous shifts – brought about, say, by deliberate counter-revolutionary action. For Godwin, society may levitate to a stable equilibrium of perfect freedom and equality, whereupon mankind is launched upon a stable growth-path of never-ending progress towards the goal of human perfectibility. As with Burke, the new equilibrium can only be disturbed by an exogenous shift: the deliberate reintroduction, say, of those pernicious 'institutions' which for Godwin are the root cause of human misery.

It is clear from this account that both Burke's and Godwin's arguments are defective in exactly the same way. For by postulating a stable equilibrium at some different state from the status quo, and by treating the latter as unstable unless constrained by institutional bonds, they leave altogether unexplained the way in which society comes to be what it actually is. Civilized society, for both, is a tightly wound spring: release the catch and the spring uncoils; for Burke into 'tyranny', for Godwin into 'equality'. Neither explains how the spring gets to be wound up in the first place.

Malthus's argument is more optimistic than Burke's, more pessimistic than Godwin's, and both more complex and more radical than either's. Like Godwin, he agrees to contemplate a transition from anarchy to a state of perfect liberty and equality, and to acknowledge the latter as superior to the status quo. Like Burke he then argues that the 'laws of nature' will bring about a state of affairs that is inferior to the status quo. But unlike Burke he goes on to show that the continued operation of the 'laws of nature' will eventually restore the status quo once again. Stable equilibrium is not to be sought, therefore, either in the superior state of Godwin or the inferior state of Burke, but in the existing state of affairs – *which is what it is precisely because the equilibrium of society is stable.* The arrow which leads downward from liberty and equality to the Hobbesian state of nature corresponds to what I have called Malthus's 'negative polemic'; the arrow which leads upwards from there to the status quo corresponds to his 'positive polemic'.

Before examining his argument in detail, we must set in their historical context Malthus's use of the concept of the 'laws of nature' and certain other related ideas.

VOCABULARY OF MALTHUS'S SOCIAL THEORY

...the Revolution was made in the name of Nature, Burke attacked it in the name of Nature, and *in eodem nomine* Tom Paine, Mary Wollstonecraft, and Godwin replied to Burke...

Willey 1940, 205

Willey might well have concluded his recitation by adding that in the name of Nature Malthus refuted Godwin. The word is used in the first *Essay* to unify a cluster of twelve other related concepts which provide the principal terms in the vocabulary of Malthus's social theory: both of his 'negative' and 'positive' counter-revolutionary polemic, and of the theodicy which the former made necessary.

'Nature' is the creature of (1) 'God' (Malthus 1798, 12, 127–8, 390) and is itself the parent of the two central concepts in the first *Essay*: (2) the 'laws of Nature' (158–9, etc.) and (3) human nature of 'the nature of man' (11, 14, 16, 19, 61, 190, 191). The laws of

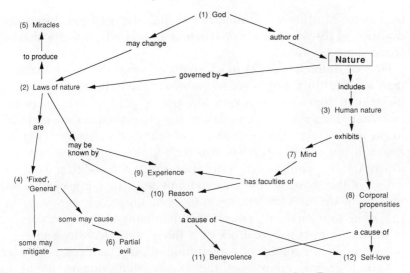

Fig. 2. 'Nature' and related concepts in the first *Essay*.

nature are (4) 'fixed' or 'general' (12, 124–8, 157–60, 363, 391–2), though they may be changed by God to produce (5) 'miracles' (127–8, 160, 239, 391). The 'general' laws of nature may cause (6) 'partial evil', though this may be (and is) mitigated or offset by the operation of other 'general laws' (294). Human nature, like the rest of nature, is governed by 'fixed' or 'general' laws, and exhibits two characteristics which jointly determine human behaviour: (7) 'mind' (221–39, 247) and (8) 'corporal propensities' (252–5). Mind has the faculty of (9) 'experience' (17, 32, 231–6) and (10) 'reason' (27–8, 177, 215–16). Reason, (or human 'rational faculties') by producing 'opinions' about the true state of affairs, may be the origin of voluntary human action; but the 'corporal propensities' act as a powerful 'disturbing force'. Both 'reason' and 'corporal propensities' determine both (11) 'benevolence' (182, 189–91, 294–5) and (12) 'self-love' (175, 190, 207, 286), which together are the proximate causes of human action. Those 'fixed' or 'general' laws by which 'human nature' is governed are known by human 'mind' through 'reason' and 'experience'. These relations are summarized in figure 2. Reference to Malthus's use of this conceptual scheme in the first *Essay* will be made in later sections of this chapter, in which his negative and positive polemic are analysed, and in chapter 3, which analyses his theology. The object of this section is to locate Malthus's vocabulary within the eighteenth-century tradition of discourse and in particular to relate it to Godwin's use of the same terms.

Godwin himself was far more chary of using the word 'nature' than was Malthus, and in general more careful in his employment of the related concepts. In a very few places 'nature' is used in the customary secondary sense to denote the phenomena of the material world as a whole: 'the phenomena of inanimate nature' (Godwin 1798a, I, 363); 'All nature swarms with life' (I, 455); 'the beauties which nature exhibits' (II, 426). But for the most part Godwin writes, in this sense, of 'the material universe' (I, 7, 367, etc.) or the 'system of the universe' (I, 332), or even simply of 'existence' (I, 171). The word 'nature' is used more frequently in its primary sense, to mean the essential qualities of a thing, and Godwin begins his discussion of 'the nature or constitution of man' in Book I, chapter v with a critical analysis of the maxim that humans ought to 'follow nature' (I, 83–4). This greater attempt at precision is of service in enabling us to see how very closely Malthus followed Godwin's usage, and just where he departed from it.

Godwin acknowledges an 'author of the universe' (I, 400) whose functions appear to have ceased after having brought the universe into existence. The 'laws of existence' are 'necessary and un-alterable' (I, 171): 'Everything is connected in the universe. If any man asserted that, if Alexander had not bathed in the river Cydnus, Shakespear would never have written, it would be impossible to prove that his assertion is untrue' (I, 160). The inevitability of cause and effect, or, more precisely, the uniformity of human experience of the succession of events, is the foundation of human knowledge: 'all that, strictly speaking, we know of the material universe, is this uniformity of events' (I, 364). Unlike Malthus, who follows him closely in his epistemology (Malthus 1798, 362–3), Godwin allows for no exceptions whatsoever on the part of the 'author of the universe': there are no 'miracles' in *Political Justice*. The necessary and unalterable laws of existence are the cause of that which humans experience as 'good', and also of that which they experience as 'evil'. Godwin makes no attempt to disguise or to justify the existence of evil, and scornfully repudiates the 'system of the optimists' (Godwin 1798a, I, 455–7). 'It may be said, with little license of phraseology, that all nature suffers... The whole history of the human species, taken in one point of view, appears a vast abortion' (1, 456–7). Though a 'sound philosophy' affords some consolation, it can never 'Vindicate the ways of God to Man'. There is no theodicy in *Political Justice*, and Godwin's attack upon theodicy is couched, characteristically, in psychological and political rather than in theological terms (1, 460).

'The nature or constitution of man' is part of the 'system of the universe', and exhibits 'external structure', 'the appetites and impressions growing out of that structure', and 'the capacity of combining ideas and inferring conclusions' (1, 84). The first two would seem to be what Malthus meant by 'corporal propensities', the last by what he called 'mind'. Godwin himself uses 'mind' in this same way, and devotes chapter IX of Book IV to showing that 'mind' is a 'mechanism' or machine for converting external stimuli into human response. 'Mind' has the faculties of 'experience' and of 'reason' (or 'understanding'). 'Experience brings in the materials with which intellect [presumably synonymous with "mind"] works' (1, 11) and is the basis of our knowledge of 'the events of the material universe' (1, 364). 'Reason' or 'understanding' – it is clear from the note to page 439 in volume II that Godwin means the same by either – is the infallible guide to all human conduct: indeed, insofar as it makes sense to say that we ought to follow 'nature', what this really means is that we ought to follow 'reason' (1, 84).

At the centre of Godwin's system is the vital argument, introduced in the new chapter v, of Book I of the second edition (1796), for the invincibility of reason and the consequent perfectibility of man.

Sound reasoning and truth, when adequately communicated, must always be victorious over error: Sound reasoning and truth are capable of being so communicated: Truth is omnipotent: The vices and moral weakness of man are not invincible: Man is perfectible, or in other words susceptible of perpetual improvement. (Godwin 1798a, 1, 86)

The third step in this argument, that 'Truth is omnipotent', is founded upon Godwin's account of 'voluntary' actions within a strictly Necessarian conception of 'mind', and is seen by his most recent commentator to have been the 'crucial move'.

voluntary action depends on our beliefs about what we are doing and what its consequences will be. It follows, therefore, that once we convince men that something is so, their voluntary actions will take account of that knowledge; their opinions will be altered, but so will their deeds. (Locke 1980, 96)

'Reason' is thus the true 'nature' of man, man is able to follow 'reason', and man ought to do so.

At first sight this seems to imply, as Don Locke has suggested, that Godwin takes issue with Hume 'in the famous debate of reason versus the passions' (Locke, 1980, 96). Insofar as the 'external structure' and the 'appetites and impressions' are the seat of the passions, these would seem to play no necessary part in determining human action; 'reason' or 'understanding' is both sovereign and sufficient. Godwin, however, defines 'passion' merely as 'a permanent and habitual tendency toward a certain course of action' (Godwin 1798a, I, 424). In this sense, 'passion' neither can nor ought to be ignored or eradicated, because it is actually the efficient cause of behaviour. 'Virtue, sincerity, justice... will never be very strenuously espoused, till they are ardently loved' (I, 81): We must learn to love virtue. This is where 'reason' plays its part, for 'the only way to conquer one passion is by the introduction of another', hence, if we employ our rational faculties we cannot fail of thus conquering our erroneous propensities' (I, 82). In chapter X of Book IV Godwin applies this analysis to a discussion of 'benevolence' – one of the 'passions' '... of the same general nature as avarice, or the love of fame' – and 'self-love'. Though both are motives of human action, 'self-love' may, by the use of 'reason', be superseded by 'benevolence' as the ruling passion and sole motive.

It would seem from this account of Godwin's use of the concepts which clustered around that of 'nature' in eighteenth-century social thought, first, that Malthus closely followed Godwin in his own usage; and secondly, that both were heirs of a tradition that runs through Priestley, Adam Smith, Hume and Hartley, and before that through Hutcheson and Shaftesbury, to Locke and Newton. Indeed, the idea of a 'science of human nature' and 'the programme of deriving from it the basic propositions of the individual social sciences are the idea and the programme of philosophers of natural law and indirectly of the scholastics' (Schumpeter 1954, 124).

The close resemblance between Malthus's conceptual scheme and that of Godwin may be seen by referring the latter to the diagram of figure 2. Malthus is found to have deviated from Godwin in only three respects. In the first place, the link between (1) God and (2) Laws of Nature does not exist in Godwin. In the second place, there is no acknowledgement in Godwin that although the 'general laws of nature' produce 'partial evil', 'we frequently observe... some bountiful provision, which acting as another general law, corrects the inequalities of the first' (Malthus 1798, 294): there is no secondary link between (4) general laws and (6) partial evil. Third, the link between (10) reason and (12) self-love, of the utmost importance for Malthus's polemic, is tenuous or absent in Godwin. Each of these requires some amplification.

Though making no use of the notion either in his polemic or in his theodicy, the Christian Malthus felt obliged to admit that 'the same power which framed and executes the laws of nature, may... change them all "in a moment, in the twinkling of an eye"' (Malthus 1798, 160). But 'The miracles that accompanied... [biblical] revelation when they had once excited the attention of mankind... had performed their part...; and these communications of the divine will were afterward left to make their way by their own intrinsic excellence' (393). The age of miracles is past, and in each of the ten references to miracles which occur in the first *Essay* (12, 127, 160, 239, 244, 246, 247, 361, 385, 392) Malthus is concerned to maintain Godwin's own position: that the 'operations of what we call nature' are conducted 'according to fixed laws'. Why then did Malthus insist on this dialectically redundant point? In part, no doubt, his cloth required it. In part, perhaps, he wished to emphasize his common ground with Godwin by introducing miracles only in order to set them aside as irrelevant. More important than either, I believe, is the contrast between his Newtonian, 'voluntarist' understanding of nature and Godwin's Leibnizian, 'immanentist' understanding derived from Priestley (1817–32). It has lately been argued by P. M. Heimann (1978) that there was a transition during the eighteenth century 'from the Newtonian view that the activity of the natural order was to be ascribed to the continued sustenance of passive matter by God's will' to the view that 'activity was intrinsic to matter and immanent in the natural order' (Heimann 1978, 272). The former is compatible with miraculous intervention, the latter is not. Priestley was an important influence upon Godwin in the 1770s (Locke 1980, 19–20). Malthus was well grounded in Newton as an undergraduate. In each of Malthus's references to miracles noted above there is clear allusion to Newton's doctrine, as set out in the *Opticks*, that God 'may vary the Laws of Nature, and make worlds of several sorts in several parts of the universe' (Newton 1952 (1730), 403; cit. Heimann 1978, 273). Behind all this is the important ideological difference, noted by J. G. A. Pocock (1985b, 548–55) following Margaret C. Jacob (1976, 1981), between the subversive implications of a pantheism more Spinozan than Leibnizian and the reassuring regularity of a transcendent creation. For 'if God stood off from His universe, surveying the operations He had set in motion, both God and reason acted through its established workings. The public Newton [as distinct from the secret, heterodox Newton] was thus a figure of the conservative and clerical enlightenment' (Pocock 1985b, 549).

The second matter on which Malthus and Godwin diverge is that of theodicy. For Godwin, theodicy is not merely otiose: it is morally suspect.

... those who believe that all the unfortunate events and sufferings that exist in the world, will be found, in some mysterious way, to have been the fittest instrument of universal good, are in danger of being less scrupulous than they ought to be, in the means they shall themselves select for the accomplishment of their purposes. (Godwin 1798a, I, 460)

The 'cosmic toryism' classically enounced in the *Essay on Man* – 'All Discord, Harmony not understood' – can too easily be used to justify inequality, luxury and other social evils; which Godwin repudiates with obvious allusion to Pope (Godwin 1798a, II, 490). For Malthus on the other hand, a Newtonian conception of God, a Christian profession and a polemical purpose alike demanded theodicy. Quoting Pope, here as elsewhere in the first *Essay* without shame and indeed with evident enjoyment, Malthus observes that 'It cannot be considered as an unimproving exercise of the human mind to endeavour to

> "Vindicate the ways of God to man"'.
>
> (Malthus 1798, 349)

The last point on which Malthus parted company with Godwin's conceptual framework is by far the most important. It is crucial to Godwin's argument both that 'reason' may be sovereign, and that 'reason' may determine pure 'benevolence' untainted by 'self-love'. Godwin believed himself to be following Shaftesbury, Butler, Hutcheson and Hume in demonstrating the 'practicability of disinterested action' (Godwin 1798a, I, 422). For Malthus, on the other hand, it is equally crucial to show that 'the inevitable laws of nature' must create economic and social conditions in which 'self-love' becomes 'the mainspring of the great machine'. *Wealth of Nations* is the most obvious source of this doctrine, though behind it lie Mandeville, Helvetius, Beccaria and Hobbes (Schumpeter 1954, 122–34). 'Benevolence' is not denied, and may be, as Godwin had suggested, 'generated perhaps, slowly and gradually from self-love' (Malthus 1798, 294). But its 'proper office' is 'to soften the partial evils arising from self-love' and 'it can never be substituted in its place' (295). The link between 'reason' and 'self-love', embarrassing to Godwin and minimized by him, is therefore essential to Malthus's argument.

Though Malthus and Godwin differed sharply in this respect, however, it is important to note that both were engaged in the same, characteristic task of eighteenth-century social theory, which was to demonstrate that

> ...God and Nature link'd the gen'ral frame,
> And bade Self-love and Social be the same.

Godwin followed the anti-Hobbesian tradition which runs through Shaftesbury's *Inquiry Concerning Virtue* (1699), according to which God 'has made it according to the *private interest* and *Good* of everyone, to work towards the *general Good*' (Shaftesbury 1699, cit. Willey 1940, 74). Though conceding – with Godwin – that

> Self-love...serves the virtuous mind to wake

Malthus denied Pope's reductionist 'but' and inclined more to the Hobbesian view of 'a general inclination of all mankind, a perpetual and restless desire of power after power, that ceaseth only in death' (Hobbes 1957, 64). Hobbes himself had failed to provide a satisfactory account of the way in which this kinetic energy could be harnessed to the 'general Good', for the political absolutism entailed by his theory of social contract was unacceptable to Enlightenment sensibility. That need was supplied by the Rational Dissenters' doctrine of 'natural liberty' which reached its full flowering in Priestley (Lincoln 1938, 175–82; Willey 1940, 178–200), powerfully reinforced by political economy, or Mandeville made respectable by Adam Smith (Schumpeter 1954, 184, n.16). In economic matters, at any rate,

> every individual...intends only his own gain, and he is in this, as in many other cases, led by an invisible hand to promote an end which was no part of his intention...By pursuing his own interest he frequently promotes that

of society more effectually than when he really intends to promote it. (Smith 1910, I, 400)

Malthus therefore reconciled 'benevolence' and 'self-love' in a way that is diametrically opposed to Godwin's. It is not so much the case that by being 'benevolent' we shall actually be practising (enlightened) 'self-love', as that, by following the dictates of 'self-love', we shall actually be practising (enlightened) 'benevolence'.

This central difference between Malthus and Godwin corresponds in some ways to that between the 'two fundamental senses of "Nature"' in eighteenth-century social theory distinguished by Willey (1940, 205): we may call them the 'historical' and the 'philosophical'. In the 'historical' sense nature means 'things as they now are or have become', *natura naturata*; in the other sense, 'things as they may become', *natura naturans*. In the former sense the concept functioned as a 'regulating principle' embodied in the 'cosmic toryism' of Pope's famous slogan: 'Whatever is, is Right'. As the eighteenth century wore on, the latter sense of the concept came to function as a 'liberating principle': 'Man is Nature's growing point... one might treat Nature as dross to be moulded in our own likeness: we must *alter* rather than explain, and *make* the future instead of letting it be' (Willey 1940, 206). Holbach and Godwin, above all, used 'Nature' in this sense as 'the creed of revolution'. According to this way of thinking, Malthus may be conceived as having reasserted the 'system of optimism' of sixty years before.

In my opinion, however, this would do less than justice either to Malthus's aims or to his achievement. Moreover it would leave unexplained his decisive victory over Godwinism. Something new had been added to the debate since the *Essay on Man*: the emergence of classical political economy. When human society is conceived as a system in stable (and stationary) equilibrium, Willey's distinction between *natura naturata* and *natura naturans* is subverted. Except when some exogenous disturbance alters the constants of the system 'things as they may become' are always going to be 'things as they now are or have become'. There is no reason to contemplate this with satisfaction, as Malthus well knew.

The view which he has given of human life has a melancholy hue; but he feels conscious, that he has drawn these dark tints, from a conviction that they are really in the picture (Malthus 1798, iv)

Theodicy still requires a demonstration that 'Whatever is, is Right'. But this is now no matter for Pope's 'chearful' smugness, but rather for the dissonant gloom with which Handel set the self-same words at the end of Part II of *Jephtha*:

> How dark, O Lord, are thy decrees!
> All hid from mortal sight!
> All our joys to sorrow turning,
> And our triumphs into mourning,
>   As the night succeeds the day,
>   No certain bliss,
>   No solid peace,
>   We mortals know
>   On earth below.
> Yet on this maxim still obey:
> WHATEVER IS, IS RIGHT.

NEGATIVE POLEMIC: THE MODEL OF POPULATION EQUILIBRIUM AND THE REFUTATION OF GODWIN

'There is a principle in human society', observed Godwin in Book VII of *Political Justice*, 'by which population is perpetually kept down to the means of subsistence' (Godwin 1798a, II, 466). It was therefore incumbent upon him to defend his 'system of equality' from 'the principle of population', to which purpose he devoted chapter IX of Book VIII. Though conceding that 'the number of inhabitants in a country will perhaps never be found... greatly to increase, beyond the facility of subsistence', Godwin believed that 'Myriads of centuries of still increasing population may pass away, and the earth be yet found sufficient for the support of its inhabitants' (516, 518). In a purely formal sense, the first *Essay on the Principle of Population* may be regarded as an attempt to undermine Godwin's defence in that chapter by a more consistent application of Godwin's own arguments.

Malthus acknowledged at the outset that there was nothing particularly novel about his theory of population.

> The principles on which it depends have been explained in part by Hume, and more at large by Dr Adam Smith. It has been advanced and applied to the present subject [as Godwin also acknowledged], though not with its proper weight, or in the most forcible point of view, by Mr Wallace: and it may probably have been stated by many writers that I have never met with. (Malthus 1798, 8)

Schumpeter has shown, indeed, that the theory had an ancestry of more than two centuries. 'Divested of nonessentials, the "Malt-

husian" Principle of Population sprang fully developed from the
brain of Botero in 1589' (Schumpeter 1954, 254). The tendency of
population to increase geometrically was suggested by Petty,
Süssmilch and Ortes as well as by Wallace; Franklin, Cantillon,
Mirabeau, Steuart, Chastellux, Quesnay and Townsend had all
maintained – though without specifying any precise mechanism –
that population tends to an equilibrium determined by the means of
subsistence (Schumpeter 1954, 255–8). The biblical source of Malthusian theory is to be found in the Book of Ecclesiastes, chapter 5, verse
11. That theory is epitomized in the concept of the 'preventive
check': which Plato clearly identified in the *Republic* (II, 372; see
Plato 1953, I, 158–9). The originality of the first *Essay* resides not in
the 'principle of population' itself but in the use Malthus made of
it in constructing both his 'negative', and more especially his
'positive', polemic.

Malthus proposed that population growth is governed by the
'fixed laws of our nature', which he expressed in the form of 'two
postulata'. 'First, That food is necessary to the existence of man.
Secondly, That the passion between the sexes is necessary, and will
remain nearly in its present state' (Malthus 1798, 11). It follows
from these that if food were freely available, a population of humans
would increase during a certain period by an amount which was
proportionate to its size at the beginning of that period. For given
the biological and institutional parameters of marriage, fertility,
longevity and the like, a certain number of live births would occur
which would exceed deaths from old age (resulting from live births
at an earlier period, when population had been smaller). Malthus
deduced from this a mathematical theorem of the greatest generality,
applicable to all populations of living organisms and later acknowledged by Charles Darwin as an inspiration of his own theories:
'Population, *when unchecked*, increases in a geometrical ratio'
(Malthus 1798, 14, my italics).

When food is scarce, however, the rate of population growth
declines as the 'positive checks' – such as malnutrition, disease,
starvation – increase the death-rate and lower the birth-rate. A
minimum 'subsistence' requirement of food per capita may be
conceived, which may be socially conditioned in light of the
'preventive check', at which the birth-rate and death-rate are equal.
If population reaches a level at which this is the case, any further
increase will depend strictly upon a subsequent increase in the
supply of food.

The food supply is itself a consequence of the application of human labour, assisted by capital goods, to the available agricultural and grazing land: if population were to increase and more labour and capital be applied to food production, formerly uncultivated land would be drawn into use and food supplies would increase. But the additional land, being of lower fertility than that already farmed, would yield less per acre, hence the increase in food would be less than proportionate to the increase in labour applied. A similar effect, noted by Turgot and subsequently identified by economists as 'diminishing returns', would occur if already cultivated land were farmed more intensively. Malthus illustrated his theory of production with the claim that 'Subsistence increases only in an arithmetical ratio': if the population of Britain were to double every twenty-five years, for example, 'The very utmost that we can conceive, is... that the whole produce of the Island might be increased every twenty-five years, by a quantity of subsistence equal to what it at present produces'. This rule is 'certainly far beyond the truth'; to imagine any greater rate of increase in food 'would be contrary to all our knowledge of the qualities of land' (22).

A detailed consideration of the implications of these propositions is contained in the Appendices. It is there shown that upon certain assumptions, later made explicit by Malthus, Chalmers, Ricardo and others – chiefly that each new entrant to the work-force can be equipped with the proper complement of housing, tools and the like – the 'ratios' of food and population growth imply a 'production function' relating inputs of labour to output of food under conditions of diminishing returns. A simple, merely ecological model of food and population equilibrium may be constructed by means of this production function together with two assumptions, one made explicit by Malthus and the other merely implicit. The first assumption is that when individuals receive a real (or 'food') income which exceeds some socially-conditioned minimum, population will increase. This is merely a corollary of Malthus's assertion that 'Population, when unchecked, increases...'. The second necessary assumption, never stated by Malthus or his contemporaries, but seemingly implied by them, is that some social mechanism exists for assigning food to individuals and for assigning individuals to food production such that the latter is maximized subject to resource and technical constraints (see Waterman 1988).

It is an important theorem of this model that in the absence of technical progress, increased capital intensity or land discoveries or improvement, *the average per capita supply of food will decrease as population increases.* When average per capita food supply has fallen to the socially-conditioned 'subsistence' level, food and population growth will cease and the system will be in equilibrium. The stability of this equilibrium is guaranteed by the two adjustment assumptions. For if any external 'shock' disturbs the equilibrium relation between food and population, population (and food production) will grow or decline until the equilibrium relation is restored.

It must be noted that Malthus did not actually construct the models presented in the Appendices. But he did make use of their more important results in his polemic, claiming or assuming that the results were entailed by his population theory. The Appendices may thus be regarded as a 'rational reconstruction' of Malthus's argument which make clear the logical relations between his stated assumptions and his stated conclusions. It is, I believe, the simple, or 'ecological' model (see Appendix 1) that was implied by Malthus when he wrote of 'This natural inequality of the two powers of population, and of production in the earth, and that great law of her nature which must constantly keep their effects equal' (1798, 16).

Chapters I to VII of the first *Essay* are devoted to a discursive exposition of the properties of this system, in particular to the tendency of the checks to population to produce 'misery' and 'vice'. The argument is then summarized in three propositions:

> That the increase of population is necessarily limited by the means of subsistence.
> That population does invariably increase when the means of subsistence increase. And,
> That the superior power of population is repressed, and the actual population kept equal to the means of subsistence by misery and vice. (140–1)

Chapter VIII deals with Wallace, and his 'error' in supposing – like Godwin who followed him – that the equilibrium of food and population belongs only to a remote future. There follow some essentially parenthetic objections to Condorcet in this and the following chapter, before what is really the centre-piece of the entire book: the demolition of Godwin's 'system of equality' in chapter x.

Exactly in the manner of Hume's essay 'Of the Balance of Trade', Malthus performs a mental experiment to investigate the behaviour of a social system in disequilibrium. The reader is invited to 'imagine for a moment Mr Godwin's beautiful system of equality realized in its utmost purity':

War and contention cease: Unwholesome trades and manufactories do not exist. Crowds no longer collect together in great and pestilent cities...The greater part of the happy inhabitants...live in hamlets and farm-houses...All men are equal. The labours of luxury are at an end. And the necessary labours of agriculture are shared amicably among all. (Malthus 1798, 181–2)

Marriage is abolished, and paternity of no consequence, for children are maintained and educated by all in the spirit of benevolence (Godwin 1798a, II, 512–13). We are to suppose the population of Great Britain at its 1798 level.

'I cannot conceive', wrote Malthus, 'a form of society so favourable upon the whole to population' (1798, 184). For in these circumstances, with all restraints removed, population might be expected to double in twenty-five years. Suppose that the production of food, too, were doubled. Population continues to grow. But 'during the next period of doubling where will the food be found to satisfy the importunate demands of increasing numbers?' (188). As population rises, the average per capita food ratio declines steadily. 'Alas! what becomes of the picture where men lived in the midst of plenty: where no man was obliged to provide with anxiety and pain for his restless wants...This beautiful fabric of the imagination vanishes at the severe touch of truth' (189).

Inexorably increasing scarcity re-awakens 'the mighty law of self-preservation' and 'expels all the softer and more exalted emotions of the soul' (190). Theft and falsehood undermine the mutual trust on which 'benevolence' depends, and 'self-love resumes his wonted empire and lords it triumphant over the world' (190). 'No human institutions here existed, to the perverseness of which Mr. Godwin ascribes the original sin of the worst men' (191). Their absence indeed, must expose humans to the worst consequences of scarcity. In eleven brilliant pages, worthy to set beside the Hume of the *Essays*, Malthus has dealt a mortal blow to Godwin's great achievement. Viewed from the standpoint of negative polemic, the remainder of the first *Essay* – almost exactly half the text – is devoted to what are essentially mopping-up operations.

As population further increases, the per capita food ratio further declines and 'In these ages want would indeed be triumphant, and rapine and murder must reign at large' (192). Long before this occurred, however 'the most active and comprehensive intellects of the society' would convene to institute 'some immediate measures to be taken for the general safety' (195). Property rights in land and its produce would have to be assigned, and sanctions imposed for theft, even the death penalty if necessary (196–7). Because of accidental differences in the fertility of land and the ability and luck of individuals, some would find themselves with surpluses to dispose of, and others be willing to offer their labour in exchange for those surpluses (198). The economic framework of a civilized society would therefore be brought about by the necessity of preventing anarchy in face of acute scarcity: private property rights in land and produced goods, a workforce consisting of those with insufficient land to provide for their own maintenance, and a market system for the exchange of goods and productive services. 'It seems highly probable', Malthus concluded, 'that an administration of property, not very different from that which prevails in civilized States at present, would be established, as the best, though inadequate, remedy, for the evils which were pressing on the society' (198).

Those 'who had turned their attention to the true cause of the difficulties under which the community laboured' would soon conclude that 'some check to population…was imperiously called for: that the most natural and obvious check seemed to be, to make every man provide for his own children' (198, 199). The 'institution of marriage' or something similar 'seems to be the natural result of these reasonings' (200). But when 'these two fundamental laws of society, the security of property, and the institution of marriage, were once established, inequality of conditions must necessarily follow'. Inheritance would ensure that some would be 'the owners of surplus'; whereas all others 'who were in want of food would be urged by imperious necessity to offer their labour in exchange for this article' (204, 205).

And thus it appears, that a society constructed, according to the most beautiful form that imagination can conceive, with *benevolence* for its moving principle, instead of *self-love*, and with every evil disposition in all its members corrected by *reason* and not force, would, from the *inevitable laws of nature*, and not from any original depravity of man, in a very short period, degenerate into a society, constructed upon a plan not essentially different from that which prevails in every known State at present; I mean, a society divided into a class of proprietors, and a class of labourers, and with *self-love* as the mainspring of the great machine. (207; my italics)

Either because he really believed it or simply for purposes of argument, Malthus agreed with Godwin to ignore 'original depravity' and to focus attention upon the 'inevitable laws of nature'. It is then seen that upon Godwin's own presuppositions his argument must collapse. This is because he has failed to understand or appreciate the 'laws of nature' he wants to talk about. 'Whatever is' gets to be the way it is because the 'laws of nature' determine a stable social equilibrium. Disturb that equilibrium, gradually as Godwin wished to do, or violently as some of the other Jacobins desired, and 'not thirty years could elapse' before we are back to the status quo ante. Godwin is wrong, but so too is Burke. Mankind has nothing to hope from revolution, to be sure; yet neither has it anything to fear.

Now it is evident that an argument of this sort is vulnerable to rebuttal of exactly the same kind as that which Malthus applied to Godwin. Suppose it were Malthus rather than Godwin who had been mistaken about the 'laws of nature'. As we have seen, Malthus considered one such line of objection in advance: that the period which must elapse before equilibrium is reached would be so great that the population-theoretic argument is irrelevant. In chapter XI he next considered another possible objection: Godwin's conjecture about 'the extinction of passion between the sexes' (Godwin 1798a, I, 72; II, 527–8) which if plausible would strike down his second postulate and undermine the entire system based on it.

In dealing with this seemingly trivial difficulty Malthus outlined two arguments which he employed in subsequent chapters for more important purposes. In the first place he once again turned Godwin's own arguments upon their author. The 'uniformity of events', the latter had said, is the 'general foundation of inference and reason' (Godwin 1798a, I, 364). But, observed Malthus, 'towards the extinction of passion between the sexes, no observable progress whatever has hitherto been made' (Malthus 1798, 216). In the second place, by exposing the absurdity of Godwin's reductionist account of sexual love (Malthus 1798, 214–16; cf. Godwin 1798a, I, 72) he illustrated the judgement to be made in chapter XIII: 'Mr Godwin considers man too much in the light of a being merely intellectual. This error, at least such as I conceive it to be, pervades his whole work, and mixes itself with all his reasonings' (Malthus 1798, 252). The first of these arguments is then used in chapter XII against the conjectures of Godwin and Condorcet concerning 'the future approaching of man towards immortality on earth'. The second is developed in the following chapter in order to administer the *coup de grâce* in chapter XIV.

Malthus admitted that 'the voluntary actions of men may originate in their opinions' but attempted to show, in chapter XIII, that 'these opinions will be very differently modified in creatures compounded of a rational faculty and corporal propensities, from what they would be, in beings wholly intellectual' (252). To ignore the 'disturbing force' of the 'corporal propensities' is like 'calculating the velocity of a falling body *in vacuo*; and persisting in it, that it would be the same through whatever resisting mediums it might fall. This was not Newton's mode of philosophizing' (253). Malthus appeals to common experience to support his psychological dualism:

A truth may be brought home to [one's] conviction as a rational being, though he may act contrary to it as a compound being. The cravings of hunger, the love of liquor, the desire of possessing a beautiful woman, will urge men to actions, of the fatal consequences of which, to the general interests of society, they are perfectly well convinced, even at the very time they commit them. (255)

If correct, 'almost all Mr Godwin's reasonings on the subject of coercion in his 7th chapter [i.e. Godwin 1798a, Book VII], will appear to be founded on error' (255). At this point in the first *Essay* the ground has been fully prepared for the final destruction of Godwin's system. At the centre of that system, as we have already seen (p. 31 above), were the five propositions respecting human perfectibility introduced in Book I, chapter v of the second (1796) edition.

(1) Sound reasoning and truth, when adequately communicated, must always be victorious over error:
(2) Sound reasoning and truth are capable of being so communicated;
(3) Truth is omnipotent;
(4) The vices and moral weakness of man are not invincible;
(5) Man is perfectible, or...susceptible of perpetual improvement.

Chapter XIV of the first *Essay* deploys the leading ideas developed in the previous chapters to subvert these.

    The first three of Godwin's five propositions form a syllogism. Malthus showed that his own, dualist account of human psychology denies either the minor premise (Godwin's second proposition) or both major and minor (first and second propositions) and hence that the third proposition falls to the ground (Malthus 1798, 264–5). Malthus correctly identified the third proposition as the 'crucial move' (Locke 1980, 96) and struck at the very heart of Godwin's argument. Godwin had also maintained that human nature is conditioned by circumstances and in particular, that 'the greater part of the vice and weaknesses of men, proceed from the injustice of their political and social institutions' (Malthus 1798, 266–7). Even if this were true, the population-theoretic argument has shown that such institutions are inevitable. But in fact it is not true: quite independently of institutions, the principle of population determines that 'the greater part of mankind ... must be ever subject to the evil temptations arising from want, besides other passions' (267). But if all or most are subject to 'such impressions, or combinations of impressions', and if we rely upon that 'uniformity of events' which both agree is the foundation of knowledge, then inevitable conditions will produce 'a variety of bad men', and 'According to Mr Godwin's own conception of the formation of character, it is surely as improbable that ... all men will be virtuous, as that sixes will come up a hundred times following upon the dice' (267). Godwin's fourth proposition must therefore go, for reasons quite unconnected with its logical dependence upon the – discredited – first three propositions. The fifth proposition follows from the first four and must fall with them. Therefore, Malthus concluded, 'As the five propositions, which I have been examining may be considered as the corner stones of Mr Godwin's fanciful structure ... he must be considered as having failed in the great object of his undertaking' (276–7). The negative polemic is complete. Political revolution, even gradual reform, is self-reversing. Social and political institutions, such as now exist, are inescapable. Not institutions, but the 'inevitable laws of nature', are the cause of human wickedness and misery. In merely temporal, political terms, human perfectibility is an unfeasible goal.

POSITIVE POLEMIC: THE 'ESTABLISHED ADMINISTRATION OF PROPERTY' AS A SOCIAL GOOD

It is unlikely that the *Anti-Jacobin* and its readers would have been so anxious for the 'exposure' of Godwin's 'whole theory' had the latter been confined to speculation upon the omnipotence of reason and the extinction of passion between the sexes. 'Jacobinism', understood broadly as 'the ideology of the French Revolution', had been identified by Burke as 'an attack on property' (Schofield 1986, 603). What made *Political Justice* a dangerous book, notwithstanding the unpopular price its author was so prudent as to ask, was its powerfully argued assault upon 'the established administration of property' in Book VIII.

'The subject of property is the key-stone that completes the fabric of political justice', Godwin saw; and with characteristic moderation he provided an analysis which afforded a justification of private property in some cases, and which disqualified a violent or even a political redistribution in cases where no justification of property rights could be found. 'Persuasion, and not force, is the legitimate instrument for influencing the human mind': though my claim be stronger than a possessor's, 'my endeavours to put myself in possession, whether effectual or ineffectual, will be attended with worse consequences, than all the good that would follow from right being done as to the object itself'. Nevertheless, the arguments for redistribution should be stated, for truth will out, 'and ultimately... produce, without a shadow of violence, the most complete revolution in the maxims of civil society' (Godwin 1798a, II, 451, 452, 453; see also Claeys 1984).

Godwin identified two cases in which a right to private property may be upheld: first, with respect to 'the means of subsistence and happiness'; secondly – by a loosely-stated version of the Lockean argument – to 'the fruits of our labours'. These are sharply distinguished from the third, unjustifiable case: the system 'by which one man enters into the faculty of disposing of the produce of another man's industry' (II, 435). As Proudhon was later to argue, Godwin regarded all accumulation of property as 'usurpation' (II, 434, 444). Even more strikingly, he foreshadowed Marx in perceiving the appropriation of surplus value to be exploitation:

Every man may calculate, in every glass of wine he drinks, and in every ornament he annexes to his person, how many individuals have been condemned to slavery and sweat, incessant drudgery, unwholesome food, continual hardships, deplorable ignorance, and brutal insensibility, that he may be supplied with these luxuries. (II, 435)

The 'master-tradesman who employs labourers', Godwin clearly saw, is able to 'tax' the result of their industry 'by the accidental advantage of possessing a capital' (II, 551). Accumulated property is thus the source of the class struggle (II, 463), of war (II, 466) and of proletarianization, for it 'forms men into one common mass, and makes them fit to be played upon like a brute machine' (II, 466).

Fascinating as these Marxian intimations may be, the main purpose of the all-important chapter III in Book VIII is to set out the

more typically Godwinian objections to 'the established administration of property' – a phrase by which both Godwin and Malthus
seem to have meant the legally-sanctioned assignment and inheritance of actually very unequal property rights in land and other
means of production. The first of these is that wealth creates a sense
of dependence in him who lacks it, a 'servile and truckling spirit'
which undermines 'the dictates of his own understanding'. Next,
that it breeds a 'desire of opulence' which directs human energy to
the acquisition of wealth. For though Samuel Johnson, voicing the
common sense of his age, had declared that 'There are few ways in
which a man can be more innocently employed than in getting
money', Godwin feared rather, that one so employed would usually
be found 'inhumanly trampling upon the interest of others'.
Godwin's third objection to accumulated property was that it
'treads the powers of thought in the dust, extinguishes the sparks of
genius, and reduces the great mass of mankind to be immersed in
sordid cares'. His fourth objection was the 'multiplication of vice'
which it generated, both the 'crimes of the poor' and the 'passions
of the rich': for 'The spirit of oppression, the spirit of servility, and
the spirit of fraud...are the immediate growth of the established
administration of property'. Finally, Godwin believed, the accumulation of property inhibits population and therefore 'may be
considered as strangling a considerable portion of our children in
their cradle' (II, 454, 455, 456, 457, 460, 462, 463, 467).

What I have called the 'positive polemic' of the first *Essay* consists
of three – less than fully realized – lines of argument in defence of
'the established administration of property', all of which are derived
in some way from the economic model of population equilibrium.
First, as we have already seen (p. 42 above), is a sociological
explanation of the 'upward arrow' which leads from a Hobbesian
state of nature to the status quo ante. (Whether we like it or not, we
are stuck with 'the established administration of property' in the
long run.) Secondly, there is an attempt by Malthus to rebut the
claim which Godwin made in chapter VII of Book VIII, namely that
'the benefits of luxury' are illusory. ('The established administration
of property' is actually a good thing because the 'owners of surplus'
spend some of it on high culture.) Finally, there is in the first *Essay* the
torso of an argument showing that under a régime of private
property in land with competitive labour and product markets the
social surplus is maximized at equilibrium of population and food

production. (The status quo is, after all, the best of all possible worlds.) The first of these arguments seeks to undermine all of Godwin's objections to property by showing them to be irrelevant. The second deals particularly with Godwin's third objection though it also bears to some extent upon the first. Malthus's third argument begins by granting the truth of Godwin's fifth objection, showing the limitation of population to be beneficial in a sense which helps to deal with Godwin's first three objections. Godwin's fourth objection – that property engenders 'vice' – was already answered generally by the explanation of 'misery' and 'vice' as consequences of the principle of population.

The first of Malthus's arguments is, in effect, a very rough sketch of an eclectic social contract theory owing something to Hobbes and Rousseau, but little if anything, to Locke. The Godwinian utopia which Malthus takes for the initial conditions of his mental experiment resembles the state of nature conceived by John Locke. For 'Men living together according to reason without a common superior on earth...are properly in a state of nature' (Locke 1967, 298). Before any contract of society is formed, however, increasing scarcity caused by the principle of population transforms Locke's state of nature into that of Hobbes. For it is inevitable 'that *nature* should thus dissociate, and render men apt to invade, and destroy one another' (Hobbes 1957, 82; my italics). Malthus seems here to have followed Rousseau, who assumed, 'for the sake of argument that a point was reached in the history of mankind when the obstacles to continuing in a state of Nature were stronger than the forces which each individual could employ to the end of continuing in it' (Rousseau 1960, 179). 'Some kind of convention would then be called', and a contract of society determined in order, first, 'to make a more complete division of land' and, secondly, 'to secure every man's stock against violation'. The latter would require 'the most powerful sanctions, even...death itself' and hence some contract of government is also implied. Once the 'established administration of property' was restored, Malthus envisaged, as we have seen, that a political society would reintroduce the institution of marriage and arrange to punish women who violated the law of chastity (Malthus 1798, 195, 196, 197, 200–3). With marriage and private property, the inheritance of the latter is tacitly assumed.

Malthus acknowledged in chapter x that 'the established adminis-tration of property' would be 'the best, though inadequate, remedy, for the evils which were pressing upon the society' (198). But he was led by an intuitive, never fully explicit grasp of the logic of his subsequent chapters to make a far stronger claim in chapter xv. The inequality caused by private property, marriage and inheritance is socially beneficent. Since the poorest must live at the subsistence level, the richer classes have a surplus to spend on all 'that distinguishes the civilized, from the savage state' (287).

Godwin had considered the objection 'from the benefits of luxury' in chapter vii of Book viii, noting that Mandeville and Hume had strongly urged the connexion between 'luxury' and 'refinement in the Arts'. 'We cannot reasonably expect', the latter had said, 'that a piece of woollen cloth will be wrought to perfection in a nation which is altogether ignorant of astronomy, or where ethics are neglected'. Nor can we expect that 'a government will be well-modelled by a people, who know not how to make a spinning wheel, or to employ a loom to advantage' (Hume 1788, I, 243, 246). Godwin had met this argument in two ways. In the first place, if inequality and luxury really were necessary to high culture, then high culture must go. It was probably this, he thought, 'that contributed to make Rousseau an advocate of the savage state'. But fortunately 'this is by no means the real alternative'. A state of inequality and luxury may be regarded as 'a stage through which it was necessary to pass, in order to arrive at the goal of civilisation'. Having arrived, 'we may throw down the scaffolding, when the edifice is complete'. All can work for the necessary half-an-hour a day at providing subsistence; then all can devote the rest of their time to those other things which though not necessary, are yet 'highly conducive to our well-being' (Godwin 1798a, II, 491, 492, 493).

Having already demonstrated, in his negative polemic, that Godwin's second – utopian – point was ill-founded, Malthus dealt with the first point partly by mere reassertion (man may not 'safely throw down the ladder by which he has risen to this eminence'), and partly by giving examples of the social benefits of surplus expenditure. Godwin (II, 458), noting the evils of government patronage, had correctly observed that 'the rent-roll of the lands of England is a much more formidable pension-list'. Malthus agreed, but took a different view of the consequences. If the surplus is merely given away to the poor 'the rich man would feel his power, and the poor man his dependence'. If it is used as formerly by the 'Great

Lords' to support armies of personal retainers the case is little better. But the growth of 'trades and manufactures' stimulated by the surplus has reduced the sense of dependence and brought about 'our present degree of civil liberty'. 'The man who does a day's work for me confers full as great an obligation upon me, as I do upon him' (Malthus 1798, 292, 293). In this, Malthus faithfully followed Hume, who had said that 'progress in the arts is rather favourable to liberty' because of the consequent enlargement of 'that middling rank of men, who are the best and firmest basis of public liberty' (Hume 1788, I, 249–50). But Malthus took the argument a stage further, for it is also the case that 'The middle regions of society seem best suited to intellectual improvement' (Malthus 1798, 367). Hence the agricultural surplus, being disbursed by landlords in part at least on clergymen and college fellows, so far from treading 'the powers of thought in the dust', is actually the final cause of 'all the noblest exertions of human genius', and of 'all the finer and more delicate emotions of the soul' (286–7).

So far none of this is more than yet another rehash of some already overcooked ingredients of eighteenth-century political controversy. Even the population-theoretic account of the degeneration of a Lockean into a Hobbesian state of nature had been noted by Wallace in 1761 (Hartwick 1988). What is entirely new in the first *Essay*, though as yet only incipient and half understood, is Malthus's third argument: that with private property in land, population dynamics maximize the surplus at equilibrium. It is this which we must now consider in some detail.

ECONOMIC ANALYSIS AND THE CHOICE OF IDEOLOGY

The model of population equilibrium which forms the core of Malthus's *negative* polemic is a simple one which deliberately abstracts from the effects of private property and factor markets. It is appropriate to the 'savage state', in which population pressures will 'dissociate, and render men apt to invade, and destroy one another'. And it is the fundamental conception of the ecological study of all living organisms.

The germs of existence contained in this spot of earth, with ample food, and ample room to expand in, would fill millions of worlds in the course of a few thousand years. Necessity, that imperious all pervading law of nature, restrains them within the prescribed bounds. The race of plants, and the race of animals shrink under this great restrictive law. (Malthus 1798, 15)

But with the emergence of private property and competitive wages the simple model is no longer adequate to capture the most important economic relations of civilized society. For the effect of these institutions is to produce a drastically different state of affairs, at equilibrium, from that which would be the case in the 'savage state'. In the first place, population will be very much lower, implying an *average* per capita food supply significantly above the socially-conditioned subsistence level. But secondly, the propertyless majority will receive *only* that subsistence wage (hence their number will remain constant), whilst the remainder, regarded as a social 'surplus', will be appropriated by the property-owning minority. Property-owners, regarded as numerically insignificant (and either immune from the propensity to procreate or as governed by a very much higher conception of 'subsistence') disburse the surplus to an 'unproductive' population, also paid at the subsistence wage, which supplies personal services, luxury goods, education, religion, national defence, and in short, 'everything...that distinguishes the civilized, from the savage state'.

All components of a more sophisticated model needed to analyse these effects are to be found in the first *Essay*. At many points Malthus writes as though the model were explicit in his mind. Yet in others he reveals clearly that it is not, and in one passage actually contradicts the logic of his own argument. Though it is important, therefore, to isolate the sophisticated model which undergirds his *positive* polemic, we must be more than usually careful to avoid what Skinner has called a 'mythology of coherence'.

The structure of the 'sophisticated' model, expressed in the terminology of modern economic analysis, is set out in the Appendices. It is sufficient here to indicate its more important features, and the results which follow from it.

In addition to the central idea of the 'simple' model – that the 'ratios' imply a theory of production which in turn implies that *average* food production per capita will fall as population grows – the crucial insight of the 'sophisticated' model is that the *increment* of production associated with an increment of population and employment will also fall as population and employment rise. Now if capitalist farmers employ landless labourers the maximum real wage at which it would be profitable to do so is the incremental

52   *The first* Essay on Population: *political economy*

contribution to production of the worker. It follows from this that as population grows – with no increase in the amount of capital per head, no technical progress and no land improvement – the maximum real wage must continuously fall. Part of this will appear in falling nominal wages, part in rising food prices.

...the price of labour must tend towards a decrease; while the price of provisions would at the same time tend to rise...it very rarely happens that the nominal price of labour universally falls; but we well know that it frequently remains the same, while the nominal price of provisions has been gradually increasing...during this period, the condition of the lower orders of the community must gradually grow worse and worse. (1798, 30, 34–5)

If a fall in the price of labour, by raising profits, encourages capital accumulation, more employment will be offered and the wage begin to rise; until further population brings it down again. Malthus sketched a theory of 'oscillations' of this kind in chapter II of the first *Essay* (Waterman 1987). But if the rate of profit falls, like the real wage, as more capital and labour are applied to a given amount of land, accumulation will eventually cease, no further employment will be offered; and no occasion afforded, therefore, for any further episodes during which the real wage is above subsistence. The 'stationary state' so produced may be disturbed by technical progress, increased capital intensity, or land improvements. But in the absence of these, 'population is at a stand' and will remain so.

Now, the agricultural population so determined is far below what would be the case if total food production were equally distributed. For if – as a result of competition in the labour market – *each* worker receives at equilibrium the value of output produced by the *incremental* unit of labour, the fact that incremental production falls as population rises must imply that total production is far in excess of the wage-bill (regarded as the product of the number of workers and the competitive wage). This excess, described by Malthus and his contemporaries as the agricultural 'surplus', is appropriated by property-owners. At stationary equilibrium, when capitalists receive only the minimum rate of profit required to sustain existing capital, the entire surplus goes to the landlords.

Two theorems of high ideological importance may be deduced from this model. In the first place, even if the whole of the surplus is spent by landlords in domestically produced goods and services, thus employing an 'unproductive' population in addition to the agricultural population (and those making necessary goods for agricultural workers), total population will still fall short of the ecological maximum which would result if food were distributed equally. Godwin had been correct to say that 'the established administration of property, may be considered as strangling a considerable portion of our children in their cradle'. It is precisely because of such 'strangulation' that average food per capita can be above subsistence when the agricultural population is stable, and hence that a surplus may be produced at all. In the second place, it can easily be shown (see Appendix 2) that *at stationary equilibrium, this surplus is at its maximum*. Not only does the principle of population determine the unfeasibility of Godwin's utopia and the inevitability of the status quo; better still, it may also be used to demonstrate that the status quo is in fact a social optimum.

In 1798 Malthus actually missed what would undoubtedly have appeared to the *Anti-Jacobin* and its readers – had they been able to follow the reasoning – as a golden opportunity to set tory principles upon the best and surest foundations. Strange as it may seem in one who later recognized that some questions in economics are like the problems 'de maximis et minimis in fluxions' (Schumpeter 1954, 481), Malthus contradicted his own logic in the first *Essay*. His argument against the 'French Economists' in chapter XVII considers the transfer of 200,000 'unproductive workers' to agriculture upon the assumption that they would 'produce only half the quantity of food that they themselves consumed' (Malthus 1798, 332). In the language of modern economics, the marginal product of labour is less than the subsistence wage: which must therefore imply that as a result of the transfer the total food production will be increased, but the food surplus *reduced*. Production now takes place with a larger agricultural *and total* population, greater food production but smaller average food per capita, a smaller gross food surplus and a *relatively* smaller 'unproductive' population. Yet Malthus blandly concludes that it will, he thinks, be allowed 'that the wealth which supported the two hundred thousand men, while they were producing silks and laces, would have been more usefully employed in supporting them, while they were producing the additional quantity of food.' (333).

That this was only a slip is seen by the fact that the example is deleted from the corresponding passage in all subsequent editions of the *Essay*. In the *Inquiry into the Nature and Progress of Rent* (1815a) Malthus conceived rent to arise from that 'quality in the soil' by which it is 'able to maintain more persons than are necessary to work it'; rent itself being a part of that 'surplus produce from the land, which has justly been stated to be the source of all power and enjoyment' (Malthus 1815a, 16). By this time, moreover, the maximum value of the surplus, and of rents, is clearly associated with population equilibrium. For 'a progressive rise of rents seems to be necessarily connected with ... the increase of population', whereas 'a fall in rents is necessarily connected with ... diminished population' (Malthus 1815a, 32). A marginal-product theory of wages, adumbrated in (1815a, 21, 22), is given a clearer expression in the latest editions of the *Essay*: 'no labourer can ever be employed on the soil who does not produce more than the value of his wages' (Malthus 1826, 154).

It would seem from this that by 1815, or at any rate by the end of his life, Malthus had a reasonably clear grasp of the properties of the sophisticated Malthusian model which lurks incognito in the later chapters of the first *Essay*. Yet he never exploited its ideological possibilities against the Jacobins and their successors, nor did any of those who erected the structure of Christian Political Economy upon Malthusian foundations. Before inquiring why this should have been, and for the light it may throw upon that important question, we must first consider another vitally important theorem afforded by the 'sophisticated' model, relating to the distribution of income, virtually neglected in the first *Essay*.

The effect of the 'preventive check' upon population is to raise the socially-conditioned subsistence wage. That Malthus was well aware of social conditioning from the outset is clearly evident in the first *Essay*.

The labourers of the South of England are so accustomed to eat fine wheaten bread, that they will suffer themselves to be half starved, before they will submit to live like the Scotch peasants. They might perhaps in time ... be reduced to live even like the lower Chinese: and the country would then, with the same quantity of food, support a greater population. But to effect this must always be a most difficult, and every friend of humanity will hope, an abortive attempt. (Malthus 1798, 132–3)

With a higher subsistence requirement, population will stabilize at a lower level, still more children will be 'strangled in their cradles' and hence the average per capita food production will be even higher.

What is more significant, what in later editions of the *Essay* and even more in the work of Chalmers came to dominate the argument, is the theorem on what would now be called the 'functional distribution' of national income (see Appendix 3). *It is an implication of the 'sophisticated' model that a voluntary limitation of the birth-rate in defence of a conventional living standard has the effect of reallocating part of the surplus, at stationary equilibrium, away from landlords and into the hands of both capitalists and labourers.* Some of the power to determine the disposal of the surplus in various 'unproductive' ways is thereby transferred from 'the rich' to 'the poor'.

If the economy is growing as the result of increasing capital intensity, technical progress or land improvement, the production available with the labour of a given population, and the incremental contribution to production, will be continuously increasing. If the socially-conditioned subsistence wage remains constant, population and capital stock will grow and the surplus available to landlords will continuously increase. But if the working class can raise its expectations and regulate the supply of labour then the 'subsistence' wage will increase and employees can secure to themselves all or at least part of the growth in the surplus. An exemplary case of 'steady-state growth' may be discovered (Eltis 1984, ch. 4) at which the rate of increase in the socially-determined subsistence wage is just sufficient to match the effects of increasing capital intensity and 'land-augmenting' technical progress: both 'productive' and 'unproductive' populations remain constant; but capital accumulation, technical progress, food production, the surplus, the output of the 'unproductive' sector and the real wage all grow at constant exponential rates.

Now it is evident that the ideological implications of this line of argument are profoundly different from the naive 'toryism' suggested by a discovery that the 'established administration of property' maximizes the social surplus. In a stationary economy, indeed, the normative implications of that proposition may even be in conflict with those which follow from the 'preventive check' theorem (raising the socially-determined subsistence wage transfers surplus from 'rich' to 'poor'). For in such a state, the lower the subsistence wage the greater the surplus and all the refinements of civilized life which the surplus makes possible. Society may therefore have to choose, to some extent, between 'civilization' and equity. It would appear, moreover, that the implications of the 'preventive check' are potentially subversive of Malthus's negative polemic. For if only Godwin's utopians can learn how to moderate, if not wholly to extinguish, the 'passion between the sexes', then average per capita income may rise by enough to stave off that 'necessity' which must vanquish 'benevolence'. Utopia can persist in (stationary) steady-state equilibrium with stable population and real income.

The analytical engine which Malthus so hastily and loosely assembled for one particular task in the first *Essay* possessed, therefore, a power and a versatility far beyond anything he could have imagined in 1798. In particular it could be used upon one set of – more or less static – behavioural assumptions to provide a cogent defence of 'the established administration of property'; or upon another – more or less dynamic – set to show how the absolute and relative position of the working classes might be improved at the expense of landlords. Neither possibility was clear to Malthus in 1798. The first, as we have seen, altogether eluded him for several years. The second is hinted at in the first *Essay* and may well have been present in its author's mind.

But in 1798 Malthus was a bachelor of thirty-two, dependent for part of his small income on a Cambridge fellowship, which must lapse with marriage. His 'pretty cousin' Harriet was then twenty-two, and Malthus could write with feeling of 'the genuine delight of virtuous love'; and with grim resignation of the abnegation required of 'a man of liberal eduction, but with an income only just sufficient to enable him to associate in the rank of gentlemen'. It is hardly possible, in the circumstances, that he should have failed to conclude that the 'preventive check' had no place in any utopia worth the name; and that its effects 'are but too conspicuous in the consequent vices that are produced in almost every part of the world; vices that are continually involving both sexes in inextricable unhappiness' (Malthus 1798, 210–11, 64–5, 69–70).

In the years immediately following 1798, therefore, Malthusian political economy was poised between alternative possibilities: a hardline, anti-Jacobin defence of the status quo, or an intellectual framework for realistic liberalism which preserved the economic benefits of private property and 'self-love' whilst distributing them more widely. That Malthus decided for the latter in his second edition is no accidental result of any failure to see the first possibility clearly, nor is it merely a consequence of the happy ending to his private story. His entire moral and intellectual formation was alien to the reactionary rhetoric of the *Anti-Jacobin*. Though merciless to Godwin, he criticized Godwin from inside the intellectual tradition to which both belonged. Marxian invective, which represents

Malthus as a hired propagandist of the land-owning classes, is wide of the mark. By the early 1800s Malthus had the ideological weapon to his hand, but he never used it.

By his choice of the 'liberal' alternative of 'moral restraint', Poor Law reform and public education, Malthus emphasized those features of his analytical schema best able to explain the dynamic, industrializing economy of nineteenth-century Britain. That he did so accounts for the otherwise puzzling fact that what began life as a hostile response to English apologetic for the French Revolution, what indeed discredited revolutionary thought for more than thirty years, became transmuted within a generation into one of the Thirtynine Articles of Philosophic Radicalism, swallowed without a qualm by Bentham, Ricardo and John Stuart Mill. More to my point in this book, it also explains how the evangelical Sumner, the sceptical and fair-minded Whately, and the social-activist Chalmers could be brought to assimilate the population-theoretic model to contemporary Christianity. At their hands, over the next thirty-five years, Malthusian political economy was first exorcized of certain theological evil spirits to be considered in the next chapter, then baptized and received into the body of Christian social thought.

CHAPTER 3

The first Essay on Population: *theology*

WHY THEOLOGY?

'It is, undoubtedly, a most disheartening reflection, that the great obstacle in the way to any extraordinary improvement in society, is of a nature that we can never hope to overcome' (Malthus 1798, 346). That obstacle, of course, is the principle of population and the political economy which it implies. No good can come of ignoring this unwelcome fact: 'on the contrary, the most baleful mischiefs may be expected from the unmanly conduct of not daring to face the truth' (346). With a right understanding of political economy 'sufficient yet remains to be done for mankind, to animate us to the most unremitted exertion' (347). But if we hasten to remedy the ills of society without proper knowledge, and so 'unwisely direct our efforts towards an object, in which we cannot hope for success', we must 'remain at as great a distance as ever from the summit of our wishes', and risk being 'perpetually crushed by the recoil of this rock of Sisyphus' (347).

With these words Malthus concluded chapter XVIII of the first *Essay*, and there, one might now suppose, he could have rested his case against the Jacobins. It is conventional to regard the last two chapters as detachable, a view which Malthus himself encouraged by his omission of their argument from later editions of the *Essay*. 'Perhaps,' conjectured Bonar (1924, 38), 'the great economist went beyond his province in attacking the problem of evil'. Little attention was paid to Malthus's theodicy in subsequent controversy, and until recently it was generally ignored in modern discussion. Though Everyman's Library republished the (seventh edition of the) *Essay* in 1914 – along with Augustine, Hooker, Boehme and Thomas à Kempis – as 'Theology and Philosophy', the image of the 'great economist' has very largely shaped modern perceptions of Malthus's work. 'In the *Essay on Population*,' Bonar maintained,

Malthus 'was inquiring into the nature and causes of poverty, as Adam Smith had inquired into the nature and causes of wealth' (Bonar 1924, 5; see also Himmelfarb 1984).

The conventional view has lately been subject to revision. Levin (1966) drew attention to a seeming inconsistency between the 'melancholy hue' of the political economy of the first *Essay*, and the more optimistic account of human perfectibility implied by the theology. Levin, Bowler (1976) and Santurri (1982) considered whether Malthus retained his putative 'theological optimism' in later recensions of the *Essay*. Bowler and Le Mahieu (1979) related 'theological optimism' to the intellectual tradition of the Scottish Enlightenment which is held to have influenced Malthus through his reading of Hume, Wallace and Adam Smith. Levin, Pullen (1981), Santurri, Waterman (1983b) and Harvey-Phillips (1984) have all attempted appraisals of Malthus's theological argument, the last four more or less contemporaneously and independently of each other. Pullen (1981, 1986) and Harvey-Phillips discussed the importance of theodicy to a right understanding of Malthusian population economics; Le Mahieu and Waterman (1983a) directed attention to the ideological function of the theological chapters. These authors are agreed in this, if in nothing else: that chapters XVIII and XIX of the first *Essay*, whether successful or not in their purpose, are an essential part of Malthus's argument and may not be detached as irrelevant appendices.

There are some fairly obvious reasons for this opinion. As I have attempted to show in chapter 2 (pp. 28–37), Malthus employed the social-theoretic language of his adversary, Godwin: and that language was rooted in post-Newtonian metaphysics and natural theology. It is this, rather than the intellectual link with the Scottish Enlightenment, which allows us to say that the theodicy was 'integral' to Malthus's 'method of social analysis' (cf. Le Mahieu 1979, 468). Indeed, it has been argued that the particular dialect in which Godwin and Malthus conducted their debate was peculiar to the 'Old Whig', 'Commonwealthman' tradition of the eighteenth-century 'country party' and hence that Malthus's 'relation to his Scottish predecessors...appears more ambiguous than his apparently straightforward acknowledgement of influence would seem to suggest' (Hont, Ignatieff and Fontana 1980, 4).

Even more fundamental than the affinity between Malthus and Godwin is the fact that both of them, like every other writer of that age, inhabited a world into which we of the present can only enter, if at all, by the most sustained and powerful act of historical imagination. For it is scarce an exaggeration to say that a transformation of consciousness has taken place since the end of the eighteenth century. No literature of pre-industrial society is intelligible, save to those who know, understand and to some extent enter sympathetically into its religious presuppositions and Christian theological categories. This has long been recognized within the 'traditional' (that is to say, pre-literary-theoretic) study of 'English literature' (e.g. Willey 1940, Lewis 1969). More recently it has begun to inform eighteenth-century political and intellectual historiography in the work of I. R. Christie (1984), J. C. D. Clark (1985) and certain others (e.g. Le Mahieu 1976; Crimmins 1983, 1986, 1989a; Hole 1989).

The decade of the 1860s, Keynes (1972, 168) predicted in 1924, 'will, I think be regarded by the historians of opinion as the critical moment at which Christian dogma fell away from the serious philosophical world of England, or at any rate of Cambridge'. The Kantian foundations of Mansel's Bampton Lectures of 1858, 'the last attempt to found Christian dogma on an intellectual basis' were undermined by J. S. Mill (1865). Meanwhile in 1859 the *Origin of Species* had appeared, followed in 1860–2 by Herbert Spencer's *First Principles*. By some time in the 1870s Henry Sidgwick, Leslie Stephen, James Ward, Alfred Marshall, W. K. Clifford and many another Cambridge luminary had forsaken Christianity. There had no doubt been many defections for at least two centuries before the 1860s. Whatever their theoretical beliefs Hobbes, Hume, Adam Smith – even Godwin himself – were 'practical atheists' (Dunn 1983, 119). As early as 1773 Jeremy Bentham was beginning to excogitate that full-scale assault upon Christianity only launched between 1817 and 1823 (Crimmins 1986). The related but heterogeneous set of phenomena labelled – and all too often hypostatized – as 'the' Enlightenment was in one sense the great turning point in European intellectual history, and the *philosophes* for the most part were no friends of orthodox religion. Yet these were outliers, even within the élites to which they belonged. 'Enlightenment was of the few. Secularization is of the many' (Chadwick 1975, 9). There is, therefore, widespread agreement about what W. O. Chadwick has called 'the secularization of the European mind in the nineteenth century', even if some reluctance to date it so precisely as Keynes attempted. As C. S. Lewis put it with more caution: 'the greatest of all divisions in the history of the West [is] that which divides the present from, say, the age of Jane Austen and Scott...somewhere between us and the Waverley Novels, somewhere between us and *Persuasion*, the chasm runs.' (Lewis 1969, 7). Malthus and Godwin were of 'the age of Jane Austen and Scott'. The presuppositions of Christian faith and culture were part of the air they breathed.

It is hardly surprising, therefore, and not particularly significant as a mark of influence, that previous population-theoretic discourse with which Malthus was familiar, such as that by Wallace or Süssmilch, should also have been constructed upon an explicitly theological framework. What is rather more to the point – the polemical point of the first *Essay*, that is – is that the attacks mounted by the English Jacobins upon 'the established administration of property' were, to a greater extent than in Godwin himself, informed by the Christian theology of the Rational Dissenters. If political economy should prove that 'a state of equal liberty and justice for all' is impossible then that proof must be rendered acceptable to contemporary sensibility by a convincing demonstration of its congruence with Christian belief. This was more than a matter either of scoring anti-Jacobin debating points, or of providing an ideological opiate for the downtrodden masses. The ruling classes and the clergy of the established church entrusted with their education, William Pitt and his former tutor Bishop Pretyman, must also be convinced.

For these reasons, as well as for the even more obvious fact that Malthus was a beneficed clergyman noted for his piety who had determined at an early age upon seeking Holy Orders (Pullen 1986, 150), we must take the theological content of the first *Essay* as seriously as its political economy. More precisely, we must recognize that what we now presume to identify as 'political economy' and 'theology' respectively are abstractions that we ourselves have made, in the light of our secularized consciousness, from the undifferentiated texture of Malthus's argument.

The 'theological aspects' of that argument are of the utmost importance to this book. As I have previously argued (Waterman 1983a, b) the theology of the first *Essay* was seriously defective. Paley provided an acceptable version in 1802; Malthus was persuaded by certain 'distinguished persons' in the Church of England to omit the 'theological' chapters from his second edition of 1803; and in 1816 J. B. Sumner published his lengthy restatement, 'a work of large and enduring influence' (Norman 1976, 43) which established the

ideological dominance of Christian Political Economy for nearly a
century. It is the purpose of this chapter, therefore, to examine the
theodicy of the first Essay in the context of late eighteenth-century
Anglican theology and of Malthus's own training in that theology.

THEODICY AND EIGHTEENTH-CENTURY SOCIAL THEORY

Unlike Viner (1972, 99), who used 'theodicy' to mean 'theological
optimism in its several varieties', I shall understand the term in a less
purely Leibnizian and now more widely accepted sense simply as
any attempt to explain the occurrence of 'evil' in a universe which
is assumed to have 'meaning' and/or 'purpose'. In this usage,
teleology is a necessary condition of theodicy, and so is a perception
of evil. The two conditions together are necessary and sufficient. If
either were lacking no occasion for theodicy would arise.

Teleology may rest upon the authority of divine revelation,
finding an answer to what is otherwise dark and mysterious in some
putative communication by the deity of His purpose in creation. Or
it may be purely naturalistic, discovering the meaning and end of
human experience by the light of reason. The boundary between the
two is not altogether clear. 'Revealed' religion must convince
sufferers that the evil they now experience is part of the providential
plan for the attainment of the greatest good. 'Natural' religion, as
Hume clearly demonstrated, implies a teleology that can never be
inferred from phenomena but is known, if at all, by faith alone.
Throughout the eighteenth century, moreover, it appears 'almost
invariably to turn out' that individual writers 'were eclectic if not
self-contradictory or undergoing changes of opinion through time'
(Viner 1978, 61).

Evil may be perceived as 'natural' (or 'physical'); as 'moral'; or
as 'metaphysical'. Natural or physical evil arises from ill effects upon
humans of their environment and their own natures: 'Pains and
Uneasinesses, Inconveniences and Disappointment of Appetites,
arising from Natural Motions' (King 1739, 103). Moral evil is the
result of free human choices: 'vicious Elections, that is, such as are
hurtful to ourselves or others' (ibid.). Metaphysical evil, associated
particularly with the *Théodicée* of Leibniz (1951) though its history
goes back at least to St Athanasius (Williams 1927, 260) and before
that to Plotinus and Aristotle (Lovejoy 1936, 64, 59), is a logical
consequence of creation: the creature must be a limited being.
William King, the original version of whose *De Origine Mali* (1702)

preceded Leibniz's more famous but somewhat similar work (Lovejoy 1936, 223; Viner 1972, 75–7) by eight years, described this class as 'the Evil of *Imperfection* ... the Absence of those Perfections or advantages which exist elsewhere, or in other Beings' (King 1739, 103). In somewhat different ways, both natural and moral evil can be considered as derivative from metaphysical evil: 'this Defect, or as we may say, Mixture of NON-ENTITY in the constitution of created Beings is the necessary Principle of all Natural Evils, and of a possibility of Moral ones' (xviii–xix).

The particular concern of the theodicy considered in this chapter and indeed throughout this entire book is with what Paley and others called *the evils of civil life*: poverty, inequality, oppression, war and so forth. Evil of this kind is logically reducible to either or both of natural or moral evil. Just where one places it, is both indicative and crucially determinative of one's ideological stance. If social evil be regarded as wholly or even largely 'natural', the political and economic status quo is shown to be an example of providence. This was the generally accepted assumption of English social theory in the eighteenth century, resting as it did for the most part upon the 'conservative' understanding of 'Nature' as *natura naturata* (Willey 1940, 205; Cassirer 1955, 40). But if social evil be seen, at least to some extent, as 'moral' evil then God can no longer be deployed in the cause of reaction and may even be supposed to will those free decisions by rational men and women which might in principle achieve reform or amelioration. This, according to Cassirer (1955, 153–8) was Rousseau's unique contribution to theodicy and the chief impetus of that 'radical' or 'Romantic' understanding of 'Nature' as *natura naturans* which inspired Godwin, Condorcet and all the other Jacobins.

Purely for convenience I shall label as 'social theodicy' all attempts to reconcile 'the evils of civil society' with a teleological view of the human condition. It is evident from the analysis so far that a four-fold taxonomy of social theodicy is available, as shown in table 1. Though most competent thinkers of this and earlier periods were too shrewd and too subtle to be boxed in completely by any of these four categories, and though many others were vacillating or inconsistent, there are clear signs of an historical progression. Broadly speaking the social theodicy of traditional, Western Catholic thinkers such as St Augustine and St Thomas belongs in class 1. The Enlightenment agreed with the Middle Ages in regarding the evils of civil life as a species of 'natural' evil, but parted company over

Table 1. *A taxonomy of social evil*

	Teleology rests upon:	
Social evil is:	Revelation	Reason
Natural	1	2
Moral	4	3

teleology. Adam Smith and Paley are most at home in class 2. Rousseau and the Romantics agreed with the Enlightenment in preferring a naturalistic teleology, but differed in their view of social evil. We may assign them, more or less, to class 3. It seems to have been left to post-Romantic Christian social thought – Christian Socialism, the Social Gospel and Liberation Theology – to occupy the hitherto vacant class 4. As I shall later show, the theologically amateurish Robert Malthus allowed himself to be trapped in class 2 with disastrous results. Why a merely naturalistic teleology should have been so important for at least one – by no means inconsiderable – late eighteenth-century British author we must now consider.

Teleology

Traditional Christianity was based almost entirely on revelation. The meaning and purpose of the universe and of human existence within that universe is to be learned from holy scripture. Though reason may be invoked in support of revelation its function is merely auxiliary. This is true even of the high Scholastic period and of its greatest ornament, St Thomas, of whom it must be said, as in Bertrand Russell's cruel but just appraisal:

He is not engaged in an inquiry, the result of which it is impossible to know in advance. Before he begins to philosophize, he already knows the truth; it is declared in the catholic faith. If he can find apparently rational arguments for some parts of the faith, so much better; if he cannot, he need only fall back on revelation. (Russell 1945, 463)

The problem of evil receives an almost purely biblical treatment in this tradition.

It is evident that the insistence of the Hebrew scriptures on the unity and omnipotence of God must rule out a dualistic, or Manichaean solution to the problem. Moreover by locating the origin of evil in a rival and malevolent deity the coherence of the biblical world-view would be threatened and its teleology under-mined. A monotheistic explanation of evil which exonerated God was supplied by St Paul. Generalizing Ecclesiasticus 25: 24 St Paul interpreted the Genesis narrative of the expulsion of Adam and Eve from Eden as the origin of evil, both natural and moral (Romans 5: 12–19; I Corinthians 15: 21–22). His theory was revived and developed by second and third-century Fathers, especially by Origen who like Pascal (Cassirer 1955, 142–4) but very few others before Pascal, 'grasped... that the Fall-doctrine really rests upon an inference from the phenomenon of evil considered in the the light of ethical monotheism' (Williams 1927, 215). Origen also saw two implications of the Pauline theory of high importance for the controversy reported in this chapter: social evil is a consequence of the Fall; and human life is a state of discipline and trial for eternity (Williams 1927, 211–3). Patristic elaboration of Pauline Fall-doc-trine was brought to its final form by St Augustine, whereupon it dominated Western thought for a thousand years.

Adam and Eve were created the *imago dei*, originally righteous and perfect. They committed the original sin (*originale peccatum*, a term coined by St Augustine), an act of infinite malice which separated God and Man. The guilt (*reatus*) of the first sin is transmitted to every human in the act of generation which is itself intrinsically sinful on account of concupiscence. As a consequence of inherited guilt, human reason and will are diseased, and humans deprived of the power to abstain from further sin. Hence all Adam's posterity are necessarily and rightfully damned: natural evil is God's punishment upon a guilty race; moral evil a consequence of moral incapacity and a further, deserved, punishment of sinful humans. Nonetheless, God selects some to be baptized, justified and to receive the gift of 'final perseverance', and so to be saved from sin and eternal punishment (Williams 1927, 317–400 *passim*).

Though St Thomas, Duns Scotus and others discovered that this formidable doctrine 'had to be perceptibly softened in order to be preserved at all' (Williams 1927, 408), it was not until the Renaissance that any substantial change became intellectually possible. By the early sixteenth century, 'The influence of Pelagi-anism in the religious position of humanism becomes increasingly evident; efforts to throw off the hard yoke of Augustinian tradition become more and more deliberate.' (Cassirer 1955, 139). The effect of the various protestant Reformations, however, was to give renewed vitality to Augustinian theology. Compelled by political necessity, the Reformers asserted the sole authority of scripture as against that not only of the Church but also of unaided human reason. St Augustine was the chief support of both Luther and Calvin, and his ultra-Pauline, biblical and anti-intellectual theodicy became the hall-mark of protestant orthodoxy for more than a century (Cassirer 1955, 138–41).

As a consequence of the disintegration of the Western church, the seventeenth century was a time of intense theological and scriptural activity, each party seeking to establish its own authenticity and to discredit that of its rivals. Two unintended outcomes of all of this prepared the ground for a transition from a revealed to a naturalistic teleology. In the first place, the unprecedented critical scrutiny to which the Bible was subjected opened the way for that radical deflation of its authority which began in Germany during the eighteenth century. And in the second, a general weariness with theological polemic and religious war produced a warm welcome for the cognitive assurance and peaceable ecumenicity of Newtonian science. A further cause operated, in the special circumstances of the Church of England, to produce a readiness to relinquish or at any rate to modify, the austerity of Augustinian-Calvinist doctrine. This was the intense and well-merited unpopularity of the presbyterian and puritan party during and after the Civil War, the grotesque violence of whose predestinarian homiletic provoked Jeremy Taylor in 1655 to compose his famous tract *Unum Necessarium* (Huntley 1970, ch. 4; Williams 1927, 441–2).

Though even St Bernard was said to have admitted that *Natura Codex est Dei* (Willey 1940, 42), and long before that the Psalmist had known that

> The Heavens declare the glory of God:
> and the Firmament sheweth his handiwork;

though 'Stoics, like their later counterparts, linked together the starry heavens and the moral law within' (Willey 1940, 14): yet it was not until the decades following the first appearance of the *Principia* (1687) – which Newton wrote with 'an Eye upon such Principles as might work with considering Men for the belief of a Deity' (Newton 1756, 1) – that the great transition came about, in Britain at any rate, from a revealed to a naturalistic teleology. John Ray, Newton's senior colleague at Trinity, published his *Wisdom of God in Creation* (1691) four years later. Derham's works of 'Physico-theology' and 'Astro-theology' appeared in 1713 and 1715 respectively. (Towards the end of his life he hedged, publishing 'Christo-theology' (1730) to demonstrate the divine origin of the Christian religion.) Newton was glorified in the *Essay on Man* (1733–4), wherein the teleological significance of his law of universal gravitation is duly celebrated:

> Look round our World; behold the chain of love
> Combining all below and all above.
> See plastic Nature working to this end,
> The single atoms each to other tend,
> Attract, attracted to, the next in place
> Form'd and impell'd its neighbour to embrace.

Within two more generations naturalistic teleology had passed into the conventional wisdom of undergraduate textbooks, as in Maclaurin's popularization of Newtonian physics, which the freshman Malthus was required to read (James 1979, 25) in his first term at Cambridge in 1784. According to Maclaurin, we learn from Newton that

Our views of Nature, however imperfect, serve to represent to us, in the most sensible manner, that mighty *power* which prevails throughout, acting with a force and efficacy that appears to suffer no diminution from the greatest distances of space or intervals of time, and that *wisdom* which we see equally displayed in the exquisite structure and just motions of the greatest and subtilest parts. These, with the *perfect goodness*, by which they are evidently directed, constitute the supreme object of the speculations of a philosopher... (Maclaurin 1775, 4; my italics)

If science can demonstrate not only the *power* and *wisdom* of God but also His *perfect goodness*, the Christian apologist can dispense with doubtful disputations over sacred scripture and the task of theodicy is made easy.

Well before Robert Malthus went up to Jesus College, of course, sceptical voices had been raised in question of this comfortable doctrine. William Derham was by no means the only theologian of the time who prudently kept at least one foot in class 1.

Edmund Law, Paley's patron and a central figure in eighteenth-century Cambridge theology (Le Mahieu 1976, 12–18), produced a translation in 1731 of William King's *De Origine Mali* with extensive notes and a 'Preliminary Dissertation' by the 'true founder' of Utilitarian philosophy (Halévy 1928, 7; Crimmins 1983, 542), John Gay. Though King's work is omitted from Pretyman's list of books which ought to be owned by every 'respectable and useful Parish Priest' (Pretyman 1812, I, xv–xvii) it is certain to have been both

well known and influential in the circle of those among whom
Malthus learned such theology as he ever knew. Viner regarded
King's *Essay* as an exposition of the 'system of optimism' (though less
'cheerful' than that of Leibniz) yet there is no attempt to palliate the
miseries of this life. The Earth 'is in a manner the Filth and
Offscouring of the *Mundane System*' and 'the Workmanship of God is
no more to be condemn'd for it, than a Judgment is to be form'd of
the beauty of an House from the Sink or the Jakes' (King 1739,
218–19). Death and disease, scarcity, the oppression of women and
certain other evils are a consequence of the Fall; though many more
are entailed by 'the necessity of Matter' and do not arise from sin
(221–2). Some evil, moreover, is a punishment of the 'depraved
Elections' of humans, and at several places (198, 444–5, 447–52 note
Y) King recognizes this earthly life as a state of discipline and trial
for eternity. It would seem from this that it is altogether too simple
to suppose that eighteenth-century theology 'rejects the dogma of
original sin' (Cassirer 1955, 159). In Anglican theology at any rate,
even in Latitudinarian circles, a more cautious and eclectic *via media*
persisted.

Sir Isaac Newton himself had been a clandestine unitarian, or
rather, in Keynes's more colourful language, 'a Judaic monotheist of
the school of Maimonides' (Keynes 1972, 368). Though Newton's
unpublished lapse from orthodoxy was the result of biblical and
patristic study, the transition from a naturalistic but Christian
teleology to pure deism is obvious enough and occurred in many of
his contemporaries. The refutation of deism was therefore high on
the agenda of eighteenth-century Anglicanism and as late as 1785
Richard Watson included anti-deist material in his collection of
Sunday readings for Cambridge undergraduates (Watson 1785, v,
vii–viii). The most famous work of that kind was Bishop Joseph
Butler's *Analogy* (1736), which argued powerfully that nature is no
more intelligible and self-evident than revelation. Since Butler also
accepted, and assumed that everyone else accepted, that nature is,
nevertheless, sufficiently reliable as evidence of the existence,
omnipotence and goodness of God, revelation is set on a secure basis.
Nature and revelation 'coincide with each other, and together make
up one scheme of Providence' (Butler 1844, 174–5; cit. Watson
1964, 107). Now 'The general doctrine of Religion' is 'that our
present life is a state of probation for a future one; moreover that '*the
present world is peculiarly fit to be a state of discipline, for our improvement in
virtue and piety*' (Butler 1844, 72, 101). Even more clearly than King,

Butler represents the Anglican determination to have the best of both worlds: to affirm the naturalistic teleology inspired by Newtonian science without giving up those biblical doctrines which alone may account for tragedy in human affairs.

The epistemological success of Newtonian science, and therefore of naturalistic teleology, was perceived by S'Gravesande as early as 1717 to rest upon the entirely arbitrary – unobservable and unprovable – axiom of the uniformity of nature (Cassirer 1955, 61). S'Gravesande took refuge in the goodness of God (who would not lie to His creatures). Three years after the first appearance of Butler's *Analogy* David Hume published the first two volumes of the *Treatise* which contained his development of the full implications of S'Gravesande's subversive insight (Cassirer 1955, 62–3). The principle of induction is to be rejected: 'from experience and observation nothing is to be learned' (Russell 1945, 672). Neither science nor religion can be found to have any rational basis. The entire enterprise of eighteenth-century natural theology, orthodox or deist, already somewhat weakened by Butler, was now completely undermined.

Hume's *Treatise* 'fell dead-born from the press'. He republished its ideas in the better-known *Enquiry* (1748). Though he seems to have violated his own principles in the essay 'Of Miracles' therein, and temporized both in *Dialogues Concerning Natural Religion* and the *Natural History of Religion* (Willey 1940, 126–35 *passim*), the evident tendency of all these works was to discredit natural theology and in particular the argument from 'design' – or 'teleological argument' – on which its entire structure rested. The *Dialogues* appeared posthumously in 1779 five years before Malthus went up to Cambridge. It is traditional to regard Hume's religious scepticism, of which this work was the culmination, as 'one of the great turning points in the history of thought' (Stephen 1876, 1, 36). After such a 'sustained philosophical criticism of the Argument from Design... there did not need to be another' (Williams 1966, 84–5). R. H. Tawney indeed, 'in his prolonged campaign to persuade us that the age of capitalism was marked by a deterioration of... social ethics', actually went so far as to assert that eighteenth-century social theory '"repudiated teleology and substituted the analogy of a self-regulating mechanism"' (Viner 1972, 59–60).

Yet natural theology did far more than merely 'linger on' (Williams 1966, 84–5) in Britain. Not only was 'Eighteenth century British social philosophy... soaked in teleology' (Viner 1972, 60): for at least a century after Hume's *Treatise* 'the argument from design flourished in orthodox circles and even, it might be claimed, experienced a renascence' (Le Mahieu 1976, 29–30). More than the usual Anglo-Saxon insularity, obtuseness and resistance to new ideas is required to explain the fact that Paley triumphed whilst Hume was ignored and forgotten.

D. L. Le Mahieu has argued convincingly that the reason for this seemingly paradoxical outcome lies in the fact that Hume missed the point of naturalistic teleology. This is because 'he never really understood the distinction between belief, which is based on knowledge and experience, and faith, which involves the total personality in a submission to what Tillich has called an "ultimate concern"' (Le Mahieu 1976, 54). In England at any rate, the eighteenth and early nineteenth century belong to the age of 'faith', which is 'the emotional and spiritual commitment which practising Christians felt (*sic*) towards God. In this sense, natural theology was an elaborate religious ritual...which was the visible and comprehensible expression of an inward, mysterious, and powerful faith.' (Le Mahieu 1976, 53). *If one already believes in God* – which Hume, it is generally supposed, did not – the 'evidence' of 'design' in 'Nature' makes sense of one's experience. Moreover, as S'Gravesande had seen, some strictly pre-rational, metaphysical commitment is always required in order to safeguard the intelligibility of science (Kolakowski 1982, 84 and *passim*). Hume's work was seen to be inimical not only to theology but also to science, and in Britain – but only in Britain – there existed a powerful alliance of natural religion and empirical science. 'The argument from design gave meaning to science, and science offered powerful ammunition for the argument from design' (Le Mahieu 1976, 39). For these reasons the naturalistic teleology, judiciously modified by revelation where the argument demanded it, survived unscathed at least until the Bridgewater Treatises of the 1830s. Paley's *Natural Theology* remained on the reading list at Cambridge until well into the nineteenth century: his *Evidences* was required for Little-go until 1920.

Social evil

No definition of 'social evil' is fully workable. In one sense all the evils which afflict the human race are 'social' for only in society can men and women exist. A preliminary sort may be had by eliminating those evils – such as 'lightning and tempest' – which occur independently of human existence. 'Plague, pestilence and famine' are more problematic, for in many cases these are clearly the outcome of *some* forms of social organization, though whether of *any* form is questionable and ideologically non-neutral. The same is true of 'battle and murder'. Other evils such as 'sudden death' may certainly be eliminated because it can be shown that they are not a consequence of social existence. Let 'social evil' be that evil, whether natural or moral, which occurs because, and only because, humans live in society. Not only are there many doubtful cases of the kind noted above: the difficulty of specifying any particular example is compounded by what A. K. Cohen (1974) has labelled the 'elasticity of evil'.

Durkheim (1938) had argued that in any society 'a process of social redefinition operates continuously to insure that all positions on the scale from wickedness to virtue will always be filled' (Cohen 1974, 5). The principle may be generalized to all evil, including social evil. Cohen suggested that there may be 'an inveterate tendency to redefine poverty, misery, injustice, oppression, and so on in a way that, *regardless of what we do about them*, we will always have a plenitude of social problems' (5; my italics). What is now called the 'rising horizon of expectations' ensures that each generation would perceive about as much social evil as its predecessors, notwithstanding any 'progress' which has actually taken place. According to this way of thinking, evil is the result of a stable human propensity to be discontented with circumstances. Therefore as social circumstances change so will the composition of that class of phenomena defined as 'social evil'.

We are thus afforded a means of explaining why 'social evil' is historically specific. The early Christian church, following the example of its surrounding culture, regarded slavery not as an evil to be justified but as a good. In the 'judgement of the Father', Viner (1978, 26) believed, slavery was 'a legitimate and useful institution'. Only much later, when moral sensibility had been refined by the removal of many grosser ills, was slavery included by Christians and others in the class of social evil.

To recognize these difficulties is to acknowledge that one can only speak in a vague and impressionistic way about the intellectual history of social evil. It is my contention, as I have stated above, that the Enlightenment agreed with antiquity and the Middle Ages in regarding social evil as generally *natural* rather than *moral*; and that this was precisely the point of departure of Rousseau, the Jacobins and the Romantic movement in general, against whom Malthus, the last major figure of the British Enlightenment, directed his polemic. But I can only urge my case by considering a more or less arbitrary shortlist of putative social evils, and even then only at the cost of much simplification. The shortlist is selected, for obvious reasons, from Godwin's *Political Justice*. The simplification is virtually to ignore as exceptions the numerous instances which can be found among authors before Rousseau of various social evils being regarded as moral rather than natural.

Godwin (1798a, I, 7) distinguished between 'the evils that arise to us from the structure of the material universe' and those which result from the existence of humans in political society. Evil is either 'physical', or it is simply a consequence of human (political, not natural) society. '*Social*' and '*moral*' *evil for him, therefore, are one and the same thing*: moreover, 'they are not the inseparable condition of our existence, but admit of removal and remedy' (I, 6). If only reason can be brought to bear on human affairs, political society will be dissolved, its institutions abandoned and the cause of moral evil thereby removed.

This is obviously the new, Rousseauvian view of social evil *in excelsis*, but Godwin was not content to leave it there. 'Everything', he believed with characteristic dottiness, 'that is usually understood by the term cooperation, is in some degree, an evil'; and in a *reductio ad absurdum* of protestant individualism declared that 'we ought to be able to do without one another' (II, 501, 503). What is more fundamental for *Political Justice*, however, is 'inequality of property', for this is the cause of political society and directly or indirectly of all other social (moral) evils. Figure 3 displays the causal relations between the chief social evils identified in that work and treated discursively in Book I, chapters II and III, and in Book VIII, chapters III, VII and VIII. Traditional social evils such as inequality, poverty, oppression and war, together with luxury and crime, commonly regarded as moral but not social evils, are shown to be a consequence of 'the established administration of property'. So are social institutions such as law, marriage, wage-labour and the market economy, not usually regarded as evil at all. With an originality seldom acknowledged by Marxists, Godwin maintained that the accumulation of capital led to the class struggle (II, 463) and the

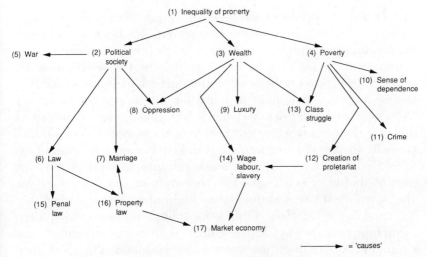

Fig. 3. Social evil in *Political Justice*.

creation of a proletariat (II, 466); but innocent of a 'dialectical' theodicy he listed each as examples of 'the multiplication of vice'. Godwin's view of marriage as a social evil was considerably modified in the successive editions of *Political Justice*: by 1798 it had become 'a salutary and respectable institution' (II, 510).

For purposes of the present inquiry it is sufficient to select the first five of Godwin's social evils, for the derivation of the remaining twelve from these is hardly a matter of controversy. Accordingly we must consider *inequality* (both of wealth and of station), *political society, wealth, poverty*, and *war*. In what follows I shall attempt to explain, with reference to these five, why I believe that Enlightenment authors, for the most part, agreed with their medieval predecessors – but not with their Romantic successors – in regarding the evils of civil life as a species of 'natural' evil (see p. 63 above). Of necessity the treatment is sketchy and can only be regarded, at best, as suggestive. Its only excuse is the absence, so far as I am aware, of any previous investigation of the question.

Inequality
Inequality of status was accepted without question by the primitive church (Romans 13: 1–2, I Timothy 2: 2, Titus 3: 1, I Peter 2: 13–17, etc.), ratified in the Constantinian establishment and joyfully celebrated in the liturgy, art and architecture of mediaeval

catholicism. It saturates the culture of post-Reformation Anglicanism, recurring continually throughout the Book of Common Prayer, finding its highest expression in the liturgy and ritual of the Coronation service and its most pointed in the selection of the scripture appointed to be read on the thirtieth of January: a day of fasting and humiliation in penance for the murder of Charles I. Deeply as Richard Price and the Revolution Society deplored all this, it is doubtful whether most, even of them, could have followed Godwin all the way to complete equality. For the vast majority of their contemporaries of all sorts and conditions, social inequality was part of the order of things. The 'principle of subordination' was almost akin to a law of nature, for as Archbishop Secker admonished his candidates for Holy Orders in 1769: 'Without union there cannot be a sufficient degree either of strength or beauty: and without subordination there cannot long be union. Therefore obey, as the apostle directs, them that have the rule over you, and promote their honour, their credit, their influence.' (Watson 1785, VI, 111).

Inequality of *station* was no evil at all. But the inequality of wealth which generally accompanies it was a very different matter. According to one eighteenth-century Anglican, 'No one thing hath more perplexed considerate men, in forming their sentiments of the Supreme Being…than the seeming very unequal distributions of good' (Edmonds 1761, cit. Viner 1972, 87–8). Yet it is doubtful if this holds good for the primitive and patristic periods of church history. Viner claimed that the Fathers 'showed no concern about economic inequality' except where excessive wealth either was morally unsafe for the rich or was the result of lack of compassion for the poor. Insofar as economic inequality was perceived as an evil at all, it was a consequence of the necessary conditions of human life after the Fall, and not normally a sign of moral evil. The fifth-century, Pelagian *Tractatus de Divitiis* which maintained that the rich are the cause of poverty in the poor was condemned as heretical (Haslehurst 1927, 30–107; Evans 1968; Morris 1965; Viner 1978, 41, n. 90) for 'Ye have the poor always with you' (Matthew 16: 11). The traditional Christian view that economic inequality is a natural evil arising from 'the various social conditions under which mankind naturally exists' survived into the twentieth century when it was enshrined in the *Catholic Encyclopedia* (1909, V, 649a).

With the exception of Theodoretus (435) Christian authors until the seventeenth century attributed inequality – and other social evil

– to the Fall (Viner 1978, 18–20). According to A. O. Lovejoy (1936) the eighteenth century sought a metaphysical explanation in a Platonist conception of dubious orthodoxy known as 'The Great Chain of Being'.

Though the Enlightenment parted company with traditional thought in the matter of *teleology*, it was Lovejoy's contention that it shared the traditional *ontology*: that of a universe created according to the principles of 'plenitude', 'continuity' and 'gradation'. The first and third of these could be mobilized in support of social distinction by implying a God who prefers variety to equality. By assimilating the 'principle of subordination' to that of 'gradation', and by a particularly flagrant misquotation of the Anglican Catechism, Lovejoy (1936, 206) argued that the conception of the Great Chain of Being could be, and was, used as a weapon 'against social discontent and especially against all equalitarian movements' (205). Soame Jenyns's (1790) preposterous *Free Inquiry* (1757), which held among other things that 'those who are *born to poverty and drudgery* should not be *deprived* by an *improper education* of the *opiate* of *ignorance*' (Johnson 1787, x, 232), lends some colour to this view. But Samuel Johnson annihilated both Jenyns and the Great Chain of Being in a profound and brilliant review, in the course of which he distinguished clearly between 'subordination in human affairs', which was 'well understood' and generally accepted by all eighteenth-century social theorists including himself (Boswell 1953, 289, 316, 360, etc.), and the metaphysical concept of 'gradation' which can 'have no meaning with regard to infinite space, in which nothing is *high* or *low*' (Johnson 1787, x, 236). Viner believed that the doctrine of the Great Chain of Being was rarely used by important writers on social issues and discovered only one example of an economist, that of Josiah Tucker, who used it to justify economic inequality. Josiah Tucker was answered by Abraham Tucker (Viner 1972, 92–4) who, as we shall later see, was an important source of Malthus's own theodicy.

There was indeed in Britain from the Restoration to the French Revolution 'a spontaneous union of theologians, philosophers, economists and intellectuals in general, maintained without serious breach of continuity for over a century and without a single heretic or dissenter,... dedicated to the justification of an existing social structure and especially of its social and economic inequalities' (Viner 1972, 95; see also Pocock 1985b, 531). All accepted without question that inequality of wealth was, for the most part, a natural and not a moral evil. But as might be expected of Englishmen of the eighteenth (or indeed of any other) century, they seldom resorted to Platonist metaphysics in order to justify it. Optimists like Adam Smith and Paley attempted to show that inequality is not really an evil at all. Pessimists like Bishop Butler and Dr Johnson confessed that 'the scheme of Providence, the ways and works of God, are too vast, of two large extent for our capacities' (Butler 1913, 193).

Political society
The traditional Christian view of this matter, as of so much else, was defined by St Augustine. The state and its institutions, especially those of private property, marriage and slavery, are willed by God as a remedy for sin. This does not mean that the state is an unmitigated good. Even when rightly administered its institutions will inflict some pain: inequality, coercion, the necessity of labour, socially transmitted disease, the human costs of maintaining internal peace and external security – and so forth. These evils are 'natural' in that they occur as the irreducible minimum of that suffering which is an inevitable consequence of the Fall. For the proposition '*from government Evils cannot be eradicated, and their excess only can be prevented*, has always been allowed' (Johnson 1787, x, 255).

Beyond this irreducible minimum, however, the evil of political society may be and is exacerbated by conscious human decision. In a rhetorical question quoted by St Thomas (*ST* ii-ii, 66: 8) and many others, Augustine asks: 'Remota itaque justitia, quid sunt regna nisi magna latrocinia?' (*Civ. Dei*, iv: 4). Because *justitia* is very often defective or absent in actual practice, political society will be the means of inflicting further evil upon those it is intended to benefit. Samuel Johnson could agree with Soame Jenyns that this latter evil, which Jenyns labelled 'Political', is not natural but moral, 'polity being only the conduct of immoral men in public affairs' (Johnson 1787, x, 255). Yet Augustine was forced to acknowledge that upon a strict (theological) construal of *justitia*, 'vera autem justitia non est nisi in ea re publica cuius conditor rectorque Christus est' (*Civ. Dei*, ii: 21). Because of sin therefore, 'political' (moral) evil is actually inevitable. As Vives put it in his *Commentaries* which were dedicated, appropriately enough, to Henry VIII: 'A weal public cannot be governed without injustice' (Tasker 1945, ii, 416).

It is essential to note in all this that it is not the state and its institutions which are the cause of moral evil as the Romantics asserted. The traditional doctrine and the Romantic are almost antithetical at this point. According to the former, sin is the cause, according to the latter, the consequence, of institutions.

The traditional theory of the state was challenged in the seventeenth century by various naturalistic accounts of the emergence of political society either directly from an hypothetical state of nature (Hobbes) or indirectly, through the intermediate but equally hypothetical stage of a natural society (Locke). Though interminable controversy surrounds all details of these theories, their ideological function and their relation to one another (e.g., MacPherson 1962 and the literature arising therefrom), one thing at least is clear: they present a secularized version of the Augustinian understanding of the state as *remedium peccatorum*. In *Leviathan*, for example, all agree to give up all power to the sovereign because of the natural propensity of humans 'to invade and destroy each other'. In the second *Treatise of Government* 'The great and chief end, thereof, of men's uniting into commonwealths, and of putting themselves under the government, is the preservation of their property' (para. 124). Like those of the Augustinian tradition which they replaced, the truth or falsity of these doctrines is irrelevant to my argument, which is merely that the transition from a biblical to a naturalistic theory of the state made no difference to the classification of social evil. Whether divinely ordained or man-made, political society and its institutions are seen as devices for minimizing, but not eliminating, the evil which must be borne if humans are to survive together. Evil of this kind is not the result of morally aberrant human decision, and therefore is to be classed as natural.

Wealth and poverty
In the Old Testament, broadly speaking, wealth is a good and poverty an evil. In the New Testament the reverse is the case. As the primitive church abandoned the naive eschatology of the first century, poverty became an evil once again but wealth was never fully rehabilitated. Though the individual possession of wealth by Christians was tolerated, provided it was rightly and charitably used, the Fathers held out to the spiritually most ambitious a way of perfection which included a literal obedience to the dominical

command to 'go and sell all thou hast, and give to the poor' (Matthew 19: 21; see Viner 1978, 14–15). Nevertheless they denied the heretical claim that the rich have no chance of salvation and the otherwise austere and rigorist St Clement of Alexandria (*c.* 150–215) was nicknamed 'Consoler of the Rich' for his tract *Quis Dives Salvetur?* (Viner 1978, 41; Quasten 1950–60, II, 15–16).

Though the New Testament ideal of a community of wealth, at least in the millennium, was generally cherished by the Fathers, the late third-century African, Lactantius, rejected even this (Viner 1978, 18). It is of some significance that the extant works of Lactantius, by no means the most profound or influential of the Fathers (Quasten 1950–60, II, 393–4), are among only six patristic authors included in the 175 theological titles of the Malthus family library (*MLC*, 91). In the following century Theodoretus argued that the wealth of the rich was positively beneficial to the poor by providing a market for their products. He also drew the important distinction, which has been noted above in connexion with political society, between the moral evil resulting from injustice of the rich, and the social effects of wealth whether good or evil, resulting from its right and proper use (Viner 1978, 18–19).

Throughout the entire period from the second century to the Reformation, indeed, the orthodox tradition of discourse considers wealth and poverty in very much the same light as the institutions of society. Any inevitable evil associated with their right use is natural. But injustice, either of the rich towards the poor (oppression, extortion, cruelty, etc.) or of the poor towards the rich (robbery and theft, poor workmanship, etc.) is moral evil, regarded as logically independent of, or at least not entailed by, the existence of riches and poverty. Those such as the Waldensians who taught that private property and its associated wealth and poverty are morally evil were repudiated as heretical (Viner 1978, 108).

Viner's opinion as to the unanimity of post-Restoration British writing on these matters has already been cited. To some extent, no doubt, it expressed a reaction to the Levelling doctrines proclaimed by extremists during the Civil War. Yet there was implicit agreement that poverty is an evil even if wealth be not. 'Sir', cried Johnson to Boswell in 1763, 'all the arguments which are brought to represent poverty as no evil, shew it to be evidently a great evil. You never find people labouring to convince you that you may live very happily upon a plentiful fortune' (Boswell 1953, 312).

Johnson dismissed Jenyns's 'gentle paraphrase' of poverty as 'want of riches', for 'in that sense almost every man may in his own opinion be poor'. 'Want of competence' and even worse, 'want of necessaries' are harder to justify, and it is 'cruel if not unjust' 'to entail irreversible poverty upon generation after generation' by denying to the poor an education by which they may rise in the world. Moreover, it 'is wholly contrary to the maxims of a commercial nation, which always suppose and promote a rotation of property, and offer every individual a chance of mending his condition by his diligence' (Johnson 1787, x, 229, 232).

Some of the evil of poverty is moral in the sense that it arises from injustice or oppression of the rich, and some in the sense that it is caused by the sloth and indolence of the poor. Yet 'the rotation of property' which takes place in 'a commercial nation' is a sign that in a world of scarcity some may be rich but many must be poor. Though Johnson rejected the particular attempt by Jenyns to establish that 'poverty is what all could not possibly have been exempted from', he raised no objection to its classification as a *natural* evil.

War

For William Godwin, war is the first and greatest of social evils. Being caused – as he fondly supposed – by a 'quarrel between two princes' (1798a, I, 11) it is, like all other social evil for Godwin, the necessary outcome of an unjust and remediable engrossment of property.

Christian theory of war began to be developed after the Constantinian establishment of the church. Obedient to Apostolic injunction, the liturgy included intercessions 'For kings, and for all that are in authority; that we may lead a quiet and peaceable life' (I Timothy 2: 2). Petitions for emperor or king are conjoined with those for his 'Christ-loving' (*philochristos*) army: 'That [God] would fight on their side and subdue every enemy and adversary under their feet' (Neale 1859, 93).

The implied concept of a *just* war was recognized by St Augustine and later developed by the Scholastics. But Augustine made no attempt to conceal the evil even of the justest war. The horrors and misery of war run like a *leitmotif* throughout human history as narrated in *The City of God*. This is because human nature, being alienated from God by the Fall, is divided in itself, 'flesh' against

'spirit'. Hence 'each good man may fight against another through
that part of him with which he also fights against himself' ('possunt
ut bonus quisque ex ea parte pugnet contra alterum qua etiam
contra semet ipsum', *Civ. Dei*, xv: 5). The disunity of man with man
which is the consequence of the disunity of Man with God is
symbolized by the murderer Cain, founder of *terrena civitas* (xv: 5),
and by the confusion of tongues at Babel (xvi: 4,5; xix: 7). Yet
every human soul longs for peace and paradoxically, tragically, it is
precisely this which is the cause of war. For the earthly city can only
understand and pursue an earthly peace, and this is only attained by
successful struggle with one's enemies 'for the things that both could
not enjoy at the same time' ('pax erit, quam non habebant partes in
vicem adversantes et pro his rebus quas simul habere non poterant
infelici egestate certantes', *Civ. Dei*, xv: 4). We may therefore say
that 'peace is War's purpose'; and 'All men seek peace by war'
('Omnis enim homo etiam belligerando pacem requirit', *Civ. Dei*,
xix: 12).

Save only for the biblical explanation of the way human nature
came to be the way it actually is, there is almost complete
correspondence between this account of the causes of war and that
supplied by Hobbes in *Leviathan*. For 'if any two men desire the same
thing, which nevertheless they cannot both enjoy, they become
enemies...and in the way to their end...endeavour to destroy, or
subdue one another'. Hence all are in continual danger of invasion
by all others, all are therefore 'diffident' of each other, and 'from
diffidence war' (Hobbes 1957, 81). War 'consisteth not in battle
only, or the act of fighting...but in the known disposition thereto,
during all the time there is no assurance of the contrary. All other
time is PEACE' (82). Peace is only possible by the destruction of all
enemies, which is impossible, or by the creation – in *Leviathan* – of a
'common power to fear'. But since sovereign states are themselves in
a state of nature (i.e. war) with respect to each other, this route to
lasting peace is also blocked. There is, in fact, no possibility of true
peace on earth, which is consistent with the biblical doctrine that
'Christ's kingdom [is] not of this world' (317). For Hobbes, as for
Augustine, war is a natural consequence of human existence,
animated by desire for good but constrained by scarcity.

Because of his inability or unwillingness to grasp the nettle of
scarcity, Locke upheld a distinction between the state of war and the
state of nature ('Men living together according to reason, without a

common superior on earth', Locke 1967, III: 19). Nevertheless, to avoid a state of war 'is one great reason of men's putting themselves into society and quitting the state of nature'. In that political society is taken by Locke as the normal state of affairs, he tacitly denies what Godwin insists: that 'reason' can actually be efficacious in maintaining peace in a state of nature.

English social theodicy in the 1780s

'Rousseau was mad but influential, Hume was sane but had no followers' (Russell 1945, 673). It is my belief that neither had begun to exert any significant influence upon English social theory by the time Robert Malthus went up to Cambridge. Hume's attack upon the naturalistic teleology which Newton had bequeathed to the age went almost unnoticed. Rousseau's determination to regard social evil as moral and therefore remediable, rather than as natural and therefore inevitable, made little headway in English letters until the emergence of the Jacobins after 1790. Before that period, Rousseau's 'absurd preference of savage to civilised life' was regarded with tolerant complacency by the enlightened as 'proofs rather of a defect in his understanding, than of any depravity in his heart' (Boswell 1953, 359). Though the eccentric Daniel Malthus, Robert's father, was a passionate admirer of Rousseau, and though by a symbolic coincidence both Hume and Rousseau spent a Sunday afternoon with the Malthuses when Robert was three weeks old (James 1979, 10–11), neither the radical scepticism of his one 'fairy godmother' (Keynes 1972, 74) nor the romantic anthropology of his other seem to have played any significant part in Robert's intellectual formation.

If I am correct in my belief, it follows that the methodological style of social theodicy current in England when Robert Malthus was a young man corresponds to class 2 of the taxonomy determined at the beginning of this part of the present chapter. *Teleology*, understood as the set of supposedly coherent beliefs about the meaning and purpose of the universe in general and of human existence in particular, rested chiefly upon a naturalistic basis derived from Newtonian physics. *Social evil*, understood as the evil which is perceived to occur because and only because humans live in society, was generally held to be natural rather than moral. Most Anglican theologians from Archbishop King to Archdeacon Paley were too wily to depend upon a wholly naturalistic teleology and reinforced their apologetic with varying doses of more or less traditional, scriptural doctrine. Virtually everyone, even Soame Jenyns, agreed that *some* social evil was moral and therefore avoidable or remediable. But virtually everyone also agreed that the irreducible minimum of evil which must occur in any society, even where no 'vicious Elections' are made, represents an optimum in this sense: that it is significantly less than the evil which would have occurred had there been no society at all.

The theodicy Malthus attempted in the first *Essay* was the outcome of his particular theological training, or lack of it, within the general intellectual climate I have attempted to describe. To some account of the former we now turn.

MALTHUS'S THEOLOGICAL FORMATION

William Cobbett, by his own account, 'detested many men'. In particular he hated 'parsons' and could think of no harsher epithet to apply to Malthus, whom he claimed to have hated above all others (Smith 1951, 120). Karl Marx followed suit. Perhaps because of this, James Bonar went out of his way to minimize Malthus's ecclesiastical career. '"Parson" was in his case a title without a *rôle*...He had hardly more of the parson than Condillac of the abbé' (Bonar 1924, 6).

Though Keynes surprised Bonar by discovering that Malthus held the rectory of Walesby from 1803 until his death, and despite the testimony of Otter (1836, liii) and Empson (*ER* 1837, 481), Bonar's biassed judgement has been generally accepted. William Petersen's biography claimed to be 'the first full and accurate exposition of [Malthus's] thought' and justly indicted the inaccuracy of much previous Malthus scholarship (1979, 22–23). Yet there is no discussion in his own work of Malthus's theological writing and only two brief and mistaken references to his ecclesiastical career (1979, 28–54). Mrs James (1979) provided more information than any previous author and gave a more balanced account of Malthus's intellectual background than Professor Petersen, yet even she was generally uncurious about her subject's theological training and interests. Only since the recent researches of John Pullen (1986, 1987) has it been possible to reconstruct even the outlines of Robert Malthus's life as a clergyman of the Church of England.

From the standpoint of this book the most important questions about that life are those which relate to what is known in clerical circles as his 'formation'. How was Malthus prepared for ordination and his clerical duties; how seriously did he take his vocation to the sacred ministry; and to what extent did he maintain or develop his theological interests in later life? There is very little direct or even indirect evidence on any of these matters but such as there is may be considered under two heads: Malthus's ecclesiastical career, and theological training in unreformed Cambridge.

Malthus's ecclesiastical career

A letter of Robert Malthus to his father dated 15 April 1783 (Pullen 1986, 150–1: Pullen follows Bonar in believing the date should be 1784) reveals that Robert had already decided upon taking Holy Orders even though, at the time, it had not yet been decided whether he would enter a university. At that time he was a private pupil of Gilbert Wakefield with whom he had studied at the Warrington Dissenting Academy immediately before its dissolution. Wakefield entered him at his old Cambridge college in the Easter term of 1784: the following November, as was then customary (Winstanley 1935, 43–4), he went into residence, being elected Brunsell Exhibitioner in 1786 and graduating BA in January 1788 as Ninth Wrangler. During his second year he sought the advice of the Master, Dr Beadon, as to ordination. Beadon 'seemed at first to advise against orders', but changed his mind upon being assured that the utmost of Malthus's wishes for preferment was 'a retired living in the country' (James 1979, 30).

Malthus remained in residence for the remainder of his fourth year and also for the greater part of the fifth year (1788–9) reading for ordination. In early May 1789 the Master and Fellows of Jesus College presented the usual testimonials to the Bishop of Winchester; John Hallam, Perpetual Curate of Oakwood (now spelt Okewood), notified the bishop that he had nominated and appointed Robert Malthus BA to the stipendiary curacy of Oakwood 'until he shall be otherwise provided of some Ecclesiastical preferment' at an annual stipend of £40; and on Trinity Sunday (7 June) 1789 the said Robert Malthus, having reached the canonical age of twenty-three the previous February, was ordered Deacon in Winchester Cathedral. The following day, having subscribed to the Thirtynine Articles and the three Articles of Canon 36 of 1603, he was licensed to serve the curacy of Oakwood (Pullen 1987, *passim*).

For the next four years this was Malthus's only occupation and only source of income. On Septuagesima Sunday (20 February) of 1791, having served twenty months in the diaconate, Malthus read his *Si Quis* 'in Oakwood Chapel where I officiate' giving notice of his intention to offer himself as 'a candidate for Priest's orders at the approaching ordination of the Bishop of Winchester'. On the same Sunday he obtained a testimonial from three neighbouring incumbents of his worthiness 'to be admitted to the sacred order of a Priest'. In fact the Bishop of Winchester, Brownlow North, held no ordination that Lent, and Malthus was ordained Priest on the Second Sunday in Lent by the Bishop of Norwich under letters dimissory from Winchester (Pullen 1987, *passim*).

At the time of his presbyteral ordination Malthus was still BA: according to Bonar – who is grievously unreliable in all other respects about the decade 1788–98 – Malthus took the MA some time in 1791 and this is confirmed by Venn (Bonar 1924, 413; Venn 1922–54, Part II, IV, 303). On 19 June 1793, he was elected a Fellow of Jesus College, which would have made a small addition to his income. In 1789 the gross income of the Master was only £120: that of a junior Fellow might have been as little as £10, together with free board and rooms when in residence (Winstanley 1935, 280–1). According to Otter, Malthus resided occasionally on his fellowship 'for the purpose of pursuing with more advantage that course of study to which he was attached'. Otter is even more unreliable than Bonar at this point, however, for he states that it was in 1797 that Malthus proceeded to the MA, was made a Fellow of Jesus, took orders, and 'undertook the care of a small parish in Surrey' (Otter 1836, xxxv). The Jesus College 'Register of Borrowers, 1791–1805' indicates that Malthus signed books out of the college library 'during the second half of November 1801' (*MLC*, xvii).

On the 21 November 1803, Malthus finally obtained the 'retired living in the country' he had envisaged seventeen years before, being instituted Rector of Walesby in Lincolnshire which carried an income of just over £300 (James 1979, 102). Presumably the stipendiary curacy at Oakwood was discontinued, though no record of a new curate's being appointed occurs until June 1806 (Pullen 1987, n. 11). This preferment enabled Malthus to marry and immediately after his marriage he and his wife resided at Walesby where he solemnized two marriages (James 1979, 164). He seems seldom to have resided thereafter (however, see Ricardo 1951–73, VI, 35, 40–4; VII, 193; VIII, 226, 349) appointing a curate at £70 p.a., raised to £80 in 1828 (James 1979, 102). His fellowship at Jesus College lapsed with marriage.

In November 1805 Malthus was appointed Professor at the East India College where he remained for the rest of his life, retaining the rectory of Walesby. In January 1824 John Hallam died, and on 5 April 1824 Malthus was licensed by the Bishop of Winchester as Perpetual Curate of Oakwood Chapel. Like his predecessor, he appointed a needy young clergyman as his stipendiary assistant (James 1979, 334). Thus, for the first fourteen years of his ministry Malthus was a resident, stipendiary curate, actually doing the duties of a cure; for the remaining thirty-two years of his life he was a beneficed clergyman though generally non-resident; and during his last eleven years he was a non-resident pluralist, employing curates to do his pastoral duties – among them his son Henry – both at Walesby and at Oakwood. The question is, just how seriously did Malthus and others take all this?

It is evident that whatever else Malthus's ecclesiastical career may have been, it was certainly in a respectable profession: a means of obtaining a comfortable, middle-class income after a fairly long apprenticeship. There is a temptation to regard the eighteenth-century church with some cynicism as a means by which the upper classes secured a maintenance of the more unwarlike of their younger sons. But as Sykes (1934, 5 etc.) has observed, this is in part the result of a church history constructed to meet the ideological needs of the Tractarians and their successors. It is unjustifiably reductionist to assume that the sacred ministry was *merely* a respectable profession for Malthus and his contemporaries.

We must consider, in the first place, the punctillious way in which it was begun. The 1604 canons of the Church of England (Bullard 1934) were scrupulously observed in the case of Robert Malthus. Canon XXXI requires that ordinations be held at the 'Four solemn Times', that is the Sundays following the Ember Weeks. Malthus was made Deacon on Trinity Sunday which follows the Whitsun Ember Days, and priested on the Second Sunday in Lent which follows the Lenten Ember Days. Canon XXXIV establishes a minimum age of twenty-three for the diaconate and twenty-four for the priesthood; specifies a degree from Oxford or Cambridge 'except he be able to yield an account of his faith in Latin'; and requires letters of testimonial 'under seal of some College in Cambridge or Oxford', or of 'three or four grave ministers'. Canon xxxiii forbids ordination without title and calls for the ordinand to provide the Bishop with 'a true and undoubted certificate' of title. Dr Pullen's recent discoveries demonstrate that all of these canonical provisions were faithfully observed, as were Canons xxxvi and xxxvii on subscription and Canon xlviii on the appointment of curates. Canon xxv stipulates that ordinands be examined by the Bishop. There is no record of this having happened in Malthus's case, but, as we shall later see, some other provision may have been made.

In the second place there is no doubt that Malthus performed the duties of Oakwood Chapel from his appointment in 1789 at least until his Scandinavian tour of 1799 and probably until preferment in 1803. Services were regularly held in the chapel except for Evening Prayer during the winter months: there was no heating until 1852 (James 1979, 45). Malthus's seeming unfamiliarity with marriage documents is explained by the fact that the chapel was not licensed for marriages until it became a parish church in 1853 (James 1979, 164, 40). His stipend depended upon the regular discharge of the curate's duties and though the testimonial letter of 20 February 1791 is in standard form it would not have been written had he been delinquent. Though elected to a college fellowship in 1793 he seems not to have resided much – if at all – before 1799 (James 1979, 71). The first *Essay* was written 'in a country situation' and only when it made him a celebrity did he begin to travel abroad and maintain a 'garret in London'.

Thirdly, the East India College was almost as clerical an establishment as any Cambridge college of the day. The Principal and many of the other professors were clergymen. Morning and Evening Prayer, compulsory for all students, were said daily in chapel. The Eucharist was celebrated and confirmations were held. According to Otter, who is more reliable about the later years, 'Mr Malthus was a clergyman of the Church of England, and during a large portion of his life read prayers and preached regularly in turn with the other professors in the chapel of the East India College at Haileybury' (Otter 1836, liii).

Finally there is the indirect evidence of Malthus's personal faith and piety. He was a friend of 'serious' men, such as the evangelical William Dealtry. His son, the Reverend Henry Malthus (1804–82), followed his father's profession and seems to have been far more carefully prepared for it than was Robert himself. All who knew Robert Malthus personally spoke warmly of his goodness and 'it was easy to perceive that spirit of the Gospel had shared largely in forming his character, and that both the precepts and doctrines of Christianity had made a deep impression on his mind' (Otter 1836, liii).

Theological training in unreformed Cambridge

From its inception until Victorian times, the University of Cambridge was first and foremost a seminary for the training of ordinands and a centre for the advanced study of theology by unbeneficed clerks. The Elizabethan statutes required resident MAs to hear lectures on theology and Hebrew and take part in theological disputations. Those who elected the Faculty of Divinity were required to continue theological studies and disputations and to preach certain public sermons. Seven years after the MA the degree of Bachelor of Divinity might be taken (Winstanley 1935, 64). Undergraduate studies for the BA were conceived as a necessary intellectual preparation of the highest and most demanding study of divinity.

Though much of this had fallen into desuetude by the eighteenth century – partly, as Watson (1785, I, viii) conjectured, because 'at the time these statutes were made, young men were admitted to the University about the age of fourteen' – the course of study prescribed for the BA had by no means ceased to be regarded as a prolegomenon to theology. Richard Watson, who became Regius Professor of Divinity in 1771, wrote of the graduate in Arts: his memory 'stocked with great abundance of Classical knowledge', his mind 'expanded by a general acquaintance with the several branches of Natural Philosophy', his reasoning faculties 'strengthened by Mathematical Researches', and 'the limits of his understanding...ascertained by the study of Natural Religion'. Such a man is 'admirably fitted to become a divine', but unless he builds on these foundations by a study of scripture and the various branches of theology 'he will never be one' (ibid.). From a superficial glance at the curriculum followed by Malthus it might appear that his studies were wholly 'secular', with a heavy dose of 'Mathematical Researches'. A more careful inspection reveals that even what we should now call its 'natural sciences' component was permeated with explicit theology and indeed that its chief object was to advance the understanding of 'Natural Religion'.

Though Keill's *Physics* deliberately abstracted from theological considerations (Keill 1776, 19) the same was not true of the other two books with which Malthus began his studies of 1784. The avowedly theological purpose of Maclaurin's *Newton*, noted above (p. 67), is declared at the outset: '...natural philosophy is subservient to purposes of a higher kind, and is chiefly to be valued as it lays a sure foundation for natural religion and moral philosophy' (Maclaurin 1775, 3). Maclaurin begins by warning against both the 'atheism' of philosophers such as Lucretius, who suppose the universe occurs by chance, and the 'superstition' (eighteenth-century code-word for Roman Catholicism) which 'discourages inquiries into nature, lest, by having our views enlarged, we should escape from her bonds' (Maclaurin 1775, 5). The entire first book is an extended critique of philosophical method with many a shrewd blow at Descartes, Spinoza and Leibniz. The final chapter of Book IV summarizes the knowledge afforded by Newtonian physics 'Of the Supreme Author and governor of the Universe, the True and Living God'. Not only does science demonstrate the unity, omnipotence, omniscience and goodness of God, it 'disposes us to receive what may be otherwise revealed to us concerning him' (Maclaurin 1775, 401) and thus provides a proper introduction to the study of scripture. We are led by science to a belief in an afterlife (Maclaurin 1775, 410–11). Finally we learn 'to consider our present state...as a state of preparation or probation for farther advancement' (411): a doctrine which, as we have seen above, was generally supposed to be revealed rather than natural. There is little doubt that Maclaurin correctly represented Newton's own aims as set forth in the *Principia* and the *Opticks*. In the latter, for example, Newton takes it for granted that natural philosophy brings us nearer to 'knowledge of the first Cause' (1952 (1730), 70); dismisses with contempt the Lucretian doctrine that the universe arises from chance (402); speaks, as Paley was later to do, of the 'Contrivance' of God (403); asserts that God might 'vary the Laws of Nature' if He chose (404); and suggests that moral philosophy might be enlarged by natural philosophy in that we learn our duty to God and our neighbours 'by the light of Nature' (405).

Aside from the theological tendency of Newtonian natural philosophy, undergraduates were expected to read Locke, Paley and

other philosophers, and to defend at public, Latin disputations
(called 'acts') theses on moral philosophy and apologetics. Gunning
(1854, I, 81, 86) recalls that for his first 'act' he was required to read
'Paley on Utility', and that at his second he was questioned about
the 'Credibility of Miracles'. When one adds to all this the fact that
undergraduates were required to attend chapel each day, permitted
to attend the public disputations for higher degrees in divinity, and
obliged to declare their bona fide membership in the Church of
England upon graduation; when one considers, moreover, that 'in
most private colleges the fundamentals of revelation itself are, by the
excellent tutors with which this place [Cambridge, 1767] abounds,
explained and illustrated in the ablest manner to their respective
pupils' (Porteus 1767, cit. Bullock 1955, 16), one is led to a
somewhat different view of undergraduate training in the 1780s than
would be suggested to the modern mind by the description 'classics,
science and mathematics'.

Nevertheless the need remained for further theological study
before ordination and it did not pass unnoticed. The Regius
Professor, Richard Watson, delivered no lectures in divinity,
excusing himself on the grounds that the obligatory Latin would
deter an audience. But in 1785 he published as *Theological Tracts* in
six substantial volumes what we should now describe as a collection
of readings for undergraduates, which included large excerpts or
complete reprintings of such well-known authors as Lardner, Locke
(*Reasonableness of Christianity*), Clarke (Boyle Lecture, 1705), Benson,
Hartley and Macknight together with Archbishop Secker's *Instructions to Candidates for Holy Orders* (1769). Watson believed that 'it
is not the reading of many books which makes a man a Divine, but
the reading of a few of the best books often over (1785, I, viii) and
recommended undergraduates intending Orders to 'dedicate a small
portion of every day, or the whole of every Sunday... in the course
of three or four years' before the BA (ibid.). Whether many did this
we do not know. What we do know from Bonar's unpublished
typescript (1956, IV–67; deposited at the University of Illinois at
Urbana-Champagne) is that Robert Malthus wrote to his father on
17 April 1788 – a few months after graduation – indicating his
intention of purchasing Watson's *Tracts*. The 1785 edition of Watson
is part of the Malthus family library presented to Jesus College in
1949 (*MLC*, 35).

The first move in modern times to provide theological lectures for baccalaureate ordinands was taken with the establishment of the Norrisian Chair of Revealed Religion in 1780, four years before Malthus matriculated. From the outset the incumbent, John Hey, lectured in English, and attracted large audiences of diligent students, which Winstanley (1935, 176) attributed to the fact that 'sometime before the end of the century, the bishops had instituted the practice of requiring all candidates for ordination to present a certificate of having attended a certain number of the Norrisian Professor's lectures'. Hey was appointed for a five-year term and reappointed twice before reaching the compulsory retirement age of sixty. In 1794 he published a seventy-six-page summary, *Heads of Lectures in Divinity*, and in 1796–8, after retirement, the full text of the lectures in four volumes (Hey 1796–8). Both titles are part of the Malthus library though the latter was among 423 titles catalogued at Dalton Hill for Bonar in 1891 which were not donated to Jesus College. It is probable that Robert Malthus acquired both the *Heads* and the complete *Lectures*, and it would seem from this that he attended the lectures himself – or later came to believe that he ought to have done so.

The canonical age of twenty-three for diaconal ordination meant that for most Bachelors of Arts in the later eighteenth century about a year must elapse between graduation and ordination. Where means afforded, it was customary to spend this year in residence, reading for Orders. Robert Malthus wrote to his father in April 1788 asking whether he should return to residence for the academic year 1788–9 (Bonar 1956, IV–67). There is no record of Daniel's reply but indirect evidence that Robert did in fact reside is provided by the Jesus College 'Register of Borrowers' for 1783–90. In 1788, in addition to volumes on history and geography, Malthus borrowed volumes I and II of Zachary Pearce's *Sermons*. In 1789 (having shown an early indication of his future researches by taking out *Wealth of Nations*), he borrowed Secker's *Sermons*, volumes I and II of Jortin's *Sermons* and Burnet *On the Thirty-nine Articles*. Burnet, Jortin and Secker appear with nine others – Pearson, Mede, Barrow, Chillingworth, Stillingfleet, Clarke, Tillotson, Taylor and Benson – listed by Watson (1785, I, xii) as eminent among 'our English Divines'. Pearce was a friend of Jortin and well respected in Cambridge. Sermons were treated as a convenient way of summarizing divinity in the eighteenth century and would correspond more closely to articles in learned journals than to the sermons of

today. All of the theological works signed out to Malthus, especially
Burnet, were much borrowed by other undergraduates and resident
BAs.

The statutes of the university presupposed that all resident MAs
who had not declared for law or medicine were candidates for a
divinity degree, the chief requirement for which was to take part, not
only as proposer but also as an opponent, in public disputations
upon theological questions. Disputations took place fortnightly in
the Divinity Schools during term and continued throughout the
eighteenth century. 'The proceedings were public and attracted
a large audience' (Winstanley 1935, 64–8). Though there is no
evidence that Malthus attended any of these, it would not have been
unusual for a resident BA reading for Orders; and in any case he
would have been made aware, by that process resembling osmosis
which determines the composition of knowledge and the climate of
opinion in any university, of the kinds of topics considered worthy of
debate.

What these were may be conveniently ascertained, for Watson
subjoined to his *Tracts* a list of 'a few' – actually 200 – which had
been disputed in Cambridge between 1755 and 1785 under his
presidency or that of the Lady Margaret Professor, Thomas
Rutherford (Watson 1785, I, xxi–xxxi). In order to support the
claim that Cambridge of his own day differed from that of the
previous century in entertaining 'a more enlarged view of the
Christian system, and more liberal notions concerning the manner in
which dissentients from our particular mode of faith and worship
ought to be treated' (Watson 1785, I, xxviii), Watson also printed
two other lists: forty-nine questions published in 1634 and fifty-two
published in 1679.

The contrast is instructive. In the seventeenth century the
questions are brief, general, and frequently polemical. Examples
such as 'Ecclesia Romana est apostatica' (1634), 'Sancti non sunt
invocandi' (1634), 'Purgatorium Papisticum est fictitium' (1679)
and 'Ministris conjugium non est interdicendum' (1679) are typical.
In 1634, 30 per cent of the questions are explicitly anti-Roman; in
1679, 17 per cent. Though strict quantitative analysis is impossible,
because of the uncertain provenance of the samples, it may be worth
noting that for 1755–85 the anti-Roman questions had fallen to 8 per
cent, and were balanced by several anti-Calvinist questions dealing
with predestination and the imparity of ministers. In the former,

moreover, the insulting adjective *papisticus* was replaced by the more courteous *pontificius*. Even more indicative of change, Watson's and Rutherford's theses were addressed to a wider variety of biblical and apologetic questions, and were more elaborately formed. 'Quod genus humanum fit laboribus et morti subjectum propter Adami peccatum, docetur in sacra pagina, nec est rationi contrarium' is typical, not least in its concern to argue that there is no contradiction between reason and revelation. Many of the questions deal with the credibility, authority and significance of miracles, and many with the divine attributes, especially goodness. The bloodier parts of the Old Testament receive special attention and one candidate even proposed that 'Filia Jephthae non fuit immolata'. The objective and eirenical spirit which Watson seems to have been eager to promote is to be seen in the question: 'Dissensiones Christianorum, de rebus quae in religione Christiana contineantur, non ostendunt religionem ipsum esse falsam'.

We may draw four conclusions from these data about Malthus's intellectual preparation for Orders: first, that he was well trained – better than would be the case with most ordinands today – in natural theology and Christian apologetics; secondly, that he was encouraged, and given opportunity, to acquaint himself with current orthodoxy respecting the Christian revelation; thirdly, that current orthodoxy, as one might expect, was much concerned with such local and contemporary issues as the relation of reason to revelation and the propriety of subscription of the Articles; and finally, that Malthus may have been less diligent than some in availing himself of his opportunity. The first two of these themes have been documented above. The third and fourth require explanation.

The Watson–Rutherford questions for disputation, as we have seen, include many which argue that the more alarming features of biblical doctrine are neither contrary to reason nor inconsistent with divine beneficence. It is evident that this is a reaction to deism, still perceived as a threat in 1785. Maclaurin (1775, 61) had quoted with approval Bacon's dictum that we ought not to suppose 'that a man can search too far, or be too well-studied in the book of God's word [scripture], or in the book of God's works [Nature]'. Watson, however, was careful to warn his readers that 'there is no certainty of truth but in the word of God. Their Bible is the only sure foundation upon which they ought to build every article of the faith which they profess, every point of doctrine which they teach' (1785, I, xii). Though freedom of enquiry had been a good thing, 'the works of our Deistical writers have made some few converts to Infidelity at home': fortunately, however, many 'distinguished characters' have exerted their talents 'in removing such difficulties in the Christian system, as would otherwise be likely to perplex the unlearned, to shipwreck the faith of the unstable, and to induce a reluctant scepticism into the minds of the most serious and best intentioned' (xii, xiii). Accordingly Watson selected readings which are chiefly concerned with removing 'difficulties in the Christian system'. Of the twenty-three printed in the six volumes, seven are expressly apologetic, such as Chandler's *Plain Reasons for being a Christian* and Locke's *The Reasonableness of Christianity*; thirteen are primarily biblical, such as Lardner's *History of the Apostles and Evangelists*; and of the latter at least eight could also be regarded as apologetic, being vindications of the truth or at least the probability of biblical history. Only two deal to any large extent with natural theology. Two others are polemical, especially Benson's *Essay on the Man of Sin*: for Watson still believed, notwithstanding his quite sincere professions of liberality, that the truth of the thesis 'Pontifex Romanorum est ille Antichristus' was 'a primary pillar of the reformed faith' (Watson 1785, v, vii).

The controversy over subscription to the Thirtynine Articles which erupted at Cambridge in 1771-2 in the aftermath of the Feathers Tavern Petition subsided soon after a grace was passed in June 1772 exempting candidates for the BA. A declaration that the candidate was '*bona fide* a member of the Church of England as by the law established' was substituted for subscription, which in 1779 was extended to candidates for bachelors' degrees in law and medicine. The issue did not altogether disappear, however, even though the movement for abolition – which had originally attracted the support of such respected figures as Watson, Edmund Law and William Paley – quickly lost credit with the defection of Jebb and others to Socinianism or infidelity. Subscription was still required for the MA and higher degrees, as it was, of course, for ordinations. Two Fellows of Malthus's college, Robert Tyrwhitt and Dr Edwards, had led the campaign for reform; and a third, his own tutor, William Frend, publicly renounced the Articles in 1787 (Winstanley 1935, 303-16; James 1979, 31-2). Considerable attention was therefore paid, in the last two decades of the eighteenth century, to the moral and intellectual problems presented to candidates for Orders by the requirement of subscription. The last book signed out to Malthus from the college library before ordination was Burnet's classic (1699)

Exposition of the Thirty-nine Articles of the Church of England (Burnet, 1819). Volume II of Hey's Norrisian lecture began with the observation that 'the great business seems to be, to give a right account of what are called *Articles of Religion*... These therefore must be considered as the *principal* objects of our attention,' (Hey 1796–8, II, 2). Volumes II, III and IV of the lectures are devoted to an exhaustive investigation, first of what it may mean to give one's assent to a theological formulary (II, 1–197), and secondly of each of the Anglican articles in turn (II, 198–end; III; IV, 1–540). Pretyman's two-volume *Elements* (1799), the third edition of which Malthus purchased in 1800, was expressly designed as a textbook for ordination candidates: all but thirty pages of its second volume 'is devoted to an Exposition of the Thirtynine Articles of the Church of England'. Pretyman concluded that

It is not indeed necessary that [the ordinand] should approve every word or expression, but he ought to believe all the fundamental doctrines, of the articles; all those tenets in which our church differs from other churches, or from other sects of Christians...
This appears to me the only just ground of conscientious subscription to the articles;...no species whatever of evasion, subterfuge, or reserve, is to be allowed, or can be practised, without imminent danger of incurring the wrath of God. The articles are to be subscribed in their plain and obvious sense, and assent is to be given to them simply and unequivocally. (Pretyman 1812, II, 571–2)

How hard Robert Malthus worked at all this during his time at Cambridge we can only surmise, but such indications as there are suggest that he was never intellectually engaged by Anglican divinity. There is no mention in the domestic correspondence of his actually attending Hey's lectures. He did not purchase Watson's *Theological Tracts* until the April after graduation at the earliest, nor is there any record of his having borrowed the library copy whilst an undergraduate – though some of his contemporaries did so. At the very moment in his career when, if at any time, he might have been expected to concentrate his whole attention upon theology, he chose to read the library's recently acquired (third edition, 1786) copy of the *Wealth of Nations*, being but the second member of his college to do so. That this suggests a particular interest in political economy rather than mere concession to current fashion is avouched by the fact that the book was only signed out again, at widely scattered intervals, five more times over the next fourteen years. For at that period it was 'a book much seen on University shelves, but seldom read' (Pryme 1870, 66). (Indeed it was precisely the success of the second edition of 'Malthus on Population' – signed out of the college library for the first time in November 1803 five months after publication – that produced an awareness of political economy at Jesus in particular and in Cambridge in general.) Though elected a Fellow of his college in 1793 he made no attempt to qualify for the degree of Bachelor of Divinity. For reasons of this kind, one is led to conjecture that Malthus, though undoubtedly sincere about his vocation to the sacred ministry, was not attracted to theological inquiry; that his postgraduate reading in divinity was undertaken from a sense of duty and/or to meet some externally determined standard of competence; and that early in adult life (perhaps even at Warrington) he was made aware of the 'new science' of political economy to which he later made such seminal contributions.

Malthus as a 'divine'

Malthus was undoubtedly a 'parson' and, so far as may be ascertained, a pious and conscientious one according to the standards of his age. In this at least the crude perceptions of Cobbett and Marx were quite correct, and the more sophisticated view of Bonar simply wrong and possibly disingenuous.

Yet in the eighteenth century, as indeed in every century of the Church's history, a man might be a cleric and even a scholar without being a 'divine'. For though, until the secularization of thought in the nineteenth century, virtually every thinker after St Augustine perceived himself and his surroundings through the mediation of Christian preconceptions, only a few made it their business to study those preconceptions themselves. The Anglican Ordinal requires a priest to be 'diligent in prayers and in reading of the holy Scriptures, and in such studies as help to the knowledge of the same, laying aside the study of the World and the flesh', but it was customary to interpret this fairly liberally. Daily recitation of Morning and Evening Prayer, in public or in private, would satisfy the first two. Archbishop Secker, in his *Instructions* to candidates for Holy Orders, interpreted the remainder as 'not making, either gross pleasures, or more refined amusements, *even literary ones unconnected with your profession*, or power, or profit, or advancement, or applause, your great aim in life; but labouring chiefly to qualify yourselves for doing good to the souls of men' (Watson 1785, VI, 112, my italics). It was genuinely difficult in the eighteenth century to draw the line between those 'literary amusements' which were and those which were not unconnected with the clerical profession. Whether it was irony that led Malthus, for example, to insert the phrase 'Particularly addressed to Young Clergymen' on the title page of one of his copies of the first *Essay*, there can be no doubt that his disciple Thomas Chalmers firmly believed that political economy was closely connected with the profession of parish minister, and a potent means of 'doing good to the souls of men'.

For reasons of this kind many in good conscience could leave the academic study of divinity – narrowly and professionally considered – to those of their colleagues who felt a particular vocation to such work. In this they were fortified by two convictions widely held in Malthus's day. In the first place the Bible alone was 'the religion of protestants' and too much divinity a cause of needless dissension. Secondly, natural theology was supposed to answer most of the important questions, and Cambridge men at any rate may well have thought themselves well qualified in this discipline. It is therefore to impute no extraordinary decadence or corruption to the Church of England in the eighteenth century to say that few of its 'parsons' were 'divines'.

All the evidence assembled in this chapter points to the conclusion that Malthus belonged to the majority of his brethren in this respect. His theological reading at Cambridge appears to have been minimal, his intellectual interests more varied than most (Otter 1836, xxxii–xxxiii), and his attraction to political economy to have come early in life. 'From the moment the principle of population had been struck out from his mind, and had taken hold of the public attention, it became to him the predominant and absorbing subject of his thoughts' (Otter 1836, xxxi). Between ordination in 1789 and the publication of the first *Essay* nine years later he seems to have acquired sixteen theological pamphlets (seven by his old tutor Gilbert Wakefield), at most three volumes of divinity (one by another Warrington Academy tutor), and the pamphlet-length outline of Hey's Norrisian lectures (*MLC*). Save for the last two chapters of the first *Essay* no other writing by Malthus attests to any special interest in or competence at theology. Unlike others among his clerical colleagues at the East India College he published no volume of sermons.

It should be no surprise, therefore, that the theological chapters of the *Essay* were so unsatisfactory that they were suppressed in later recensions. To the problems they addressed and the failure of the solutions they proposed, we are now in a position to turn.

THEOLOGY IN THE FIRST *ESSAY*

At the beginning of this chapter I argued that it is anachronistic to create too sharp a distinction between the so-called 'scientific' and 'theological' features of eighteenth-century social theory. Though the last two chapters of the first *Essay* are almost entirely what we should now call 'theology' the previous seventeen, which are largely what we should now call 'politics', 'philosophy' or 'economics', are at least as well supplied with 'theological' terms and concepts as, say, Maclaurin's *Newton*. 'God', 'Heaven' (generally used as a synonym, like 'Buckingham Palace' for the Queen), 'Nature' (another synonym for God), 'miracles', 'revelation', 'temptation', 'evil' and 'sin', 'natural religion', 'soul' and 'immortality' are introduced without explanation or apology, in complete confidence that readers will be inward with their universe of discourse. The principal theme of chapter XVIII is anticipated by a long footnote in chapter XII (1798, 246–7). As I have demonstrated in chapter 2 (see pp. 29–37), the entire argument of the first *Essay* is couched in a metaphysical and theological vocabulary which closely resembles Godwin's.

Nevertheless, chapters XVIII and XIX form a more or less self-contained theodicy of scarcity which Malthus had originally conceived 'as a kind of second part to the essay' but which, because of 'a long interruption, from particular business' was laid aside in favour of the 'sketch' actually published (356). It is therefore defensible to examine the theodicy as a specimen of late eighteenth-century divinity, appraising it according to the standards of theological scholarship then current. The examination may conveniently follow three general questions: what was Malthus trying to achieve; how did he go about his task; and how far was he successful?

What was Malthus trying to achieve?

It was the ostensible purpose of Malthus's theological chapters to reconcile his view of 'the situation of man on earth' – which he had drawn with 'dark tints, from a conviction that they are really in the picture' – with 'our ideas of the power, goodness and foreknowledge of the Deity' (iv, 349). It was his declared secondary object to replace the doctrine that human life is a state of discipline and trial for eternity with the less familiar theory that it is, rather, 'the mighty process of God ... for the creation and formation of mind' (353). The presentation of each of these theses is vague, not to say muddled. In my opinion this is less a consequence either of the 'interruption, from particular business' or of his elementary theological technique – though both have obviously played a part – than of the fact that Malthus had a more or less hidden agenda in these chapters. An important purpose I believe, like that of the political economy of chapters I to XVII, was *further to undermine Godwin's attack on private property*. Whereas the 'positive polemic' in the political economy showed that private property and inequality were beneficial because they maximized the surplus upon which civilization depends, the corresponding theological argument held that they were beneficial because they furthered the Divine plan 'to sublimate the dust of the earth into soul'. The effect of this argument, together with its corollaries, is to replace or supplement Godwin's 'optimistic' doctrine of Man with a more 'pessimistic' anthropology better suited to Malthus's ideological needs. The relation between Malthus's ostensible and his covert or unconscious theological aims is suggested diagrammatically in figure 4.

'The constant pressure of distress on man from the difficulty of subsistence' (349) is the cause of that 'misery' and 'vice' which Malthus deliberately opposed to the 'happiness' and 'virtue' that Godwin (1798a, I, 382; II, 528; etc.) predicted. 'Misery' is here a shorthand for 'those roughnesses and inequalities in life which querulous man too frequently makes the subject of his complaint against the God of Nature' (Malthus 1798, 356): that is, for *natural evil*. 'Vice' arises from 'the temptations to which Man must necessarily be exposed, from the operation of those laws of nature which we have been examining' (348) and is a species of *moral evil*. Malthus argued that 'it seems highly probable, that moral evil is absolutely necessary to the production of moral excellence' (375). In order to justify both natural and moral evil Malthus employed the 'creation of mind' hypothesis. This permitted him to deal with *social evil* (which he regarded, of course, as natural rather than moral) in a way that directly contradicted Godwin. For the inequality inevitably associated with private property is necessary for the creation of mind. As a corollary to this hypothesis Malthus was able

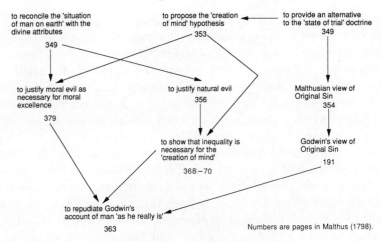

Fig. 4. The aims of Malthus's theodicy.

to assert a demythologized account of original sin – more serviceable for his ideological programme in the first *Essay* – as against both the traditional Augustinian belief in 'original depravity' (207) and Godwin's own brief statement (Malthus 1798, 191; Godwin 1796, II, 340). The combined effect of his justification of moral evil, his defence of inequality and his account of original sin is to set against Godwin's presentation of man 'for what he really is, a being capable of rectitude, virtue and benevolence' (Godwin 1798a, I, 436) a different through not strictly contradictory vision of 'man as he really is, inert, sluggish, and averse from labour unless compelled by necessity' (Malthus 1798, 363).

Though it is evident that the 'creation of mind' hypothesis is superficially well-suited to an anti-Godwinian theodicy of social evil, the more acceptable 'state of trial' theory could be made to serve as well if not better, as Paley and Summer later demonstrated. The question therefore arises as to why Malthus should have picked upon this theological oddity for his purposes.

By his own not very convincing account he selected the theory because it seemed to be 'more consistent with the various phenomena of nature which we observe around us, and more consonant to our ideas of the power, goodness, and foreknowledge of the Deity' (Malthus 1798, 349). In particular it would seem that 'A state of trial...indicates something like suspicion and want of foreknowledge' in the Supreme Being (353). Bonar (1885, 324, n. 8) stated that Malthus owed the idea to the writings of Abraham Tucker; others (Santurri 1982, 321) suggested less plausibly that he employed 'a mentalistic language which is decidedly Humean'; or (Harvey-Phillips 1984, 598–9) that the 'theory of mind' has 'much in common with the tradition of the Cambridge Platonists' especially Cudworth. But neither they nor any other recent commentator offer any hint as to why Malthus felt the need to incorporate the 'growth of mind' theory, however derived, into his theodicy.

In my opinion the key to this puzzle, as with most of the other puzzles presented by the first *Essay*, is to be found in the work of William Godwin that Malthus set out to refute. it is as clear from the last two chapters of the *Essay* as from the previous seventeen that Malthus wrote with *Political Justice* at his elbow. Here as elsewhere he takes Godwin's own ideas, words and phrases and uses them to undo him. Book VIII, 'Of Property', is 'the key-stone that completes the fabric of political justice'. One of the most important objects of that Book is to show that 'inequalities of property perhaps constituted a state, through which it was... necessary for us to pass, and which constituted the true original excitement to the unfolding the powers of the human mind' (Godwin 1798a, II, 448) but that 'though inequality were necessary as the prelude to civilisation, it is not necessary to its support. We may throw down the scaffolding when the edifice is complete' (II, 492). This is because 'love of distinction' would be a sufficient stimulus to intellectual exertion under a regime of equality (II, 485–7). Eventually this too would be recognized as a 'delusion' and 'will take its turn to be detected and abjured' (II, 486). It would be replaced by 'justice': provided 'monopoly' has been banished. 'Truth, the overpowering truth of the general good, then seizes us irresistibly' (II, 488). 'Mind would be delivered from her perpetual anxiety about corporeal support and free to expatiate in the field of thought which is congenial to her' (II, 463). What that might be is determined by 'truth', once we see 'how multitudes and ages may be benefited by our exertions' (II, 488). 'Mind... will perhaps at no time arrive at the termination of its possible... improvements', hence we may reasonably entertain 'the sublime conjecture of Franklin... that "mind will one day become omnipotent over the matter"' (II, 486, 520).

Whatever literary encouragement Malthus may have received from his reading of Abraham Tucker, Hume or the Cambridge Platonists, it was, I believe, Godwin's conception of the development of mind which determined his choice of a particular, Tuckerian form of the theodicy. It was essential to show that inequality is a perennial requirement of human intellectual and spiritual development, and hence that man may never safely 'throw down the ladder by which he has risen' (Malthus 1798, 287) to the civilized state.

How did he go about it?

'In all our feeble attempts... to "find out the Almighty to perfection" it seems absolutely necessary, that we should reason from nature up to nature's God' (Malthus 1798, 350). Whether because he really believed it or, more likely, because here too he had determined to fight Godwin with Godwin's own weapons, Malthus deliberately ignored the cautious orthodoxy of his Cambridge seniors. Watson, Hey and Pretyman maintained that 'there is no certainty of truth but in the word of God' (Watson 1785, I, xxii): Malthus proposed that we should 'turn our eyes to the book of Nature, *where alone* we can read God as he is' (Malthus 1798, 351, my italics).

Though this position had become a cliché long before 1798, it is at least possible that Bonar was correct in stating that Malthus owed his epistemology and the rest of the theology of the *Essay* to the writings of Abraham Tucker. The latter bought Betchworth Castle near Dorking in 1727, married in 1736 and lived at Betchworth until he died in 1774. Daniel Malthus bought Chert Gate Farm (the Rookery) at Wotton, four miles away, in 1759 and lived there with his family until 1768. Thus the two were near neighbours for the nine years immediately preceding the first publication of Tucker's *magnum opus*, *The Light of Nature Pursued*. Given the customs of their time and class it is inconceivable that they should not have met socially; given Daniel Malthus's passion for philosophic speculation it is improbable they should not have become friends. Though *The Light of Nature Pursued* is not to be found in the Malthus library, chapter XXII on *Freewill, Foreknowledge and Fate* published in 1763 as 'a sample from the loom' is among the collection. We may conjecture that the larger work was originally in the family library, that Robert Malthus may have learned of it and its argument from his father, and that Bonar had some authority, now lost, for his statement.

Tucker began with the premise that 'reason cannot work without materials, which must be fetched from nature'. We must begin with the things lying nearest to us...which must help us to investigate others more remote'. Moreover, since 'nature exhibits nothing abstracted to our view' we must accept that 'the abstract must be learned from the concrete' (Tucker 1768, I: I, xxv, xxviii). Though Tucker was prudent enough to admit that he would not reject 'what other help may be afforded us from elsewhere' such as 'from supernatural existence if any such be at hand' (xii) he made no use of scripture in that portion of his work published in his own lifetime. The second part (confusingly called a 'volume' but actually three volumes) on theology, acknowledges that 'we are taught to believe a resurrection of the body': but Tucker treats this as an 'opinion' which 'it is obvious...cannot fall within the compass of my present plan' (II: I, 7).

Tucker's object was to find a rational basis for ethics. In the first part ('volume' I, *Human Nature*, in two volumes) he showed that without the prospect of an after-life there are no compelling grounds for right behaviour. The second part attempts to demonstrate, depending as far as possible on 'the meer light of reason' that human immortality, and thus the 'Re-enlargement of Virtue' is possible. Crucial to Tucker's vast system is his concept of *mind*, in which he located human identity; which is 'spiritual' rather than 'corporeal'; related to, but not to be confused with the 'vulgar' notion of the soul, and of which, 'from [her] individuality and distinct existence... may be inferred her perpetual duration' (II: I, 6, 87, ch. v *passim*, 117, 112).

Tucker considered the attributes of God and the problem of evil at considerable length. The latter 'remains an inscrutable mystery which has perplexed the thoughts of men from the days of Job...and probably will continue to do so' (II: I, 257). Noting that 'evil is so interwoven into our nature that the business of mankind would stagnate without it; he postulated that

If man were placed in such a situation as that no pain or mischief, no satiety or uneasiness, no loss or diminution of enjoyment could befal him, he would have no inducement ever to stir a finger: but 'tis the perishable nature of our satisfaction that urges us to a continual exertion of our activity to renew them. (II: I, 227)

Tucker was led irresistibly to the conclusion that 'God created evil as well as good' (II: I, 236), where 'evil' is conceived as a kind of estate tax upon 'happiness': 'since then we find the estates of happiness in this sub-lunary kingdom subject to taxes we must take the whole together, the rents and the profits together with the disbursements' (II: 1, 256). Because it is 'probably the use of evil ... to excite the mind to bestir herself in avoiding it' (II: 1, 306) he winds up his discussion of immortality, mind and the problem of evil in this way:

> we may gather from the perishable nature of our bodies and the durable nature of our minds...from the method constantly taken by Nature to bring her work to perfection slowly through several stages...from the nature of mind that it was designed for action, from the nature of action that evil is a necessary inducement to excite it... that a very little quantity of evil may suffice to set the spiritual world in motion. (II: 1, 311–12)

Tucker's theory of the evolution of mind under the stimulus of evil is summarized in a gargantuan ten-page footnote – omitted when the entire work was published in 1768 – at the end of the 1763 fragment found in the Malthus library (Tucker 1763, 258–68).

Either because he was directly or indirectly familiar with Tucker's doctrine, or because by sheer coincidence he hit upon the same idea independently, it was this that Malthus made the central feature of his own theodicy.

Godwin had admitted that 'Mind... will improve more in a calamitous, than a torpid state' but had asserted that he 'who has nothing to provide for but his animal wants, scarcely ever shakes off the lethargy of his mind' (Godwin 1798a, II, 336, 427). Malthus followed Tucker's view that 'the perishable nature of our satisfaction...urges us to a continual exertion' and countered Godwin with an image of the savage who 'would slumber for ever under his tree unless he were aroused from his torpor by the cravings of hunger, or the pinchings of cold;...the exertions that he makes to avoid these evils...form and keep in motion his faculties' (Malthus 1798, 357). If all were granted the leisure that Godwin supposed would follow from equalization of property 'we have much more reason to think that they would be sunk to the level of brutes...than that they would be raised to the rank of philosophers' (358). It would seem in fact, that 'some of the noblest exertions of the human mind have been set in motion by the necessity of supplying the wants of the body' (358).

As against Godwin, who had argued that necessity should and would be replaced by higher motives under a 'system of equality', Malthus, like Tucker, generalized the observation to utter what almost amounts to a cosmology. From the proposition, 'The first great awakeners of the mind seem to be the wants of the body' Malthus was led to suppose that 'the world, and this life' are 'the mighty process of God...for the creation and formation of mind, a process necessary, to awaken inert, chaotic matter into spirit, to sublimate the dust of the earth into soul; to elicit an aethereal spark from the clod of clay' (Malthus 1798, 356–7, 353). He then deduced from this an explanation of original sin, a theodicy and an eschatology.

'Is there any innate perverseness in man that continually hurries him to his own destination?' Godwin had asked in a passage deleted from the third edition of his book.

This is impossible; for man is thought, and, till thought began, he had no propensities either to good or evil. My propensities are the fruit of the impressions that have been made upon me, the good always preponderating, because the inherent nature of things is more powerful than any human institutions. The original sin of the worst men, is the perverseness of these institutions, the opposition they produce between public and private good, the monopoly they create of advantages which reason directs to be left in common. (Godwin 1796, II, 340)

Malthus, who appears to have worked with the 1796 edition of *Political Justice,* alluded to this paragraph in the course of his attack in chapter X upon the stability of Godwin's model (Malthus 1798, 191: his footnote ought to read 'B. 7. C. 3. P. 340'.). In chapter XVIII he opposes to Godwin's belief that institutions are the cause of human misery an alternative (but equally heterodox and anti-Augustinian) suggestion that 'The original sin of man, is the torpor and corruption of the chaotic matter, in which he may be said to be born' (354).

Because scarcity is requisite 'in order to rouse man into action, and form his mind to reason', the principle of population is 'part of the gracious designs of Providence'. For 'it has been ordained, that population should increase much faster than food' precisely 'to furnish the most unremitted excitement of this kind' (361). Now scarcity 'undoubtedly produces much partial evil': but 'evil seems necessary to create exertion; and exertion seems evidently necessary to create mind' (361, 360). Not only the physical evils of starvation and disease, but also the social evils of poverty and inequality are justified in this way. Though 'the middle regions of society seem best suited to intellectual improvement' and more equality therefore beneficial, yet 'If no man could hope to rise, or fear to fall in society; if industry did not bring with it its reward, and idleness its punishment' this would no longer be the case (367, 369). Leisure, on the whole, is a bad thing; 'talents are more common among younger brothers [like Robert], than among older brothers'; great achievements are to be attributed more 'to the narrow motives that operate upon the many, than to the apparently more enlarged motives that operate upon the few' (370).

The physical and social evils of scarcity serve to effect the creation of 'mind' (that is, in Tucker's conception, genuine human beings), so justifying *natural* evil in general. It turns out that the justification of *moral* evil may be derived from the same set of ideas. For the 'sorrows and distresses of life' caused by natural evil 'seem to be necessary...to soften and humanize the heart, to awaken human sympathy' and 'to generate all the Christian virtues' (372). So far so good. There are some, however, who respond perversely to misfortune and who produce 'evil proportionate to the extent of their powers'. These 'vicious instruments' nevertheless perform 'their part in the great mass of impressions, by the disgust and abhorrence which they' excite: whence 'it seems highly probable that moral evil is absolutely necessary to the production of moral excellence' (347–5). Scarcity is the cause of moral as well as natural evil; natural evil is a necessary stimulus to intellectual development; moral evil is a necessary stimulus to moral development.

This neat simultaneous solution of the problem of natural and moral evil still leaves one end untied, however. Those 'vicious instruments' who 'misapply their talents' and create moral evil may be doing others a service: but 'both reason and revelation seem to assure us, that such minds will be condemned to eternal death' (374). This raises the question, of course, of why a good and foreknowing God would create human beings predestined to damnation.

Tucker had questioned 'the absolute perpetuity' of divine punishment but had been at pains to argue that this in no way lessened 'the discouragement against evil-doing' (II: III, 448–9). Malthus's Cambridge tutor, William Frend, had abandoned belief in eternal punishment, along with much else, on becoming a unitarian in 1787, as had his private tutor, Gilbert Wakefield, some years earlier. Though Otter discounted the influence upon Malthus of 'the persons to which he had been entrusted for the specific purposes of education' (1836, xxiv) the approximation of their views on this matter to that of Tucker may possibly have weighed with him. At any rate, Malthus firmly rejected the possibility that any of 'the creatures of God's hand can be condemned to eternal suffering' (1798, 389). His actual solution, however, seems to owe nothing to these three but rather to be original, not to say eccentric.

Malthus took it to be a 'moral certainty' that in the process of creation of mind 'many vessels will come out of this mighty creative furnace in wrong shapes'. It is inconceivable to 'our natural conceptions of goodness and justice' that God would punish these; 'it is consonant to our reason' that those vessels which emerge with 'lovely and beautiful forms, should be crowned with immortality'; and that those who are 'misshapen' (that is, 'whose minds are not suited to a purer and happier state of existence') 'should perish and be condemned to mix again with their original clay' (388–90). Malthus thus committed himself to the 'annihilationism' which Tucker (II: 1, 229) attributed to Seneca and rejected, and also to a pair of still more doubtful propositions: that God may require time to achieve His ends (Malthus 1798, 352); and that even then, God may, and in fact does, make mistakes.

The upshot of the matter is, nevertheless, a conclusion which paraphrases Tucker: 'We may have every reason to think that there is no more evil in the world, than what is absolutely necessary as one of the ingredients of the mighty process' (391). Like Tucker (II: 1, 227) moreover, Malthus, seeing evil as the divinely ordained – or at least permitted – spur to human achievement, supposes that the proper moral response is engagement: 'Evil exists in the world, not to create despair, but activity. We are not patiently to submit to it, but to exert ourselves to avoid it' (Malthus 1798, 395).

How far was he successful?

Three criteria ought to be employed in appraising the theological work of an earlier period. First, we must inquire whether, in view of his assumptions, the author is internally consistent and successful in achieving his announced purpose. Secondly, we must consider whether those assumptions, and necessary inferences from them, are consistent with the contemporary canons of orthodoxy by which the author was bound. Finally, if the contribution is to have any applicability to our own day, we must ask whether it meets the standards both of intellectual coherence and of orthodoxy now current. For purposes of this chapter only the first two criteria apply.

In applying the criterion of internal consistency and success within his own terms of reference we must note that the cogency of the theological portions of the first *Essay* is weakened by self-contradiction and confusion; that the theodicy, if taken seriously, seems to imply that God's purpose for mankind can be defeated by His creatures; and that the upshot of Malthus's argument is to render vacuous the concept of 'evil'.

Malthus cites Locke as saying that 'the endeavour to avoid pains, rather than the pursuit of pleasure, is the general stimulus to exertion in this life' whence 'evil seems necessary to create exertion; and exertion seems necessary to create mind' (Malthus 1798, 359, 360). There are three objections to Malthus's use of this idea. In the first place, it does not seem to make sense to hold that evil, which must be perceptible by humans in order to be effectual, is God's way of creating that 'mind' by which, we must suppose, the evil alone is perceived. In the second place, Malthus elsewhere asserts that virtuous acts are produced by *love*, and not *fear* (387–8), despite his general theme, consistent with the 'creation of mind' hypothesis, that God compels us to action of any kind by threat of starvation. In the third place Malthus repeatedly tells us that *self-love* is actually 'the main-spring of the great machine' (175, 207, 286, 370) without relating this motive clearly either to *love* or to *fear*. Other less damaging contradictions recur. The foreknowledge of God is used to rule out the 'state of probation' theory of evil, but not the 'creation of mind' theory in which God can and does make mistakes (353, 375; cf. 388–90). The claim that human misery proceeds 'from the inevitable laws of nature, and not from any original depravity in man' (207) appears to conflict with the assertion that 'the original sin of man is the torpor and corruption of the chaotic matter, into which he may be said to be born' (354) and which is the explanation of God's allowing evil. And Malthus's approval of the middle class seems inconsistent with the view that 'uniform prosperity' tends rather 'to degrade than exalt the character' (368, 372–3).

Even if none of these objections applied, it has been remarked that 'the Malthusian theodicy affords no defence against the charge that God's act of bringing evil into the world may have been performed in vain' (Santurri 1982, 330). This is because the function of scarcity in that theodicy is to stimulate man 'to remove evil from himself, and from as large a circle as he can influence' (Malthus 1798, 305) which requires the capacity of reasoning from cause to effect: 'Consequently, it is the foresighted and prudent individual whose creation constitutes the fulfilment of God's plan, and who may hope for the salvation of immortality' (Santurri 1982, 323). Now the Poor Laws 'prevent members of the lower classes from considering the ultimate consequences of their acts', and so 'impede the formation of mind intended by divine creation' (324). The Poor Laws ought therefore to be abolished and social institutions fostered that encourage prudence and foresight. But this means that 'the formation of mind, the *telos* of divine creation' is contingent upon an appropriate social policy which might never be implemented, hence 'God's purpose will be frustrated and ... the suffering occasioned by the population principle will have been, and will continue to be for naught' (328).

Another author (Harvey-Phillips 1984) has recently put forward an almost opposite objection which nevertheless has somewhat the same effect as the former. In the first chapter of the first *Essay* Malthus wrote darkly of 'Necessity, that imperious all pervading law of nature' that '*the race of man cannot, by any efforts of reason, escape from it*' (Malthus 1798, 15; my italics). We may regard this as an *ad hoc* assumption necessary to preserve the integrity of the 'growth of mind' theodicy. For 'If this were not the case, the presence of the principle of population could itself lead to a rational solution of the principle's dilemmas and consequently the dissolution of the principle itself; God's design for the formation of mind/spirit would be self-defeating and contradictory of his omniscience' (Harvey-Phillips 1984, 596). Even if the former objection did not apply – indeed, precisely if it did not – then the consequent development of rational human behaviour, by taking away the spur of 'necessity' would stultify the 'growth of mind'.

More serious than any of these objections, however, is Malthus's failure to achieve his endeavour to 'vindicate the ways of God to man' within his own conceptual framework, even granting its coherence. Unlike Butler, Paley or even Abraham Tucker (not to mention Watson, Hey and Pretyman), Malthus was obsessed with the heuristic power and efficacy of natural theology. His more professional and more cautious predecessors carefully hedged their treatment of evil, and were not ashamed to fall back, when necessary, upon the authority of sacred scripture. But Malthus chose solely to 'reason up to nature's God' and so was betrayed into a non-solution of the problem of evil. For in his system, everything that is commonly thought of and experienced as 'evil' has to be regarded as a necessary part of the providence of God, and hence is not *really* an 'evil' at all, but a 'good'.

Writing in 1885 James Bonar felt able to declare that 'we cannot find anything in the writings of Parson Malthus inconsistent with his ecclesiastical orthodoxy' (1885, 367). This generous view is, I believe, impossible to sustain if we submit the theological content of the first *Essay* to serious examination. The criteria to be applied are first, the Thirtynine Articles of the Church of England to which Malthus would have subscribed formally on at least four occasions before 1798; and second the Vincentian canon – we must hold as *de fide* only those beliefs *quod semper, quod ubique, quod ab omnibus traditum est* – which as Manning and Marriot (1839) and More and Cross (1935) have argued was the first principle of Anglican theology from the Reformation to the Tractarians.

It has lately been suggested (Harvey-Phillips 1984, 601), following Halévy (1949, 392) and Sir Leslie Stephen (1876) that the Articles were regarded in Malthus's day as 'an almost vacuous political formula' and hence ought not to be used as a standard with which to appraise his orthodoxy. However it is evident from the previous section of this chapter (see pp. 90–4 above) that Halévy was simply wrong to suppose that 'nobody was obliged to believe the Thirty-nine Articles or even to read them'. As for Stephen's work, it was written to demonstrate the benign efficacy of Hume's scepticism in rescuing the British intelligentsia from darkness and error, and the facts are bent whenever necessary to support his thesis. John Hey's Norrisian lectures are grievously misrepresented as casuistical and crypto-Socinian. Hey's careful analysis of assent to unintelligible propositions (1796–8, II, ch. x) is reduced to the gibe that 'talk about the Trinity is little better than unmeaning gibberish' (Stephen 1881, I, 426). Hey's own position – 'I am not the person who would insinuate, that any of our own Articles stand in need of anything beyond plain interpretation' (1794, II, 48) – is of course ignored. I shall therefore take it that Pretyman spoke for ecclesiastical authority in his day when he admonished the ordination candidate that he must

peruse carefully the articles of our church, and...compare them with the written Word of God. If upon mature examination, he believes them to be authorized by Scripture, he may conscientiously subscribe them; but if, on the contrary, he thinks that he sees reason to dissent from any of the doctrines asserted in them, no hope of emolument or honour, no dread of inconvenience or disappointment, should induce him to express his solemn assent to propositions, which in fact he does not believe. (Pretyman 1812, 571)

According to the criteria of the Articles and the Vincentian canon the first *Essay* would seem to be clearly heterodox on four points and of doubtful orthodoxy on a number of others.

In the first place, by following too closely Tucker's speculations on the immortality of 'mind' whilst ignoring the way in which that author carefully hedged his position (Tucker 1768, II: 1, 7), Malthus actually denied the resurrection of the body (Malthus 1798, 246). This is a mere slip, however, and is in no way essential to his argument. Far more serious is the denial of the incarnation implied by his uncompromising devotion to natural theology. By asserting that 'it seems *absolutely necessary* that we reason up to Nature's God' (350, my italics) he seems to deny the possibility of revealed knowledge. His assumption that 'in the book of nature...*alone* we can read God as he is' (351, my italics) contradicts the New Testament teaching that God is known in and through the Son (John 10: 30, 14: 8–11, etc.). Malthus's decision to abstract from the incarnation is consistent with his soteriology. The key passage here is: 'Evil exists in the world, not to create despair but activity. We are not patiently to submit to it, but to exert ourselves to avoid it' (395). If 'avoid' in this context means 'get out of the way of' and 'evil' includes the infliction of suffering and death, this would seem to be inconsistent with the willing acceptance of suffering by Christ, who did *not* 'exert himself to avoid it' (e.g. Heb. 5: 7–8, 9: 26–8; Mark 14: 36; John 18: 4–8, etc.). Because Malthus emptied the concept of evil of all content, Christ is redundant in his soteriology, which no doubt explains why he is never mentioned or alluded to in the entire *Essay*. Insofar as there is any need for or possibility of 'salvation' at all in Malthus's system, it is a Pelagian 'salvation by works': for 'it is the duty of every individual, to use his utmost efforts to remove evil from himself' (395). The last point on which Malthus was unmistakably heterodox was his denial of the divine omnipotence: God needs time to create man (352); 'evil seems necessary...to create mind' (360);' God makes mistakes (388–90); and 'the works of the creator are not formed with equal perfection' (379: cf. Gen. 1: 31, etc.). Ignoring Tucker's naive speculation that in view of the problem of evil we must postulate some as yet undiscovered attribute which reconciles goodness with omnipotence, Malthus chose rather to hold that the traditional attributes 'must be in some respects limited' (James 1979, 118).

The foregoing opinions are demonstrably inconsistent with Articles IV and VIII (the resurrection); II (the incarnation); XV, XXXI and IX (salvation from sin only by the atonement of Christ); and I (unity and omnipotence of God). Moreover the doctrines of the resurrection of the body, the incarnation, the atonement and the omnipotence of God would almost certainly have been held by Anglican theologians of Malthus's day to be authenticated by the Vincentian canon. It is remarkable indeed that even his free-thinking economist friends, David Ricardo and James Mill, could see clearly that Malthus's position on the last of these matters was simply Manichean (Ricardo 1951–73, VII, 212–13).

On three other matters where the generally accepted teaching was neither specified by the Articles nor guaranteed by the Vincentian test, Malthus's theology is of doubtful orthodoxy. His doctrine of 'man as he really is, inert, sluggish, and averse from labour', useful as a counter to the secular optimism of Godwin and Condorcet, seems to call in question the Christian optimism of the *imago dei* which Malthus himself showed awareness of in a previous chapter (294). His view of original sin precludes prelapsarian bliss – and even existence – and seems to imply that creation itself overcomes original sin, which takes away the need for any further redemption. And his 'annihilationist' theory of divine punishment (390), which despite Frend's *Thoughts on Subscription* is not literally ruled out either by the Articles or the Athanasian Creed, is nevertheless at variance with what was to remain for another half-century the generally accepted Anglican position.

It has been suggested that the theology of the first *Essay* was passed over without comment at the time, and hence that its seeming heterodoxy ought not to be considered an important reason for its subsequent omission (Harvey-Phillips 1984). However, this is to neglect the fact that the periodicals which noticed the *Essay* were with one exception among those stigmatized by the *Anti-Jacobin* as subversive: organs of the Dissenting literary intelligentsia, the least likely in Britain to be perturbed by infidelity to the Articles. Moreover, even two of these regarded the theology as unsatisfactory. Though the *Analytical* indeed was bland and non-committal the

Monthly Review thought that the 'creation of mind' doctrine 'leads to difficulties as great as those which it is adopted to evade (*MR* September 1798, 9), and the *New Annual Register* that 'the author advances certain notions... no less fanciful than the hypotheses of his opponents' (*NAR* 1798, 229). The organ of Anglican orthodoxy, the *British Critic*, noticed the *Essay* very belatedly and was understandably less than flattering about the theology: 'our readers may expect from what precedes, that Mr M. is an enemy to the idea of perfectibility; but in this they will be deceived: he denies it to the human species indeed, but liberally confers it upon every particle of matter' (*BC* 1801, 278).

At any rate, within less than a year of publication Malthus himself had been brought to see that his theology would not do. The April 1799 number of the *Monthly Magazine* printed a letter by 'the Author of the Essay on Population' which announced his intention 'to enlarge and illustrate, by a greater number of facts, the principal part' of his essay. Because 'the subject of the last two chapters is not necessarily connected with it' he would, 'in deference to the opinions of some friends whose judgement' he respected, 'omit them in another edition' (*MM* April 1799, 179). Who those 'friends' might have been we can only guess. Malthus much later referred to them as 'a competent tribunal' and Otter described them as 'some distinguished persons in our church'. It is at least possible that one of them was Bishop Pretyman, Pitt's Cambridge tutor, friend and adviser on ecclesiastical patronage. Pretyman would certainly have known of the Prime Minister's favourable reaction to the *Essay* (James 1979, 91–2), would almost certainly have read it himself, grasped its ideological importance, and seen the need for a drastic revision of its theological portions. One of the very few theological works that Malthus acquired at this time was the third (1800) edition of Pretyman's textbook on the Thirtynine Articles.

A year or two later at least one very 'distinguished person' in the Church of England, Archdeacon William Paley, decided that he must do something about the matter himself.

CHAPTER 4

The reconstruction of Malthusian theodicy: Paley and Sumner

MALTHUS AFTER 1798

The order of generation proceeds by geometrical progression: the increase of provisions can only assume the form of an arithmetic series. Hence population will always overtake provision, will pass beyond the line of plenty, and continue to increase till checked by the difficulty of procuring subsistence; from this, springs poverty, which imposes labour, servitude and restraint. It is impossible to people a country with inhabitants, who shall be all in easy circumstances... (Joyce 1807, 110)

Jeremiah Joyce's *Full and Complete Analysis of Dr. Paley's Natural Theology*, in reality a digest for the penurious or feeble-minded student, affords a précis of Paley's already terse summary of Malthusian social theory. By the first decade of the new century the process of assimilation and vulgarization had begun, together with reappraisal and amendment both by Malthus and by others.

It is important to note that Paley published his *Natural Theology* in 1802, about twelve months before Malthus's second edition, and referred his readers only to 'a statement of this subject, in a late treatise upon population' (Paley 1825, v, 351). Having formerly taken a very different view of the matter in his celebrated *Moral and Political Philosophy* (1785) he was thus one of Malthus's earliest and most distinguished converts.

Another was Dugald Stewart, who in his 'Plan of lectures on Political Economy for the Winter 1800–01' included a 'Critical Examination of a late *Essay on the Principle of Population as it Affects the Future Improvement of Society*' (Stewart 1855, VIII, xvii, xviii). Stewart admired the first *Essay* which he judged to be 'distinguished by originality of thought, and which (among some general speculations, more plausible, perhaps, than solid) contains a variety of acute and just reflections': its reasonings 'in so far as they relate to the Utopian

113

plans of Wallace, Condorcet and Godwin, are perfectly conclusive, and strike at the root of all such theories'. However, 'they do not seem to justify those gloomy inferences which many persons are disposed to draw from them concerning the established order of nature'. The author of the *Essay* made no attempt to argue against 'the expediency of meliorating, to the utmost of our power, the real imperfections of our existing institutions'. Stewart was 'disposed to differ' in one point only: the author 'seems ... to lay ... too little stress on the efficacy of those arrangements which nature herself has established for the remedy of the evils in question' (VIII, 203, 207).

It is remarkable that Stewart has very shrewdly identified, in this lecture, precisely those features of the first *Essay* which had to be strengthened or modified before it could become fully acceptable to the leaders of informed opinion at that time. The 'general speculations, more plausible ... than solid' (Malthus's confused and ineffectual theology) must go, and must be replaced by something better. The crucial argument which 'strikes at the root' of all utopian theories must stay, but it must be carefully guarded against an ultra-tory, *Anti-Jacobin* mode of interpretation: for surely there is work yet for whigs to do, 'meliorating ... the real imperfection of our existing institutions'. The 'gloomy inferences' which appear to follow from Malthusian population theory must be resisted; and the self-correcting function of 'nature' asserted and explained, both in political economy and in social ethics. These tasks constituted the programme of Christian Political Economy. In the last thirty pages of his work, William Paley sketched an outline which Summer, Copleston, Whately and Chalmers were later to amplify and supplement.

Before considering Paley's contribution some attention should be paid to his place in English letters at the beginning of the nineteenth century.

PALEY AND MALTHUS

William Paley went up to Christ's College, Cambridge in 1759, was Senior Wrangler of 1763 and became a Fellow in 1766, the year in which Robert Malthus was born. Ten years later he quitted Cambridge for a North Country rectory, having worked out in the lecture room the outlines and essential argument of his most famous works. His years at the university therefore coincide with the high summer of the English Enlightenment, a time in which all men of taste and letters however disparate in faith or morals could meet in urbane society – Hume and Rousseau at the home of Daniel Malthus, Jack Wilkes and Samuel Johnson at the table of Mr Dilley – not yet knowing that the day must soon come when such amenities would cease. For with hindsight the year 1776, or at any rate the decade of which it is the mid-point, looms up as a watershed in intellectual history. Before that date the 'ideology of "politeness"', identified in recent scholarship as 'an equivalent of "enlightenment" in England' (Pocock 1985b, 537 and *passim*, and references; see also Gascoigne 1989) united Christian, specifically Anglican orthodoxy both with modern science and with an unprecedented freedom of opinion. The English Enlightenment was conservative, clerical and 'Magisterial' (Jacob 1981).

The failure of the Feathers Tavern Petition four years earlier compelled the Anglican élite to make up its mind about subscription and even, to a considerable extent, about trinitarian orthodoxy (Clark 1985, 311–15). The failure in 1773 of the first of many petitions to Parliament for relief forced the Dissenting Interest into detachment and disaffection: 'an alienation from the House of Hanover and their ancient loyalties which grew progressively more complete' (Lincoln 1938, 22). The American Declaration of Independence gave heart to 'patriots' and 'friends of liberty' at home and abroad, being followed by the Gordon riots four years later and the storming of the Bastille after another nine. *Wealth of Nations* and Bentham's *Fragment on Government*, both of which appeared in 1776, symbolically inaugurate a fundamentally new way of looking at human society and its ills. Watson's *Apology for Christianity* (1776) written in answer to Gibbon's *Decline and Fall* marks the beginning of a growing tendency among Cambridge moderates to close ranks against the enemies of the Church. Modern labels such as 'conservative', 'radical' or 'progressive', hopelessly anachronistic before 1776, gradually became more applicable to a generation forced to take sides during an increasing polarization of belief and opinion.

For it is well known that by the end of the century a correlation existed between theological orthodoxy and political conservatism on the one hand, and between atheistic philosophy and some species of Jacobinism on the other (e.g. Crimmins 1989a). But it has lately been proposed by J. C. D. Clark (1985, 330–46) that the theological

– by no means atheistic – writings of Richard Price and Joseph Priestley exhibit not merely a correlation, but a causal connexion between anti-trinitarian heterodoxy and political 'radicalism'. From the late 1750s to the early 1790s, Clark argues, Socinian theology 'entailed' a credo of political revolution. Such entailment need not and does not imply that political 'radicalism' was *uniquely* determined by Socinian theology. Wilkes is an obvious counter-example. But it does mean that men like William Paley were gradually compelled to commit themselves one way or the other.

As always Cambridge both mirrored, and in certain ways helped to create, the larger world of English letters. Much has been made, usually out of uncritical deference to the authority of Leslie Stephen, of the subversive influence of such as Blackburne, Jebb and Edmund Law upon Cambridge thought in the third quarter of the century. The Hyson Club, a society of former Wranglers founded in 1758 to drink China tea and engage in rational conversation, has been regarded as a latitudinarian conventicle, possessing 'a coherence and unity of purpose that indicate strong ties of sympathy and collaboration' (Le Mahieu 1976, 14). Yet its membership 'usually consisted of some of the most respectable members of the university' (Wakefield 1792, 126) several of whom, such as Beadon, Pretyman and Isaac Milner, were afterwards powerful in stamping out heterodoxy at Cambridge and beyond.

When Jebb resigned his preferments in 1775 he was followed by others into Dissent or infidelity. Two younger members of the Hyson Club, Gilbert Wakefield (BA 1776) and William Frend (BA 1780), each of whom as is well known played a part in Robert Malthus's education, eventually gave up the struggle to reconcile mind and conscience to Anglican orthodoxy. Wakefield went quietly in 1779. At Milner's instigation Frend was ejected with much screaming and kicking in 1793, having been dismissed as a college tutor in 1788 by Beadon, who was at that time Master of Jesus (Knight 1971).

The men in the middle – Hey, Watson, Paley and John Law (BA 1766) – found themselves inexorably drawn towards theological orthodoxy and political conservatism during the last quarter of the century. In part, no doubt, this was the mere consequence of advancing years and respectability. In 1780 Hey, who was then forty-six, became the first Norrisian professor. Two years later Watson, aged forty-five, was made Bishop of Llandaff; Paley, aged thirty-nine, Archdeacon of Carlisle: and Law, aged thirty-seven,

Bishop of Clonfert. But in larger part their seeming change of position was a response of clear, honest and critical minds to the pharisaical scruples of the theological objectors and the naive delusions of political Jacobinism. It is perfectly true, as Le Mahieu (1976, 15) asserts, that Paley and his friends believed in 'tolerance, in promoting rational inquiry by creating an open market-place of ideas' and that they 'demanded a climate of understanding if they were to survive and advance in the ecclesiastical hierarchy'. But they also believed with Watson (1776, 2) that 'free disquisition is the best means of illustrating the doctrine and establishing the truth of Christianity'. It is a fact which eluded Sir Leslie Stephen and those who have followed him that 'rational inquiry' and 'free disquisition' in the two decades after 1780 could induce Hey, Watson and Paley to part company with Jebb and his followers and ally themselves with the unashamedly conservative Pretyman and Isaac Milner.

The beginning of this process is well illustrated in Paley's first book, *The Principles of Moral and Political Philosophy* (Paley 1825, IV), which became a textbook at Cambridge within a year of its publication in 1785. To George III and other timorous folk the *Principles* might well have seemed alarming. As late as 1802 the *Anti-Jacobin Review* 'hesitated not to affirm' that in the *Moral and Political Philosophy* 'the most determined Jacobin might find a justification of his principles, and a sanction for his conduct' (*AJRM* 1802, 528). The famous parable of the pigeons satirizes the 'paradoxical and unnatural' distribution of property, ninety-nine out of a hundred 'gathering all they got into a heap' and keeping it for 'one, and that the weakest, perhaps worst pigeon of the flock'. The oath of allegiance 'permits resistance to the king, when his ill behaviour or imbecility is such, as to make resistance beneficial to the community'. Slavery is an 'abominable tyranny'; the poor have a claim on the rich 'founded in the law of nature'; inequality of property is an evil; and 'it is a mistake to suppose that the rich man maintains his servants, tradesmen, tenants and labourers: the truth is, they maintain him' (1825, IV, 72, 137, 157, 162, 75, 154). In chapter XI of Book VI on 'Political Philosophy' Paley made proposals for a progressively graduated income tax with exemptions for marriage and child-support which were later advanced by Tom Paine: as a result of which their permanent implementation was delayed until the twentieth century (1825, IV, 511–12; Clarke 1974, 86–7). In theological and religious matters there was the same deceptive appearance of adventure, not to say 'radicalism'. 'Whoever expects to find in the Scriptures a specific direction for every moral doubt that arises, looks for more than he will meet with'. The Thirtynine Articles were 'articles of peace' intended to comprehend in the national church all save those, such as papists and puritans, who would have destroyed it by their intolerance. Yet there should be with respect to public office 'complete toleration of all dissenters from the established church' (1825, IV, 4, 145, 477).

It is not in the least to disparage either Paley's integrity or the coherence of his arguments to observe that beneath this whiggish surface there subsisted a devotion to accustomed ways as secure as that of Burke or Samuel Johnson. A distinguished author has lately remarked indeed that the *Principles* afford 'a more systematic exposition of the intellectual tradition upon which Burke and other conservative writers of the 1790s drew' than Burke's own work. 'It is evident that it provided a quarry for arguments paraded by anti-revolutionary publicists after 1789' (Christie 1984, 160–1; see also Crimmins 1989a). The parable of the pigeons is immediately followed by an exposition of the expediency of private property which might have been (but probably was not) taken from the *Summa Theologiae* (1825, IV, 73–5; cf. *ST* II-ii, 66: 2). Abominable though it be, 'no passage is to be found in the Christian Scriptures, by which [slavery] is condemned or prohibited' (1825, IV, 158). Whether he realized it or not, Paley's defence of the claims of the poor follows that of St Ambrose, and its corollary – that 'the real foundation' of property rights in real estate 'is the law of the land' (80) – is Augustinian. Moreover, though 'a poor neighbour has a right to relief, yet if it be refused him, he must not extort it' (61). Though inequality be an evil 'abstractedly considered', it 'flows from those rules concerning the acquisition and disposal of property, by which men are united to industry, and by which the objects of their industry is rendered secure and beneficial' (75). The rich man is maintained by his servants but is no happier than they, and probably less so, for 'the luxurious receive no greater pleasure from their dainties, than the peasant does from his bread and cheese: but the peasant, wherever he goes abroad, finds a feast, whereas the epicure must be well entertained to escape disgust' (25). Toleration of religious dissenters must be qualified by the exception of 'what arise from the conjunction of dangerous political dispositions with certain religious tenets'. It was usual to suppose that this refers to the connexion between popery and Jacobitism (Clarke 1974, 84) but John Ehrman (1983, 63) has recently pointed out that Paley's qualification was 'a significant statement in the middle eighties, for it was just then that doubts were being voiced about the "dispositions" of Dissent'.

Paley's *Principles*, like Watson's *Apology* (1776), is only the beginning of that emergence among the Cambridge moderates of increasingly conservative convictions. And in the case of the *Principles* it is confined to political theory. Not until *Horae Paulinae* (1795) and the *Evidences* (1794) did Paley expound what he took to be Christian orthodoxy in response to the objections of Hume and lesser men (Le Mahieu 1976, 90–114). It has been suggested by M. L. Clarke (1974, 73) that some of this was inspired by Paley's 'discussions in the Hyson Club and his defence of the *status quo* against reformers such as Jebb'. What does seem to have been the case is that Paley, like all intellectuals of goodwill, tried very hard during his early years to maintain communication with and to do justice to the deeply held convictions of all his friends and colleagues; that this was feasible in the eirenical climate of the 1760s and early 1770s; but that from the late 1770s he was increasingly forced by the logic of his own spiritual and intellectual commitments into criticism of and confrontation with the 'reformers'. Something of the same kind may well have happened in the case of John Hey and even, to a lesser extent, notwithstanding Stephen's cynical presuppositions (Stephen 1876, 1, 454–8, 464; see also Gascoigne 1989, ch. 8), in that of Richard Watson.

All commentators from his own day to the present agree in describing Paley as 'influential' (e.g. Ehrman 1983, 62, 163 n.1) and this was specially so in his own university, for his style of thinking is deeply congenial to the Cambridge mind. Sir Leslie Stephen wrote of Paley's 'utter inability to be obscure' (Annan 1984, 244) and Lord Keynes (1972, 79), describing the *Principles* as an 'immortal book', deemed that it 'must be placed high... amongst the intellectual influences on the author of the *Essay on Population*'.

This observation of Keynes is perfectly true, yet it must be pointed out that the 'influence' that Paley exerted upon Malthus's first *Essay* is closely akin to the 'influence' of Ricardo upon Karl Marx; not merely as the standard authority to be cited with respect, but also as the clearest exponent of a doctrine urgently in need of correction and restatement at certain vital points. For in 1798 Malthus constructed his argument upon an explicit rejection of two crucial propositions on which the entire structure of Paley's teaching was based: the populationist account of social utility and the belief, which Paley shared with Butler, and every other orthodox theologian of the day, that human life is a state of probation and trial for eternity. As we shall see, Paley immediately accepted Malthus's correction on the first point, though he did not live to incorporate the necessary amendments in his *Principles*. Malthus finally backed down on the second point, somewhat ungraciously, many years later.

In a now much-quoted passage of his unpublished pamphlet, *The Crisis* (1796), Malthus had boldly announced:

> On the subject of population I cannot agree with Archdeacon Paley, who says, that the quality of happiness in any country is best measured by the number of people. *Increasing* population is the most certain possible sign of the happiness and prosperity of a state; but the actual population may be only the sign of the happiness that is past. (cit. Keynes 1972, 83; my italics)

It is evident that this astute – and characteristically 'fluxionist' – distinction between the *rate-of-change* and the *level* of the population variable adumbrates the political economy of the first *Essay* as summarized in chapter 2. For supposing real incomes of the poor to be positively correlated with 'the happiness and prosperity of the state', which both Malthus and Paley accepted, the latter emerges not so much as the outcome as the cause of 'increasing population' (see Malthus 1798, 137). But if 'actual population' were at or near stationary equilibrium this would imply that real incomes of the poor were at subsistence level. Paley ignored the distinction, not because he was not as good at calculus as Malthus (in fact he was probably better) but rather because like Wallace (1761) before him and Godwin (1798a, 518) after, he conjectured that 'the number of the people have seldom, in any country' arrived at the limits to growth set by 'all the provisions which the soil can be made to produce' (Paley 1825, IV, 480).

Though the political economy of Paley's *Principles*, chiefly found in chapter XI of Book VI, is largely devoted to a discussion of policies for encouraging population, much of the analysis is separable from his empirical assumptions and remains valid. It is evident that Malthus borrowed some of this material in 1798, such as the remark that the subsistence wage is culturally determined (Paley 1825, IV, 482) and that the preventive check will operate for prudential reasons among the middle classes (484–5). Other more pregnant ideas, such as those which relate employment to effective demand and effective demand to income distribution (491–501), a non-Physiocratic distinction between 'productive' and unproductive or 'instrumental' labour (496), and the dictum that 'the soil will maintain many more than it can employ' (494–5), were only later to become important in Malthusian and subsequent theory. It is probable that it was the first of these which inspired Keynes (1972, 79 n.2) to suggest that 'Perhaps, in a sense' it was actually Paley rather than Malthus who was 'the first of the Cambridge economists'.

We may also see some reflection of Paley in Malthus's defence of private property (1798, 194–8), and of 'the whole system of barter and exchange' as the means of income distribution (187–9; cf. Paley 1825, IV, 491). But Malthus was not one of the 'anti-revolutionist publicists' who sought in the *Principles* that 'quarry for arguments' so described by Professor Christie. Far more original than they, and more radically 'anti-revolutionist', Malthus constructed his own more powerful arguments from a new and carefully chosen combination of materials, only a few of which were supplied by Paley.

Nowhere is this more obvious than in Malthus's treatment of the case for transfer payments to the poor. Paley had argued in the *Principles* (1825, 159–71) that 'the poor have a claim founded in the law of nature' upon the resources of the rich, and that the 'Christian Scriptures are more copious and explicit upon this duty' of the rich to relieve the poor 'than upon almost any other'. Though Paley did not explicitly say so, it has been convincingly argued by Thomas A. Horne (1985, 59) that his 'purpose was to enjoin private charity along with the Poor Laws' and not as a substitute for them. Malthus did not deign even to notice Paley's arguments, convincing as they may well have appeared to conventional minds. With the ruthlessness of youthful genius he cut straight to the heart of the matter with a demonstration that money transfers are powerless (in the short run) to increase the supply of food: cash payments can only result in such increase in food prices as will leave the poor pretty much as they were before. It is irrelevant whether the transfer results from legislation or from private charity. 'No possible contributions or sacrifices of the rich, particularly in money, could for any time prevent the recurrence of distress among the lower members of society' (Malthus 1798, 75–6, 78–9). As for the Poor Laws themselves, they 'create the poor which they maintain', partly because their tendency is 'to increase population without increasing the food for its support', and partly by creating a welfare dependency that saps the 'spirit of independence' (83, 84–5).

The most explicit repudiation of Paley did not come until the second (1803) edition of the *Essay*, and that in a passage subsequently deleted because of the rage and detestation it brought down upon its author. Paley (1825, IV, 79) had illustrated his doctrine of the 'natural' (i.e. God-given) right of all to subsistence with the analogy of a banquet given for the free-holders of a district. No one need ask permission to eat, for the food and drink were provided for that purpose. Malthus simply denied this.

A man who is born into a world already possessed, if he cannot get subsistence from his parents on whom he has a just demand, and if the society do not want his labour, has no claim of right to the smallest portion of food, and, in fact, has no business to be where he is. At nature's mighty feast there is no vacant cover for him. (Malthus, 1803, 531–2)

The passage was unnecessary to his argument, and could only have been intended as a provocation; or more probably, as his biographer suggests (James 1979, 100), to have been a reflection of his own misery and bitterness at the time.

Less than two years after the publication of Malthus's revised *Essay* Paley died of a lingering and painful disease, and it is doubtful whether he ever read this brutal dismissal of the traditional Christian doctrine of almsgiving. He had certainly read the first *Essay*, however, and with characteristic percipience and largeness of mind immediately accepted its central message. Meadley (1809, 152) testifies that

Mr Malthus's *Essay on Population* had recently thrown light on a subject, which Dr Paley had himself discussed with his usual acuteness, before the important facts, by which the author's great argument is supported, had been so minutely examined. But he spoke with much approbation of the ability displayed in the Essay, in opposition to the common notion, that an increase of inhabitants is invariably beneficial.

Malthus, as is well known, regarded Paley, along with Pitt, as one of the two converts of whom he was most proud (James 1979, 53).

As we have already seen, Paley incorporated the Malthusian 'principle of population' into the last chapter of his last work.

Though counter-revolutionary polemic was no part of his purpose in *Natural Theology*, he was alert to the ideological implications of the new doctrine. 'It seems impossible to people a country with inhabitants who shall be all in easy circumstances' (Paley 1825, v, 351). But as an experienced and highly professional theologian he would see at once that Malthus's bizarre theodicy was a serious liability. It is just conceivable that he was one of those 'distinguished persons' in the Church who privately persuaded Malthus to drop the theological chapters from the *Essay*. There is, however, no evidence of any communication between Paley and his pupil's pupil. At any rate he determined to do something about it himself, and in the closing pages of *Natural Theology* sketched a more orthodox theodicy, to which we must now attend.

PALEY'S THEOLOGY

Paley claimed that *Natural Theology* completed a system of theological work composed in the reverse order from that in which it should be read. *Natural Theology* demonstrates the existence and other attributes of God from the 'book of nature'. Given these, *Evidences* and *Horae Paulinae* demonstrate 'a future state of rewards and punishments' from holy scripture. Given a future state, *Moral and Political Philosophy* elucidates the principles of private and political conduct most conducive to future rewards; for 'Virtue is "the doing good to mankind, in obedience to the will of God, and for the sake of everlasting happiness"' as Edmund Law had put it. It was Paley's intention to apply the test of human experience in essentially the same way to the 'evidence' of God afforded both by 'nature' and by 'revelation'. As Stephen (1876, I, 415) correctly observed, the entire structure stands or falls with the teleological argument which Hume had challenged and which *Natural Theology* was written to reaffirm (Addinall 1986, 233).

Rather more questionably Stephen conjectured that 'some of the dogmas' of Paley's professed creed 'must certainly have sat very loosely upon him'. 'His methods of reasoning lead naturally to the Unitarianism which presents the nearest approach to a systematic evolution of opinion in the latter half of the eighteenth century' (Stephen 1876, I, 420). This would seem to be yet another example of Stephen's willingness to consider only those data which confirmed his view of the 'evolution' of eighteenth-century theology toward the *telos* of nineteenth-century agnosticism. The 'method of reasoning' actually employed by Paley in his books depended upon the ruthless application of Ockham's razor to every dialectically redundant concept. His terse dismissal of the 'moral sense' at the very beginning of his first work (Paley 1825, IV, 13) is a typical example. But Christian theology, purporting to be knowledge of God, is more than a 'method of reasoning' and is in part expressed in other discourse such as prayer, liturgy and the rhetoric of preaching. Paley and those like him in the church differed sharply from the 'Unitarians' by their unhesitating willingness, when occasion required, to employ such discourse in its most orthodox and traditional forms (Le Mahieu 1976, 21–3, 114).

A striking example of this is to be found in a sermon on the 'Unity of God'. Having expounded the Hebraic tradition of monotheism and shown that 'the Christian dispensation entirely confirms and repeats what the Jewish Scripture of the Old Testament had before delivered', Paley declared that

We hear, nevertheless, of three divine persons – we speak of the Trinity. We read of the 'Father, Son, and Holy Ghost'... What is that union which subsists in the divine nature; of what kind is that relation by which the divine persons of the Trinity are connected, we know little – perhaps it is not possible that we should know more: but this we seem to know, first, that neither man nor angel bears the same relation to God the Father as that which is attributed to his only-begotten Son, our Lord Jesus Christ... (Paley 1825, VII, 426)

The language, though deliberately rhetorical, is carefully used. We 'seem to know' because of the witness of the scriptures, which for Paley, as for Watson, was final. We 'speak of the Trinity' because the word is used in the formularies and liturgy of the Church to which Paley had given his solemn assent. If the New Testament really 'attributes' to 'our Lord Jesus Christ' a unique relationship with 'God the Father' then we must simply accept this essentially mysterious dogma. Too much subtle theology may be unhelpful: 'perhaps it is not possible that we should know more'.

In very much the same manner, Paley dealt with the doctrine of the atonement in a sermon for Good Friday. 'The full magnitude and operations of those effects which will result from the death of Christ we can only comprehend...from general expressions used in the Scripture'. Certain theories, such as that God is a 'harsh and austere character' whose 'enmity was to be reconciled by the blood of his Son' can be ruled out: not because they are irrational (which they need not be) but because they are unscriptural. 'God is never said to be *at enmity with us*... but we are said to be *at enmity with God*'. It is probable that Christ was sent to teach holiness to the human race 'lost in an *almost total depravity*', but 'we are not to stop at this'.

...in various declarations of Scripture concerning the death of Christ... there are other and higher consequences attendant upon this event: the particular nature of which consequences, though of the most real and highest nature, we do not understand, nor perhaps are capable of understanding... until we be admitted to more knowledge than we at present possess of the order and economy of superior beings, of our own state and destination after death, and of the laws of nature by which the next world will be governed, which are probably very different from present.

The sermon ends with a scriptural doxology glorifying God in Christ 'in whom we have redemption through his blood' (VII, 175–6, 177, 178, 180, 181, 182). It may be noted here that even in his *Natural Theology* Paley was willing to speak, though in a footnote, of the 'propitiatory virtue' of Christ's passion (V, 368 n.).

It is true that by comparison with earlier or later generations of Anglican divinity the use of liturgical and mystical language by Paley and his Cambridge contemporaries is slight. But it is not negligible and there is a difference between their didactic, and their homiletic or pastoral writing. In the former the conceptual apparatus is stripped down to the bare minimum required to sustain the argument. Wherever possible it is naturalistic. The authority of the scripture is invoked only where no other argument will do, as in Paley's defence of the killing of animals for food (IV, 65–6). In the latter sort of writing the traditional dogmas of the church – incarnation, atonement, trinity – are presented inasmuch, and only inasmuch, as they seem to be required by the liturgy and are consistent with scripture. The authority of scripture is absolute in either case and is congruent with a deep-seated protestantism taken for granted by the Cambridge moderates. It was certainly not intellectual laziness that induced Watson, as moderator, to settle arguments in the Divinity Schools by holding up the New Testament and exclaiming 'En sacrum codicem!' (Watson 1818, 35). Yet in Watson's case this protestantism was consistent with his recommending the '*Summa Theologica* [*sic*] of *Thomas Aquinas*' to his students

(Watson 1785, I, xxxii); and in Paley's with his reissuing, for the clergy of Carlisle, a Caroline compendium of high-church pastoralia, *The Clergyman's Companion* (Paley 1808) which his father had used in Giggleswick.

In all this we see that the Cambridge moderates of the later eighteenth century were following a somewhat different *via media* from that traditionally associated with Anglicanism (see Waterman 1991a). There was no desire to steer a course between Rome and Geneva for both were tarred with the same brush. Calvin, Watson noted, 'thought it almost impossible that the Scriptures could ever have been so far perverted as to afford the *Romanists* any handle for their doctrine of Transubstantiation'. Yet 'this same *Calvin* followed *St Augustine* in the doctrine of absolute personal reprobation and election, inculcating it as a fundamental article of faith, with nearly the same unchristian zeal which infatuated him when he fastened *Servetus* to the stake' (Watson 1785, I, xiv). Paley, Watson and Hey sought the middle ground along a different continuum: that of which the 'blind attachment to system' evinced by both Calvinism and Popery represented one extreme; and the sterile infidelity of Hume, Gibbon, the '*Esprits forts* of France, and the *Frey-Geisters* of Germany' represented the other. The danger in one direction lay in a false biblicism which attempted to extract more information from holy writ than the nature of the data allowed. The danger in the other direction was of an exclusive reliance upon the light of nature which altogether ignored the data of revelation and therefore produced either the scepticism of Hume or the theological nonsense of Malthus.

Though it is most improbable that correction of the latter formed any part of Paley's motive in writing *Natural Theology*, it is almost certain to have been in his mind as he worked at its penultimate chapter XXVI, 'Of the Goodness of the Deity'.

Theodicy in Natural Theology

Paley's theodicy bears a family resemblance to the 'system of optimism' of William King and Leibniz. It is highly probable that he was familiar with King's *Origin of Evil* for it was translated and edited by his friend, mentor and patron, Edmund Law. Paley's treatment of the relation between 'design' and goodness of God is explicitly based upon Thomas Balguy's *Divine Benevolence Asserted*

(Paley 1825, v, 336 n., 337–8, 341). Balguy (1781, 74) agreed with 'Leibnitz' that 'the best system possible has actually taken place'.

Yet chapter xxvi of *Natural Theology* is both more and less than a popularization of these distinguished exemplars. Deference is paid to the King–Leibniz doctrine of *metaphysical evil* but the reader is quickly hurried on to considerations of a 'more limited, but more determinate, kind'. *Physical* or *natural* evil is treated in a way that emphasizes pain, disease and death, with only passing reference to other 'difficulties, wants and inconveniences'. *Civil* evil is distinguished from physical evil and given extended treatment. *Moral* evil is treated conventionally, though war is included in this, rather than the previous category. There follows a detailed consideration of chance, which is evidently required in a theodicy developed upon the argument from design. The entire argument concludes with a discussion of human life as a state of *probation*. Each of these stages in Paley's exposition must be examined in more detail.

Like Malthus (1798, 361–2) and just about every English writer of the eighteenth century, Paley (1825, v, 342–3) affirmed that the universe is beneficently governed by 'general laws' but these 'however well set and constituted, often thwart and cross each other', from which 'frequent particular inconveniences will arise'. Though this 'serves rather to account for the obscurity of the subject' it does suggest that 'apparent evil' may be explained by 'views of universal nature'. A single paragraph lucidly summarizes the 'scale of being' as an explanation of evil. Paley ignored Samuel Johnson's damning objections (see pp. 75–9 above). The next paragraph, a single sentence, summarizes even more briefly the doctrine of 'finiteness' which King and Leibniz had laboured over for thousands of words. Though these *metaphysical* answers to the problem of evil 'are not the worse for being metaphysical' they are 'of a nature too wide to be brought into our survey' (v, 344). Paley made no attempt to analyse the concept of metaphysical evil so as to show how particular evils may be derived as special cases. Instead he turned at once to that evil with which, from his own experience, he was most familiar: 'bodily pain'.

The justification of pain, disease, death and all other *physical* evil is closely related to the naturalistic teleology of the previous twenty-five chapters. All must be shown, so far as possible, to be consistent with the 'design' or 'contrivance' of a beneficent creator. Paley quoted Balguy on pain: 'that it is seldom the object of contrivance;

and that when it is so, the contrivance rests ultimately in the good'
(v, 345). For example, pain serves as a useful warning; it is not
without its alleviations; disease is seldom fatal; when it is it may
reconcile us to death; death is a necessary part of the order of nature;
animals are preserved from the fear of death; humans can look
beyond death; the pain of bereavement is softened by time and
probably serves a moral purpose (v, 345–9). Paley, like Malthus
(1798, 395), followed Abraham Tucker in supposing that the
purpose of much physical evil is to elicit 'engagement' and thereby
serve human development.

A world, furnished with advantages on one side, and beset with difficulties,
wants and inconveniences on the other, is the proper abode of free, rational
and active natures, being the fittest to stimulate and exercise their faculties.
The very *refractoriness* of the objects they have to deal with, contributes to
this purpose. A world in which nothing depended upon ourselves... would
not have suited mankind. (Paley 1825, v, 350)

Paley had favoured 'engagement' as the sovereign means to
happiness in his earliest work (IV, 24–5). The passage I have cited
from *Natural Theology* is the nearest he ever came to the Tucker–
Malthus theory of the creation of 'mind'.

Having seemingly equated 'physical' and 'natural' evil (v, 349),
Paley's location of *civil* evil 'or the evils of civil life' (v, 350) is
equivocal, for it is evident that he meant to distinguish these from
moral evil (which follow from 'the character of man as a *free agent*' (v,
355)). However, it appears that 'they result, by a kind of necessity,
not only from the constitution of our nature, but from a part of that
constitution which no one would wish to see altered... Mankind will
in every country *breed* up to a certain point of distress' (v, 350). The
Malthusian argument is invoked to prove the inevitability 'in every
old country' of poverty, labour, servitude and restraint. What Paley
really meant to say, therefore, is that 'the evils of civil life' are
'natural' after all, even though they be not 'physical' as he had used
that word in the previous pages. The equation of 'physical' and
'natural' was a slip. In effect Paley used 'physical' and 'civil' as
subdivisions of 'natural' evil.

Paley's strategy for justifying civil evil is based partly on the
putative consistency of evil with 'design' already outlined in
connexion with physical evil, and partly on his analysis of happiness
first worked out in *Moral and Political Philosophy*. The latter is used to
show that many supposed 'evils' are not evil at all. Teleology is used

to mop up the residue which cannot be dealt with in that way. Moreover the cruel edge of the Malthusian argument is blunted by a reaffirmation, in almost the same words, of Paley's original (1785) population theory: 'there may be limits fixed by nature...but they are not yet attained, nor even approached, in any country of the world' (v, 352; cf. iv, 480). This is a clear contradiction of the accurate summary of Malthus's argument that Paley had used, on the previous page, to explain the origin of social evil.

In the *Principles* Paley had argued convincingly that happiness is not to be found in pleasures of the senses, in exemption from pain, labour, care or business, or in greatness, rank or elevated station. Rather it is to be found in the exercise of the social affections, exercise of our faculties in pursuit of some engaging end ('engagement is everything'), good habits, and good health of body and spirits. Much of this was reproduced, some of it word-for-word, in a sermon preached at Dalston in 1790 and later printed as the pamphlet, *Reasons for Contentment* (iii, 317–31) in response to Paine's *Rights of Man* (1791–2). Though there is no reference to these works in *Natural Theology* it is evident that Paley assumed his readers were familiar with them for his use of the corresponding material is extremely brief. He correctly noted in reference to the Malthusian argument that many sources of human happiness are not subject to scarcity. In addition to good habits and desires, he adds to previous lists the benefits of good government, of religion and of a sense of security (v, 352). The 'distinctions of civil life', though 'apt enough to be regarded as an evil' are dealt with in two short paragraphs which summarize portions of the *Reasons for Contentment*. 'The gifts of nature always surpass the gifts of fortune' (v, 352). 'Habit...is a great leveller' (v, 353). In the latter Paley shows awareness, as in his earlier works, of the socio-psychological phenomenon much later to be noted by Durkheim and labelled the 'elasticity of evil' by A. K. Cohen (see pp. 70–1 above). As Viner remarked there was a 'spontaneous union' of virtually all intellectuals in eighteenth-century Britain 'dedicated' to this kind of social apologetic. Most authors were far less restrained in their rhetoric than Paley. Adam Smith, for example, declared in a famous passage of *The Theory of Moral Sentiments* (1759) that 'in what constitutes the real happiness of human life' the poor 'are in no respect inferior to those who would seem so much above them. In ease of body and mind all the different ranks of society are nearly upon a level, and the beggar, who suns himself by the side of the highway, possesses that security which kings are fighting for' (Smith 1976, 185).

Whether or not Paley had actually read Smith – and it would seem very likely that he had at least read *The Theory of Moral Sentiments* – he resembles Smith not only in his socio-psychological treatment of civil evil but also in his use of teleology. Adam Smith had argued that 'the pleasures of wealth and greatness', though illusory, served an important purpose. '…it is well that nature imposes on us in this manner. It is this deception which rouses and keeps in continual motion the industry of mankind' (Smith 1976, 183). The poor are enticed by it to labour. The 'natural selfishness and rapacity' of the rich is harnessed by it, and they are 'led by an invisible hand' to 'advance the interests of society' (183–5). As poverty, for Malthus, was a stick; so inequality, for Adam Smith, was a carrot. By means of the two mankind is propelled, despite its brutish inertia, toward the higher possibilities of earthly existence.

There is no doubt that the kind-hearted Paley preferred to emphasize the carrot and to hide the stick. '*Money* is the sweetener of human toil; the substitute for coercion; the reconciler of labour with liberty'. Distinctions of property and rank 'are subjects much more of competition than of enjoyment… It is not… by what the *Lord Mayor* feels in his coach, but by what the *apprentice* feels who gazes at him, that the public is served'. But it is actually better to be subordinate, for 'command is anxiety, obedience ease'. Moreover, 'artificial distinctions sometimes promote real equality' for they traverse the inevitable economic distinctions created by unequal ownership of property. This completes the justification of civil evil, in all of which Paley was more scrupulous than many of his contemporaries to remind his readers that some evil of this type, being neither inevitable nor benign, ought to be remedied by 'public law' (Paley 1825, v, 354).

Paley's treatment of *moral* evil is extremely brief, and conventional in that like that of King and Leibniz it rests upon 'the character of man as a *free agent*' (v, 355). In two respects, however, it differs from what we might expect. In the first place, as we have seen above, Paley included 'wars' under this head rather than under civil evil. Malthus (1798, 47–52) had made it clear the much, if not all war can be explained by the pervasive scarcity caused by population pressures. Either Paley had not read the *Essay* very carefully or he simply forgot. At any rate it suggests, together with his self-contradictory qualifications already noted, that Paley was a less than whole-hearted 'convert' to the new political economy of scarcity. Secondly, Paley accounted for moral evil 'without having recourse to any native, gratuitous malignity in the human constitution' (1825, v, 356). It is not quite clear what he meant by this. King had attributed moral evil to 'vicious' or 'evil' or 'depraved' 'elections', and had been careful to limit the evils resulting from the Fall to those specified in chapter 3 of Genesis. Yet one of these is open-ended: the withdrawing of supernatural grace, whence 'come all the Errors and Follies of our lives' (King 1739, 781). Paley's Good Friday sermon shows him willing to describe the human race as 'lost in an *almost total depravity*' (see pp. 124–5 above), and it is certain that the moderate biblicism he shared with Watson would have commanded his assent both to the Genesis account of the Fall and to St Paul's use of it in the epistle to the Romans. Perhaps the remark was an attempt to distance himself from Calvinism. So the *Christian Observer* June 1803, 372–3) appears to have thought. Perhaps it is an oblique reference to 'the torpor and corruption of chaotic matter' which Malthus thought of as the 'original sin of man'. More probably it is simply one last flourish of Ockham's razor.

Having thus dealt with the traditional concerns of theodicy, Paley turned to a relatively detailed account of 'the appearance of *chance*'. First, 'there must be chance in the midst of design' (1825, v, 357). His explanation refers only to multiple, uncoordinated acts of 'design', and therefore fails to reconcile chance with the singular 'design' of a divine creator. Secondly, 'the *appearance of chance* will always bear a proportion to the ignorance of the observer'. This is a more fruitful line though it is all too easy, if not merely tautologous, to maintain 'the ignorance of the observer…applied to the operations of the Deity' (v, 357, 358). Paley is happiest in his third argument, returning to that teleology which informs his entire book with the claim that 'in a great variety of cases it is better that events rise up…with the appearance of chance, than according to any observable rule whatever' (v, 358–9). For example, 'it seems expedient that the period of human life should be uncertain'. The irregularity of the weather induces 'activity, vigilance, precaution' among 'cultivators of the soil'. More social apologetic is generated: necessary 'disparity of *wealth* and *station*' is better left to chance, for those who 'would have all the virtuous rich' fail to perceive the consequence, 'that all the poor must be wicked'. Finally, the appearance of chance may be explained by supposing that divine providence, 'which always rests upon final good, may have made a *reserve* with respect to the manifestation of his interference' for our moral and intellectual good (v, 359, 360, 361–2, 364).

The importance of 'chance' in Paley's apologetic is made clear in the final section of his theodicy. Having agreed with Malthus – though somewhat less than whole-heartedly – in ascribing civil evil to the principle of population, Paley parted company with him over the 'creation of mind'. 'Of all the views under which human life has ever been considered, the most reasonable, in my judgement, is that which regards it as a state of *probation*' (v, 365). Joseph Butler had expounded the official doctrine with great authority. Because of the first *Essay on Population* it was now necessary to reassert that doctrine, and to do so in a way that guarded against what was already becoming a popular misconception among 'serious' churchmen. The 'appearance of chance', Paley recognized, is an essential ingredient of a well-formed theory of the 'state of probation'.

It had been part of Butler's purpose, in the *Analogy*, to show that God rewards and punishes humans in this life (but 'particularly... the latter'), and hence that there is 'nothing incredible' in his doing so 'hereafter' (Butler 1844, I, 39). In 'the present state, all which we enjoy, and a great part of what we suffer, is *put in our own power*. For pleasure and pain are the consequences of our actions' (I, 34). For example, 'vice and folly and extravagance' lead to 'poverty and sickness, remorse and anguish, infamy and death' (I, 44). This was profoundly appealing to that morbid addiction to punishment which, as Boyd Hilton (1988) has lately shown, lay deep in the evangelical consciousness. Butler, however, had guarded himself against the view that *all* human misery is a disclosure of the wrath of God. 'It is not in any sort meant, that... men are always uniformly punished in proportion to their misbehaviour' (Butler 1844, I, 44). Indeed, 'happiness and misery appear to be distributed by other rules, than only the personal merit and demerit of characters'. We will often see 'the *rewarding of some actions*, though vicious, and *punishing other actions*, though virtuous' (I, 58, 59). Butler's explanation of the anomaly was less than clear however, and was not connected in any essential way with his account of the 'state of trial'.

Paley had already worked out a resolution of this difficulty in his sermon on 'This Life a State of Probation' (1825, VI, 42–50) and it was this that he reasserted in *Natural Theology*. As one might expect, the argument is based on his unshakeable conviction of the goodness of God. It is actually best for us, in this life, that there should be such a low correlation between 'happiness' and 'virtue', 'vice' and 'misery'. For if this life were simply a state of 'retribution' (perfect correlation between 'vice' and its consequent 'misery'), then 'we could not actually succour or relieve, without disturbing the execution' (VI, 45): human 'benevolence would only stand in the way of justice' (V, 371). Moreover, the *'Passive* virtues' – by which Paley meant not merely submission but 'a steadfast keeping up of our confidence in God, and of our reliance upon his final goodness, at the time when everything present is adverse and discouraging' (V, 370) – would be ruled out. Cruelly tortured by cancer as he was, Paley's doctrine of 'chance' was a glowing testimony to his faith and devotion.

Of course he was misunderstood by evangelicals eager to invoke the support of Butler, whom they also misunderstood, for their theological sado-masochism. Much of what Butler had chosen to describe as divine punishment – such as the fact that fire will burn one foolish enough to approach it too nearly (1844, I, 38) – Paley had treated in his reconciliation of physical evil with 'design'. Important as the difference may appear in emotional overtones, the analytical distinction between Butler and Paley is trivial or non-existent at this point. Yet the *Christian Observer* (June 1803, 373), probably Wilberforce, solemnly rebuked 'Dr Paley' for failing to advance 'those tendencies of virtue to produce happiness, and of vice to produce misery...so unanswerably enforced by Bishop Butler'. The *Christian Observer* believed that natural and moral evil is a 'sufficient proof' that the human race is in 'a corrupt and depraved state, and consequently obnoxious' to God. It is a melancholy sign of the power of ideology and of the unwillingness of authors to make use of primary sources, that later generations have often supposed evangelicals to have introduced a new moral seriousness lacking in 'the school of Paley'.

Paley's contribution to Christian Political Economy

Paley included a brief discussion of the population issue in his *Natural Theology* of 1802, making it clear that although ostensibly a convert, his real intention was to subvert the spirit of Malthus' doctrine and incorporate it into the traditional argument from design. (Bowler 1976, 645)

This snap judgement, summarizing three pages of a more careful yet essentially one-sided treatment by Robert M. Young (1969), is typical of the reductionism which afflicts the historiography of ideas of this period. Though not exactly 'wrong', it leaves out so much of what was vitally important to Paley and his contemporaries that it can scarce be regarded as 'right'. Any who have followed this chapter thus far may agree that Paley's 'real intention' in chapter xxvi of *Natural Theology* was probably more complex: and that at the very least it might be rationally reconstructed upon a putative agenda similar to that of Dugald Stewart. Whether any such intention was in Paley's mind – and I believe it was – it is important in view of the further course of Christian Political Economy to appraise Paley's contribution in the light of that agenda.

The first task, it will be recalled, was to purge Malthusian doctrine of those 'general speculations, more plausible... than solid' which, by inviting the ridicule of the hostile, might deflect attention from the anti-utopian argument. Paley reasserted the widely accepted 'state of trial' theory which Malthus had rejected, and did so in a context that referred to the main stream of eighteenth-century Leibnizian theodicy. However he failed to satisfy those evangelicals who demanded some explicit acknowledgement of an Augustinian theodicy based upon the Fall. Furthermore, his well-meaning and necessary amendment of Butler's account of the 'state of trial' was misunderstood and gave offence.

The second item on Stewart's agenda was the protection of the anti-utopian argument from an ultra-tory interpretation. There seems no doubt that Paley was always ready to grant the need of 'meliorating... the real imperfections of our existing institutions' and in chapter xxvi acknowledged the function of 'public laws' in regulating the distribution of wealth. He did indeed provide additional 'reasons for contentment' under the 'evils of civil life', but his ill-deserved reputation as a dangerous author would have preserved him from any imputation of favouring too much the pretensions of the *ancien régime*. Nevertheless, his treatment of Malthus's population theory in *Natural Theology* is altogether too brief to go very far in meeting Stewart's second requirement.

The same is true of the third task, that of dissipating the 'gloomy inferences' which 'many persons are disposed to draw' from Malthus's argument. Though Malthus himself had written of a 'melancholy hue' and of 'dark tints' in his picture of human life, Stewart appears the first to have employed the words 'gloom' or 'gloomy' which were to become habitually attached to Malthusian population economics. No one has ever accused Paley of being 'gloomy', but his resolute 'optimism' was not available as an antidote. His work appeared too soon after the first *Essay*, and referred to it briefly and elliptically. *Natural Theology* was noticed, respectfully and at length, in the *New Annual Register* (1802: 2), the *Annual Review* (1802), the *Christian Observer* (1803), the *Critical Review* (1803), the *Edinburgh Review* (1802), the *Monthly Magazine* (1803: 1) and the *Monthly Review* (1803: 3). None of these made the least allusion to the fact that Paley had incorporated the principle of population in his theodicy.

The last item on Stewart's agenda was a demonstration of 'the efficacy of those arrangements which nature herself has established for the remedy of the evils' of population dynamics. Paley worked manfully at this task, especially in that section of chapter XXVI (V, 325–35) which deals with animal predacity. He produced a social apologetic based almost entirely on a naturalistic teleology. Yet it was felt at the time, as a modern historian puts it, that he was offering an 'eighteenth-century anodyne' perceived to be 'inadequate to the needs of an age in which natural suffering and individual depravity were only too apparent' (Hilton 1988, 5). The reason for this, I believe, is that Paley provided no theory of social process which could subsume Malthus's political economy under a more general, and less inevitably 'gloomy' explanation. Signs are not lacking in Paley's writing, especially the *Principles*, of an incipient social theory in the modern or Smithian sense. There is in *Natural Theology* a justification of 'idleness' as a Newtonian *vis inertia* which in the civil, as in the material world 'keeps things in their places' (1825, V, 356). But the hint is left undeveloped. Whether or not he had read *Wealth of Nations*, the task of reconstructing a social theory based on Malthusian population economics was one which Paley in 1802 was no longer able to attempt.

It would appear from this summary that Paley's *Natural Theology* came too soon after the first *Essay on Population*, and too late in Paley's own career, to be more than a preliminary sketch. It was left to younger men to carry out the work of forging an ideological alliance of Christian theology and the new political economy of scarcity. The first to begin was Robert Malthus himself.

Just over a year after Paley's *Natural Theology* appeared Joseph Johnson published a new recension of the *Essay on Population*. Malthus acknowledged authorship, the content was drastically changed, and the title altered to indicate a changed polemical purpose. The 'Speculations of Mr Godwin, M. Condorcet and Other Writers' upon the 'Future Improvement of Society' were removed from the limelight. In its place readers were offered 'A View of its Past and Present Effects on Human Happiness' of the principle of population and an 'Inquiry into our Prospects Respecting the Future Removal or Mitigation of the Evils which it Occasions'. Malthus himself was evidently aware of the need to 'dissipate the gloom' which hung over his political economy.

Much ink has been spilt over the relation between the first and subsequent versions of the *Essay*: whether Malthus changed his mind (or his approach to 'economic analysis'), whether 'moral restraint' subverted or strengthened his argument, whether he recanted his heterodox theology. For purposes of this study three things only need be noted, but they are of the utmost importance to the development of Christian Political Economy. In the first place, the specification of 'moral restraint' as a species of the preventive check makes no difference whatsoever to the body of 'economic analysis' we may abstract by the use of modern concepts from the *Essay on Population*. Secondly, 'moral restraint' does make a very great difference to the normative implications of that economic analysis. Finally, the 1803 recension marks a decisive rejection of the 'growth-of-mind' theodicy and the first step towards its more complete repudiation twenty years later. Each requires more detailed consideration.

'Moral restraint' and economic analysis

By an unaccountable slip, the 'positive' and 'preventive' checks to population presented in the first *Essay* were supplemented by 'vicious customs with respect to women, great cities, unwholesome manufactures, luxury, pestilence, and war' (Malthus 1798, 100). This taxonomy was traversed by an alternative, mutually exclusive and exhaustive classification of 'misery and vice' (100). Five years later Malthus altered this in two ways. The 'positive' and 'preventive' checks were made exhaustive in sum, and the 'engaged' or normative categories which traversed this 'neutral' taxonomy

(Flew 1957, 1970) enlarged by the addition of a new check, 'moral restraint', mutually exclusive with respect to 'vice' and 'misery'.

It would appear that 'moral restraint', defined to mean abstinence from marriage 'which is not followed by irregular gratifications' (Malthus 1803, 11), is a species of the 'preventive check' discussed in chapter IV of the first *Essay*. In 1803 Malthus acknowledged that the concept might be at least notionally purged of the 'misery' and (or) 'vice' he had formerly supposed inseparable from it. It is evident from chapters IV and V of the first *Essay* that Malthus believed prudential postponement of marriage to be a function of some socially-determined target real income that might far exceed the biological minimum required for 'subsistence' even when the latter is augmented by the provision of non-food 'necessities' such as clothing and shelter.

The analytical structure of the first *Essay*, as the Appendices demonstrate, permits us to deduce 'comparative statics' theorems of the kind which are so typical of present-day economics. In the simple, ecological model a once-for-all increase in target real income (starting from a position of equilibrium) will bring about a decline in production and therefore in population, leading to a new equilibrium with higher production per capita. In the more sophisticated model of capitalist production a similar behavioural change will bring about a new equilibrium at which production and population – both 'productive' and 'unproductive' – are lower, the real wage of labour higher, and the share of social surplus appropriated by labour and capital increased at the expense of the landlords. Given the stability of these models – which can be deduced as a consequence of Malthus's assumptions (Waterman 1988) – such theorems are 'operationally meaningful' in Samuelson's sense. Notwithstanding the objections of Schumpeter (1954, 579–80), Blaug (1978, 72–4) and many another eminent anti-Malthusian, the theory we may legitimately abstract from the first *Essay* is just as 'scientific' as – no more and no less than – any other example of 'comparative statics' in economics.

It should now be transparent that the introduction of 'moral restraint' leaves the 'economic analysis' which may be abstracted from the *Essay on Population* exactly where it was before. For in economic theory a behavioural change that alters one of the parameters of a system in equilibrium is of interest solely because of its effect upon the value of that parameter. Whether that behavioural change is ethically good, bad or neutral is irrelevant to the new equilibrium values of the dependent variables. If an upward revision of the target real income, causing an increase in the average age of marriage, brings about changes in population, production and real incomes, the magnitude of these induced changes will be the same whether deferment of marriage be accompanied by misery and vice or whether it be purely the consequence of 'moral restraint'.

Viewed from the present-day, and therefore anachronistic, standpoint of 'positive economics', there is no difference between the first *Essay on Population* and any later recension. Certain analytical ideas, such as that of diminishing returns at the extensive margin implied by the 'ratios', are made more (but not fully) explicit. Certain logical slips are corrected. The claim that at the end of each period of 'oscillation' the means of subsistence 'become in the same proportion to the population as at the period from which we set out' (Malthus 1798, 31), which as I have elsewhere argued (Waterman 1987) would subvert the anti-Godwin polemic if taken seriously, was modified by insertion of the all-important auxiliary 'may' (Malthus 1803, 13). The passage in chapter XVII of the first *Essay* (1798, 332–3) which was shown above (pp. 50–3) to imply self-contradiction was quietly modified in the corresponding chapter in the new edition (1803, Book II, ch. VIII) and eventually dropped altogether. In all such amendments Malthus made the smallest change necessary to cover himself, and did so without calling attention to the fact. We may conclude from this, I believe, that the analytical core of the first *Essay* gradually became clearer to Malthus as his attention focussed more narrowly upon political economy during the last three decades of his life. In that sense at any rate it is misleading to suggest, as Bonar (1924, 45), McCleary (1953, 34) and many others have done, that Malthus had 'second thoughts' in 1803.

However, from the standpoints both of ethics and of theology the case is very different. The idea of a 'moral restraint' from marriage which can be entirely free of vice and misery completely alters the terms of the debate with the Jacobins and drastically reduces the problem of evil created by the principle of population. Whether or not he consciously intended it in 1803, Malthus sacrificed some of the temporal and temporary advantages of complete victory over Godwin and Condorcet in exchange for the more lasting benefits of theological integrity.

'Moral restraint' and Godwin

It was remarked by Bonar that 'what Godwin had said to him about Prudence' in a letter to which Malthus replied on 20 August 1798 'may well have suggested the "other check" by which in the Second Essay our author softened the harshest conclusions of the first' (Bonar 1924, ix, iii–viii). In this he has been followed by others including Kenneth Smith (1951, 38) and Patricia James (1979, 68–9). Yet it has been shown (see pp. 37–57 above) that Malthus clearly envisaged a prudential restraint upon marriage in the first *Essay*, 'and this restraint *almost* necessarily, *though not absolutely so*, produces vice' (1798, 29; my italics). Because the 'tendency to a virtuous attachment' usually prevails however (thereby weakening the prudential check), the result of such attachments 'tend to subject the lower classes of the society to distress' (29). Even if prudence dominates and even if it does so without 'vice', yet 'every the slightest check to marriage, from a prospect of the difficulty of maintaining a family, may fairly' be regarded as 'a species of misery' (1798, 108). It is clear from this, first, that the prudential restraint of marriage was an integral part of Malthus's argument from the outset; secondly, that he was aware from the beginning that the preventive check is a parameter of the equilibrium real income; thirdly, that he realized even in 1798 that prudential restraint need not necessarily entail vice. Only in the fourth respect can Malthus really be said to have changed his mind in 1803: by then he was willing to postulate a prudential restraint free both of vice *and* misery.

It is true that this does 'soften the harshest conclusions' of the first *Essay*, though by no means as much as Malthus pretended in 1803. For as Samuel Hollander (1986, 210) has unanswerably demonstrated, 'Malthus had not shown in 1798 that "the poverty and misery that prevail among the lower classes of society are absolutely irremediable" – only that they are so in the absence of prudence'. Malthus himself exaggerated the 'dark tints' both in 1798 and in retrospect; and correspondingly exaggerated the amelioration offered by his – only partially – new concept. Moreover as Flew (1970), Levy (1978), Hollander (1986) and many others have seen, Malthus recognized a trade-off between vice and misery. In 1798 'he had intimated a deliberate preference for prudence – albeit accompanied by vice – as an alternative to misery'. And 'since Malthus was never to put great faith in "moral restraint"... the somewhat greater optimism regarding future prospects in later editions is largely unrelated to the allowance for moral restraint strictly defined' (Hollander 1986, 188–9).

Nevertheless, Malthus's claim to have softened the conclusions of the first *Essay* has generally been taken at its face value by all those who have followed Southey (*AR* 1803, 299) in supposing that Malthus retreated from his 'negative polemic' against Godwin. Godwin had answered Malthus, along with several other detractors, in his *Thoughts on Parr's Spital Sermon* (1801, 72). The destructive effect of population growth upon utopia might be prevented in several ways: one 'which operates very powerfully and extensively in the country we inhabit, is that sentiment, whether virtue, prudence or pride, which continually restrains the universality and frequent repetition of the marriage contract'. It is probable, thought Godwin, that in his ideal society these motives would operate even more strongly. Hence 'Malthus capitulated, while still claiming victory, when in the second edition of the *Essay* (1803) he gave special prominence to a new preventive check...Given the possible... efficacy of moral restraint, Godwin had carried this issue' (Stigler 1952, 191). As Bagehot put it in a famous aphorism: 'In its first form the *Essay on Population* was conclusive as an argument, only it was based on untrue facts; in its second form, it was based on true facts, but it was inconclusive as an argument' (Bagehot 1889, v, 387; cit. Himmelfarb 1968, 108–9).

That this influential opinion is inadequately founded upon what Malthus actually wrote will already be apparent. Even Godwin himself seems not to have read the first *Essay* with ordinary attention. However, Godwin was certainly entitled to ask Malthus what would become of his negative polemic if prudential restraint were both powerful and prevalent enough to stabilize population and output per capita at a point where the latter is above the critical value at which utopia disintegrates. The question gave Malthus an opportunity to repair a deficiency in the first *Essay*, and in so doing to strengthen the *positive* polemic in support of private property and the market economy. Chapter III of Book III in the 1803 edition was given to his 'Observations on the Reply of Mr Godwin'.

The essence of Malthus's rejoinder is very simple. In a society with private property and a market for labour services, and in which the institution of marriage assigns the cost of procreation to the parents, it would be rational to defer marriage. Hence self-love reinforces the duty of moral restraint. But in a world without property, without any predictable reward to labour services and without any legally enforced obligation to recognize, let alone support, one's children, 'the passion between the sexes' – often in conflict with social duty – would operate with no economic sanction to constrain it.

Mr Godwin acknowledges that in his system, 'the ill consequences of a numerous family will not come so coarsely home to each man's individual interest as they do at present'. But I am sorry to say that, from what we know hitherto of the human character, we can have no rational hopes of success, without this coarse application to individual interest, which Mr Godwin rejects. (Malthus 1803, 385–6)

Malthus's new argument may be stated more formally without violence to its intent. Consider a market economy in which the *actual* wage for labour services exceeds the biological 'subsistence' level but is below a target wage required to support a wife and family without indigence. An individual who postpones marriage may save the margin above subsistence until he has accumulated that capital sum which yields an annuity supplementing the *actual*, or market wage by enough to bring it up to the target; which will itself be reduced by the lower life expectancy of the prospective husband and consequently smaller number of expected dependents. This is what Malthus meant, I believe, when he said, of such a person, 'It is clearly his interest... to defer marrying, till, by industry and economy, he is in a capacity to support the children that he may reasonably expect from his marriage' (1803, 506; cit. Hollander 1986, 231). Evidently this can only be the case in a society in which there is a market for the services of labour, in which the worker has property rights in his accumulated savings, and in which he is legally responsible for his offspring. All these conditions are absent by assumption from Godwin's state of 'equal liberty and justice'. Hence Malthus can reassert the positive polemic of the first *Essay* with even greater assurance and with one significant improvement.

To *the laws of* property *and marriage*, and to the apparently narrow principle of self-love *which prompts each individual to exert himself in bettering his condition*, we are indebted for all the noblest exertions of human genius, for everything that distinguishes the civilized from the savage state. *A strict inquiry into the principle of population leads us strongly to the conclusion, that* we shall never be able to throw down the ladder by which we have risen to this eminence; *but it by no means proves that we may not rise higher by the same means.* (1803, 604; cf. 1798, 286–7: italicized passages added in 1803)

The terms of the debate with the Jacobins have indeed been altered. For 'moral restraint' reopens the possibility of continuous improvement in the human condition, which in the end was all that Godwin had really meant by 'perfectibility'. But the negative polemic is saved by a device which actually strengthens the positive polemic. Perfectibility may be a feasible goal after all, *but not by the route Godwin proposed.* It is precisely those 'institutions' that Rousseau, Godwin and all the other Romantics hated, above all the institutions of private property and marriage, which alone may harness ineradicable 'self-love' to the goals dictated by 'benevolence'. The achievement of Malthus's second *Essay*, in some ways even greater than that of the first, was to wrest the idea of 'progress' from the grasp of the Jacobins and to make it instead the legitimate property of reformist whigs and subsequently of a new generation of post-war 'liberal conservatives'.

The positive aspect of this achievement has sometimes been threatened by a theoretical objection first clearly formulated by W. F. Lloyd (1833). Though all workers can gain at the expense of landlords if all defer marriage, it may be the case *even under a regime of private property and wage labour* that 'there is a want of appropriation to each person of the consequences of his own conduct' and hence 'no encouragement to moral restraint is offered to individuals' (Lloyd 1833, 482). Professor Samuel Hollander (1986, 231 n.40) has recently lent his authority to the view that Malthus neglected this 'obvious problem'.

That Malthus was aware in general of the 'free-rider' problem is shown by a passage in the first *Essay* dismissing the possibility that the 'lower classes of society' could agree to restrict the supply of labour (Malthus 1798, 298–9). But in 1803 he quite explicitly rejected this objection to the efficacy of moral restraint.

The happiness of the whole is to be the result of the happiness of individuals, and to begin first with them. *No co-operation is required.* He who performs his duty faithfully will reap the full fruits of it, whatever may be the number of others who fail. (1803, 505; my italics)

His reason for believing that a motivation for moral restraint could exist independently of others' behaviour lay in the conception of a target income discussed above. Whether others are practising moral restraint or not, the rational individual has a motive for deferring marriage if he has a reasonable prospect of achieving his target income before it is too late to be worthwhile. Lloyd accepted that this would be the case with 'all the higher and middling classes of society' but doubted whether the labouring class could entertain with equal confidence an 'assured prospect of an advance in circumstances with the advance in age' (Lloyd 1833, 491, 492). His difference with Malthus was therefore empirical rather than theoretical. Whether moral restraint was or could be effectual among the labouring class depended upon whether social institutions did or might exist for assigning to labourers as individuals the costs of procreation and the benefits of abstinence. Evidently Malthus assumed an affirmative answer to this question. Moreover he believed that he had formulated an 'invisible hand' theorem. As a result merely of self-love, individuals defer marriage to achieve a *target* income; this restricts the supply of labour, raises its price and thereby brings about an unintended – and beneficent – outcome: *actual* income from labour is brought nearer *target* income. When therefore, by moral restraint, an individual pursues 'as his primary object, his own safety and happiness, and the safety and happiness of those immediately connected with him... the most ignorant are led to promote the general happiness, an end which they would totally have failed to attain, if the driving principle of their conduct had been benevolence' (Malthus 1806, II, 522–3: cit. Hollander 1986, 206 n.21).

Malthus was well aware from the outset that the institution most relevant in his own day to the 'free-rider' problem was the Poor Law. For a guaranteed support of the indigent as of right is the most powerful of all disincentives to moral restraint. He launched his attack in the first *Essay*. Poor Laws 'create the poor which they maintain' (1798, 83–4, 87, 134–5); they confer a power upon what we should now call the 'welfare bureaucracy' to tyrannize over the poor, that power is used and is unjust (92–3, 98–9); they interfere with freedom of the labour market (95, 320); they sap the spirit of independence and enterprise (84–6); outdoor relief should be replaced by the provision of deliberately uninviting workhouses 'where *severe* distress might find some alleviation' (97, my italics). The anti-Poor Law theme was taken up in the second *Essay* (1803, Book III, chs. V, VI), and the disincentive to moral restraint developed. Thereafter it became a permanent feature of Malthusian political economy.

It is important to notice in all this that Malthus was already beginning to mark out that course which was later to become characteristic of the new political orthodoxy. A way was to be sought between romanticism and reaction: between Godwin's wholesale repudiation of institutions on the one hand, and an ultra-Burkean defence of the *ancien régime* on the other. Malthus defended certain specified institutions against Godwin and the Jacobins, but he attacked certain others for essentially the same reasons as Godwin had: because they were a cause of, rather than a remedy for, social evil. Thus he was willing to admit that the 'tyranny of Justices, Churchwardens and Overseers' who administer the Poor Law is not the fault of such persons 'who probably before they were in power, were not worse than other people; but *in the nature of all such institutions*' (1798, 93; my italics). Where the need existed for new institutions, moreover, Malthus was ready to propose them. Having shown that moral restraint is 'the only effectual mode of improving the condition of the poor' he followed Adam Smith in recommending universal education through a system of parochial schools (1803, 553–7).

In terms of Dugald Stewart's ideological programme we may at this stage assess the second *Essay* on three points. The 'gloomy inferences' have been at least partially dispelled by the introduction of moral restraint. The 'efficacy of those arrangements which nature herself has established' are suggested, if not conclusively demonstrated, by the invisible hand theorem. The 'expediency of meliorating...the real imperfections of our existing institutions' is validated by the attack on the Poor Law and the proposal for public education. It remains to consider the 'general speculations, more plausible perhaps, than solid'.

'Moral restraint' and the problem of evil

One of the principal reasons, which had prevented an assent to the doctrine of the constant tendency of population to increase beyond the means of subsistence is, a great unwillingness to believe, that the Deity would, by the laws of nature, bring beings into existence, which, by the laws of nature, could not be supported in that existence. That if, in addition to *that general activity and direction of our industry put in motion by these laws*, we further consider, that the incidental evils arising from them, are constantly directing our attention to the proper check on population, *moral restraint*; and if it appear, that by a strict obedience to those duties which are pointed out to us by the light of nature and reason, and are *confirmed and sanctioned by revelation*, these evils may be avoided, the objection will, I trust, be removed, and all apparent imputation on the goodness of the Deity be done away. (Malthus 1803, 494; my italics)

This passage at the beginning of chapter II of Book IV of the 1803 recension, reprinted without significant change in all later editions, marks the decisive switch in Malthusian theodicy which followed Paley's contribution to the debate.

It has lately been shown by Robert Hole (1989, ch. 10, (c) and (d) *passim*) that Pretyman's view of Christianity as 'the religion best adapted to restrain men's passions and control their appetites', though commonplace for most of the eighteenth century, was asserted with much greater frequency, centrality and intensity after 1790 as a result of the French Revolution. In the *Reflections* and subsequent anti-Jacobin writing Burke argued that social order depended upon internal restraints, which could only be inculcated by religion, to the 'lust of selfish will'. The vast majority of writers of the period agreed with Burke and the thesis was argued by such otherwise very disparate authors as Gisborne (1797), Paley (1794; see 1825, III, 317–31) and Wilberforce (1797). It seems probable that Malthus's incorporation of the concept of moral restraint into his second edition was a particular, though slightly belated mani- festation of this general tendency among all English anti-Jacobins.

As I have already remarked Malthus made his tactical concession to Godwin in order to repair the theological foundations of his social theory. And though moral restraint meant that 'perfectibility', at least in a qualified sense, was now admitted to be feasible, Malthus was able to turn even that admission to his own advantage, as we have seen (pp. 139–42 above). Meanwhile the 'growth-of-mind' theory could be dropped, a theodicy of social evil reconstructed along Paleyesque lines, and useful work found for that Christian 'revelation' which in 1798 had been treated as redundant.

The ideological benefits of all this were very great. One can almost hear a sigh of relief from the high-church *British Critic* (1804, 245) at the end of a long and respectful review:

It is but justice to this author to declare, that in this edition of his *Essay*, we do not find any trace of what we conceived to be intimated in the former; a notion that human minds were framed, by some natural process, from inert matter. On the contrary, he seems here to write as impressed with a due sense of religious as well as moral truths.

Among those publications associated more with Dissenting and radical opinion, on the other hand, only the *Monthly Review* (December 1803, January 1804) was warmly favourable. The *New Annual Register* (1803) was distinctly cool and the *Annual Review* (1803) bitterly hostile.

It has been correctly pointed out by John Pullen (1981, 51–2), following Levin (1966), that in 1798 the growth-of-mind theodicy 'introduces an optimistic dimension which counter-balances whatever pessimism is implicit in its socio-economic aspects'. Bowler (1976), Le Mahieu (1979) and Santurri (1982) also contrast theological 'optimism' with political 'pessimism' in the first *Essay* and consider whether it is in net more or less 'optimistic' than later versions. All this is but a cumbersome, secularized way of stating the truism that a Christian author in the eighteenth century would as a matter of course attempt to preserve his social theory from impugning the divine attributes. In a fundamental sense the *Essay* of 1803 is no more and no less 'optimistic' than that of 1798. Only the method of vindicating the 'goodness of the Deity' has been brought more into line with the requirements of contemporary orthodoxy. We may understand how this was done by attending to six theological features of the second *Essay*: the treatment of 'mind', moral restraint, the divine injunction to 'replenish the earth', the state of probation, celibacy and religious education.

It has been suggested by Dr Pullen (1981, 49) that although the growth-of-mind theodicy was not explicit after 1798, 'it was referred to in several places in the form of an assumed background position'. Two references to Book IV, chapter I support this claim. The first is a very general remark upon the effect of scarcity in 'producing that general activity so necessary to the improvement of the human facilities' (Malthus 1803, 491). Later in the same paragraph we read 'it is more conducive to the formation and improvement of the human mind, that the law [of population] should be uniform, and evils incidental to it, under certain circumstances, be left to be mitigated or removed by man himself' (1803, 492). There is no allusion here to the hypothesis that 'God is constantly occupied in forming mind out of matter' or to the alternative theory of 'state of trial' which Malthus deliberately rejected in 1798 in favour of the 'process necessary, to awaken inert, chaotic matter into spirit' (1798, 355, 353). The third reference supplied by Pullen is to the appendix to the fourth (1807) edition reprinted with a short addendum from the third (1806) edition. Here Malthus affirmed his belief that the 'struggle' produced by population pressure is 'calculated to rouse the natural inactivity of man, to call forth his faculties, and invigorate and improve his mind' (1807, II, 478; 1806, II, 553). The entire appendix was intended to clarify Malthus's position in response to criticism and misunderstanding. We should therefore understand the isolated phrase about the 'formation ... of the human mind' in the light of this later clarification: as a self-indulgent attachment to a form of words, the substance of which he had been obliged to abandon. What Malthus meant in 1803 and after by 'the formation and improvement of the human mind' is no different from what Paley had meant when he wrote of this world, with its 'wants and inconveniences' as 'the proper abode of free, rational and active natures, being the fittest to stimulate and exercise their faculties' (Paley 1825, v, 350; see pp. 126–33 above). One may infer Malthus's new position from the passage cited at the head of this subsection. A 'general activity and direction of our industry' is 'set in motion' by the principle of population. His capitulation to Paley is made explicit at the end of the paragraph cited from the appendix: for there Malthus admits that the 'difficulty' which rouses 'the natural inactivity of man' is 'most eminently and peculiarly suited to a state of probation' (1806, II, 553). We must therefore conclude that the *British Critic* was right; and that Dr Pullen, like so many other commentators, has been deceived by Malthus's less than candid mode of recanting. For though in the attack Malthus was an admirable, indeed exemplary controversialist, courteous, magnanimous and fair-minded; in retreat he was less gracious, correcting logical slips by minimal, unadvertised amendments, and camouflaging retraction by a verbal smokescreen.

It seems not to be widely recognized that even the crucial idea of 'moral restraint' itself is heavily dependent upon Paley, though Malthus cannot be faulted here, for he quoted an important passage from chapter XXVI of *Natural Theology* in explication of his new concept.

Human passions are either necessary to human welfare, or are capable of being made, and, in a great majority of instances, in fact made, conducive to its happiness. These passions are strong and general; and, perhaps would not answer their purpose unless they were so. But strength and generality, when it is expedient that particular circumstances should be respected, become, if left to themselves, excess and misdirection. From which excess and misdirection, the vices of mankind (the causes, no doubt, of much misery) appear to spring. This account, whilst it shows us the principle of vice, shows us, at the same time, the province of reason and of self-government. (Paley 1802, 547; cit. Malthus 1803, 490)

The quotation of this paragraph is the most convincing of several indications that Malthus had read and taken to heart the social theodicy of *Natural Theology* before completing and publishing his revised *Essay* one year later. *Pace* Peter Bowler (pp. 133–44 above), not only Paley but Malthus himself evinced a 'real intention to subvert the spirit of Malthus' doctrine and incorporate it into the traditional argument from design'. Immediately after this quotation from Paley, Malthus wrote:

Our virtue…as reasonable beings…consists in educing, from the general materials which the Creator has placed under our guidance, the greatest sum of human happiness; and as all our natural impulse are abstractedly considered good, and only to be distinguished by their consequences, a strict attention to these consequences, and the regulation of our conduct conformably to them, must be considered as our principal duty. (Malthus 1803, 490–1)

'Moral restraint' is located clearly within the conceptual framework of Paley's 'theological utilitarianism', and at just that point where the latter intersects with the same author's naturalistic teleology. God has endowed us with *passions* but also with *reason*. It is part of God's 'design' that the former should afford occasion for the exercise and development of the latter. By this means *vice* and *misery* are reduced or eliminated, *virtue* established, and 'human happiness' or *welfare* achieved, both in this life and the next.

Failure to grasp the essentially theological nature of moral restraint has blinded several generations of Malthusian scholarship, bemused by Bonar's distorted image of Malthus 'the great economist' but seemingly unaware of Bonar's careful analysis of the intimate relation between Malthus's and Paley's moral theory (Bonar 1924, 319–34). The second *Essay*, we were told by one author of the 1950s, is 'interspersed with occasional exhortations, somewhat more appropriate to the pulpit than to a treatise on political economy' (Smith 1951, 41). This grievous misperception, all too typical even now, is in urgent need of correction.

The third ingredient in Malthus's revised theodicy, Paleyesque in spirit though not by direct derivation, is the idea that the 'passion between the sexes' is part of God's design to 'replenish the earth'. This idea was explicit in the first *Essay* (1798, 361, 365) but not fully integrated into the theodicy because of the central importance of the growth-of-mind theory. In his 1806 appendix Malthus noted that 'The first grand objection made to my principles is, that they contradict the original command of the Creator, to increase and multiply and replenish the earth' (1806, II, 506). Though Malthus had retained the idea in the second *Essay* (1803, 491–2) in close contiguity with the passage from Paley cited above, this is evidently an objection to prudential and/or moral restraint. He answered the objection with the Paleyesque (Bonar 1924, 323–33) belief that 'it is the intention of the Creator that the earth should be replenished; but certainly with a healthy, virtuous and happy population, not an unhealthy, vicious, and miserable one' (1806, II, 509).

It will be recalled that Malthus had explicitly rejected the 'state of trial (probation, discipline)' doctrine in 1798 in favour of 'growth of mind'. Though the former was often claimed to be demonstrable by reason alone (e.g. Maclaurin 1775, 411; see p. 88 above) it was generally agreed to be scriptural in a way the latter is clearly not. I have argued above that the *British Critic* was correct in supposing that Malthus dropped growth-of-mind in 1803, though he temporized with an ambiguous form of words. In the same temporizing spirit he merely hinted at state-of-trial in 1803 (494), surreptitiously inserting the idea at the tail end of the 1806 appendix (1806, II, 553). Nevertheless he was able to say with a totally clear conscience in 1803 that the moral implications of the principle of population are 'confirmed and sanctioned by revelation'.

This was much clearer in the use Malthus made of scripture in 1803 to reinforce the duty of at least temporary celibacy (1803, 499, 501, 506), and to invoke authority of St Paul for the doctrine that 'If a man will not work, neither shall he eat' (II Thess. 3: 10; cit. Malthus 1803, 566). The *British Critic* (1804, 243–4) disagreed with Malthus's 'ideas of extending the period, and even the habit of celibacy...unless monastic institutions for the female sex were revived (an event neither likely to occur, nor fit to be recommended)'. Thirty-seven years later, Edward Pusey received the vows of the first Anglican nun since the Dissolution of the Monasteries.

The last respect in which Malthus moved, in 1803, to accommodate contemporary religious sensibilities, was to advocate a national system of education for the lower classes which would train up a rising generation 'in habits of sobriety, industry, independence and prudence, and in a proper discharge of their religious duties'

(1803, 557). But even in later editions of the *Essay* there is little more than a hint of the importance this theme was to assume for Christian Political Economy. It remained for Chalmers to demonstrate much later its relation to Paleyesque teleology. For as moral restraint is the sole and infallible method of raising the general standard of 'comfort and enjoyment', it is 'a wise and beautiful connection in the mechanism of society, that the most direct way to establish it is through...efficient Christian institutions' (Chalmers 1832b, 32).

Christian Political Economy in 1803

The second *Essay on Population* completed the foundations of Christian Political Economy. Reduced to essentials, these are Malthus's economics and Paley's theology. It was left to others to erect the super-structure. The doctrine that inequality is both inevitable and beneficent would be greatly amplified, the futility of legislation to achieve economic goals explained, and the validity and importance of private charity reinforced. The Smithian idea of an 'invisible hand', hardly more than implicit in Malthus, would be made explicit and given theological significance. The view of human life as a state of probation, together with other features of Paley's theodicy, would be developed along lines that the new generation of 'serious' Christians could approve. As the anti-Jacobin theme became less relevant with changing political conditions it would be generalized by a more comprehensive, less historically specific critique of 'radical' social theory.

The first substantial author to address these tasks was John Bird Sumner.

JOHN BIRD SUMNER: 'AN ABLE AND INGENIOUS EXPOSITOR OF THE WHOLE SYSTEM'

Theodicy of the civil evils 'occasioned by the principle of population', said Malthus in his fifth edition of 1817, 'has lately been pursued with considerable ability in the Work of Mr. Sumner on the Records of the Creation; and I am happy to refer to it as containing a masterly developement and completion of views, of which only an intimation could be given in the Essay' (Malthus 1817, III, 425). This opinion was widespread among respectable churchmen. Edward Copleston deemed that in Sumner, Malthusian political economy had found 'not only an advocate, but an able and ingenious expositor of the whole system – one who has beautifully developed the high moral and religious blessings which lay involved in this germ, and has *dissipated that gloom* which in the eyes of many candid persons still seemed to hang over that discovery' (Copleston 1819b, 23; my italics). The *Treatise on the Records of the Creation* (Sumner 1816) met with a chorus of approval from the reviewers. *The British Critic* (1816: 2, 477) regarded Sumner as 'the first to develope, in its full extent, the additions' which the principle of population 'afforded to the proofs of the comprehensive and infinite wisdom of the Creator'. The *British Review* (1817, 492) welcomed his 'vindicating Mr Malthus from the imputations... unjustly thrown upon him'. The *Christian Observer* (1817, 187, 185), though not entirely satisfied with Sumner's 'view of the scheme of redemption', yet commended his 'good sense... clear judgement and comprehensive observation'. The *Monthly Review* (1817: 1, 297) praised his 'important service to the cause of truth'. Even the *Quarterly Review* (1816–17, 50), which at that time was still implacably hostile to Malthusian theory, was delighted that 'although Mr Sumner has brought himself to admit the truth of Mr Malthus's principles, he can yet have derived from them the same conclusions respecting the wisdom and goodness of God which we have ourselves derived from what we conceive to be a refutation of those principles'.

In all this there was no mention of Paley, though it is quite clear from Sumner's references (1816, 1, xii, 21, 27; 11, 251, 255, 262, 296–7, 361–2, 371–2) that he was thoroughly familiar with the 'recent and popular work of Dr Paley' (1, 27) and deeply dependent upon the latter's specific arguments and general theological style.

In order to understand the 'development' of Christian Political Economy in the years after Waterloo we must therefore answer two pairs of questions. First, why did Sumner issue his work in 1816, nine years after Malthus's latest edition and fourteen years after *Natural Theology*; and what were his qualifications for doing so? Secondly, just what did Sumner achieve in the *Records*, and what is the relation between that work and the social theodicy sketched by Paley in 1802?

Sumner in 1816

Malthus wrote his first *Essay on Population* in the heat of the moment. It was, as I have argued in chapter 2, the crucial contribution to a great debate which raged at the centre of English life in the decade after 1789. Paley's *Natural Theology* was the culmination of more than three decades of useful scholarship, written to secure the intellectual underpinnings of its author's lifework, and also to afford 'engagement' with which to soften the pangs of terminal cancer. *A Treatise on the Records of the Creation: with particular Reference to the Jewish History, and the Consistency of the Principle of Population with the Wisdom and Goodness of the Deity*, in two volumes, was neither a tract for the times nor a component of an academic system. It was, in fact, a piece of literary 'speculative building', composed by a schoolmaster in his leisure hours over several years in the hope of winning a valuable prize.

An advertisement had appeared in the newspapers in 1807, announcing to the literary world a competition for a treatise upon

The Evidence that there is a Being, all-powerful, wise and good, by whom every thing exists; and particularly, to obviate difficulties regarding the wisdom and goodness of the Deity; and this, in the first place, from consideration independent of written Revelation; and in the second place, from the Revelation of the Lord Jesus; and from the whole, to point out the inferences most necessary for, and useful to mankind. (*BC* 1816: 2, 333)

In due course Sumner submitted an entry and was awarded the second prize of £400. The first prize of £1,200 went to a Wm Laurence Brown DD of Aberdeen, one of the trustees of Burnett's will under which the competition was established. Brown's (1816) work was soon deservedly forgotten, but Sumner's launched him on a course which led him from almost complete obscurity to the throne of St Augustine in thirty-two years.

For in 1816 Sumner was an assistant master at Eton, aged thirty-six, having occupied that position with no other regular source of income since 1803, when he resigned his fellowship at King's upon marriage to the daughter of a Scotch naval officer. Thereafter things moved quickly. In 1817 he was elected to a fellowship at Eton, in 1818 nominated to the valuable college living of Mapledurham, and in 1820 to the ninth prebendal stall at Durham. In 1826 he moved to the more lucrative, fifth prebendal stall and in 1828 was nominated by the tory Wellington to the see of Chester. Twenty years later, with no evident change in his voting behaviour, he achieved a rare political double, being nominated to Canterbury by the whig Russell: at last outstripping his more brilliant and ambitious younger brother, Charles Richard. Meanwhile the *Records* went through seven editions and other, even more popular, publications appeared from the same pen. Seldom can the second prize in a literary competition have conferred such lasting benefits upon its recipient.

Sumner's belated success was no fluke. In 1798 he had been first in his year at Eton and gone up to King's where he won the Browne Medal for a Latin ode in 1800 and the Hulsean Prize for 1801. His prize essay, 'tending to Shew that the Prophecies, now accomplishing, are an Evidence of the Truth of the Christian Religion' dealt with 'the deplorable contempt of all Religion and authority which has taken root in France' and 'the precipitate decline, and still sinking state of the Papal power' (1802, 12): so pressing contemporary history into the service of natural theology. Nor was this his only literary production before 1816, for his important theological analysis of *Apostolical Preaching* was first published in 1815, and by his own account at least one article on political economy had appeared in the *Quarterly Review* by 1814. Both of these were published anonymously however.

There is no biography of J. B. Sumner, no collection of letters or other papers, and few if any recollections of his Cambridge and Eton days in others' published works. Of his formative years from 1798 to 1816 we can only conjecture for the most part. Three very significant features of his spiritual and intellectual formation may, however, be established with tolerable assurance. He was an evangelical. Yet his theology was continuous with that of the school I have labelled (p. 125 above) the 'Cambridge moderates': Paley, Watson and Hey. And he was, like Malthus, unusually committed to the serious study of political economy.

Sumner's obituary in *The Guardian* (10 September 1862, Supplement) remarked his 'strong bias in favour of those doctrines called Evangelical'. His patronage was cited as evidence of this bias, and in all the many crises of his episcopal and archiepiscopal career he came down – generally with reluctance – on the side of the 'Evangelical' party in the Church of England. It is probable that this allegiance, as in so many similar cases, was an accident of time and place. Had Sumner gone up to Oxford in the mid-1830s he may well have become a moderate Puseyite. But King's College, Cambridge in 1798 was a tiny, close-knit society of exclusively Etonian scholars and fellows, seldom more than twelve of the former, exempt by statute from most of the ordinary activities of the university and dominated by the powerfully charismatic figure of Charles Simeon, Dean of Divinity (1789), Vice-Provost (1790–1), Tutor, and Second Bursar (1798–1805). W. H. Tucker's unpublished memoir of 'King's Old Court, 1822–5' suggests that Simeon had separated himself from college life before the 1820s and that his influence upon King's men was by then negligible (Tucker, ts. 12–14). But the 1790s and early 1800s were the years of his greatest involvement in college affairs. As early as 1789 Simeon had been assured that '...the Provost is willing to co-operate with you in reforming the College' (Carus 1847, 83). What Simeon meant by 'reforming' was turning the hearts and minds of his colleagues and their pupils to 'serious' religion. In 1798 he had not, as yet, abandoned that impossible task. His port-sodden brethren were beyond persuasion no doubt, but the scholars might yet be amenable. The gentle Sumner was not of such stuff as rebels are made of. His reference in his Hulsean Prize essay to 'the propitiatory sacrifice of our Saviour's death' (Sumner 1802, 12), together with other similar usages in this early work, suggest that he had attended the sermon classes which Simeon had been conducting in King's since 1792 (Pollard and Hennell 1959, 142).

It has often been remarked that evangelicalism was a far from unitary phenomenon in the nineteenth century. Boyd Hilton's recent study (1988, 7–26 and the references therein) presents a useful summary of the broad divisions. The older generation of evangelicals, whose intellectual roots lay in the eighteenth century, were divided between Calvinists of varying degrees of rigour, and Arminians or crypto-Arminians. Those whose formation was purely of the nineteenth century were divided between what Hilton calls the 'moderates' and the 'extremists'. The moderates were respectable churchmen with strong academic connexions: Wilberforce, Thornton, and John Venn of the Clapham sect, Isaac Milner and Charles Simeon of Cambridge. The extremists were 'pentecostal, pre-millenarian, adventist and revivalist' (Hilton 1988, 10), a whole class lower in the social scale and much less nice about the boundary between Church and Dissent. The Calvinist/Arminian distinction was still a live issue among the 'moderates' (Hilton 1988, 8–10), but 'extremists' lacked either the taste or the equipment for theological subtlety. John Bird Sumner was an evangelical of the most 'moderate' and respectable kind, whose religious preferences were chiefly displayed in the piety and simplicity of his life and a certain nervousness about surplices and daily services. In theology, moreover, he was strongly critical of Calvinism. Here, as in other important respects, his work may properly be seen as a continuation of the Cambridge tradition discussed above in this and the previous chapter (pp. 123–6; see also Waterman 1991a).

Strong dissonance between evangelicalism and Cambridge theology had appeared as early as 1802 in a work by John Overton, *The True Churchman Ascertained: or An Apology for those of the Regular Clergy of the Establishment who are sometimes called Evangelical Ministers* (1802). Overton sought to establish that 'evangelical ministers' read the Articles in 'the literal and grammatical sense'; that attacks upon Calvinism both by high-church men such as Daubeny and by the Cambridge moderates impugned that sense; and hence that the 'evangelical ministers' were 'true churchmen', and 'Drs Paley, Hey, Croft; Messrs Daubeny, Ludlam, Polwhele, Fellowes; the Reviewers, etc., etc.' were not. There was a grain of truth in this, but also much paranoia, confusion and serious misrepresentation. The central issue was whether the Articles imply, *and only imply*, a Calvinist doctrine of justification, predestination and election. The Cambridge moderates were reviled for asserting, 'with almost one voice, like the papists, the doctrine of *freewill*: our Reformers say, that the Papistical doctrine of freewill is *abominable* in the sight of God, and to be *abhorred* by all Christian men' (Overton 1802, 156). Watson's charges and Hey's lectures were selectively quoted in ways that destroyed their careful balance; Paley was smeared by association with his 'great model, the late Bishop Law', and condemned for his 'Jacobin' parable of the pigeons which puts St Paul on the 'same footing' as Tom Paine (19, 24, 141; 129, 245–7).

In profound contrast to such intemperate vituperation, Sumner began his *Apostolical Preaching* with the aim of '...a complete freedom from all party designs, and without aiming either to defend or confute any man or set of men. He reverences no party...and appeals to no authority, except that which all profess to acknowledge' (Sumner 1815, v; cf. Paley, 1825, i, 70–2). In particular, and in very much the same spirit as Watson, he repudiated the authority of Calvin. In the matter of predestination, Sumner preferred 'the examples of our own Church...who, in her Articles, considers this doctrine separately, as a speculation distinct from the essential points of the Christian faith' (Sumner 1815, 29). Calvin's doctrine of 'decrees' is at variance with the idea that this world is a 'probationary state' (58–60). The doctrine of election is as objectionable as that of predestination for it implies that Christ's propitiatory sacrifice is not efficacious for all (61–2). In the chapter on justification, however, his principal target is the Church of Rome. ('The fatal, though predicted, apostasy in Papal Rome' recalls Sumner's early Hulsean essay.) 'It is the nature of the Roman Catholic religion silently to undermine the true nature of Christian justification' (179). His final chapter displays precisely that desire to find a middle way between 'blind attachment to system' and the 'meer light of reason' which, as I have argued above, was characteristic of Watson, Paley and Hey. 'There are two characters of preaching...at opposite extremes equally removed from the spirit and practice of the Apostles'. The first presents the Gospel through the distorting lens of the Calvinistic system. Though 'Calvinistic tenets' *may* be deduced from scripture, may be consistent with one possible interpretation of the Articles, they are nothing but conjecture: and 'as far as concerns the Christian preacher or teacher, these doctrines are as if they were not true' (250). The other 'very different character of preaching', equally unsatisfactory, fails to see that the Gospel unfolds to mankind 'certain terms and means of entering into everlasting life, which their natural reason would never have discovered' (251, 252). Sumner had in mind 'what Priestley called rational Christianity...not deduced from Scripture, but the coinage of his own imagination' (241).

Sumner's apparent continuity with the Cambridge moderates is confirmed by an examination of his use of their work in his own writing. Paley's *Sermons* and *Horae Paulinae* were cited with approval several times in *Apostolical Preaching* (1815, 24, 33, 69, 147) alongside such Anglican authorities as Burnet, Butler, Hall, Hooker, Horsley, Milner, Taylor, Warburton and Wilberforce. Overton (1802) was altogether ignored. *Natural Theology* was cited eight times in the *Records* (1816, I, xii, 21; II, 251, 255, 262, 296–7, 361–2, 371–2), more than any other authority, and *Moral Philosophy* once. In his slightly later work, *The Evidence of Christianity* (1824), Sumner cited Paley's *Moral and Political Philosophy*, *Evidences* and *Horae Paulinae*, Watson's *Letters to Gibbon*, and Hey's *Lectures*. The last is his chief authority in that work, cited respectfully and often at length in five places (Sumner 1824, 162, 192, 205, 329–30, 407). That his use of Paley, Hey and Watson was no mere resort to the authorities he had read as an undergraduate is shown by the complete absence of any reference to Pretyman's (1812) conservative and highly popular textbook which first appeared (1799) in Sumner's second year at King's. It is, however, consistent with the surmise that he was much influenced as a young man by Charles Simeon. For like the Cambridge moderates, the latter based his 'sentiments' not on 'the dogmas of Calvin or Arminius, but in the Articles and homilies of the *Church of England*', being persuaded that these are 'manifestly contained in the Sacred oracles' (Carus 1847, 178).

Even more significant than quasi-statistical data of this kind is the general intellectual style apparent (save in his youthful Hulsean essay) in all of Sumner's writing: lucid, balanced and peaceable. More prolix than Paley, less subtle than Hey and far more 'serious' than Watson, yet he comes unmistakably from the same stable. It is no accident that two of his most considerable productions, the *Records* and *Evidence of Christianity*, should have been works – at least in part – of natural theology.

The remaining feature of Sumner's formative years which may be inferred from the scanty evidence now available is his undoubted affection to the study of political economy.

'I am sorry to hear', wrote David Ricardo to Hutches Trower in January 1818, 'that Mr Sumner does not intend writing any more on Political Economy – his whole attention in future is to be devoted to the study of Theology. Whether in this future pursuit he will have an equal chance of benefiting mankind, as in the former, I have great doubts, or rather I have no doubt at all; and I very much regret that the science will no longer be assisted by his distinguished talents' (Ricardo 1951–73, VII, 247–8). Ricardo referred in the same letter to Sumner's 'clever book on the Records of the Creation', to its review in the *Quarterly* by Weyland which 'does not do the author justice', and to the fact – which he supposes his correspondent to know – that it was Sumner himself who wrote the long and favourable review of Malthus's *Essay* (1817) which marked the *Quarterly*'s temporary reconciliation to Malthusian economics.

By 1818, this is to say, Sumner was well-known and highly respected within the small and select circle which founded the Political Economy Club three years later. Despite Ricardo's information, moreover, Sumner had not wholly withdrawn from that circle by the mid-1820s. For Macvey Napier secured his services, in company with Buchanan, Lowe, Malthus, M'Culloch, James Mill and 'the late Mr Ricardo', in preparing the section on political economy for the *Supplement* to the *Encyclopaedia Britannica* (1824). 'The important and fruitful doctrine more particularly connected with the name of Mr Malthus' was given 'a correct and comprehensive summary...from his own pen. Closely connected with this subject is that of the article by Mr Sumner' (*EB* 1824, I, xxiv), which was on the Poor Laws (*EB* 1824, VI, 293–306).

It is clearly the case that Sumner's commitment to political economy must antedate the *Records* by several years at the very least. Unfortunately, there is very little direct evidence of Sumner's doings between 1803 and 1816. We must surmise that the *Records* itself was very long in gestation, for the competition for which it was written was advertised seven years before the due date of 1 January 1814 (Sumner 1816, I, vi) and nine years before its publication. Sumner referred in the *Records* (1816, II, 306) to an article he had written in the *Quarterly Review* (October 1814, 146–59) 'On Improving the Condition of the Poor'. It is conceivable, from stylistic resemblances, that he could also have been the author of the review of Ricardo's *High Price of Bullion* which appeared in the February 1810 issue of the *Quarterly*; and considerably more probable that he wrote the article on Savings Banks in the October 1816 number of the same periodical (*QR* February 1816, 152ff.; October 1816, 89ff.). In a letter of 25 April 1822 to Macvey Napier, Sumner remarked that his principal difficulty in writing an article on the Poor Laws 'arose from having written a great deal on the subject before' and mentioned in particular an article in the *British Review* for 1817 (BL, Add. MSS. 34613, f. 53).

Indirect evidence of Sumner's interest in political economy may be sought, as with that of his theological inclinations, in the use he made of other authors. It is no surprise to discover that the *Records* makes considerable reference to Malthus. Sumner relied to an even greater extent, however, on Adam Smith and other luminaries of the Scottish Enlightenment: Reid, Hume, Robertson, Ferguson, Millar and Dugald Stewart (Sumner 1816, I, 4, 46, 48, 212, 236, 251, 254, 258, 260; II, 51, 67–74, 88, 94, 95, 98, 121, 148, 242, 284–5, 287, 340, 346, 360). Adam Smith was even invoked in support of evangelical theology. 'Some other intercession, some other sacrifice, some other atonement, it appears, must be made for sin, beyond what man himself is capable of making, before the purity of the divine justice can be reconciled to his manifold offences' (Smith 1976, 206). 'Who will not regret', asked Sumner 'that the judicious and natural sentiments which accompany the sentence here quoted, were omitted in the subsequent editions? It is well known to the friends of that great philosopher, that he himself lamented, when it was too late, many similar alterations which he admitted into his works' (1816, II, 242 n.). Small wonder that *The Times* (8 September 1862, 12) obituary observed that the *Records* 'might displease a good many of his friends among the so-called Evangelical party, but... would commend him to more liberal thinkers'. Even more remarkable is Sumner's willingness to cite the same 'liberal' authorities in his anonymous *Apostolical Preaching* of 1815. Reid and Stewart are brought forward to counter 'the strong language of our venerable Reformers' on the 'corruption of human nature' (1815, 108–9, 162); and both *Moral Sentiments* and *Wealth of Nations* used in evidence against the Calvinists (1815, 141, 222).

How the evangelical King's Scholar, Fellow and Etonian schoolmaster should have come by such eccentric tastes can only be guessed at. There are one or two straws in the wind but these are nothing more. Among the very few books (483 titles) acquired by the library of King's College in the twenty-six years between 1776 and 1802 are works by Robertson later cited by Sumner, and Stewart's life of the author; the 1793 edition of *Wealth of Nations* (acquired 1796) and *Moral Sentiments* (acquired 1798); the first *Essay on Population* (acquired 1799); and the *Encyclopaedia Britannica* (acquired 1801). Apart from Sumner's own *Records* (acquired 1816) there are no other acquisitions of the Scotch authors or of English political economy between 1776 and 1820. Someone at King's was interested in the Scottish Enlightenment during the period of Sumner's residence from 1798 to 1802. (Note that even Malthus's own college acquired no copy of his first *Essay*.) It may well have been the case, of course, that Sumner deliberately read and made use of Scottish authorities for an essay to be judged in Aberdeen. He was evidently a diligent reader of the *Edinburgh Review* and may even have made the acquaintance of Malthusian economics from that periodical. One other fact which may be of relevance is Sumner's marriage in 1803 to Marianne, daughter of Captain George Robertson RN of Edinburgh. It is possible that Sumner may have visited Scotland either then or later, and that his interest in Scottish social theory was awakened or encouraged by his new connexions. George Pryme, Simeonite evangelical, first Professor of Political Economy at Cambridge and a contemporary of Sumner at Cambridge, recorded that Dugald Stewart's political economy lectures in 1800–2 'attracted so much attention, that several members of our own university went from the south of England to pass the Winter in Edinburgh' (Pryme 1823, vii). We may conjecture (but only conjecture) that Sumner was among those who braved an Edinburgh winter.

It seems reasonably clear from all this that the *Records* was written over a six or seven year period from 1807 to the end of 1813; that its author was a moderate and theologically sophisticated, anti-Calvinist evangelical, first formed by Charles Simeon; and that he had developed an interest in and proficiency at the new science of political economy quite unusual among churchmen of any party at that time. It seems equally clear that it was not written to address any new ideological need, for none had emerged in the years between the peace of Amiens and Waterloo. Paine, Godwin and the Jacobins were still bogeymen, or at least Aunt Sallies, though Robert Owen's *New View of Society* had appeared by 1814 and was soon to present a more tempting target to critics of utopian thought. We may say therefore that although Sumner's contribution to Christian Political Economy was an outcome both of Malthus's refutation of Godwin and of Paley's lifelong devotion to a social theory both rational and Christian, its appearance in early 1816, and its evident flavour of Scottish Enlightenment, were essentially fortuitous.

Sumner on *the* Records of the Creation

The shape of Sumner's *Records* was governed by the terms of the competition for Burnett's prize. Volume I is concerned with the *existence* of God; volume II with His *wisdom* and *goodness*. To a large extent the argument is based on 'considerations independent of written Revelation'. A chapter is included in the second volume however which justifies the divine goodness by means of 'the Revelation of the Lord Jesus'.

The existence of God is suggested first by 'metaphysical reasoning, that something must have existed from eternity' (1816, I, 247). The reader is than referred to 'the various instances of design with which the world abounds'. But 'the chief marks of contrivance which the world exhibits' are passed over very quickly, for 'the recent and popular work of Dr Paley seems to render any fresh enumeration of these instances quite superfluous' (1, 27). The great bulk of volume I (which contains part I) consists of 'an inquiry, whether no historical record has been preserved' of creation. '...the result has proved to be a moral certainty, that the Creator did originally reveal himself to the patriarchs of the human race, and afterwards caused a mode of government and a form of religion to be instituted, which should commemorate the creation of the world, and preserve the worship of the Creator' (1, 248). For in a manner similar in spirit to that employed by Paley with New Testament records in his *Evidences* (Paley 1825, II), Sumner argued that 'the principal facts recorded by Moses, have more testimony, historical or moral, positive or collateral, in their favour, than any other events in the annals of the world' (Sumner 1816, I, 37). Like Paley, he was much concerned, in this part of his inquiry, to answer the sceptical objections of Hume. The latter was treated with great respect, and wherever possible Sumner agreed with him (e.g. I, 236). But Hume's own friends and fellow-countrymen – Robertson, Reid, Adam Smith and Stewart – were skilfully mobilized against him (e.g. I, 250–1), and his writings made to yield orthodox conclusions. 'It is curious to observe how Hume contrived to escape from the argument in favour of the authenticity of Hebrew Scriptures, which arises so regularly from his course of reasoning as if he had written his *Natural History of Religion* to prove it' (1, 236–7).

All this is good, clean fun and intellectually at least on a level with Paley. No other Anglican evangelical of his generation, moreover, could have come anywhere near Sumner in theological learning and philosophical sophistication. But though this volume gave his famous work its misleading short title it was not particularly original, and by itself would have attracted little attention. What made the *Records* 'a work of large and enduring influence' (Norman 1976, 43) was its second volume, which expounded 'the consistency of the Principle of Population with the Wisdom and Goodness of the Deity'.

The treatments of the divine wisdom and goodness are separated in volume II. That of the former (part II) is tightly constructed, daring in its conception, and executed with as near an approach to brilliance as its temperate author would ever allow himself. That of the latter (part III) exhibits a lower level of literary inspiration, is dependent in part on the previous section, and sandwiches a chapter on 'the Christian Dispensation' between largely naturalistic accounts of the 'State of Moral Trial' and the 'Evils of Civil Life'. It is possible nonetheless, that its recognizably 'evangelical' flavour was at least as important as the dialectic skill of the previous part in commending the *Records* to a wider public. Both parts II and III are of high importance for Christian Political Economy and must now be examined in more detail.

Sumner's argument in part II is audacious both in its affirmation and in the stark simplicity of its analysis. 'Inequalities of Ranks and Fortunes' is the condition best suited both to the development of human faculties and to the exercise of virtue. It is proof of the divine wisdom that this order of things is 'universally established, by the Operation of a single principle': the principle of population.

The argument begins by noting that 'the complete developement of the Newtonian theory' brings 'the mechanism of the natural world' under the operation of a 'single and universal law' (Sumner 1816, II, 7, 8). It might be expected that 'right government of the universe' would also require with respect to human societies what 'the free agency of man seems to forbid': laws of 'the same general and comprehensive nature' (II, 14–15). Now it seems to be the 'Design of the Creator' in creating humans that their life on this earth should be 'a state of discipline, in which the various faculties of mankind are to be exerted, and their moral character formed, tried, and confirmed, previous to their entering upon a future and higher state...life, therefore, is with great propriety described as a race in which a prize is to be contended for' (II, 25). This is known from the fact that man, unlike all other creatures, is endowed with 'improvable reason' and hence may become 'the artificer of his own rank in the scale of beings' (II, 21).

The next step is to show that inequality of rank and fortune is in fact best suited first, to the development of human faculties and secondly, to the exercise of virtue.

The first, which is expounded in part II, chapter III, begins with a fairly conventional attack upon Rousseau's doctrine of the savage state. The nearer the approach to equality 'the more stagnant and inactive is the human mind' (II, 37). Humans are induced to change their habits by example and emulation. But this will not happen until 'the first blow has been given to the system of equality, by recognizing that division of property which secures every man the fruit of his labour' (II, 42). Once this has occurred, 'he is continually impelled by his desires from the pursuit of one object to another' (II,

46–7). Hence may arise societies of 'unequal fortunes, ranks and conditions', which by affording the maximum stimulus to exertion, is 'best calculated to improve by exertion the faculties of man' (II, 74). The argument is supported by recent geography and by Robertson, Wallace, the *Edinburgh Review* and Millar on the *Origin of Ranks* (1779). Having apologized for paying attention to 'a writer now so completely forgotten as Mr Godwin' Sumner disposed of the latter's ethical objections to 'the established administration of property'.

That inequality is most conducive to the exercise of virtue (part II, chapter IV) is proved by the fact that it affords the rich an opportunity by their benevolence to relieve want and alleviate misery, and to the 'middling and lower ranks' an opportunity for frugality, temperance and 'a prudential restraint upon the passions' (II, 89). The 'lowest ranks' have abundant opportunities to practise those virtues by which 'poverty may be rendered tolerable and indigence avoided' (II, 91). Virtue, in general, is 'an active and energetic habit, arising from the various relations of human life, and exercised in the practice of real duties; so that, as you increase the number and variety of those relations, you enlarge its sphere of action' (II, 78).

All this is routine eighteenth-century apologetic. Chapter III is based on Adam Smith's carrot and Malthus's stick; chapter IV on Paley's 'Reasons for Contentment'. Sumner's 'crucial move' comes in the next chapter. Given that social and economic inequality is 'the state best suited' to human development both intellectual and moral, 'it might naturally be expected that the Creator would devise a mean' for bringing this about. 'And this in fact, I believe to be the final cause of that "principle of population" with whose powerful agency we have recently been made acquainted.' (II, 101). The pressure of population against subsistence leads inevitably to private property in the means of production (II, 101–18). Once this has occurred, natural inequality, 'moral differences in the character of men', luck and inheritance lead to 'very unequal shares' in the ownership of land and to the 'subordination of ranks' (II, 118–22). Legislation is futile to prevent it (II, 124–8). Hence 'in the gradual process of time the inequality becomes more and more striking, and all the arts of cultivation follow in its train'. And so

The Deity has provided, that, by the operation of an instinctive principle in our nature, the human race should be uniformly brought into a state in which they are forced to exert and improve their powers: the lowest rank, to obtain support; the one next in order, to escape from the difficulties immediately beneath it, and all the classes upward, either to keep their level, while they are pressed on each side by rival industry, or to raise themselves above the standard of their birth by useful exertions of their activity, or by successful cultivation of their natural powers. (II, 133)

Part II concludes the account of divine wisdom by an enumeration of the 'collateral Benefits derived by the human Race from the Principle of Population' (part II, chapter VI). Though the Fall of Man and the Curse of Adam, by condemning the human race to scarcity, is the cause of 'much want and misery', the 'present state affords only a partial developement of the Creator's designs' (II, 137–8). Meanwhile the principle of population brings about 'the establishment of universal industry' and 'the quick and wide diffusion of the beneficial results of that industry' (II, 139). The first of these benefits occurs because the 'inherent principle of indolence' is expelled 'by the operation of a still more powerful desire' (II, 143). And by the 'quick multiplication of the species' division of labour may occur, increasing productivity and thereby raising living standards 'infinitely above any benefits that could be expected to result from a different system' (II, 171). A famous passage from *Wealth of Nations* is quoted in support. (Analytically, Sumner here assumed that increasing scale shifts the production function by more than enough to offset falling productivity caused by diminishing returns to the variable factors. The proposition, if true, would seriously complicate the 'Malthusian' implications of population theory. But it was passed over without comment in all discussion of Sumner's book.) The second benefit occurs through migration and international trade, which serve to disseminate the blessings of Revelation. Hence 'through the influence of the principle of population ... civilization becomes the instrument of diffusing Christianity' (II, 163).

Part II ends with a 'concise recapitulation of the general argument' which is worth quoting in full.

It is apparent then, first, to be the *design* (a) of the Creator to *people the world* (b) with rational and improvable things, placed there, it would seem, in a *state preparatory* (c) to some higher sphere of existence, into which they might, hereafter be removed. With this in view, he implanted in the first progenitors of the species a *passion* (d) transmitted by them to their descendants, which in the outset prompts the finest feelings of the mind, and leads to that close union of *interests* (e) and pursuits, by which the domestic comfort and harmony of the human race is most effectively promoted. The operation of this *principle* (f), filling the world with *competitors* (g) for *subsistence* (h), *enforces* (i) labour and *encourages* (j) industry, by the *advantages* (k) it gives to the industrious *at the expense* (k) of the indolent and extravagant. The ultimate effect of it is, to foster those arts and *improvements* (l) which most dignify the character and refine the *mind* (m) of man, and lastly, to place mankind in that *situation* (c) which best enables them to improve their natural faculties, and at the same time best exercises, and most clearly displays, their *virtues* (n).

The collateral benefits derived from the same principles were shown to be the promotion of universal comfort, by ensuring the most effective *disposition of labour* (o) and skill; and the diffusion of the *civilization* (p) thus attained, by gradual and steady *progress* (p), throughout the various regions of the habitable globe.
Such is the omniscience and comprehensive *wisdom* (q) of the Creator, deducible from the facts respecting *population* (f) ... (II, 172–3; my italics and letters)

Most of the major terms in contemporary political discourse are fitted neatly into this summary. The principle of population (f) and its related concepts of the 'passion between the sexes' (d), replenishing the earth (b), competition (g) and subsistence (h), are shown to produce inequality (k) which is beneficial because it fosters civilization (l) by the Malthusian 'stick' of disincentives to idleness (i) and the Smith–Paley 'carrot' of incentives to industry (j). Civilization encourages the development of mind (m) and virtue (n); and the latter is consistent with 'interest' or self-love (e). It also leads to the division of labour (o) and progress (p). The whole exemplifies the divine wisdom (q) within a Paleyesque argument from design (a) which accommodates the doctrine of a probationary state (c) strongly favoured by evangelicals. No single element in this is new and most are very familiar. But the whole is greater than the sum of its parts. For whereas Malthus himself and virtually all of his readers had looked on the principle of population as producing an uncommonly nasty case of the problem of evil to be reconciled as well as might be with the divine *goodness*, Sumner lifted it out of the icy realm of theodicy altogether, transplanting it to the genial soil of Paley's teleology, there to flourish as an example of divine *wisdom*.

Part III, though containing much judicious discussion of eighteenth-century theodicy, lacks a central unifying argument and therefore presents as a whole a less compelling literary composition. The *British Critic* (1816: 2, 478) was 'generally... inclined to say, that nothing useful can be learned from such discussions', but excused Sumner, who was 'compelled to notice it by the express words of Mr Burnett's bequest'. The *Monthly Review* (1817: 1, 296–7) decided 'to omit a notice of the remainder of the Volume' and complained of its 'want of a distinct separation between the subjects of the different chapters'. Only the *Christian Observer* (1817, 185–91), wishing to quibble over 'the scheme of redemption', devoted more than a page or two to part III.

Sumner began (part III, chapter I) by arguing 'from the Constitution of Mankind' that God intended the happiness of His creatures, and that this is therefore evidence of His goodness. An attempt was made to answer Bolingbroke's objections but the treatment is brief, for the subject is one 'which so many excellent writers have occupied'. Sumner's argument is evidently based on Balguy and Paley.

Next (part III, chapter II) comes an extended account of 'the present Existence of Mankind considered as a State of Moral Trial'. Butler and Abraham Tucker are cited in support of the doctrine that God has made it clear to human reason that He is on the side of virtue and against vice. William King's justification of moral evil in terms of free will is questioned (II, 197–201). But 'The infinite wisdom of God supposes an infallible prescience of all future events; and must clearly have seen, that a being, liable to vice and temptation in the degree to which man was liable, would inevitably fall into it' (II, 202). How then can the inevitability of human moral failure be 'part of God's general scheme in the creation of man'? Boyle's conclusion that reason is powerless and 'only faith can support us' is rejected. Soame Jenyns's use of the Great Chain of Being is countered by Samuel Johnson's 'masterly review' (see pp. 75–9 above). Sumner's own treatment is ingenious and, so far as I have been able to discover, original. Suppose that humans were given the choice of being placed in a state of trial. The rewards are such that 'all would joyfully embrace it, notwithstanding the difficulties that might oppose the attainment, and the dreadful evils awaiting a failure' (II, 223). But God, being omniscient, already knows that humans would make this choice if they were free to do so: hence it is not unjust or cruel of Him actually to expose them to risks they would freely have chosen. This austere doctrine is leavened by illustrations from scripture and early church history showing that 'trial, severe trial, is absolutely requisite to purify and establish the human character' (II, 210–11). Sumner's rhetorical technique is clearly visible in this chapter, wherein the bare bones of Paleyesque naturalism are endued with a scriptural and homiletic phraseology congenial to the new 'serious' sensibility.

In the following chapter (part III, chapter III) Sumner turned, in obedience to Burnett's mandate, to a task Paley never attempted: the integration of the results of natural theology with the 'Christian Dispensation'. 'Whatever doubts the permission of evil might excite, whatever clouds it might appear to cast over the plan of God's moral government, are dispersed by the view which the Scriptures present of the mission and sacrifice of Christ' (II, 230). 'Christian revelation steps in to confirm our confidence' wrote Sumner. We learn as certain 'what reason before showed...to be probable: that this earthly state is preparatory to a superior state' for which we are designed. Now 'in the very notion of a state of trial, evil must be included' (II, 235). The Creator, having foreseen this, provided a remedy. First, the sacrifice of Christ affords 'a vicarious atonement for repented sins'; mankind are 'redeemed...from the consequences of their guilt' and a 'way of eternal happiness' opened to them (II, 232, 237). Secondly, 'gracious assistance' is offered for all who have been placed this way, enabling them 'to fulfill those commands which, as the descendants of guilty parents, they would otherwise be disqualified from obeying' (II, 232). At this point Sumner quoted a long passage from his anonymous *Apostolical Preaching* in explication.

It is notable that both in this chapter and in various earlier places, Sumner explicitly invoked the doctrine of the Fall to account for moral evil. The scheme of redemption contained in scripture is 'mercifully devised to meliorate man's condition, and obviate the fatal effects of sin' (II, 231). Though, as I have argued against Cassirer (pp. 62–82 above), Anglican theologians from King and Derham to Paley and Hey were always willing, when pressed, to fall back upon this doctrine, the work of Sumner marks a much more decided return to a pre-Enlightenment teleology based on revelation. Yet as his decided anti-Calvinism confirms, this was no mere turning back the clock. An Enlightenment natural theology based on Newtonian science was here to stay, Sumner obviously believed. Moreover, the morally repugnant features of the Augustinian-Calvinistic theodicy clearly had to go. Sumner's eminent predecessors, Watson, Paley and Hey, had attempted to steer between the opposite errors of proving too much from scripture on one hand,

and of ignoring it altogether on the other. But in truth their use of scripture was often less than whole-hearted, and their intellectual energies were chiefly engaged elsewhere. John Bird Sumner, immunized by his King's scholarship from the cerebral attractions of the Tripos, impelled by evangelical sentiments to close study of holy scripture, was the first English theologian of stature to carry out the programme of the Cambridge moderates with complete success.

This alone would not have sufficed to win for his book the universal approbation it received. Sound theology was necessary, but so was a firm grasp of political economy. As an economist Sumner was not a seminal thinker like Malthus, nor even a brilliant amateur like Paley, Copleston and Whately. There are no analytical innovations in his work, and the only respect in which his analysis diverges from that of Malthus – the case described above in which increasing returns to scale are assumed to outweigh diminishing returns to the variable factors – is vague and unsatisfactory. Yet Sumner had a clear understanding of the broad outline of classical political economy (as it had evolved to about 1807) and of its principal implications for public policy. Ricardo's approval was not lightly bestowed.

Though the principle of population figures largely in the discussion of divine wisdom in part II, it is in the final chapters (IV, V and VI) of part III that political economy is most evident.

Natural evils such as death and pain are dealt with in very much the same way as by Paley. But 'poverty, dependence, servitude', are divided into two classes: 'those which in the opulent states of society press heaviest upon the inferior stations; and those which in rude and unsettled countries press more uniformly upon the whole population (II, 263). The distinction corresponds precisely to that between the sophisticated and the simple models of population equilibrium in Malthus's *Essay* (pp. 37–57 above). In the latter, all incomes tend to bare subsistence level. In the former, private property in land and wage-labour of a landless proletariat operate through market forces to bring the incomes of labourers to a socially-conditioned minimum, to restrain population below the ecological maximum, and to generate a social surplus, controlled by property-owners and available for support of the civilized state. Sumner provided a justification of 'the Evils of an uncivilized State' (part III, chapter IV), the chief element in which is that the populations of such countries being small, stationary and poor, they are the more likely to be conquered and civilized by their large, dynamic and affluent neighbours. (There is no mention of war among the evils considered by Sumner, nor was this remarked by any of his reviewers. For Godwin, it will be remembered, war was the greatest of all the evils of civil life.) But the treatment was essentially negative and residual, briefly captured in the final sub-heading, 'No situations inconsistent with a State of Probation'. Of much more interest, both to the author and his readers, was the previous chapter (part III, chapter v) 'On the Capabilities of Improvement in a State of Advanced Civilization'.

It is in this chapter, more than any other in the *Records*, that Malthus would have found that 'masterly developement and completion' of his views which he acknowledged in 1817. Political economy provides an explanation of why some must be poor in a civilized society. However, *political economy also reveals that the genuine evil associated with this inevitable outcome is remediable.* 'The fundamental cause of the greatest evil of the poor is ignorance' (II, 292). With proper education this can be overcome, which not only may reconcile the poor to their lot in this life by fixing their attention upon the next, but may 'make them agents in bettering their own condition'. For the educated man 'sees his own interest more clearly, he pursues it more steadily, he does not study immediate gratification...or mortgage the labour of his future life without an adequate return' (II, 298–9). Secondly, irremediable poverty caused by 'sickness, infancy, and old age' can and might be dealt with by private and local charity, and by Friendly Societies. (Poverty caused by the Poor Laws can be eradicated by the gradual elimination of the latter.) Best of all is growth of the market economy and widespread participation in ownership. 'The security of capital in this country, the facility of turning it to the best use, the quick and ready communication of labour throughout the whole kingdom, afford inestimable facilities to...the improvement of the state of the mass of the community' (II, 303). The poor must be encouraged to save by the creation of parochial savings banks. At this stage Sumner provided an arithmetical illustration of Malthus's 'moral restraint' theorem that I have analysed in the previous section of this chapter (see pp. 142–3). The weekly wage for a labourer aged 18 averaged 12s. per week; 6s. was required for support of a single man, leaving 6s. per week to be saved, or 4s. allowing for lost time. £10 saved per annum for seven years would accumulate with interest to £80 by the age of 25. If marriage then took place, and the wife had accumulated enough capital to furnish the cottage, the interest on capital will pay rent until the family increases. Capital must be drawn on while the children are dependent, but about half should remain 'towards setting forth the children in life'.

Sumner therefore imbedded the concept of moral restraint within a larger theodicy which included the beneficence of the market economy, the key importance of universal public education, the need for accident and sickness assurance and of financial institutions to mobilize the savings of the poor, and with private charity as the last resort. Most of the argument in this chapter is adapted from his anonymous article in the *Quarterly Review* (October 1814, 146–59) 'On Improving the Condition of the Poor'. Though there is little evidence that Sumner ever grasped the analytical point that moral restraint actually redistributes part of the social surplus from landowners to workers, there is a strong flavour of 'progress' in his political economy; and no doubt that he deserved Copleston's praise for having 'dissipated that gloom' which, until his *Treatise*, still surrounded Christian Political Economy.

CHAPTER 5

Oxford contributions: Copleston and Whately

CHRISTIAN POLITICAL ECONOMY AFTER 1816

Sumner's *Records* completed the assimilation to sound doctrine of the first anonymous and provocative 'Remarks on the Speculations of Mr Godwin'. The anti-utopian argument was retained, and the case for private property strengthened by relating it to benign inequality. The dubious theology of the first *Essay* was replaced by a combination of Malthus's own new concept of 'moral restraint' with the orthodox notion of a 'state of discipline and trial'; and the principle of population, exonerated from the charge of impugning the divine goodness, was employed in defence of the divine wisdom. 'Gloomy inferences' were dispelled in part by Sumner's transposition of the theology to a cheerful, Paleyesque conceptual framework, and in part by his emphasizing the possibilities of economic, social and religious amelioration opened up by moral restraint. The whiggish appetite for orderly reform was acknowledged by correlating moral restraint with institutional *encouragements*, such as parish schools and savings banks, and *discouragements*, of which the greatest was the Poor Law. The former must be fostered, the latter amended or repealed.

What came next was a final re-shaping of the *Essay on Population* by Malthus himself; then the correction of certain themes and amplification of others by two of the most brilliant and powerful of that now almost legendary society of Oriel fellows which dominated the intellectual life of Oxford from Copleston's appointment as tutor in 1797 to Whately's departure for Dublin in 1831. This chapter contains a detailed review of their contributions. By way of preliminary it is necessary first to examine Malthus's response to Sumner; then to consider the changing social and political circumstances of post-war Britain, and to identify those issues of public policy on which the new science of political economy was to cut its teeth.

171

Malthus and Sumner

A fifth edition of the *Essay on Population* appeared in 1817 'with important additions' and a new publisher. As the recension of 1803 must be seen to a significant extent as a response to Paley's *Natural Theology*, so that of 1817, in some degree, is a response to Sumner's *Records*.

This is clearly the case, as may well be supposed, in the theological matter. Malthus paid tribute to Mr Sumner's 'masterly developement and completion' of his views (Malthus 1817, III, 425), and in the extended Appendix made a belated and somewhat misleading recantation of his views on the 'state of trial'. 'I have always considered the principle of population', wrote Malthus disingenuously, 'as a law peculiarly suited to a state of discipline and trial. Indeed I believe that, in the whole range of the laws of nature with which we are acquainted, not one can be pointed out, which in so remarkable a manner tends to strengthen and confirm this scriptural view of the state of man on earth' (1817, III, 426). But in 1798 Malthus had argued not from scripture but from 'the book of nature, where alone we can read God as he is'; and had deliberately rejected the 'state of trial' as indicating 'something like suspicion and want of foreknowledge' in the 'Supreme Being' (1798, 351, 353). In 1798, moreover, Malthus had purported to resolve all checks to population into misery and vice. Yet in 1817 he was able to assert that he had '*never* felt any difficulty in reconciling to the goodness of the Deity the necessity of practising the virtue of moral restraint in a state allowed to be a state of discipline and trial' (1817, III, 423; my italics). These are extreme examples of that want of perfect candour with which, as I have noted in the previous chapter (see pp. 146–7 above), Malthus approached the painful task of retraction.

In the other substantial changes in the fifth edition the influence of Sumner is less obvious, but often discernible. The chapter on 'Increasing Wealth, as it affects the Condition of the Poor' (1817, book III, ch. xiii) was rewritten to make it appear that economic growth might after all bring with it 'advantages to the lower classes of society which may fully counterbalance the disadvantages with which it is attended' (1817, III, 25). A supplement was added to the chapter on 'Effects of the Knowledge of the Principal Cause of Poverty on Civil Liberty' (1817, book IV, ch. vii) asserting that 'universal suffrage and annual parliaments' were powerless to remedy post-war unemployment, and that popular clamour for revolutionary changes merely afforded an excuse for repressive measures by a government which 'during the last twenty-five years has no very great love either of peace or of liberty' (1817, III, 170). Some changes and additions, however, were made in response to other authors. A large part of the 1817 appendix consists of replies to Grahame's *Inquiry* (1816) and Weyland's *Principles* (1816). 'Observations on the Reply of Mr Godwin' (1807, book III, ch. iii) was replaced by a new chapter 'Of Systems of Equality' (1817, book III, ch. iii), in which Robert Owen's *New View of Society* (1814) and the communistic Society of Spencean Philanthropists were criticized. Even in this chapter, however, Malthus gave pride of place not to the 'pessimistic' anti-populationist argument he had used against Godwin, but rather to the 'optimistic' justification of inequality presented by Sumner. Inequality of conditions 'is unquestionably the best calculated to develope the energies and faculties of man, and the best suited to the exercise and improvement of human virtue'. Though here too Malthus had the audacity to claim that the argument had 'always appeared to my own mind sufficiently conclusive' he did at least give proper credit, directing the reader to 'this subject very ably treated in a work...by the Rev. John Bird Sumner,...a work of very great merit, which I hope soon to see in as extensive circulation as it deserves' (1817, II, 277n.).

In addition to such large, structural changes as these, Malthus continued the process, begun in 1806, of watering down the more outrageous expression of his unpopular opinions. It was probable, he said with some justice, 'that having found the bow bent too much the one way' he was 'induced to bend it too much the other'. He was always ready to defer to a 'competent tribunal', and had already 'expunged the passages which have been most objected to'. And he had 'made some few further corrections of the same kind in the present edition' (1817, III, 427). The most notorious of these objectionable passages were the anti-Paleyesque vision of 'nature's mighty feast' (see pp. 119–22 above), and a delicious homily in praise of spinsterhood and old maids which ends with a paragraph strongly suggesting the nuptials of Wickham and Lydia Bennet:

...It is perfectly absurd as well as unjust, that a giddy girl of sixteen should, because she is married, be considered by the forms of society as the protector of women of thirty, should come first into the room, should be assigned the highest place at table, and be the prominent figure to whom the attentions of the company are more particularly addressed...(Malthus 1803, 552)

Each had been removed in the 1806 edition, but the first especially was long remembered against him.

These changes were noted with approval by Sumner, who reviewed the fifth edition for the *Quarterly* (July 1817, 369–403): '...it must be owned that no pains were originally employed to win an easy way...Every succeeding edition has been improved in this respect; and in the present especially the author has equally gratified our self-complacency and displayed his own candour, by expunging those passages to which we had most pointedly objected' (374). It is hard to know just what Sumner could have had in mind by the word 'especially', for the merely verbal alterations between 1807 and 1817 were slight and for the most part insignificant. A clue may be found in his criticism in the *Records* of Malthus's equivocal discussion of moral restraint in book II, chapter xi of the second, third and fourth editions. In 1803 and 1806 Malthus had retained – though with one highly significant addition – a typically 'melancholy' passage from the first *Essay*:

> Famine seems to be the last, the most dreadful resource of nature. The power of population is so superior to the power of the earth to produce subsistence to man, that, *unless arrested by the preventive check*, premature death must in some shape or other visit the human race. The vices of mankind are active and able ministers of depopulation.... But should they fail in this war of extermination, sickly seasons, epidemics, pestilence and plague, advance in terrific array, and sweep off their thousands and ten thousands. Should success still be incomplete, gigantic inevitable famine stalks in the rear, and, with one mighty blow levels the population with the food of the world. (1798, 139–40; my italics, italicized passage added in 1803)

Sumner felt that the insertion of the italicized phrase was inadequate to modify the psychological effect of this passage. 'If prudential restraint, i.e., the *preventive check*, is disregarded, who can doubt that famine, war, or epidemic will arise?...But it is *not necessary* that the prudential check should be violated; neither, therefore, is it necessary that famine and pestilence should carry off a redundant population'. It would be desirable that Malthus should 'correct or qualify those expressions' in this chapter, which 'have created a wrong impression in the minds of many readers' (Sumner 1816, II, 165).

Now the passage objected to is indeed absent from the 1817 edition, but it is *also* absent from that of 1807. It is clear from

Sumner's references to Malthus in the *Records* (1816, II, 104, 110, 165) that he was working with the *third edition of 1806* and unaware of the differences which were made in 1807. He was therefore deceived into supposing that Malthus had deleted the offending portion in deference to his own advice. In fact it had been removed ten years earlier. With less excuse Bonar was even more deceived. Citing Otter's memoir, he surmised that the cancellation of 'nature's mighty feast' was 'probably due to Sumner' (Bonar 1924, 307 n.2). But there is no evidence of any communication between Sumner and Malthus from 1803 to 1806, nor is it probable that there should have been.

The recension of 1817 contained the last considerable revisions to the *Essay*. The only later edition to appear in Malthus's lifetime was that of 1826, containing some additional material and a few 'inconsiderable alterations and corrections', but no structural or thematic change. But in 1821 Malthus was invited by Macvey Napier to contribute an article on 'population' to the *Supplement* to the fourth, fifth and sixth editions of the *Encyclopaedia Britannica* (1824). A revised and abbreviated version (Malthus 1986, IV, 179–243) was published over the author's name as a *Summary View of the Principle of Population* (1830). The geometrical ratio of potential population growth was retained in a subdued form, but the arithmetical ratio of induced growth in subsistence was suppressed. In its place, the law of diminishing returns implied by the two ratios was made a little more – but not fully – explicit. There is an 'absolute want of power to prepare land of the same quality, so as to allow the same rate of progress': it is impossible 'to make all the soil of the earth equal in fertility to the average quality of land now in use' (1986, v, 181). These amendments are strictly in accordance with the advice Sumner tendered in his review of the fifth edition. 'We have always regretted the place which these calculations hold in the head and front of the essay'. Had Malthus 'contented himself with beginning from the propositions which he really proves, his work would have had the same utility... with the additional advantage of less outraging the feelings of his readers' (*QR* 1817, 375–6, 380).

The final pages of the *Summary View* are pure Sumner.

First, it appears that the evils arising from the principle of population are exactly of the same kind as... those arising from the excessive or irregular gratification of the human passions in general... Secondly, it is almost universally acknowledged, that both the letter and spirit of revelation represent this world as a state of moral discipline and probation... Lastly, it will be acknowledged, that in a state of probation, those laws seem best to accord with the views of a benevolent Creator, which, while they furnish the difficulties and temptations which form the essence of such a state... reward those who overcome them with the happiness in this life as well as in the next. (Malthus 1986, v, 240)

The 'dark tints' and 'melancholy hue' have finally been painted out of the picture.

Economics and politics in post-war Britain

The *Treatise on the Records of the Creation*, as befits a work of natural theology, was composed in Olympian detachment from the excitement and the squalor of Regency Britain. Not so the fifth edition of the *Essay*, which abounds in references to contemporary controversy and the violent economic changes which gave rise to it. For the world had changed since 1798, and though even Lord Grey had grown to perceive the menace of Jacobinism (Trevelyan 1929, 182–9) the Jacobins of 1817 were a different breed from Richard Price, James Mackintosh and Mary Wollstonecraft. Genteel Dissenters who looked to 1688, aristocratic poets who hated Malthus for denying the romantic vision and ambitious Scotchmen with Enlightenment sensibilities were not to be found in the ranks, or even at the head, of the starving mobs who set fire to barns, smashed machinery and looted bakeries. Major Cartwright (now in his mid-seventies) and Sir Francis Burdett had organized the Hampden Club to focus popular discontent upon demands for constitutional reform. But the movement boiled over in a renewal of Luddism and of revolutionary violence, and its new leaders were much more in the mould of Tom Paine whose bones were symbolically repatriated by Cobbett in 1819. When Orator Hunt addressed his open-air mass meetings he was attended by a standard-bearer carrying a tricolour flag. His 'Loony Left' of Spencean communists stormed the Mansion House with stolen weapons. As Southey wrote to Lord Liverpool in March 1817, 'The Spirit of Jacobinism which influenced men in my sphere of life four-and-twenty years ago (myself and men like me among others) had disappeared from that class and sunk into the rabble, who would have torn me to pieces for holding those opinions

then, and would tear me to pieces for renouncing them now'
(Halévy 1949, II, 19 n.1).

Economic circumstances during the first years after Waterloo
afforded the rabble some occasion for its belated intoxication with
the Spirit of Jacobinism. The condition of the poor in many, but not
all, parts of Britain was depressed by an evil coincidence of four more
or less independent causes. A major recession was created by
demobilization and the sudden termination of government contracts
for war goods. The seasons of 1814 and 1816 had been exceptionally
poor, but farm prices fell with all others and the latter was 'one of
the blackest years in agricultural history' (Hilton 1977, 30). The
Napoleonic Wars fostered a wide diffusion of labour-saving
machinery in manufacturing and agriculture, and the effect was felt
in technological unemployment even before, but especially after
1815 (Tunzelmann 1981, 161). Underlying these short-term effects
and exacerbating their power to create misery were those vast
structural changes, greatly accelerated by the wars, by which
Britain was transformed into the first industrial state (Rose 1981,
251–75).

The acute suffering of the poor in these years has been well
documented, and the repressive response of government to their
protest imbedded in the folklore of 'the making of the English
working class' (Thompson 1968, 660–780). But in 1820 the economic climate improved and workers in employment began to enjoy
some of the fruits of industrialization. The best available index of
real wages shows an increase of 9.3 per cent between 1820 and 1824;
and in the latter year the average real wage stood at 33 per cent
above the level of 1790 (O'Brien and Engerman 1981, 169, table
9.1). 'The darkest hour of our domestic history was over' (Trevelyan
1929, 198): two years later Peel succeeded to the Home Office,
began to dismantle Sidmouth's system of espionage and coercion,
and embarked upon his life-work of tory reform. Jacobin agitation
faded away. On 16 August 1820, barely a thousand could be
assembled in Manchester to observe the first anniversary of Peterloo.
Meanwhile in London, a vast procession, stretching from Hyde Park
Corner to Hammersmith, paid its respects to Queen Caroline. For
once again (see p. 22 above) the British public afforded 'proof of its
ingrained devotion to monarchy even in its attack upon George IV,
by dropping the cause of manhood suffrage to display its sympathy

with a persecuted Queen...The Radical agitators found themselves relegated to the background' (Halévy 1949, II, 103).

The response of government to the turmoil of the first five post-war years was not confined to the preservation of law and order. But the upper classes were not of one mind as to the causes of, or the cure for, the popular disaffection.

The attempt to relieve the agricultural sector by restricting importation of grain set manufacturers against landlords, alienated many of the most powerful members of the whig party (Hilton 1977, 10–15) and divided even the tiny fraternity of economists. Ricardo's *Essay on the Influence of a Low Price of Corn on the Profits of Stock* (1815) argued for the 'inexpediency of restrictions on importations'. Malthus's *Grounds of an Opinion on the Policy of Restricting the Importation of Foreign Corn* (1815b) which took the opposite view, was the cause of his excommunication by the *Edinburgh Review* (Fontana 1985, 75, 139–40).

Virtually all supposed that nothing could be done by government to reduce unemployment: the secure believed that temporary misfortune must be weathered before natural forces reasserted themselves; the sufferers and their radical leaders put their trust in the magic of parliamentary reform. But there was some awareness that financial policy has what would now be identified as a macro-economic effect. Abolition of the property tax (now known as 'income tax') was forced on the government in 1816 and the budgetary deficit financed by loans from the Bank of England. At least since the report of the Bullion Committee of 1810, moreover, there had been growing awareness that the wartime expedient of an inconvertible paper currency was linked to domestic inflation and external depreciation; and that these effects had serious conse-quences for the economy. Division of opinion, in this case, cut across the lines drawn by the Corn Law controversy. In part it was merely the understandable reluctance of Vansittart and his cabinet colleagues to make drastic changes in their empirical approach to public finance in response to the technical criticisms of monetary theorists like Horner and Ricardo. More fundamentally it reflected a conflict of interest between those whose nominal incomes varied with the general level of prices – not only merchants and manu-facturers, but also the landlords to whom they were opposed on the issue of protection – and those with fixed nominal incomes: fundholders, other creditors and officials (Hilton 1977, 31–66).

The condition of the poor made itself felt by the upper classes, if in no other way, by the cost of maintaining them. The poor-rate rose from £5.4 million in 1815 to £7.9 million in 1818 (Halévy 1949, II, 40), an average annual increase of 13 per cent. Even when allowance is made for price changes as recorded in the Gayer–Rostow–Schwartz index of domestic and imported commodity prices (Mitchell and Deane 1962, 470), the real burden rose by 36 per cent over these years, an average annual increase of 11 per cent. Here too there appeared a conflict of interest, in this case between land-owners, on whom the tax chiefly fell, and the new urban upper class, more able to entertain liberal sentiments.

At a theoretical level, debate was waged between the 'humani-tarians' such as Weyland (1807, 1816) and Whitbread, and the 'natural law opposition' of Malthus and his followers who held that the Poor Law was actually a cause of poverty (Cowherd 1977, chs. 1–3). On this matter, at any rate, economists were agreed. Malthus received the enthusiastic support of the *Edinburgh Review* (March 1817, 28: 1ff.; February 1818, 29: 261ff.), and a tactical alliance of Christian Political Economy and Philosophic Radicalism was sealed by Sumner's article on the Poor Laws in the 1824 *Supplement* to *Encyclopaedia Britannica*.

The leadership of the former tradition was of purely Cambridge origin; that of the latter quite detached from either university. It is not to be supposed, however, that at Oxford there was none to rise to the intellectual challenge presented by post-war economic policy. In Oriel College, at any rate, political controversy had been followed with keen attention at least since the Bullion Committee of 1810, and by no-one more than its formidable Provost, Edward Copleston.

In 1819 Copleston, then aged forty-three, was the most powerful man in Oxford. Ten years before he had engineered the election of Lord Grenville as Chancellor, and a year later single-handedly vanquished the *Edinburgh Review*. In 1814 he was unanimously elected Provost of Oriel, and immediately after made DD by diploma, the highest honour the university could bestow. His two *Letters to the Rt. Hon. Robert Peel, MP for the University of Oxford*, which dealt with the nexus between protection, currency reform and the Poor Law in relation to the principles of Malthus and Sumner, raised Christian Political Economy to a new level of analytical sophistication.

COPLESTON, OXFORD AND POLITICAL ECONOMY

There is no biography of Edward Copleston, who was born in 1776 the son and grandson of West Country clergymen and who died in 1849 as Bishop of Llandaff. Yet by the unanimous consent of his contemporaries he was a man of commanding powers, brilliant achievement and great personal attraction. Decades later men recalled his 'majestic figure... monarch in his day alike of Oriel and of Oxford, dethroner of uncreating Chaos, supreme for twenty years over the new *saeclorum ordo*' (Tuckwell 1909, 17). His voice possessed a 'richness and melody' that 'surpassed any instrument.... It penetrated everybody, entered into the soul' (Mozley 1882, 384). He could add long columns of pounds, shillings and pence at sight with perfect accuracy (206). During his six years stewardship as Bursar he trebled the annual revenues of his college and liquidated all its debts (Tuckwell 1909, 31–2). His personal fortune grew from £21 on 1 January 1800 to more than £20,000 by 1821 (Copleston 1851, 96). He raised his company of Volunteers to a high degree of efficiency in drill and marksmanship, and he walked from Oxford to his parents' home at Offwell, in Devon, the first twenty-two miles in five hours.

Copleston's intellectual prowess was of a piece with these prodigies. Elected Professor of Poetry at the age of twenty-six he attracted the favourable attention of the two Edinburgh Francises, Jeffrey and Horner (Horner 1843, I, 257), and his *Praelectiones* (1813) were much admired by J. H. Newman (*DNB*). Undergraduates would 'limp upstairs on one leg to hear a lecture of Copleston' (Tuckwell 1909, 54). Having undertaken to revive the teaching of logic in Oxford (Checkland 1951, 50) he devastated the pretensions of *Logic Made Easy* by his former rival for the Chair of Poetry, one Henry Kett (Copleston 1809). Whately, a former pupil and lifelong friend, always insisted that his own immensely successful *Logic* owed everything to Copleston (Whately 1875, 49), and declared in 1845 that '...from you I have derived the main principles on which I have acted and speculated through life' (Copleston 1851, 103). When in 1808 and 1809 the *Edinburgh Review* was incautious enough to print a series of articles impugning Oxford education, Copleston set about the three anonymous reviewers with the calculated ferocity of a heavyweight champion punishing the insolence of an upstart contender. The superficiality, bias, defective classical scholarship and plain ignorance of Playfair, Knight and Sidney Smith were exposed without mercy (Copleston 1810). After a further brief exchange the *Edinburgh* retired licking its wounds and all Oxford rejoiced.

Copleston, who was described by Whately (1854, 28) as 'a most decided tory', had used his already considerable prestige to secure the election as Chancellor of Lord Grenville, who by comparison with the other two candidates – Eldon and Beaufort – was almost a reformer, or at any rate a whig. Horner (1843, II, 6) regarded the election as 'a victory both over the Court, and over the worst prejudices of the Church'. From that time he was a frequent guest in 'the refined and intellectual society of Dropmore', and also at such other whiggish-tory, or tory-whig seats as Althorp (Copleston 1851, 20; Tuckwell 1909, 48). Canning, Peel, Baring and Huskisson sought his advice (Copleston 1851, 86, 105). For though a devout and faithful cleric of the pre-Tractarian, high-church tradition, his grasp of affairs was widely recognized and he was very much a public figure: of 'august and commanding presence, with the air and polish suggesting a man of fashion rather than a university don' (Tuckwell 1909, 49).

Beneath this tremendous persona there lurked a darker side. Copleston, who never married, appears to have suffered occasional spells of depression, and his correspondence and diary hint at the loneliness and deprivation of the single state (Copleston 1851, 68, 87, 104, 125). Though the victim generously remembered only 'the kind courteousness which sat so well on him' (Newman 1950, 45), Copleston's brutal correction of the shy, young Newman's table manners is well known (Tuckwell 1909, 46). The streak of cruelty is apparent in his polemic. Kett and the *Edinburgh* reviewers richly deserved the flagellation they received, but there is no mistaking the relish with which Copleston enforced the uttermost stripe. (Even his friends thought that he had gone too far in his treatment of the long-faced Kett – nicknamed the 'Horse' – in printing the tag *equo ne credite, Teucri* on the title-page of his pamphlet.) Withal he possessed an endearing love of modern invention, and a properly donnish absent-mindedness. 'His first experience of the railroad filled him with an astonishment bordering on awe, and the invention of the electric telegraph so stirred him as for some nights to banish sleep' (Tuckwell 1909, 47). A son of Sidney Smith was at Oxford during his last years at Oriel, and a frequent visitor. 'Mr Smith', announced

Copleston with much solemnity, 'next Thursday the college will be
fifty and I shall be five hundred years old' (Mozley 1882, 384; cf.
Copleston 1851, 109).

The college over which Copleston presided as Provost from 1814
until his elevation to the see of Llandaff in 1827 had been pre-
eminent in Oxford since the reforms of his predecessor, Eveleigh, at
the end of the eighteenth century. Having persuaded a reluctant
university to adopt the new examination statutes but not to provide
any fee for the examiners, Oriel volunteered six of its fellows to serve
gratuitously. But the entire fellowship (eighteen in all) was
distinguished by learning and intellect, and by a zealous commitment to free inquiry at any cost. Observers spoke of a 'fine
dialectical cut and thrust of men brought together by intellectual
force rather than by social amenity' (Tuckwell 1909, 19).

> ... its most prominent talkers, preachers and writers seemed to be always
> undermining, if not actually demolishing, received tradition and insti-
> tutions; and whether they were preaching from the University pulpit, or
> arguing in the common room, or issuing pamphlets on passing occasions,
> even faithful and self-reliant men felt the ground shaking under their feet.
> (Mozley 1882, 19)

So competitive was this society that it is said that at least two of its
members, Davison and Whately, 'crammed habitually for post-
prandial talk'. Guests 'whose digestion of the dinner and relish of the
port wine were spoiled by these animated dialectics, went away
complaining that Oriel Common Room *stunk* of logic' (Tuckwell
1909, 59).

In view of the prominence of two of its members in the
development of Christian Political Economy it is pertinent to inquire
what was the state of theological opinion in Oriel at that time, and
what knowledge of, and interest in political economy was evinced by
the fellowship.

It is common knowledge that Oxford in the eighteenth century
was the home of high-church Anglicanism, based on patristic
learning, the Laudian divines and Butler's *Analogy*, flavoured with
Cavalier piety and spiced with a pinch of Jacobite nostalgia. This
pleasing picture is apt to blur under magnification. The 'Register of
books taken out of the library' reveals that there were many years
during the 1770s and 1780s in which the sombre ranks of theological
scholarship slept undisturbed on their shelves in the Oriel College

Senior Library. Yet virtually every resident fellow had borrowed Robertson's *America* within a year or so of its acquisition in 1777. There are clear signs, moreover, of a gradual penetration of Oriel by the new theology of what I have called the 'Cambridge moderates' (see pp. 114–19 above). Paley's *Principles, Evidences* and *Horae Paulinae* were acquired by the library in 1786, 1796 and 1794 respectively, the *Natural Theology* in the year of publication, 1802. Watson's *Theological Tracts* were acquired in 1791 and the first edition of Pretyman's *Elements* in 1799. In the early 1820s E. B. Pusey, then a newly-elected fellow, recommended the purchase of 'Dr Hey's Norrisian lectures' (the 1822 edition was acquired) and 'Bp Watson's collection of Theological tracts', not realizing that the latter had been held by the library since before he was born. Newman records that Hawkins persuaded him to read Sumner's *Apostolical Preaching* – acquired by the library in 1817 – 'from which I was led to give up my remaining Calvinism and accept the doctrine of Baptismal Regeneration' (Newman 1950, 39–40). Sumner's *Records of the Creation* was acquired by 1818 and his *Evidence* in 1824, the year of its publication; Copleston as we have seen (pp. 150–70 above) had mastered the former by the beginning of 1819.

Though Newman (1950, 39–40) credited Hawkins with introducing him to the doctrine of tradition, and Whately with teaching him 'the existence of the church', it is clear that Oriel theology by the 1820s was much closer in spirit to the 'school of Paley' than it was to the ultra-Laudian Tractarian Movement which emerged in the following decade. Mozley (1882, 23) recalled that 'Whately – for Copleston was now content to be represented, not to say personated, by his disciple – regarded High Church and Low Church as equal bigotries', though he had some respect for the former which was at least 'learned and cultivated'. Newman himself was thoroughly acquainted with Gibbon and with Hume's essays: but he kept Paine's works under lock and key, and 'lent them with much caution to such as could bear the shock' (Mozley 1882, 40). The 'broad-church' school later associated with such former Oriel fellows as Arnold, Hampden and Baden Powell had its roots in the Cambridge theology which flourished in their youth.

It would appear from the library records that a similar penetration by Scotch political economy had been going on since the acquisition in 1795 of Dugald Stewart's *Life* of Adam Smith. Other works by Stewart followed between 1801 and 1828; Smith's *Posthumous Essays* were acquired in 1795, *Wealth of Nations* in 1805 and *Theory of Moral Sentiments* in 1812. The register shows that *Wealth of Nations* was first borrowed in October 1806. The *Edinburgh Review* was taken from the outset and scrutinized for each new outrage. Copleston's 'Commonplace book' reveals that he was reading the *Edinburgh* at least since number XII (1806) and he noted 'a long list of Americanisms' in number XXIX. The 'Commonplace book' contains several references to *Wealth of Nations*, mentions of works by Stewart and Reid, and an allusion to 'the principle of population, as explained by Malthus' with an illustration of Malthusian theory from statistics of the London cattle market for 1810.

Copleston was not alone in his attention to political economy. His prize essay on agriculture of 1796, which according to Bonar (1894) 'shows that his attention was early directed towards the topics afterward treated in his "letters to Sir Robert Peel"', is unlikely to have been written in isolation. Henry Beeke (1751–1837), a fellow since 1775, was Professor of Modern History from 1801 to 1813. His *Observations on the Produce of the Income Tax* (1799) incorporated his own estimates of national income and was regarded by M'Culloch as the 'best example of the successful application of statistical reasoning to finance that had then appeared' (*DNB*). He was frequently consulted by Pitt, Vansittart and other ministers. Beeke gave his lectures in Oriel College hall and during their course, Copleston (1810, 154) informed the *Edinburgh* reviewers, 'the doctrines of Political Economy have…been much introduced and discussed'. John Davison (1774–1834), a fellow from 1800 to 1819 and a distinguished Old Testament scholar, addressed his *Considerations on the Poor Laws* (1817) to Henry Sturges-Bourne, Chairman of the parliamentary Select Committee; and later published *Some Points on the Question of the Silk Trade* (1826). Whately's devotion to the new science is well known and will be considered below. That of Thomas Arnold (1795–1842), a fellow from 1815 to 1820 and Regius Professor of History 1840–2 is attested by his biographer (Stanley 1881, I, 174–5, n.). The college library contains two volumes of *Pamphlets on the Bullion Question* (1810–11) by Bosanquet, Vansittart, Canning, Huskisson and others. Each pamphlet is marked 'Oriel College Common Room' on the title page in ink, and there are numerous pencilled sidelinings and marginal comments, some by Copleston and some in other hands. It is improbable that financial and economic matters should have escaped the intellectual furnace in which all other questions, sacred and profane, were then being tried.

In his first *Reply to the Calumnies of the Edinburgh Review* Copleston assigned a chapter to the 'course of studies pursued at Oxford'. On the subject of political economy he deplored the fact that 'the attainment of this science seems almost to have supplanted all the other branches of knowledge requisite for a statesman' (1810, 172). To argue for the 'utility' of such inquiries is to beg the question, for political economy is a means to an end – the increase of 'national wealth' – and 'It is the value of the end, which must determine the value of the means' (165). Other studies, such as religion, ethics and the knowledge of the human condition which is mediated by classical literature are requisite. But political economy is 'prone to usurp over the rest', hence 'the pedant in political economy is not disagreeable only, but dangerous' (174). Nevertheless, 'the science has a tendency, if rightly studied, to enlarge the mind', and though the student should 'lay the foundation ... by exercising his mind in sound logic and in mathematical reasoning', yet its 'leading principles are soon acquired: the ordinary reading of the day supplies them' (172, 175).

It is clear from a passage which occurs in this context that Copleston regarded the 'leading principles' of political economy as supplying what we should now describe as the equilibrium outcomes of market processes. 'But by far the greater part of those who are educated for the active professions have less occasion for contemplating these abstract notions', being chiefly concerned with 'the remedy of evils caused by the *friction of the machine* and by external accident' (174, my italics). Copleston was one of the first to see clearly that in the analytical 'short period' (which in reality may last for years) between one socially optimum equilibrium and another, substantial costs of adjustment must be borne by society, and that these would in all probability be shifted to the poorest and therefore weakest of its members. The violent economic upheavals of the first two decades of the nineteenth century provided a string of 'external accidents' to disturb market equilibrium. Social institutions such as the Poor Law, and the rigidities introduced by more recent legislation suspending sterling convertibility and restricting the grain trade, added to the 'friction of the machine'. Stirred to activity by Sumner's success and no doubt encouraged by the 'refined and intellectual society of Dropmore' at which Francis Horner had been a frequent guest until his death in 1817 (Horner 1843, II, 150, 281), Copleston composed his two *Letters to the Rt. Hon. Robert Peel* upon these matters, the immediate occasion of which was a revival of parliamentary interest in the bullion question early in 1819.

COPLESTON'S LETTERS TO PEEL

The first *Letter* (1819a) analysed the 'Pernicious Effects of a Variable Standard of Value, especially as it regards the Condition of the Lower Orders and the Poor Laws'. The *Second Letter* (1819b) considered the 'Causes of the Increase of Pauperism and... the Poor Laws'. Though the second may have been an afterthought it is clear from the summary of the first with which it begins that the two must be considered as a single argument. Reduced to its bare essentials that argument shows that the Poor Laws themselves have not been the cause of poverty (though ill-administered they may have aggravated or prolonged it); that the chief cause of grievous poverty is inflation; and that the wartime expansion of Britain's inconvertible paper currency was the source of the most recent inflation. The argument is informed throughout by 'that principle of self-correction which the analogy of nature teaches us is the universal law of her constitution' (1819a, 37), and the motto *laissez-nous faire* was inscribed on the title-page of the first *Letter*. However, the *Second Letter* carried a quotation from Burke:

It is one of the first problems in legislation, 'What the State ought to take upon itself to direct by the public wisdom, and what it ought to leave with as little interference as possible to individual discretion'

and the *Eclectic Review* (1819: 1, 422) sarcastically congratulated the author on the progress he had made in political economy between the two publications. But Copleston knew what he was about. 'Pure theory inculcates the natural and necessary tendency towards an equitable adjustment; it leaves the intermediate difficulties and delays out of the question, as frictions in a mechanical problem' (1819a, 35). Thus it is the aim of economic legislation that 'those very frictions and disturbing forces may possibly by care and skill be diminished'.

Most of the first *Letter* is given to monetary theory. It was expedient to resort to inconvertible paper currency during the wars (1819a, 5–7), but Vansittart's reasons for its continuance in peace are both a 'perversion of law' and a 'perversion of reason' (7–8).

Precious metals are most suitable for use as money; their value in terms of other goods (and hence its inverse, the general price level) is determined by demand, which is a function of population and the volume of trade, and supply, which is given by mining (11–13). Paper currency is part of the 'circulating medium' and its great increase at the end of the eighteenth century and during the wars was 'precisely equivalent to the multiplication of the metals' (20) and hence a large cause of the late inflation (17–21). It was this insight, in retrospect, that Copleston regarded as his 'grand discovery in those currency pamphlets' (Copleston 1851, 86).

The evil of inflation arises because the value of money is expected to be constant. In Copleston's day indeed, its constancy was regarded almost as a 'law of nature'. Hence when prices begin to rise expectations are falsified, and redistributions in income and wealth occur which are arbitrary and unjust in that they bear no relation to economic performance (1819a, 13–17, 22–7). It is true that monetary expansion stimulates the economy in the short run, but this is because of what is now called 'money illusion' in the labour market: 'The mere circumstance of a fall in the value of money creates…a demand for labour – and that labour being really underpaid brings unusual profit to the employer' (81). Hence inflation 'deceives men to their own advantage' (24), but the real cost is borne by the labouring class and others whose incomes are fixed, at least for some time, in nominal terms and who lack the bargaining power to re-contract. Copleston, who had supported Lord Harrowby's Curates' Bill of 1812 (Copleston 1851, 46), used the case of the assistant curate to illustrate inequality of bargaining power: 'the superior may be petitioned but he cannot be threatened into equity. The competition of the market offers no resource here' (1819a, 38). The poorest classes, having the least bargaining power, are the 'last to obtain redress' during inflation (33). Periods of rapid inflation in England have thus been associated with the depression of real wages below the current socially-determined subsistence wage. 'It is the intimate connexion of this fact with the much agitated question of the Poor Laws, that gives it a commanding claim on the attention of the legislature' (33).

It is of course possible, in terms of Copleston's own argument, that a steady rate of price inflation might eventually create the expectation of its permanence in the minds of all transactors, in which case all contracts might fully anticipate its effects and thus avoid the unrequited redistributions justly complained of. Apart from the fact that Copleston, like all his contemporaries, did not believe that the public would ever relinquish its expectation of price stability (22–4), he declined to consider this possibility for two reasons, one empirical, the other theoretical. In the first place, inflation may and does occur 'naturally' as the result of new gold discoveries which are unpredictable (13–14, 37), hence the rate of inflation is unlikely to remain constant. Secondly, it is the nature of an inflation which is primarily 'artificial' (that is, the result of an expansion of inconvertible paper currency), to accelerate. Copleston quoted a speech of Canning to this effect published in one of those *Pamphlets on the Bullion Question* that he and his colleagues had read and annotated eight years before. 'Every day new contracts must necessarily be made; and every day successively (as it is of the essence of depreciation to go on increasing in degree) at rates diverging more and more widely from the real standard from which we have departed' (77). 'Depreciation' referred to the gold value of the paper currency, and its rate was taken to be more or less equivalent to the 'artificial' component of the rate of inflation.

Two important conclusions follow from this line of reasoning. In the first place, the possibility of 'artificial' inflation must be removed by restoring 'cash payments', that is, by making banknotes freely convertible into gold or bullion upon demand. In the second place, the Poor Laws may not be regarded as the *cause* of poverty, but as an inefficacious *remedy*. The ultra-Malthusian demand for repeal ought therefore to be resisted, and attention concentrated upon reform. Copleston devoted the remainder of the first *Letter* to a detailed examination of the mechanism of monetary creation, inflation and foreign exchange rates as a preliminary to his demand for the restoration of convertibility. The *Second Letter* begins with a summary of the first which leads to a recommendation that no change be made in the Poor Laws until convertibility has been restored and the consequent deflation runs its course (1819a, 13–15). The Corn Bill of 1815 is to be seen in this light as a '*set-off* against the advantage enjoyed by the commercial interest'. But both it and (inconvertible) paper currency are an 'unnatural state of things' and must gradually be removed (9–10). Copleston then turned, for the remainder of the *Second Letter*, to the causes of and remedies for poverty.

When 'poverty' is understood as the condition of those at the margin of subsistence, its cause is evidently the Malthusian principle of population. But Malthus himself explicitly recognized that the conception of a 'subsistence' standard of living is conventional and culturally determined. A large gap may exist in a civilized and prosperous society between the *socially-determined* subsistence wage and the *biological* subsistence requirement which would obtain in the absence of the preventive check. Hence wages may fall below the socially-determined subsistence level and so exacerbate poverty for reasons which have nothing to do with population pressures. Only if low wages persist for long enough for the socially-determined subsistence wage to be brought down to the market level would the explanation of poverty again be purely Malthusian.

This essential analytical point was clearly grasped by Copleston in the *Second Letter*, more clearly indeed than it was by Malthus himself. Whilst deferring to Malthus – whose *Essay* was 'an original well-head of political truth' (15) – and his 'able and ingenious expositor' Sumner, Copleston showed that poverty *of the kind the Poor Laws were intended to remedy* could not be, and was not in fact, caused by the Poor Laws themselves. Here too his argument had both a theoretical and an empirical component.

If the entire working class were fully employed at Malthusian equilibrium there would be no need of legislation, for each family would receive an income sufficient for its freely-chosen size and standard of living. Relief in such a case would be needed only for those incapacitated from joining the work-force, who might be supported by their own families assisted by private charity. Systematic public relief would be called for only if the able-bodied poor were unable to earn the current socially-determined subsistence wage. This could occur either because of involuntary unemployment or because of the erosion of real incomes by unanticipated inflation. Though Copleston did not ignore the possibility of the former (1819b, 36–9), he concentrated on the latter. The greater part of the *Second Letter* is given over to a review of the English Poor Law since Elizabethan times. The increase of poverty in the early sixteenth century 'cannot be attributed...to the Poor Laws themselves' because those laws did not then exist (46). It arose instead from 'the depreciation of money' (47). The Elizabethan Poor Law was enacted as a remedy. Since that time, Copleston demonstrated from such statistical evidence as then existed, public attention has been drawn to the problem of poverty and the Poor Laws during and after periods of severe inflation (47–63, 69–73, 83–8).

'If the alarming pressure of the Poor Rate arises...not from the principle of the laws themselves, but from temporary causes' such as inflation, it follows that 'All plans for a gradual abolition of the laws, besides the objections, insurmountable as they seem to me, which have been urged against them, must under this view of the subject be regarded as needless' (91). The Poor Laws should be reformed, not repealed. The Malthusian concept of a socially-determined subsistence wage implies that 'it may be possible to provide by law for *preserving* life, without encouraging the *propagation* of it' (28). It is essential to attempt this, for 'unless we do undertake in every case to support life, vagrancy and mendicity cannot be punished' (94). The level at which life may be *preserved* without *propagation*, moreover, is itself a function of the socially-determined subsistence wage. If by parish schools and the like , 'a spirit of industry and self-respect, of moral decency' (103) is fostered in the poor, then 'in proportion to the moral improvement of society, in proportion to the prevalence of a taste for the comforts and decencies of life among the lower orders...in the same proportion might the rate of allowance be safely raised' (29). In taking his leave of these investigations the (moderately) tory Copleston expressed his 'satisfaction at finding that no violent remedy seems to be called for, but the chief benefit will arise from knowing our constitution more accurately, and from discovering the true seat of the disorder' (110).

Malthus, ever sensitive to the criticisms of others and genuinely appreciative of their improvements, deferred to Copleston in his (anonymous) review of Godwin's *Population* (*ER* 1821, 362–77) by abandoning, at last, his insistence on repeal of the Poor Laws.

...even should the legislature determine...to make no essential alteration in them; yet if, instead of asserting that the poor have a mortgage *to an indefinite extent* on the land, and a full claim of right to support, the poor rates were called a compulsory charity, limited by the necessity of the case, and the discretion and resources of society...the present evils arising from them might not only be prevented from increasing, but might be gradually diminished. (*ER* 1821, 377, my italics)

Copleston's two *Letters* to Peel represent a considerable advance for Christian Political Economy. Important improvements were made in economic analysis. And further refinements and correction were introduced into the theological framework constructed by Paley and Sumner.

Copleston was not an original thinker. His economic analysis was indeed learned from 'the ordinary reading of the day': Horner's digest of Thornton (1802) in the *Edinburgh* (Fontana 1985, 57-9), Ricardo's pamphlets of 1810, 1811 and 1815, Canning's speeches, the economic publications of his Oriel colleagues Beeke and Davison, and of course Malthus on population. Even his most interesting theoretical contribution, the discussion of monetary disequilibrium and the cost of adjustment had its immediate origin in Hume's essay 'Of Money'. But he was gifted with one of the most powerful minds of his generation and what he grasped, which was a great deal, he held with a lucidity and penetration exceeding anything achieved by the more truly original Malthus or Thornton.

The most important of Copleston's analytical contributions to Christian Political Economy was his account of disequilibrium. Dugald Stewart, it will be recalled, had criticized Malthus for laying 'too little stress on the efficacy of those arrangements which nature herself has established for the remedy of the evils in question' (see p. 114 above). Though Stewart alluded here to the evil of population pressures, the point is more general. The Smithian conception of a beneficently self-regulating economy is part of the Lakatosian 'hard core' of that 'scientific research programme' which Stewart and his disciples of the *Edinburgh Review* sought to recommend. Malthus and Paley were unable fully to incorporate this idea into the system, the former because of his un-Ricardian concern for 'the economy in which we happen to live' (Keynes 1972, 97), and Sumner made no attempt to do so. Copleston faced the challenge head-on, and in looking back to Hume formulated the analysis later made famous by Keynes. Of course 'the analogy of nature teaches us' that the 'principle of self-correction' is the 'universal law of her constitution' (Copleston 1819a, 37). However, 'self-correction' takes time and only occurs, if at all, in the long run. But as Keynes wrote in a famous passage, 'this *long run* is a misleading guide to current affairs... Economists set themselves too easy, too useless a task if in tempestuous seasons they can only tell us that when the storm is long past the ocean is flat again' (Keynes 1971, 65). Copleston too wrote in a 'tempestuous season'. Ricardo's account of the immediate adjustment to equilibrium, he surmised, 'was not perhaps intended to be taken literally' (Copleston 1819a, 25). Copleston's few paragraphs on monetary disequilibrium in the first *Letter* subsume the analytical apparatus of Keynes's *Tract on Monetary Reform*. His treatment of 'money illusion' in the labour market foreshadows academic discussion of the *General Theory* after the Second World War (e.g. Patinkin 1956, 23–4, 197–200). Yet at no point did he lose sight of the fact that disequilibrium phenomena can only be analysed within a conceptual framework of stable equilibrium. 'All payments, sooner or later, find their proper level' (Copleston 1819a, 24), for 'Profit is in mercantile dealings, what *gravitation* is in the system of the universe: and no problem is worth listening to, which supposes the absence of that universal principle' (61–2).

Aside from his insight into the central concept of equilibrium Copleston had a more complete mastery of Malthusian population theory than Malthus himself and an apparent familiarity which such technical matters as arbitrage (1819a, 12), the demand for money (13), velocity of circulation (18), the cash reserve ratio (19), market power (28), functional income distribution (36), the balance of payments (46) and foreign exchange rates (50–1). He implicitly challenged Adam Smith's notion of a 'propensity to truck and barter', correctly pointing out that many prefer to rely upon custom or bargains once made (26–7). In only two respects was Copleston's analysis short of the very highest standard. His neglect of Hume's 'specie-flow' mechanism of international price adjustment rendered the account of domestic price movements less than fully convincing, rescued only by the *ad hoc* assumption of falling world prices in a post-war recession (1819b, 10). And his explanation of the potential consequences of deflation (1819b, 7–8, 35–6) is seemingly self-contradictory. In the first of these at any rate he was at one with all other participants in the 'bullion' debate.

The theological aspects of Copleston's two *Letters*, though occupying far less space than the economic analysis, are at least as important. The doctrine of human life as a state of discipline and trial is again affirmed (1819b, 17). The essentially theological conception of 'moral restraint' is acknowledged (103). More significant is the reintroduction of natural law and a further move, along the lines of Sumner's, to display the Malthusian results as a specimen of Paleyesque teleology.

It will be recalled that Paley had argued that the poor have a claim to relief 'founded in the law of nature' (see p. 121 above; Horne 1985). This Malthus appeared to deny on the grounds that there can be no 'right' to that which may be unobtainable. Sumner avoided the question. Copleston clarified it by distinguishing clearly

between the 'right to self-preservation' which is what Paley had
meant, and which is defensible; and the right to a particular level of
support, which is what Malthus had meant, and which is not. The
'natural law of *self-preservation*... is universally allowed to supersede
the positive restraint of other laws' and may even 'render a violation
of property excusable' (1819b, 32). Hence 'if we deny to any human
being the means of support ourselves, we have no right to deny him
the chance he may have of finding it elsewhere' (94). This venerable
maxim of Christian social thought must be affirmed if 'Political
Economy' were to be 'Christian'. But on the other hand 'the absurd
notion... of a *right* to a full supply of wheaten bread must be steadily
denied or disregarded' for 'in the case of scarcity, nature dictates
that the allowance should be shortened in proportion to the
exigency' (97). Moreover, the poor can possess no 'positive rights
and interests in their corporate capacity' for they are 'merely the
aggregate' of a continually changing set of individuals who have –
in many cases temporarily – lost the power of supporting themselves.
In effect Copleston denied the seeming implication of Malthus's
argument that an actual person now living, but without the means
of subsistence, might have no right to live; but upheld the genuinely
Malthusian doctrine, first, that the level of support must of necessity
be constrained by the actual supply of food, and, secondly, that even
in the absence of this constraint support should not be set so high as
to encourage population and so aggravate the problem.

As far as possible, Copleston argued, relief of the poor should be
undertaken by private charity. *For their own good* the rich ought to
give up some of their income to the poor. (When he became a bishop,
Copleston spent every penny of his income from the episcopate upon
charities within his diocese.) But 'an action to be virtuous must be
voluntary': hence legislation cannot compel virtue, it can only
punish vice and 'prohibit injustice' (18–19). Not only 'common
sense' but the 'divine purpose and declared end of our being' forbid
the idea that we can be 'charitable by proxy' (19). Laws therefore
have little direct effect upon human happiness or goodness. 'Active
virtue, generosity, benevolence, forgiveness, hospitality, piety, all
that constitutes the charm, the beauty, the dignity of life – all that
can develope the best part of a man's nature, or that can hope to be
acceptable in the light of his Maker, must be derived from another
source' (21). Here Copleston made a Sumner-like move. 'What is
thus proved to be true theoretically, and by a kind of *a priori*

argument, Mr Malthus has shown to be deducible from the actual constitution of things. And in this lies the great merit and the everlasting value of his work' (22). We ought to suppose that the universe is so constructed that 'all truths would be harmonious and consistent'. It should be possible to see the divine wisdom and goodness wherever we look.

It is the high distinction of the Essay on Population to have demonstrated, that such is the fact – that all endeavours to embody benevolence into law, and thus impiously as it were to effect by human laws what the Author of the system of nature has not effected by his laws, must be abortive – that this ignorant struggle against evil really enlarges instead of contracting the kingdom of evil. (22)

As Sumner had shown that inequality, being beneficent and designed by God, is actually brought about by the principle of population, so Copleston argued that the principle of population ensured that men and women could only do good to one another by those free, unlegislated initiatives intended by God as a means of human fulfilment. Malthusian political economy was fitted even more comfortably into the teleological framework of Paley's *Natural Theology*.

After publishing his two *Letters* Copleston was much in demand by the ministry as an economic adviser. Whately (1854, 27) judged that the 'work on the Currency … attracted much attention and probably exercised no small influence on the public mind'. Ricardo thought so highly of the *Second Letter* that he made a detailed paragraph-by-paragraph summary (Hollander 1932, 135–45). Other than his 'Dissertation upon the State of the Currency' (1822), however, which appeared in the *Quarterly Review* and was published separately by John Murray in 1830, Copleston wrote no more on political economy. In 1821 he brought out his learned and subtle *Inquiry into the Doctrines of Necessity and Predestination* regarded by the *British Review* as the best work since Butler on the 'correspondence of natural and revealed religion' (Copleston 1851, 88–9). And in December 1827 he quitted his much loved college to become Bishop of Llandaff. For the next twenty-two years he laboured devotedly in his diocese, repairing the neglect and reforming the abuses of centuries. He died in October 1849 at the age of seventy-three, and was buried in the ruins of his yet unrestored cathedral.

In relation to Christian Political Economy, Copleston's two *Letters* to Peel represent as near an approximation to what Lakatos called a 'progressive problem-shift' as may be found in any discipline so vague and unscientific as social theory. In order that an intellectual development may count as 'growth of knowledge', it will be recalled (Lakatos and Musgrave 1970, 118, *passim*), the replacement of one 'theory' by another must be *progressive* rather than *degenerating*. For this is to be the case two criteria must be satisfied. The new theory must have 'excess empirical content over its predecessor', that is, it must 'predict some novel...fact'. And some of the excess empirical content must be corroborated: there must be 'the actual discovery of some *new fact*'. It would seem that in the case of a heterogeneous discipline such as Christian Political Economy these criteria ought to be applied both to the *positive* and to the *normative* components of the programme. The 'problem-shift' must be progressive in at least one of these components and ought not to be degenerating in the other.

So far as the positive (political economy) component is concerned, Copleston's contribution appears to have been progressive.

Disequilibrium monetary dynamics within the institutional framework postulated by Copleston predicts that periodic inflation will inflict distress upon the poor by depressing their incomes below the socially-determined subsistence wage. These predictions Copleston corroborated with such empirical data as were then available. Malthusian population dynamics are not replaced but subsumed. All genuine facts predicted by the principle of population are left undisturbed. But the evident 'anomaly' (that is, that there existed poverty before the Poor Laws) is corrected by the newer theory.

In the case of the normative (theological) component something analogous seems to have been achieved. Copleston's amended account of Malthusian population theory is consistent with the right of the poor to self-preservation and with the Christian duty of private charity, both of which crude Malthusian theory had called in question. Yet the genuine theological insights of Malthusian theory – moral restraint is compatible with divine goodness and wisdom; legislated benevolence is futile and harmful – are affirmed in such a way as to reinforce Sumner's assimilation of the principle of population to Paley's teleological scheme.

In terms of their intellectual achievement, Copleston's two *Letters* to Peel measure the high-water mark of Christian Political Economy.

POLITICAL ECONOMY AND IDEOLOGY IN THE 1820s

Though a small rift had appeared in 1815, it is broadly true to say that when Copleston wrote in 1819 political economy still united all who studied it. Bentham, then aged 71, Ricardo (47), James Mill (46) and M'Culloch (30) were joined by many ties of mutual respect, friendship and common purpose with such as Malthus (53), Copleston (43), Sumner (39), Chalmers (30) and Whately (32); as all had been with Horner and with Thornton before the latters' deaths a few years previously. Within a decade this unity was to disappear. Though all British economists continued to adhere to the same scientific method – of a different nature, it was supposed, from that of the 'foreign school' (*ER* October 1837, 77) – they were increasingly divided by ideology. The crisis over political reform in the years 1817 to 1819 produced somewhat the same effect upon economists as the subscription controversy had upon Cambridge theologians forty years before (see pp. 114–19 above). Men felt themselves forced to take sides. By the end of the 1820s both 'Philosophic Radicalism' and 'Christian Political Economy' had emerged as recognizable and in some ways sharply opposed schools of thought. The task of defining the latter fell to Richard Whately.

Before examining Whately's contribution in detail, it is necessary to review the various elements which composed the ideological conjuncture in Britain of the 1820s. The most important of these may without risk of gross misunderstanding be labelled as (1) 'orthodox' Christianity; (2) 'liberal' or critical theology; (3) 'romanticism'; (4) 'whiggism'; (5) political 'radicalism', and (6) 'political economy'. The categories described by these labels were not in every case mutually exclusive. Thus religious orthodoxy for example might co-exist with romanticism, or even with whiggism. Much political theorizing of the 1820s lay in deciding just which of these categories were compatible and which were not.

'*Orthodox*' *Christianity* was understood in that time and place to be trinitarian protestantism, chiefly but not exclusively associated with the high-church party in the established church and with the evangelical movement, both Methodist and Anglican. There was a high correlation between theological and political orthodoxy, and J. C. D. Clark (1985, 235ff.) has lately argued that the evangelicals 'inherited almost intact the political theology of mainstream Anglicanism'. In essence, this was the belief that 'in a Christian

commonwealth the Church and State are one and the same thing'
(Burke 1792, cit. Clark 1985, 250). Underlying Burke's seemingly
facile identity is a long tradition of anti-puritan (and anti-
republican) discourse which has its origins in Richard Hooker's
careful analysis of the concepts of 'church' and 'commonwealth' at
the beginning of book VIII of *Ecclesiastical Polity*. Whatever might
have been the case elsewhere and at other times, 'within this realm
of England...one society is both the Church and commonwealth'
(Hooker 1888, III, 340). The theory appeared to entail, on a strict
construal, the doctrine of passive obedience and the permanent
exclusion of papists and Dissenters from public life. In practice these
doctrines were held by orthodox churchmen and Methodists with
greatly varying degrees of rigour, and there were some who sought
to defend theological orthodoxy whilst tolerating or even welcoming
political reform.

What I mean by *'liberal'* or *critical theology* is the Newtonian
reliance upon the 'meer light of reason' both to make independent
discoveries about God from the Book of Nature, and to evaluate the
evidence of divine revelation supposed to be contained in scripture.
Liberal theology was closely associated with, and to some extent a
predictable consequence of, the Cambridge Tripos. It is commonplace that Cambridge theology in the eighteenth century
frequently led to deism or Socinianism, or even to complete
infidelity. It is less generally realized that there was intellectually
defensible middle ground between Hume and Godwin on the one
hand and 'two-bottle orthodoxy' on the other. I have argued in
chapter 4 and elsewhere (see pp. 114–19 above, and Waterman
1991a) that from about 1776 the Cambridge 'moderates' attempted
with considerable success to retain the *methods* of liberal theology in
defence of, or at least without damage to, the beliefs of orthodoxy. In
so doing, they achieved for themselves a measure of intellectual and
political liberty without deserting the Establishment, and they
strengthened the latter by meeting its adversaries on their own
ground. It is an essential part of the argument of this chapter, indeed
of my entire book, that the intersection of orthodox Christianity with
liberal theology provided the mental space within which Copleston
and Whately could guarantee the acceptability of political economy
to their fellow churchmen. This is not to say that it was either
logically or psychologically impossible for an orthodox Christian
innocent of Cambridge theology to accept political economy. It is

rather that a naturalistic teleology, which was the hallmark of the former, served as a perfect instrument for the incorporation of the latter. But that instrument could only be used for the purpose if its compatibility with orthodoxy had first been proved.

'*Romanticism*' is generally used in an English context to describe whatever common vision it was which at some time or other united authors so diverse as Wordsworth, Scott, Coleridge and Southey on the one hand, and Byron, Shelley, Blake and Hazlitt on the other. An important ingredient of that common vision, it was suggested in chapter 3, is the Rousseauvian belief that 'social evil' is moral and not natural. Inequality and other forms of injustice ought never to be accepted as inevitable. Somehow or other those constraints upon human fulfilment which seem to be set by physical limitation and even by human nature itself must be transcended. For in England as in Germany, romanticism was a 'revolt against the finite' (Lovejoy 1941, 263–4). In 1789 all English romantics were Jacobins. Within a decade most had defected to some variety of political and theological conservatism. Yet the old instinct remained. Abhorrence of Malthus in particular and of political economy in general was a common element in romantic thought (Kinnaird 1978, 114–28). Southey's review of Malthus (*AR* 1803, 292–301), said to have been inspired by Coleridge, is typical. Wordsworth attacked economists in his second 'Address to the Freeholders of Westmorland' of 1818 (1974, III, 162–89); and in one of the 'Ecclesiastical Sonnets' written in 1820 and published in 1822 (Wordsworth 1950, 354–5) gave classic utterance to the romantic refusal to compromise with scarcity:

> Tax not the royal Saint with vain expense,
> With ill-matched aims the Architect who planned –
> Albeit labouring for a scanty band
> Of white-robed Scholars only – this immense
> And glorious Work of fine intelligence!
> Give all thou canst; high Heaven rejects the lore
> Of nicely calculated less or more:
> So deemed the man who fashioned for the sense
> These lofty pillars...

By contrast with romanticism, '*whiggism*' was regarded by its adherents as fully compatible with political economy. This was especially the case after the absorption by the Holland House circle of Francis Horner and Henry Brougham (Fontana 1985, 112–46; Sanders 1908, 255–71). 'With them came the full force of the Scottish Enlightenment which, they believed, could substantiate

Whig ideas on an almost scientific basis' (Mitchell 1980, 37). The *Edinburgh Review* gave coherence and publicity to the cause of reform from its inception in 1802. Moreover, though the Hollands and many another whig grandee were indifferent or hostile to religion, and though much the same has lately been claimed of the *Edinburgh* reviewers (Fontana 1985, 87), there was no necessary incompatibility between whiggism and Christianity. Even Lord Holland believed that 'there was a natural affinity between Whig politics and Dissenting religion' (Mitchell 1980, 108); and whereas Sydney Smith's attachment to orthodoxy might well be questioned there is no reason to believe that every whig clergyman of those days was a secret Socinian or deist. There is little doubt, on the other hand, that whiggism and romanticism were fundamentally opposed. The *Edinburgh*'s hostility to the Lake Poets (Mitchell 1980, 190–3; Fontana 1985, 176–8) was inevitable.

The word '*radical*' was first used in a substantive sense in 1819, though it had been used adjectivally since 1798 (Halévy 1952, 261) to describe those who sought 'radical reform' of British institutions as contrasted with 'moderate reform' desired by most whigs. Between those dates an alliance generally subsisted between all reformers, whether whig, romantic, scientific or demagogic. By the early 1820s this had disintegrated. The whigs, and most romantics who had not already been cured of Jacobinism in the 1790s, were alienated by the violence of popular protest in 1817 and after. And in the decade between 1808 and 1818, as Halévy (1952, 249–64) has shown, the 'philanthropy of Bentham inspired by Helvetius' became clearly separated from 'the christian philanthropy of Wilberforce'. But though Bentham also severed his connexion with the Holland House whigs and became a radical by 1820, he and his friends quickly dissociated themselves from the plebeian radicalism of Cobbett and Hunt. Under the influence of James Mill and Francis Place Bentham was turned into the leader and chief theoretician of a new force in British politics, later to be known by the name invented in 1837 by John Stuart Mill: 'Philosophic Radicalism' (Thomas 1979, 2, 32–42; Halévy 1952, 260ff.). In 1824 a new periodical, the *Westminster Review*, was founded to represent the doctrines of the radicals as against those of the whig *Edinburgh* and the tory *Quarterly* (founded in 1810). Philosophic Radicalism was a highly-seasoned mixture, repulsive to all save its devotees, of Benthamite (as distinct from Paleyesque) utilitarianism, Ricardian economics and James Mill's puritanical hatred of the arts (Thomas

1979, 100–5), with a strongly anti-clerical, even anti-religious bias. It was this last, as we shall see, that made it essential in the later 1820s for Whately to defend political economy from the charge that it was hostile to Christianity.

'*Political economy*' was generally supposed to be both a recent and a British discovery. George Pryme, who lectured at Cambridge from 1816 and was made first Professor of Political Economy in 1828, declared in his *Introductory Lecture* (1823) that 'Little more than half a century has passed since Political Economy has attained any degree of security'. For in 1776 Adam Smith published his *Wealth of Nations*: 'Political Economy may be said before that time to have had no existence'. Dugald Stewart had been more circumspect, acknowledging that the French 'Economists' had played a key role in the formulation of 'this new science' (Fontana 1985, 100). His disciples were less scrupulous. Francis Horner was 'reluctant to expose Smith's errors before his work has operated its full effect. We owe much at present [1803] to the superstitious worship of Smith's name' (1843, I, 229). The work of Quesnay and Turgot was little read by the educated public, and that of Beccaria, not to mention Bodin, Botero and Cantillon, almost completely unknown. But from the end of the French wars interest in political economy grew rapidly in Britain. The stimulus of the bullion controversy has already been noted. In 1815 Malthus, Ricardo, Torrens and West each formulated independently the classical theory of rent. Ricardo's *Principles of Political Economy* appeared in 1817 and Malthus's in 1820. The Political Economy Club was founded in 1821; the Drummond chair at Oxford, with Senior as first incumbent, in 1825. University College, London was established in the following year and shortly thereafter M'Culloch, whose *Principles* were published in 1825, became its first Professor of Political Economy. The 1824 *Supplement* to the *Encyclopaedia Britannica* contained articles on political economy by Malthus, Ricardo, James Mill, M'Culloch, Sumner and other leading authorities. Barry Gordon (1976, 1979) has fully documented the increasing attention paid by Parliament to economists and political economy from 1819.

The various and complex relations between these six strands of ideological tradition in Britain of the 1820s may be illustrated graphically. Figure 5 is a Venn diagram in which orthodoxy (1), liberal theology (2), romanticism (3) and political economy (6) are represented as solid rectangles, intersecting or not as discussed above. Whiggism (4) is the dotted rectangle superimposed upon

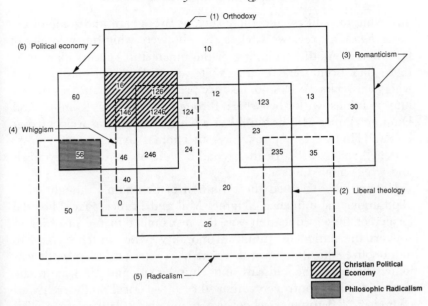

Fig. 5. An ideological map of the 1820s.

parts of 1, 2 and 6. What is to be understood as *toryism* in the 1820s
is thus implicitly defined as *all the orthodox who are not whig*: a
heterogeneous and incompatible assortment of romantics, political
economists, liberal Anglicans, evangelicals and 'high-and-dry'
churchmen, represented by the union of classes 10, 12, 123, 126, 13
and 16. Radicalism (5) is illustrated by the irregular dotted area
comprising classes 235, 25, 35, 50 and 56. Like toryism it was
fundamentally divided at this period because of the inclusion within
its ranks of members drawn from the mutually exclusive classes of
political economy and romanticism. Whiggism, by repelling most of
the romantics, was to that extent ideologically more coherent.
Unlike toryism however, it comprised a potentially divisive alliance
of orthodox churchmen (classes 124, 1246 and 146), heterodox
Christians (classes 24 and 246), and infidels (classes 40 and
46).

It is possible to see by aid of the diagram how economists and
those who believed in political economy came to be ideologically
divided in the 1820s. There were always some, such as Ricardo (class
60), who were neither orthodox nor liberal in religion and neither
whig nor radical in politics. There had been those such as Adam
Smith and Dugald Stewart (class 246) who were liberal in religion

and whig in politics, and those such as Brougham and some of the other *Edinburgh* reviewers (class 46) who were whig but virtually of no religion. At the beginning of the nineteenth century, however, there had been some overlap between radicalism (class 5) and whiggism (class 4). Despite his tory prejudices Bentham was drawn into relations with the whigs through his friends Romilly and Dumont. James Mill began life as a whig. Burdett was welcomed at Holland House (Halévy 1952, 254–6; Thomas 1979, 21, 44–5, 56–7; Mitchell 1980, 26–8). In the second decade of the century radicals and whigs moved apart.

Halévy has described the evolution of Bentham's thought after 1808 under the influence of James Mill and Francis Place. For the former of these 'education was the instrument to use in order to convert the nation to utilitarian morality'; the church's claim to monopolize education must therefore be resisted; by 1813 battle was joined between the radicals and churchmen, and 'it was in the course of this controversy that the anti-clerical and irreligious character of Bentham's school was manifested' (Halévy 1952, 282, 291, *passim*). *Church-of-Englandism* (1818) attacked the catechism and the creed; *Analysis of the Influence of Natural Religion* (1822) showed that the latter 'invariably leads its votaries to ascribe to their Deity a character of caprice and tyranny'; *Not Paul, but Jesus* (1823) demonstrated that the apostle was an imposter and the true Anti-Christ. The worst effect of religion, Bentham taught, was the creation of a clerical class whose interest 'is irreconcilably at variance with that of society' (Halévy 1952, 291–4). The support given by Bentham, Mill and Grote to the atheist publishers, Hone and Carlile, confirmed the radicals in their anti-religious attitude.

Now it was at just about this time that James Mill largely succeeded in annexing political economy to the radical cause. He had published pamphlets in defence of free trade in 1804 and 1808 and Bentham's own *Manual of Political Economy* had been written as early as 1795 (1952–4, I, 219–74). Mill introduced Ricardo to Bentham in 1811, and in the (somewhat overstated) view of Halévy (1952, 266) 'All the actions in Ricardo's life, after 1811, were willed by James Mill'. Mill's *Elements of Political Economy* was published in 1821. The Ricardian method of analysis was congenial to the abstract, *a priori* bent of radical political theory; and the 'Ricardian vice' – the formulation of policy recommendations upon the basis of simple, deductive models (Schumpeter 1954, 473) – was its chief intellectual characteristic. By 1826 a biassed but perceptive observer could feel that it was precisely this assimilation of political economy by 'The New School of Reform' which had destroyed the unity of the progressive movement.

The obvious...effect of the Westminster tactics is to put every volunteer *hors de combat*, who is not a zealot of the strictest sect of those they call Political Economists...to strip the cause of Reform...of everything like a *mésalliance* with elegance, taste, decency, common sense, or polite literature...to leave nothing intermediate between the Ultra-Toryism of the courtly scribes and their own Ultra-Radicalism. (Hazlitt 1928, 183)

By the mid-1820s, therefore, political economy was coming to be seen by many as uniquely associated with *Westminster* radicalism: and *Westminster* radicalism as characteristically anti-clerical, even godless. Political economy became tainted by association. As Godwin's *Political Justice* had largely neutralized the immediate ideological effect of Burke's *Reflections*, so thirty years later the hijacking of political economy by the Philosophic Radicals eclipsed for the time being the efforts of Sumner and Copleston to reconcile the new science with orthodoxy.

From the romantic radicals' point of view the result was indeed, as Hazlitt complained, 'to leave nothing intermediate' between the *Quarterly* and the *Westminster*. For Hazlitt and his friends (classes 235 and 35) were absolutely separated by their loathing of political economy from the Philosophic Radicals (class 56). And the whiggism of the *Edinburgh* (classes 1246, 146, 246 and 46) – which in any case held no charm for them – must now be regarded as a weaker, less cogent version of the New School of Reform. Yet there was no reason in general why an intellectually satisfactory middle way should not be sought, for despite the pretensions of the New School, the science of political economy had in fact been regarded by many of the (more or less) orthodox for more than twenty years as wholly compatible with Christian belief. What was needed was a methodology of political economy which demonstrated that its epistemic claims were not, and could not be, at variance with those of theology. It was this that Whately supplied: indirectly, through his sponsorship and encouragement of his former pupil, Nassau Senior, in the Drummond chair; and directly by his own literary contributions. His achievement defined an intersection of orthodoxy and political economy which could unite politically liberal but theologically orthodox tories such as Canning, Peel and the Claphamites (class 16), and theologically liberal-but-orthodox tories such as Sumner and Copleston (class 126), with orthodox whigs if any (class 146) and liberal-but-orthodox whigs such as Malthus and Whately himself (class 1246). The resulting coalition, which excluded only radicals and romantics, recaptured political economy for the orthodox and remained ideologically dominant, or at any rate influential, for most of the nineteenth century.

WHATELY ON THE RELATION BETWEEN POLITICAL ECONOMY AND CHRISTIAN THEOLOGY

He was not profound or very learned. He was not original or even brilliant. But his clear and strong intellect grasped calmly and firmly whatever it did grasp within an unusually wide range of interests. And in his age, country, and world, he was a leader of the formative type, an ideal illustration of what it means to be a key man. (Schumpeter 1954, 483–4)

Schumpeter's appraisal of Richard Whately (1787–1863) was based on the latter's contributions to ecclesiastical affairs and 'the *Sozialpolitik* of his age', to logic, theology and political economy. In the last, however, his 'most important service…was that he formed Senior, whose whole approach betrays Whately's influence'. The judgement would have been true *a fortiori* had it referred to Whately's part in the development of Christian Political Economy.

In some measure this was an accident of time and place. Notwithstanding the examples of Tatham, Copleston, Beeke, Davison and West (Checkland 1951, 44–5), Oxford had yet to set its seal of approval upon political economy in the mid-1820s. Traditionally reluctant to degrade education by being useful (Checkland, 53), it was the less inclined to do so because of the alarming antics of the *Westminster*. Moreover, as Barry Gordon (1979, 43–5 and *passim*) has shown, the financial crisis of December 1825 inflicted serious damage upon the prestige of Ricardo in particular and of political economy in general. Whately was ideally placed to convert the university. For though Copleston did not quit Oxford until 1827, he had resigned intellectual leadership to his former pupil some years before; and from 1825 when he became Principal of Alban Hall until his own departure in 1831, Whately ruled the roost, fertile in expedients for preserving religious and social order yet terrorizing all who fell back on a mindless affection to the past (Mozley 1882, 23,18; Corsi 1980, 114–16).

Whately's willingness to entertain new ideas has been described as 'a sophisticated form of political opportunism of a basically conservative kind'. Wherefore 'His intellectual vigour was consciously directed to counteracting new social and intellectual ferments forcefully emerging at the surface of British society' (Corsi 1980, 127). Though this may have been true at times during the 1820s and even later, it would be reductionist to suppose that Whateley's 'intellectual vigour' was merely a response to current political provocation. For though like Copleston he exhibited 'a constitutional tendency to indolence' (Corsi 1980, 114; Whately 1866, I, 13) his substantial literary output from 1819 to 1829 was far more than reactionary polemic, however 'sophisticated'.

Historic Doubts Relative to Napoleon Buonaparte (1819) applied the *reductio ad absurdum* to Hume's sceptical account of miracles: the history of Buonaparte must be incredible, for it is clearly 'miraculous' by Hume's definition. In this his earliest work Whately perceived 'the weak epistemological status of inductive investigations' (Corsi 1980, 186) which he later made the basis of his crucial distinction between 'scientific' and 'theological' knowledge. His edition of *King on Predestination* (1821) was routine scholarship; his celebrated review of Jane Austen in the same year, though published in the tory *Quarterly* (1821) was innocent of ideological purpose. The *Sermons* (1823) and *Scripture Revelations Concerning a Future State* (1829) were the fruits of his labours to repair the effect of decades of pastoral neglect in the parish of Halesworth of which he became Vicar in 1822 (Whately 1866, I, 44–5). The Bampton Lectures of 1822 on *Party Feeling in Matters of Religion* foreshadowed Whately's later disapproval both of 'Tractites' and evangelicals. The *Elements of Logic* (1826a), his most famous book, was actually a work of 'moral metalogic' which 'explained what logicians should have been doing' by supplying an acceptable demarcation of the subject matter (Prior 1967, 287–8). Its appendix on definitions in political economy was the first-fruit of Whateley's collaboration with his former pupil Naussau Senior (1790–1864), who became first Drummond Professor in 1825. The *Elements of Rhetoric* (1828a), a textbook, was intended as a companion to the *Logic*. *Difficulties in the Writings of St Paul* (1828b) contained the notorious essay on the Lord's Day which single-handedly liberated educated opinion of that time from the oppressive sabbatarianism then inculcated by evangelicals and reluctantly tolerated by high-church men (Whately 1866, I, 41, 103–5). In none of this work is there evidence of any purpose to counteract the threat of subversive new ideas. (In criticizing Hume's scepticism Whately was following an intellectual tradition that went back fifty years to Watson and Paley.) In all of it there are abundant signs of a striking individuality and a refusal to be tied down by loyalty to any school or party in Church or State that all who knew Whately were agreed in ascribing to him.

The first outward sign that Whately was disturbed by the 'new social and intellectual ferments' of the 1820s appeared in the anonymous – and never acknowledged – *Letters on the Church. By an Episcopalian* (1826b). According to this work 'there were clear signs that in the near future the State could be dominated by forces hostile to the Anglican establishment' and hence the church must regain its independence (Corsi 1980, 117). Two years later Whately's review of Senior's first political economy lectures alluded to the 'many crude and mischievous theories afloat', as a result of which 'the science is in danger of falling into disrepute'. 'Not only may just views of Political Economy be neglected, but false ones may gain currency; and if the cultivation of this branch of knowledge be left by the advocates of religion, and of social order, in the hands of those who are hostile to both, the result may easily be foreseen' (*ER* 1828, 171). The clearest expression of Whately's apprehension is contained in a letter written in 1829 to 'a friend whose name is not given' explaining his reasons for accepting nomination to the Drummond chair. 'Religious truth... appears to me to be intimately connected, at this time especially' with political economy. '*For it seems to me that before long, political economists, of some sort or other, must govern the world...*Now anti-Christians are striving very hard to have this science to themselves, and to interweave it with their own notions.' Whately was thinking, in the event of his appointment, 'of making a sort of continuation of Paley's "Natural theology", extending to the body-politic some such views as his respecting the natural' (Whately 1866, I, 66–7). The appointment was made, and Whately delivered his *Introductory Lectures* in the Easter term of 1831, barely three months before a totally unexpected elevation to the see of Dublin abruptly terminated his academic career.

Whately's Introductory Lectures

As with all who must defend middle ground, Whately's grand strategy required at least the possibility of a war on two fronts. On the one side lay tories, romantics and disillusioned legislators who wanted to repudiate political economy altogether. On the other were the Philosophic Radicals who wanted to annex political economy to their own subversive ends. As against the first, Whately had to demonstrate that political economy is not in conflict with religion; that its method and findings are in fact 'value-free'; that its subject matter – wealth – is not an evil; and that its principal theoretical achievement (the model of the self-regulating, market economy) is of service to natural theology. As against the radicals he had to show that political economy *by itself* can be of no use in public policy formation; that additional value premises are necessary; that atheism must have as much difficulty in justifying value premises as religious belief has in accounting for evil; and that knowledge of the good may come from natural law or scripture, but cannot be had from utilitarian principles alone. The greater part of the *Lectures* is addressed to the first of these sets of objectives, though in some cases the results obtained are serviceable for the second. For though Whately was intellectually and temperamentally far closer to Bentham and Mill than to most of his Oxford colleagues, he saw little hope of converting the radicals to Christianity and for the most part was content merely to indicate the more obviously untenable of their doctrines. But high-church men – of the 'learned and cultivated' kind – were his natural allies and it was essential to convince them that the objections brought against the new science by romantics and obscurantists could be met.

The form of the *Lectures* is not obviously determined by Whately's polemical aims, and many important ideas are dealt with in more than one place. It will be most convenient therefore to consider their content under seven principal objects, noting wherever necessary their connexion with those aims: (1) to dispel the prejudice against political economy arising from the supposition that it is hostile to religion: (2) to explicate the scope and method of political economy; (3) to defend the usefulness of political economy; (4) to argue that wealth and virtue are not necessarily incompatible; (5) to reinforce the original claim of Christian Political Economy, namely that property rights are beneficial; (6) to exhibit the results of political economy as serviceable to natural theology; and (7) to reassert a natural-law view of ethics (as against the utilitarians) by arguing for the logical necessity of a 'moral sense'.

(1)   At the heart of Whately's entire argument is a fundamental epistemological distinction, borrowed from his former pupil Samuel Hinds, between 'secular knowledge' or knowledge of nature, and 'sacred knowledge' or knowledge of God (Whately 1831, 140–1; cit. Hinds 1831, 4–5). The two are not mutually exclusive and indeed their intersection is precisely the domain of natural theology. What

makes the difference is the method of inquiry. Secular or *scientific* knowledge – of 'Historical or physical truth' – consists of 'theory' which may turn out to be true or false. But its truth or falsity must be established by 'our own natural faculties' on the basis of 'proper evidence'. 'For if we really are convinced of... the falsity of any theory... we must needs believe that the theory is also at variance with observable phenomena' (Whately 1831, 19, 20, 22). Subject to the uncertainty which attends all scientific knowledge the latter may throw light on the existence and attributes of God. But the only *certain* knowledge we can have of God comes by 'Faith', by means of which we can see His self-revelation in 'Scripture' (19, 20, 141). Thus 'Scripture is not the test by which the conclusions of Science are to be tried'; its purpose rather is 'to reveal to us *religious* and moral truths' (19, 20).

Now as Copleston had argued against the *Edinburgh* (see pp. 180–6), political economy, though its deals with human behaviour and actually may prescribe conduct, concerns itself solely with the *means* of achieving those *ends* which are given by value axioms (such as those supplied by the moral 'principles' found in Scripture). A legislator may seek the public good 'with the best intentions', but actually fail to promote it 'from not perceiving in what way this or that enactment affects the community'. Hence it must be our duty not only to 'understand in what their good consists', but also 'how it is promoted'. The latter *and only the latter* is the business of political economy: which is declared to be a study of 'the nature of wealth, its production, the causes that promote or impede its increase, and the laws which regulate its distribution'. *Whatever the end proposed by moral principles*, political economy is necessary for its efficient pursuit (23, 24, 25). Political economy is clearly like scientific and historic inquiry in that it depends upon theory and observation and neither depends on nor encroaches upon the authority of divine revelation. Hence, 'That Political-Economy should have been complained of as hostile to Religion, will probably be regarded a century hence... with the same wonder, almost approaching to incredulity, with which we of the present day hear of men's having sincerely opposed, on religious grounds, the Copernican system.' (18). The ostensible purpose of Whately's demarcation of 'scientific' and 'theological' knowledge was to defend the former, in particular political economy, from an illegitimate assertion of scriptural authority. Quite as important to his ideological programme, however, was the other side of the coin: the consequent insulation of theological knowledge from scientistic encroachment by the radicals.

(2) Whately's account of the scope and nature of political economy is in part a corollary of his epistemology. The science is technical and value-free: its 'strict object is to inquire *only* into the nature, production and distribution of wealth; *not*, its connexion with virtue or happiness' (32, my italics; see also 13). Though it is 'a science which professes to have its foundation on *facts*' (1855, 148) it is actually a matter of '*theory*': the 'collecting, arrangement, and combining whatever general propositions on the subject can be well established' (1831, 50; see also 1855, 158). This is quite inescapable, for all 'facts' are theory-laden. Physicians remark that 'no patient can ever be brought to give such a description of any case of sickness as shall involve no theory'. But in all matters 'men are so formed as...to reason...on the phenomena they observe, and to mix up their inferences with their statements of those phenomena; so as in fact to theorize (however scantily and crudely) without knowing it'. In all scientific inquiry, the only choice is between 'a more imperfect and crude theory' and 'one more cautiously framed' (1831, 44; see also 155). As with all good theory the method of political economy is analytical. We are 'more likely to advance in knowledge, by treating of one subject at a time' (14). It is essential to distinguish the effect that a cause would have 'if *operating unimpeded*' from what we actually observe when it is modified by 'accidental circumstances' (120–1, 164–5).

The point was illustrated by a methodological exoneration of Malthus's population theory. But although it is completely erroneous to describe the *Lectures* as 'an animated assault on Malthus's theory of population', and misleading to suggest that Whately and Senior were 'opposed to Malthus on this score' (Fitzpatrick 1864, 1, 68; Checkland 1951, 52) it is nevertheless true that Whately was the least Malthusian of all who contributed to Christian Political Economy. This is because of his failure to grasp (or at any rate to articulate) the logical priority and practical centrality of *scarcity* in economics. Though his proposed name for the subject, 'catallactics' (Whately 1831, 4) implies relative scarcities, it rules out any consideration of the economizing actions of Robinson Crusoe (5) and hence the point is blurred. The focus of attention, as in Adam Smith, is on *wealth* which Whately believed had a natural tendency to increase (108, 119). Smith's analysis of the effects of division of labour is carried further by showing that the latter generates economies of scale (87). There is no trace of the central Malthusian idea – which by 1831 had been fully incorporated into English political economy through the work of Ricardo (1815, 1817) and West (1815) and soon after was classically enounced by Senior (1836) – of diminishing returns to variable labour and capital applied to fixed land.

Whately was thoroughly familiar with Sumner's restatement of Malthus (Whately 1831, 66, 89–91, 137) and of course would have known of Copleston's further refinement. In view of his intimacy and close collaboration with Senior he must have been aware of the latter's fourth 'elementary proposition' (Senior 1836, 26, 81ff.; Schumpeter 1954, 575–88) long before its publication in 1836. It is inconceivable that he should have ignored this crucial theme either from ignorance or incompetence. Two possible explanations remain. He may have intended to deal with diminishing returns and scarcity in his second course of lectures (Whately 1832, xi–xii). Long after, in his lecture on *Dr Paley's Works* (1859a, 33–4), he spoke of Malthus, 'that eminent and most valuable writer' in glowing terms. Alternatively, Checkland (1951, 52) may have been correct in thinking that Oxonian opinion regarded Malthus's '"un-Godly" theory of population' as 'one of the pillars of the Ricardian system' which they detested, and hence that Whately felt it inexpedient to give it any prominence in his exposition.

(3)   Though political economy is a theoretical science it is useful, for 'whether wealth be a good, or an evil, or partly both, the knowledge of all that relates to it is not the less important' (Whately 1831, 31). Moreover it is useful to Christians for 'the world always in fact has been, and must be, governed by political-economists' (cf. Keynes 1936, 383) and 'if none of these should be friendly to christianity... it is easy to foresee what must be the consequence' (Whately 1831, 53). This is because political economy is necessary but not sufficient for the formulation of public policy. Precisely because it is a value-free study of *means* (13) and nothing more, a knowledge of *ends* is also required. This cannot be supplied by science but must be sought among 'religious and moral truths'. If Christians abdicate from the study of political economy they incur the risk that public policy, being left in the hands of non-Christian economists, will be formulated by default in the light of theologically unacceptable ends.

That this was a matter of considerable anxiety for tories at that time is illustrated by the review of Whately's *Lectures* which appeared in the *Quarterly* (1831–2, 46–54). Though Whately and Senior were commended for distinguishing between 'wealth' as the province of political economy and 'virtue or happiness' which lie beyond it (*QR* 1831–2, 51), the reviewer thought that Whately had 'somewhat slurred over the difficulty' and had 'not expressed himself with the clearness and decision which this important point... undoubtedly required of him'. The *Quarterly* liked Whately's minimalist name, 'catallactics', and proposed that it should be regarded as a subset of 'political economy' (or 'social economy' as they preferred to call it), the latter to 'comprehend in it' not only catallactics but 'moral and religious education' (54).

(4)   The *Quarterly's* unease may have been aggravated by Whately's willingness to argue that wealth and virtue are not necessarily incompatible. Those who have claimed that they are have often been inconsistent (Whately 1831, 25–7). The chief exception, Mandeville, argued merely hypothetically: '*if* the notions... were admitted, respecting the character of virtue and vice, and respecting the causes and consequences of wealth, then national virtue and national wealth must be irreconcileable' (28). But in fact there is no such incompatibility and no one really believes there to be. 'I never heard of any one, even of those who in theory deprecate the increase of national wealth as an evil... advocate any measure on the ground that it tends to destroy wealth' (36–7). Wealth is in fact a good (38). Luxury and poverty are relative terms (33–4). The desire of wealth, and emulation, like all other human propensities, are morally neutral (94). What keeps the savage poor, remarked Whately echoing Malthus (1798, 357), is not virtue but rather 'a love of sluggish torpor and present gratification' (Whately 1831, 97). In general there is a coincidence between 'Man's duty' and 'his real interest both in this world and the next' (110).

(5)   The detectably apologetic flavour of Whately's discussion of wealth and poverty is also evident in his treatment of property rights. Defence of private property against the Jacobins was the primordial task of Christian Political Economy which Malthus and Sumner had dealt with so thoroughly that very little remained to be said. Whately cited a long passage of Sumner's *Records of the Creation* (1816, part II, ch. III), 'a book probably so well known to most of you', in praise of the inequality produced by property rights. Whately's own contribution was to link property, progress and civilization explicitly

to Adam Smith's concept of the division of labour. Smith had explained the division of labour as a consequence of the uniquely human propensity to truck and barter, and was somewhat cool towards large accumulations of property (Smith 1910; book I, ch. I; book III, ch. II). As against Smith, Whately regarded property rights as necessary and sufficient for the division of labour. 'I have spoken of *security of property* as the most essential point, because, though no progress can be made without a division of labour, this could neither exist without security of property, nor could fail to arise with it' (Whately 1831, 86–7).

(6)   Even before his appointment as Drummond Professor was confirmed, it will be recalled (see p. 206 above), Whately had premeditated the use of his lectures as 'a sort of continuation of Paley's "Natural Theology"'. This object was acknowledged at the end of lecture III and addressed at large in the next and subsequent lectures. Biological science is found 'to throw more and more light on the stupendous contrivance which the structure of organized bodies displays' which as Paley showed furnished 'a most important portion of Natural-Theology. And it might have been anticipated, that an attentive study of the constitution of Society, would bring to light a no less admirable apparatus of divinely-wise contrivances, directed to no less beneficial ends' (Whately 1831, 56).

Contrivance in the 'body politic' is discovered in the operation of the invisible hand: 'that by the wise and benevolent arrangement of Providence, even those who are thinking only of their own credit and advantage, are, in the pursuit of these selfish objects, led, unconsciously, to benefit others' (95). Lecture IV contains Whately's celebrated example, incorporated in the most famous modern textbook (Samuelson 1958, 37–8), of 'the problem of supplying with daily provisions of all kinds such a city as our metropolis': 'one of the most beautiful pieces of Sunday reading it ever fell to the lot of the *Westminster Review* to recommend' (*WR* January 1832, 16). Though participants in the market 'are merely occupied in gaining a fair livelihood', the operation of the price mechanism ensures that in reality they are performing the important service of husbanding the supply in accordance with its deficiency' (Whately 1831, 63). There is 'no human wisdom' in this arrangement for it is not deliberately planned; nor could it be, for 'the anxious toil such a task would impose on a Board of the most experienced and intelligent commissaries' would achieve nothing like the same efficiency (62).

Yet '*wisdom* there surely is' of 'Providence' in contriving a harmonious and efficient outcome of the innumerable, self-directed actions of 'rational free agents'. Hence 'Man, considered... as a rational agent, and as a member of society, is perhaps the most wonderfully contrived, and to us the most interesting, specimen of divine Wisdom that we have any knowledge of (63, 64).

Whately supplemented the central core of this economistic theology with accounts of the human 'capacity of *improvement*', the origin and progress of civilized society, the social benefits of emulation, and the reconciliation of wealth and virtue discussed above. In all of these he was explicitly indebted to Sumner, whose work he had 'much pleasure in referring to the reader' (66 n.1). Like all natural theologians he was compelled to acknowledge 'the *existence of evil* in the Universe', which he regarded a 'the *only* difficulty in theology' (67). Like Sumner, but unlike Malthus and Paley, he invoked the doctrine of 'original-sin...not a matter of Revelation...but of experience' (109) as the residual explanation of moral evil. For though indeed 'Man's evil propensities' become 'less mischievous as wealth increases' Scripture does teach us that 'this corruption...arises from something inherent in the human breast'. Unlike Sumner however there is no explicit recognition of redemption from sin by the 'propitiatory sacrifice' of Christ.

(7)   The last of Whately's objects was more obviously connected with the radical challenge than any of the first six. The Philosophic Radicals based their programme of reform on Bentham's secularized version of Paley's utilitarian ethics (Crimmins 1989a). The latter afford the ends: political economy the means. Whately completely agreed with the radicals that political economy is a valid and useful science of means. The principal thrust of his *Lectures*, indeed, was to convince (and reassure) the Establishment in that matter. But he repudiated the utilitarian claim to supply the ethical basis of policy formation. Paley's 'theological utilitarianism', though practically harmless, can not be operational without a 'moral sense' which Paley rejected. Bentham's atheism must of necessity deny any 'design', meaning or purpose in human existence, and must therefore evacuate the 'good' of any moral significance.

Paley's maxim 'of doing to others as we would have them do to us' is all very well, 'Yet if we imagine this maxim placed before a Being destitute of all moral faculty...he would evidently interpret it as implying, that we are to do whatever we should *wish* for, if in another's place.' This is clearly absurd, for 'our conduct will affect two or more parties, whose wishes are at variance with each other'. Fortunately in practice 'everyone feels that what he is bound to do, is, not necessarily what would be agreeable to his *inclinations* were he in the other's place, but what he would think he might justly and reasonably expect. Now this very circumstance implies his having already a notion of what is just and reasonable.' (Whately 1831, 21, 22). Whately was much concerned at this fatal weakness in Paley's thought. He first noted it in his edition of *King on Predestination* (1821, 119–24); and returned to the theme thirty-eight years later in his lecture on and annotations of Paley's works. Paley's denial of the moral sense, which I have suggested above (p. 124) was a consequence of his 'method of reasoning', was borrowed from Abraham Tucker and 'the infidel Hobbes'. But 'He would have found a much safer guide in Bishop Butler' (Whately 1859a, 31). For not only is the denial subversive of Paley's moral philosophy: it also undermines his natural theology. It 'would be impossible for Man, if he were really such a Being as Paley represents him to be, to form those notions of the divine benevolence which Paley himself contends for' (1859a, 17). Moreover the 'theological' character of Paley's utilitarianism is destroyed, for his distinction between 'prudence' and 'virtue' breaks down and so, accordingly, does his attempt to base morality upon rewards and punishments in 'a future state' (22–4).

But the Benthamite programme of dispensing with religious sanctions and looking only to the greatest good of the greatest number fares no better. Paley had defined virtue as 'the doing good to mankind, in obedience to the will of God, and for the sake of everlasting happiness' (Paley 1825, IV, 28). No doubt Bentham was correct to regard all that follows 'mankind' as redundant to a utilitarian ethic. The difficulty arises however with the idea of 'good'. In a materialist universe presupposed by Bentham (Crimmins 1989a) human pleasure and pain are reducible to the interaction of 'discrete physical objects'. The effect of this can be evaluated – subjectively and provisionally – by each individual. But without some *necessarily theological* understanding of a 'meaning' or 'purpose' to human life, it is impossible for anyone to be sure about the value even of his own pleasures and pains, let alone those of anyone else. 'For as the believer in God is at a loss to account for the existence of *evil*, the believer in *no* God, is equally unable to account for the existence of *good*: or indeed of anything at all that bears marks of *design*' (Whately 1831, 68). Philosophic Radicalism, therefore, stands doubly condemned. Without the idea of a 'moral sense' men and women cannot discern good and evil. Thus far Bentham and Paley are on all fours. Paley, however, had the virtue of inconsistency. His belief in God was central, and his rejection of 'moral sense' a mere tactical error. Hence his system may be rescued by correcting that error. But Bentham's atheism must logically entail the absence of a genuine (non-illusory) 'moral sense'. Therefore his system can afford no information about what *ought* to be in public affairs; and his advocacy of political economy in policy formation is at best unhelpful and at worst a mere fraud.

It should be noted that Whately's argument in this connexion is a two-edged sword, one edge of which was used to cut the ground from under the feet of the utilitarians, the other to smite low-church bigots who pretended that scripture was the only source of knowledge.

I have said that the object of the Scriptures is to reveal to us religious and moral truths; but even this, as regards the latter, must be admitted with considerable modification. God has not revealed to us a system of morality such as would have been needed for Beings who had no other means of distinguishing right and wrong. On the contrary, the inculcation of virtue and reprobation of vice in Scripture are in such a tone as seems to pre-suppose a natural power, or a capacity for acquiring the power, to distinguish them. (21)

OXFORD AND CHRISTIAN POLITICAL ECONOMY

In a nutshell, the essential Oxford contribution to Christian Political Economy lay in Copleston's correction of Malthus's economics and Whately's correction of Paley's theology. The former showed that indigence is not the equilibrium outcome of Malthusian population dynamics and is not caused by the Poor Laws, but is an effect of disequilibrium against which the state may legitimately and usefully afford protection. The latter showed that both Paley's theological utilitarianism and his natural theology must fail without some Butlerian assumption of a 'moral sense', but can be rescued by means of it.

There were valuable secondary contributions moreover. Copleston refined Sumner's theology by including the theme of the futility of legislated benevolence within the framework of Paley's teleology.

Whately defended Christian Political Economy from confusion with Philosophical Radicalism by his demarcation of 'scientific' economics from 'theological' ethics, and he applied Paley's method to the evidence of 'design' in the body politic.

But if intellectual history be narrowly construed as a rational reconstruction of the development of a set of related ideas, then the work of Copleston and Whately, distinguished and significant as it undoubtedly was, must be regarded as essentially auxiliary. What gives it such high importance in the story of Christian Political Economy is not so much its part in the origin and filiation of ideas as the sanction of respectability it conferred upon those ideas during the last decade of the *ancien régime*. For new ideas must make their way in society like new aspirants to patrician status, depending at least as much upon the accidents of patronage and fashion as upon their intrinsic merit and potential usefulness.

Notwithstanding such as Horsley and Pretyman, Cambridge was thought to be a whiggish place. The essentially conservative work of Watson, Paley and Hey was still widely regarded with suspicion, and Malthus remained a bogyman to multitudes of the godly. But Oxford was the spiritual home of the English Establishment, and more than that. It was a filter through which all new ideas must pass before they could be assimilated into official ideology (Sutherland and Mitchell 1986; Taylor 1988, 976–80).

Copleston and Whately were among the first at Oxford to grasp the opportunity that the theological work of the 'Cambridge moderates' had made possible: that of defending orthodoxy (in politics as well as in religion) not by denying but by incorporating the social and physical science of the Enlightenment. Their strategic location at the centre of the 'Noetic' society of Oriel Common Room, their enormous personal prestige and subsequent political power, and the brilliance and lucidity of their writing guaranteed the success of their enterprise. This was not so much the conversion of Oxford to the new ideas, for that would hardly have been possible in the circumstances of the time, as the neutralizing of its opposition to them. By reassuring Oxford that Cambridge theology and Cambridge political economy were not utterly subversive of religion and good order – and by well-advertised corrections of their more obnoxious features – Copleston and Whately enabled Christian Political Economy to pass through the filter and enter the mainstream of respectable opinion.

CHAPTER 6

Chalmers and the establishment

THOMAS CHALMERS AND THE 'GODLY COMMONWEALTH'

'See Dr Chalmers' excellent Work on Endowments', noted Whately in the preface to his *Introductory Lectures* (1831, x). His advice contains, in the smallest possible compass, the essence of Chalmers's contribution to Christian Political Economy.

This is not to say that the particular book referred to – *On the Use and Abuse of Literary and Ecclesiastical Endowments* (1827), a copy of which Chalmers had presented to Whately when they met at Oxford in 1830 (Hanna 1849–52, III, 278–9, 288–9) – contains the clearest or the fullest statement of Chalmers's position. It is rather that his chief contribution to the ideological alliance between political economy and Christian theology consists of an altogether novel defence of the established churches in the British Isles. For during the final decades of the *ancien régime* there was mounting attack upon the establishment in church and state, particularly upon the Churches of England and Ireland. And Chalmers – not to put too fine a point upon it – attempted to prove *by means of economic theory* that church establishment was the only way to raise the condition of the poor and so to make the world safe for property.

With the solitary exception of his ill-starred *National Resources* (1808), Chalmers's intellectual achievements were distinctly inferior in quality to those of his predecessors considered in this book. Yet far more has been written about him, especially in the way of biography, than any, with the possible exception of Malthus. This is partly because he himself wrote a very great deal. *The Published Writings of Dr Chalmers* (Watt, 1943a) is itself a volume listing some 200 separate publications, many of inordinate length. The fairly substantial outputs of Paley, Malthus, Sumner and Whately are dwarfed in comparison: the elegant but meagre productions of Copleston overwhelmed. This gargantuan literature, however, is but a sign of Chalmers's exuberant vitality, industry and hunger for recognition, which continually embroiled him in controversy, thrust him to the centre of Scotch ecclesiastical politics from the mid-1820s until his death in 1847 and made him a national figure by 1838, compelling the often reluctant attention of Melbourne and Russell, Peel and Aberdeen. Chalmers was a public man in a way that not even Whately was.

But more significant than this, I believe, is the attraction or at any rate the fascination of his turbulent life and character. Paley and Malthus lived peaceful, domestic, and largely private lives. So private and uncontroversial was Sumner's life that practically nothing is known about him, though he was Archbishop of Canterbury for fourteen years. Copleston and especially Whately were more colourful and more engaged in affairs, but they were essentially 'smooth men': insiders with predictable careers and a recognized position in church and state. But Chalmers was 'an hairy man': for though a highly successful ecclesiastical politician, a Moderator of the General Assembly (1832) and Professor of Divinity at Edinburgh (1828–43), he was by nature a disturber of the peace, never more dramatically signified than at the Disruption of the Kirk in 1843.

Chalmers was born in the same year as J. B. Sumner, being four years younger than Copleston, and seven years older than Whately. He read and admired *Political Justice* at the age of fourteen, quarrelled with the family who hired him as tutor, and gave rival lectures in mathematics at St Andrews when denied an appointment in the university. He fell deeply in love with a beautiful childhood friend, wilfully quarrelled with her, fell sick and had a nervous breakdown – aggravated by the failure of his first book – in the course of which he experienced an evangelical conversion. His sermons suddenly became famous, and for the next three decades he wielded almost hypnotic power as preacher and lecturer. Vast crowds flocked to hear him in Scotland, and in England too. Glasgow merchants gave their clerks half-holidays to attend his lectures. When Chalmers preached in London, Castlereagh was moved and Canning wept. He dominated General Assembly from the mid-1820s to the Disruption. 'He buried his adversaries under the fragments of burning mountains.' One of his hearers recalled the effect that Chalmers produced when in full flight: of more than 'mere eloquence' but rather 'some great force of nature' '...the whole assembly were catching the inspiration of the master; a strange afflatus filled the hall. Peal after peal, becoming almost ceaseless, not of applause – the word is too cold, but where is the word sufficiently glowing?' (Dodds 1870, 208–9). He spoke with an uncouth, Fifeshire accent, his eyes bulged when he became excited in the pulpit, and Melbourne thought him a madman and a rogue. Mad he almost certainly was at times, but no rogue. Though devious and unscrupulous in manipulating the administrative machinery of the Kirk, there is no denying the passionate sincerity of his evangelical faith nor the single-mindedness of his social vision. It is hard not to sympathize with his 'deep moral loathing' of the corrupt and perfidious 'Whugs'.

Chalmers loved good cheer, young children, old friends and the study of political economy. Unlike many a social reformer, he actually loved the poor. In his early years as Professor at St Andrews (1823–8) he played golf 'almost daily' on the historic links. 'He afterwards gave up the practice, imagining that it weakened his capacity for study' (Hanna 1849–52, III, 223).

Chalmers's biography begins with his son-in-law, William Hanna's four-volume *Memoirs* (1849–52) supplemented by a volume of selected correspondence (Hanna 1853) and the edition of posthumous works (Hanna 1847–9). Hanna made piously selective use of a vast quantity of letters, journals and other papers, most of which are now held in New College, Edinburgh (Butt 1985). He was followed by Dodds (1870), Walker (1880), Fraser (1881), Oliphant (1893) and Blaikie (1896). Broadly speaking, the aim of all of these is hagiographic. Most twentieth-century writing has focussed upon various aspects of Chalmers's work and has ventured some evaluation. J. Wilson Harper (1910), Wood (1912), Stewart Mechie (1960), R. A. Cage and E. O. A. Checkland (1976), and J. F. McCaffrey (1981) deal with Chalmers's social theory and practice, and H. Watt (1943b) with his part in the Disruption of 1843. J. W. Nisbet (1964) produced the only contribution so far to a long overdue reappraisal of Chalmers as an economic theorist. D. Cairns (1956) and D. F. Rice (1971, 1979) have written on Chalmers's theology. The Bicentenary essays (Cheyne 1985) contain material on these and other topics.

By far the most important study of Chalmers is the recent biography by Stewart J. Brown (1982). It is the central thesis of this illuminating work 'that Chalmers's life and career must be understood in terms of his struggle to realize an ideal Christian society – a "Godly commonwealth" – in response to the social dislocations of early nineteenth-century industrialization and urbanization' (Brown 1982, xv). From his conversion at Kilmany in 1810 until the 'fading of vision' in the last year of his life, Chalmers sought to revitalize the parochial community of pre-industrial Scotland and transplant it to the slums of Glasgow and Edinburgh. By a combination of evangelical fervour and improved organization – judiciously assisted where necessary by initial, temporary doses of capital and volunteer labour – small communities were to be revived or newly created all over Scotland, centred upon parish church and school. In such communities the mutual interdependence in Christ of all human souls could be realized, the rich knowing and respecting their poor neighbours and encouraging them in that sturdy self-sufficiency thought to be the peculiar glory of the Scotch peasantry. The whole of Chalmers's often tempestuous involvement in ecclesiastical and national politics, including the tragic episode of the Disruption, and a large part of his voluminous writing, are to be explained by this single, over-arching vision.

The thesis is compelling and in general entirely convincing. In one respect only, I believe, has Professor Brown been seduced by its appeal into a neglect of certain facts which are of the highest importance to my own work.

Before the end of the nineteenth century Chalmers's authority was claimed for the entirely un-Chalmerian 'social gospel' movement in America (Brown 1982, 375, 377). The most audacious attempt to harness Chalmers to Christian socialism in Britain was made by J. Wilson Harper (1910) in his Chalmers Lectures, encouraged and possibly abetted by Sidney and Beatrice Webb, who lectured in Edinburgh during the same year and who prepared the Minority Report for Scotland of the Poor Law Commissioners (Wood 1912, 1, 90–102). Chalmers was made by these to appear as though he had approved of government regulation of wages, subsidized housing for the poor, old age pensions, unemployment insurance and the nationalization of land. The lectures provoked an indignant response from Grace Chalmers Wood, a granddaughter, who published *The Opinions of Dr Chalmers Concerning Political Economy and Social Reform* (1912) in order to demonstrate, with copious extracts from his own works, her ancestor's uncompromising devotion to private property,

free enterprise and *laissez-faire*. Properly disclaiming any qualification for adjudicating the arguments themselves, she correctly
insisted that the doctrines of Harper and the Webbs were 'singularly
unlike the political economy of Dr Chalmers'. 'Thus, if I am not
mistaken, the social reformers of today have little to do with Dr
Chalmers, except to lament his errors and refute his reasoning'
(Wood 1912, 100). Notwithstanding Miss Wood's publication the
view has somehow persisted that Chalmers was an apostle of the
welfare state, or at any rate a hostile critic of the market economy.
'His advocacy of the social gospel is well known' we are told in the
first of the Bicentenary essays (McCaffrey 1985, 51). It is this
erroneous conception, or something like it, which mars Stewart
Brown's otherwise exemplary biography.

Chalmers's social vision, Brown claims, was communitarian: 'his
purpose was ultimately to subsume economic individualism in a
parish communal ideal, and control industrial development for the
elevation of the labouring orders'. Hence his 'ideal of the godly
commonwealth was in fact fundamentally opposed to Whig faith in
economic individualism and industrial expansion'. At several other
points we are reminded of this theme. Once even, there is mention
of 'Chalmers's Malthusian critique of laissez-faire capitalism'
(Brown 1982, 147–8; 189; 117, 225, 371, 372; 199). Brown is constrained to perceive Chalmers in this way because of the peculiar
understanding of the 'Godly Commonwealth' he ascribes to his
subject. According to Brown, Chalmers 'meant essentially the
sixteenth- and seventeenth-century Calvinist social ideal' in terms of
which 'Under Christian discipline, people would learn to live in
unison, sharing nature's bounty for the common welfare, *suppressing
usury and mandating a "fair price" for goods and services*, practising
benevolence towards the sick and indigent poor, and cultivating
their spiritual, moral and intellectual natures to the service of God'
(Brown 1982, xv, xvi; my italics). None of this is uniquely 'Calvinist'. On all such matters the Reformers were at one with popery.
Of course Chalmers – who was never a very strict Calvinist – would
have gone along with most of it. But he would most emphatically
have repudiated the clause italicized. For though his 'ideal of the
godly commonwealth' was indeed 'fundamentally opposed to the
Whig faith in...*industrial expansion*' it does not follow from this, and
is not in fact the case, that it was 'fundamentally opposed to the
Whig faith in *economic individualism*'.

In part the confusion arises from a seeming ambiguity in both the method and the tendency of Malthusian political economy, still a matter of lively debate among historians of economic thought. But in part it springs from the undoubted fact of Chalmers's social paternalism. How could someone who believed so fervently in 'improving' the poor be a friend of *laissez-faire*? The answer to this question has lately been supplied by Boyd Hilton (1988) in his masterly study of evangelical social thought. Chalmers was a *moral paternalist* but an *economic individualist*. 'The combination was typical of the period. By and large economic paternalists tended to be relatively indifferent to the need for moral reform, while individualists enthused about it'. In Hilton's opinion, which I wholly share, Chalmers would have seen no contradiction between 'the radical individualism of *laissez-faire* capitalism' and his 'vision of the nation as a Godly Commonwealth' (Hilton 1988, 87). It is clear therefore that Brown's thesis remains undisturbed by this modification. The modification is essential, however, to reconcile the picture presented by Brown with the part actually played by Chalmers in the development of Christian Political Economy.

As I have indicated above, that part consisted chiefly in constructing a new line of defence for those historic institutions increasingly threatened in the first two post-war decades by a tactical alliance between the whigs and a new, more virulent strain of radicalism. With sublime effrontery characteristic of his gigantic ego, Chalmers perpetrated the most outrageous, most heroic example of the 'Ricardian vice' ever attempted. The unconditional necessity of church establishment was to be proved by means of classical economic theory. In order to understand this enterprise, its successes and its failures, we must first examine Chalmers's credentials and achievements as an economist.

CHALMERS AS AN ECONOMIST

To the extent that any 'view' persists of Chalmers as an economist, it is unflattering. An improbable conjunction of M'Culloch and Marx has created the vague impression that Chalmers was a very minor figure, and that he was unoriginal or wrong or both. According to M'Culloch, his *Political Economy* (1832a)

displays in an eminent degree that tendency to rash generalization, and that striking declamatory style, which...has contributed to the popularity of the author's other writings. The principles which pervade the work are mostly borrowed from the Economists and Mr. Malthus; and are frequently either wholly unsound or carried to such an extreme as to become inapplicable and absurd. (1845, 19)

Marx's jeering allusion (1954–9, I, 578 n.2) to 'Parson Malthus and his pupil, the arch-Parson Thomas Chalmers' has become a cliché. It is less well-known that he cited Chalmers at various other places in *Capital* with at least as much respect as he accorded M'Culloch. Schumpeter's 'not so left-handed compliment' – had there been a 'Malthusian' school of theory 'Chalmers would have to figure as its McCulloch' (1954, 487) – has done little to improve the picture. D. P. O'Brien's perfunctory biography in the *New Palgrave* (1987) accurately displays the current view. Only J. S. Mill appreciated the originality and merits of Chalmers's contributions and took them seriously (J. S. Mill 1909, 75–8, 424, 690–1, 727 etc.). Now that Mill's *Principles* are no longer part of the formation of a professional economist Chalmers has been lost to sight. There is no mention of his name in Marshall.

Yet a case could be made for suggesting that of all Chalmers's manifold claims to be remembered his work in what we now recognize as 'economic analysis' is the strongest. He at any rate regarded that work as a central, at times obsessive, part of his life, and it is incorrect to say that 'political economy was secondary to, and grew out of, his lifelong crusade to correct the problem of poverty in industrial cities' (Hilton 1988, 64; cf. Furgol 1985, 116–19). Seven years before his earliest urban incumbency he wrote of his first book (1808): 'It contains discussions of permanent importance; and not a person who is profoundly versant in the writings of Dr Smith who does not see that if my principles are found to be conclusive, they will give a wholly different aspect to the science of political economy' (Hanna 1849–52, I, 136). It was the unmerited failure of that ambitious work which in part produced the emotional crisis and conversion experience, and ultimately therefore, his 'lifelong crusade' (Brown 1982, 39–50; Furgol 1985, 116–21). Long after his conversion political economy continued to occupy Chalmers's mind to an extent that he sometimes felt to be spiritually dangerous. 'Let my adoption of Political Economy' he prayed in 1825, 'set me to the vigilance of one who is fearful of and resolved in the strength of Thy grace against all secular con-tamination' (Hanna, 1849–52, III, 93). Yet in 1827 his 'chief earthly ambition' was 'to finish a treatise on Political Economy' (III, 298). He wrote up his Edinburgh University lecture notes on political economy in 1831–2 'by way of bidding a last adieu to the subject' (Chalmers to Babington, 8 February 1832, cit. Hilton 1988, 64); but contributed seven articles on that same subject to the *North British Review* during the last three years of his life (Watt 1943a, 73–4).

Chalmers's interest in political economy began at the early, not to say precocious age, of twelve-and-a-half. At any rate he borrowed *Wealth of Nations* from St Andrews University Library on 13 August 1792. His subsequent undergraduate borrowing shows more interest in mathematics however. During the Winter of 1800–1 he attended Dugald Stewart's Edinburgh University lectures. James Brown's testimonial of December 1801 noted that 'he is at present...investigating some of the difficult and interesting questions of Philosophy and Political Economy' (Hanna 1849–52, I, 490–1). It will be recalled (pp. 113–14 above) that Dugald Stewart's lectures of 1800–1 are notable as among the earliest to consider the significance of Malthus's first *Essay*. Whether Chalmers read Malthus at that time or 'in about 1807' as Stewart Brown (1982, 117) conjectures, his first and in some ways most important book on economics, *An Inquiry into the Nature and Stability of National Resources* (1808), shows an almost complete understanding of the 'sophisticated' model of population equilibrium latent in the *Essay*, and is the first substantial attempt to consider the impact of Malthusian theory upon the economic analysis of *Wealth of Nations*. The characteristically Malthusian flavour of Chalmers's Christian social thought appeared soon after his conversion in a pamphlet upon *The Influence of Bible Societies on the Temporal Necessities of the Poor* (1814); and this theme was continually enlarged in the many volumes and pamphlets that followed during the next two decades. By 1817 Chalmers was writing for the *Edinburgh* on the 'Causes and Cures of Pauperism' (*ER* 1817, 28: 1–31).

Opportunity to devote himself more fully to political economy was afforded by his chair in Moral Philosophy at St Andrews from 1823 to 1828. The second volume of *Christian and Civic Economy of Large Towns* was published in mid-1823. In the Spring of 1824 he began to read James Mill's *Political Economy*; by the following Autumn he was reading Ricardo, Say, Sismondi and Spence. In August of 1825 he read 'Bicheno on the Poor Laws' and the *Britannica* Supplement on political economy and 'Tooke on Prices' in November (St Andrews

Library 'Receipt book 1821–32', 476–82). Ricardo gave Chalmers a great deal of trouble and the journal records renewed efforts to master him in August 1825 and June 1826 (Hanna 1849–52, III, 92–5, 103). In November 1826 he enrolled 'a numerous class' for what was one of the first formal courses in political economy to be offered at any university. *Wealth of Nations* was the textbook, but Chalmers 'refuted or modified... the views of the text-book as they seemed to require it' (Hanna 1849–52, III, 64; cf. Brown 1982, 166).

Manuscript notes from this period include an outline of the 'Chief Peculiarities of the Course of Political Economy' (CHA 6.8.5, 6.9.1). Chalmers summarized his teaching in twenty-six propositions, all of which are included, nineteen of them verbatim, in the slightly longer 'Synoptical View' – containing thirty-six propositions – at the end of *Political Economy* (1832a, 551–66). Eight of these first appear in *National Resources* (1808) to which, despite its failure, Chalmers continued to refer for the rest of his life.

The central thesis of this book – not a 'Spencean pamphlet' but a substantial treatise owing nothing to Spence (Hilton 1985, 143; 1988, 66; cf. Chalmers 1808, 343) – is that at Malthusian equilibrium of population and production in a closed economy the total population must consist of four components: the *agricultural* population, employed directly in food production; a *secondary* population employed in producing non-labour inputs into agricultural production; a negligibly small class of landlords, capitalists and rentiers who collect the agricultural surplus over and above what is required to maintain equilibrium values of the agricultural and secondary populations; and a *disposable* population maintained by a distribution of the surplus determined by the preferences of the propertied classes. The disposable population may supply personal services, luxuries, and public goods such as law and order, national defence, education and religion. Chalmers deliberately eschewed (1808, ch. 5) the ambiguous and analytically worthless distinction between 'productive' and 'unproductive' labour (population) employed by classical economists from the Physiocrats to Marx. For to describe the first two categories of population as 'necessary' (1808, 6) and the last as 'disposable' does not mean that the goods produced by the latter are any less real or valuable than those produced by the former; only that those who command the surplus may exercise choice over the goods for which it is to be exchanged.

Government commands part of the surplus either directly from crown lands or indirectly by revenue from taxation. Part of the disposable population may thus be employed in national defence. When external security is threatened, as is now (1807) the case, 'The Tax which I give to government, goes to purchase my security. I balance the enjoyment I derive from luxuries which I have been forced to abandon; and if the one enjoyment outweighs the other, I do not feel that the tax has either done an injury to myself, or produced any derangement in the circumstances of the nation' (1808, 38). Now at equilibrium (which Chalmers assumed to be the ordinary state of affairs) both wages and profits are at the minima required to maintain the current flow of inputs into production. Thus neither workers nor capitalists receive any part of the surplus. Since taxation must necessarily be a transfer of part of the surplus from private to public sector it follows that the whole burden of taxation falls upon land. The Physiocrats were right but for the wrong reasons. Taxation, therefore, does not 'exhaust and impoverish the country', it only 'turns the expenditure of the country to a different object' (1808, 38).

The argument is sustained with much sophistication and analytical skill, and with few traces of that 'striking declamatory style' of which M'Culloch complained in his later work. The characteristic method of economic analysis, invariably attributed to Ricardo, is found here in developed form. Chalmers repeatedly abstracts a 'strong case', investigates its properties, then progressively relaxes assumptions to take account of greater realism. First a closed economy is considered; then a trading economy self-sufficient in agriculture; then 'the case of a country which has to import agricultural produce' (1808, chs. 1–3). The analytical distinction between the short and the long run is recognized (1808, 25, 27, 261); the classical assumption of the neutrality of money upheld (28); technical progress and the division of labour are recognized as causes of increasing labour productivity (4, 60); and the stability of Malthusian equilibrium very explicitly recognized (257). It is a remarkable achievement for its date and Chalmers was quite justified in expecting that it would 'give a wholly different aspect to the science of political economy'. Seven years before the pioneering studies of Malthus, West, and Ricardo on rent, and nine years before Ricardo's *Political Economy*, Chalmers had perceived at least in outline the shape of 'the canonical classical model of political economy' which appears when *Wealth of Nations* is modified by the Malthusian insight of diminishing returns to population (Samuelson 1978; Waterman 1991b).

Yet *National Resources* was a complete failure, noticed adversely by the *Eclectic* (1808, 575–89) and the *Farmers' Magazine* (1808, 221–44) and otherwise ignored. Only Lord Selkirk was favourably impressed and began an appreciative review for the *Edinburgh* which unfortunately he did not complete (Hanna, 1849–52, III, 129). No London publisher could be found to distribute the first edition, nor any Edinburgh publisher for a second. In part this was a mere consequence of Chalmers's provincial obscurity. Had he, like the equally obscure Malthus ten years before, been fortunate enough to interest a fashionable metropolitan publisher like Joseph Johnson, the case might have been different. Had Selkirk's review appeared in the *Edinburgh* it almost certainly would have been. But in larger measure the failure was caused by an accident of timing.

A few months before, William Spence (1807) had argued that the Continental System would benefit rather than harm the British economy by stimulating more balanced development. He was decisively answered in the *Edinburgh* (1808, 429–48) by Malthus, who showed that foreign trade and industrialization increased domestic employment and raised living standards for all. James Mill (1808) made similar points in a pamphlet. Now Chalmers had used his model to show that exclusion from foreign markets would inflict no significant economic loss on Britain. His argument was subtle where Spence's had been simple-minded. Wealth is subjectively determined by the 'enjoyment' that goods afford (1808, 202). Hence a diversion of domestic production and consumption from internationally traded to home goods need not reduce welfare if tastes change and the public comes to prefer home goods (1808, 220–1, 345–8). Chalmers explicitly acknowledged the potential advantages of specialization and trade but made the empirical judgement that these were severely limited in Britain's case by transport costs (1808, 141–6). He also recognized that imported food may support a 'redundant' or 'excrescent' population, but for the above reason did not think this would much exceed three per cent of the total and thus could easily be absorbed in home production under autarky (1808, 146–55). An appendix considered Malthus's (anonymous) objection to Spence's argument, to the effect that without the stimulus of foreign trade 'unproductive' expenditure of landlords would fall and the economy decline. If landlords will not spend the surplus,

Chalmers suggested, let government appropriate it as a tax and expend it on public goods (1808, 351).

Economic reasoning so far in advance of contemporary wisdom was bound to fall on deaf ears, and it is a tragic irony, therefore, that it was Malthus himself who unwittingly administered so great an initial setback to one he would later describe as his 'ablest and best ally' (CHA 4.21.51, f.2). It is less plausible to suppose, as Brown suggests, that the book failed because it was 'fundamentally opposed to the emerging doctrines of economic individualism, free trade, pacifism, and limited government' (Brown 1982, 41–2). For Chalmers maintained that

Government should take no interest in the preservation of a manufacture which is deserted by the free and voluntary support of the people. Every man is the best judge of his own wishes and enjoyments. Leave him to himself and he will consult his happiness and interest, to much better purpose than the interference of policy can ever provide for them. (1808, 18)

It is true that Chalmers vigorously advocated pursuit of the war with France (e.g. 1808, 294), but that was hardly an unpopular position in 1808.

Whatever the reasons , the book had no effect, Chalmers became an evangelical and never again produced a work on political economy of such originality and sustained analytical brilliance. The deadly pulpit manner cast its blight, and he increasingly distanced himself from 'a mere political economy' (1832a, 420), pretending to have a theological joker up the sleeve of his Geneva gown. The opportunity to establish himself with Adam Smith, Malthus, Thornton, and Ricardo as one of the founding fathers of classical political economy, once real but cruelly denied in 1808, was never more vouchsafed.

Nonetheless there are many traces in his later writing of great insight. The third volume of *Christian and Civic Economy* (1826), published after he had begun his study and teaching of economics at St Andrews, is almost wholly concerned with political economy, in marked contrast to the 'social-work' character of the first two volumes. The long footnote on pages 125–8 epitomizes Chalmers's political economy with the greatest clarity, and shows that despite his misgivings he had in fact mastered Ricardo by that date and seen clearly the relation between Ricardo's work and his own. It was noted above that he had read Tooke's earliest publication on prices

(Tooke 1823) the previous November. Chapter XXI of *Christian and Civic Economy* contains a discussion of the determination of market price by supply and demand (1826, 306–10) possibly suggested by Tooke's historical data, which calls in question the priority assigned by Schumpeter (1954, 839, 992) to Cournot and J. S. Mill in the formulation of the concept of price elasticity. In volume II of his Bridgewater Treatise, Chalmers constructed a two-sector model of a trading economy under flexible exchange rates, with empirical assumptions about the range of demand elasticities, in order to demonstrate the power, wisdom and goodness of God (1833, II, 33–47). Chalmers was also among the first to formulate the characteristically classical doctrine that the growth-rate of the capital stock, like that of population, is a function of the difference between its market rate of return and its 'natural' or equilibrium price (CHA 6.8.5; 1826, 302–12). The appendices to *Political Economy* (1832a, 458–551), especially (A) 'On the Rent of Land' and (B) 'On Machinery', are at the highest contemporary level of technical competence.

In the light of this evidence it is difficult to know what meaning to give to the distinction repeatedly drawn by Boyd Hilton between 'professional economists like Ricardo', and 'christian' or 'devotional' or 'clerical' or 'evangelical' economists (Hilton 1985, 142–51; 1988, 37, 47, 65, 67, 69) such as Chalmers and the other authors considered in this book. As that word is used today, there were no 'professional economists' anywhere, not even in the United States, much before the 1880s. If by 'professional' we are simply to understand 'philosophic radical' the distinction is clear though the terminology somewhat misleading. But if we are to understand that 'Few "Christian economists" displayed much analytical rigour or really understood what political economy is about' (Hilton 1988, 37) the facts speak otherwise. Chalmers at any rate displayed as much 'analytical rigour' as Ricardo. When he was wrong it was for exactly the same reason as Ricardo: from a willingness to apply the policy implications of a rigorously specified model at long-period equilibrium to the vastly more complex social reality from which it had been abstracted. To the most signal example of the way in which adherence to 'Ricardian' method seduced Chalmers into 'Ricardian vice', we now turn.

THE POLITICAL ECONOMY OF CHURCH ESTABLISHMENT

Adam Smith recognized that religion has economic value, for it internalizes the restraints on behaviour necessary in any society and so reduces the cost of government. Malthus argued that a 'moral restraint' of procreation raised the equilibrium real wage and so permanently transferred a portion of the surplus to the working class. Chalmers married these insights to produce the hard core of his theory of church establishment, 'one of the simplest and most uncompromising approaches to this difficult subject that has ever been presented to government for adoption' (Chadwick 1985, 71).

Reduced to essentials the argument consists of a chain of putatively causal links. (1) A nationally established church can teach a common religion. (2) Religion inculcates morality and self-restraint. (3) Morality and self-restraint cause the poor to defer marriage until they see a reasonable prospect of supporting a family. (4) Deferred marriages reduce population. (5) Reduced population, and correspondingly reduced work-force, increases the real wage. (6) An increase in the real wage (at equilibrium, when the return to capital is at the minimum required to maintain the capital stock in optimum relation to work-force) must be at the expense of rents. (7) Hence a portion of the surplus is transferred from the (rich) landlords to the (poor) workers. (8) The consequent prosperity of the working class reduces social unrest and therefore legitimatizes, or at any rate safeguards, property rights. (9) It also eliminates pauperism and the need of a compulsory levy upon property for poor relief. (10) Because the Poor Laws are an ineffectual means of relieving the poor and actually increase pauperism, an easing of the burden of poor relief would more than offset the transfer of surplus from rents to wages resulting from 'moral restraint'. (11) Therefore the cost to society of an established church is worth incurring for two reasons: first, because it protects property; secondly because it reduces the net burden of poor relief.

It is evident that this argument is vulnerable at several points. To begin with, as Owen Chadwick remarked in his Bicentenary essay (1985, 73–4), there is the problem of deciding, out of several rival claimants, just which 'church' to establish. Even more serious for the structure of the argument as a whole is the question of whether the causal links (if they exist at all) are unique. Can *only* an established church teach morality and self-restraint? Can *only* moral restraint restrict the supply of labour and so raise wages at the expense of rents? Chalmers's critics raised such questions with damaging effect. Yet from the first volume of *Christian and Civic Economy* (1821) to his Bridgewater Treatise (1833) his theory was an important element in the ideological defence of the *ancien régime*.

This was gratefully acknowledged in England. Despite his support of catholic emancipation Chalmers was warmly welcomed on his two visits to London in 1830. During the first he dined or breakfasted with numerous bishops, peers and cabinet ministers, presented his views on the Irish Poor Law at the request of a parliamentary committee, and spent an evening with J. B. Sumner disputing the alleged advantages of 'latitudinarianism and laxity' with several other friends: Chalmers and Sumner agreed that 'it is godliness which exalteth a nation' (Hanna, 1849–52, III, 249–63). During the second he was made chaplain to the king, dined at the Mansion House, and spent a few days at Oxford where amongst other luminaries he met Whately, 'a very powerful and original man' (III, 266, 276–89). When invited to preach at a Dissenting chapel near Bristol he concluded his sermon with a ringing affirmation of the value of an establishment. The function of Dissent was strictly auxiliary (III, 266–7). As late as 1838, 'dukes, marquises, earls, viscounts, baronets and members of Parliament' crowded into his London lectures on what was by that time a lost cause: the *Establishment and Extension of National Churches* (Chalmers 1838; Chadwick 1985, 65–7). Three years earlier, he had been made Doctor of Divinity by the University of Oxford, the first presbyterian ever to be so honoured.

By the end of the 1830s, however, Chalmers and his argument for the establishment were largely discredited. To the more acute observers the weakness of his position had been evident at least since 1831. We must now consider that position in more detail, and it will be convenient in doing so to refer from time to time to propositions (1) to (11) above.

Like every educated man of his age, Chalmers was familiar with Hume's *History*. He first borrowed it as an undergraduate in 1796 and the work is listed in the 1840 catalogue of his own books (St Andrews Library records; CHA 6.3.9–14). In volume III, Hume had ventured a 'Digression concerning the ecclesiastical state' which argued for an established church. Because 'in every religion, except the true', zeal is 'highly pernicious', state support of the clergy would be a good thing. For it would take away the temptation to attract 'customers' by 'practising on the passions and credulity of the populace', which perverts true religion by 'infusing into it a strong mixture of superstition, folly, and delusion' (Hume 1778, III, 134–5). Adam Smith quoted at length from this passage in *Wealth of Nations* (1910, II, 272–3) in order to counter it. Though it is certainly the case, as Smith had maintained in *The Theory of Moral Sentiments* (1976, 281) that 'religion enforces the natural sense of duty', he sought to argue in the later work that 'free markets in preaching tended to generate socially efficient religious doctrine' because competition 'would tend to restrain, not encourage, religious fanaticism' (Anderson 1988, 1073).

Chalmers was no enemy of 'zeal' in religion and could therefore accept neither Hume's argument for, nor Smith's against, an establishment. But he wished to adopt and to amplify Smith's view of the social utility of religion, whilst at the same time making a case for establishment which did not altogether ignore Smith's central insight of the benefits of free competition. Chalmers's willingness to allow that Dissent is useful 'to supplement the deficiencies, and to correct and to compensate for the vices of an Establishment... under the evil of a lax and negligent ministration' (Hanna, 1849–52, III, 267) is a concession to the virtues of competition. But he held that there were what we should now describe as 'externalities': the social benefits of religion exceed the value captured by its market price, hence a completely free market in religion would fail to serve the Smithian end of internalizing social restraints. 'Individuals... had no natural inclination to sacrifice for the ideals of Christian civilization, and would not adequately support churches and universities if they were placed on a purely voluntary basis' (Brown 1982, 174). The urban middle classes, who are the chief producers and consumers of religion, would provide proprietary chapels for their own use, but the urban poor and the rural population would be neglected. 'The cities might indeed continue to be supplied with regular preaching, but innumerable villages and hamlets... would be speedily reduced to the condition of a moral waste.' It is for this reason that Chalmers believed 'the Establishment to be... indispensable to the upholding of a diffused christianity throughout the land' (Hanna, 1849–52, III, 267, 266).

Propositions (1) and (2) were established, therefore, by a theoretically satisfactory modification of Adam Smith's doctrine. Proposition (3) is of course Malthusian and its development by

Malthus and Sumner has been considered at length in chapter 4 above. Together with propositions (4), (5), (6) and (7) – all of which are at least implicit in Malthus – it constitutes the fundamental theme of Chalmers's social theory, a ground bass upon which he erected the immense passacaglia of his published works.

The theme is stated, or at any rate suggested, in Chalmers's first book. 'Accomplish a change in the general taste of the people, and you accomplish a corresponding change in the wages of labour.' For the real wage is determined at equilibrium by the supply of labour; and to the workers themselves 'belongs the mighty power of regulating the supply of labourers'. This is effected through population. 'The refined habits of a people may lead them to indulge in a certain degree of splendour and luxury; and if the expense of a family should force them to forgo this splendour, they will rather choose to remain single.' Labour supply is therefore regulated by a 'general though tacit combination, which is produced by the tastes and habits which are diffused through the mass of people'. Now by 'exalting the taste of a people, you add to the extent of the population who work for their secondary enjoyments'. Some part of the national surplus, that is, is diverted to the working class, which uses it to employ part of the 'disposable' population to produce luxury goods for its own needs (1808, 259, 256, 255, 256, 258). Propositions (4), (5), (6) and (7) are explicit.

The theme reappears in summary form in one of the earliest publications of Chalmers after his evangelical conversion. *The Influence of Bible Societies on the Temporal Necessities of the Poor* (1814) was written to meet the objection that 'every shilling given to the Bible Society is... an encroachment upon that fund which was before allocated to the relief of poverty'. But religious instruction may inculcate moral virtue. 'Could we reform the improvident habits of the people, and pour the healthful infusion of Scripture principle into their hearts, it would reduce the existing poverty of the land to a very humble fraction of its present extent.' Moreover, since the existing legal provision for the poor produces 'an increased number of improvident marriages' and so raises the cost of relief, religious instruction is a good investment. Social institutions which supply it may be 'a burden upon the landed property of Scotland' but are 'a cheap defence against the poor-rates, a burden far heavier and which is aggravating perpetually' (1814, 1, 14, 18, 11). Propositions (3), (9) and (10) have been added to the argument.

Not until 1821, however, after Chalmers had ministered for

several years in two Glasgow parishes, do we find a clear statement of that combination of 'economic individualism' and 'moral paternalism' which characterizes his theory of establishment. Adam Smith was correct to recommend that *trade* should 'be left to the operation of nature's own ... process'.

To bring the economy of the nation's wealth into its best possible condition, it may suffice to go up to the legislature, and beg that she may withdraw her intermeddling hand from a concern, which her touch always mars, but never medicates.

Malthus has shown that after a certain fashion the same is true of *population* and poor relief.

To bring the economy of the population into the best possible condition, it is right to go up to the legislature, and beg that she may recal the mischief of her own interferences.

Thus far *economic individualism* is justified. But 'there is one wide and palpable distinction between the matter of commerce, and the matter of population', as implied by the 'Essay of Mr Malthus' 'whose theory of population, had it been present to the mind of Mr Smith, would, we think, have modified certain of those doctrines and conclusions, which he presented to the world ...' For population can only be contained at a level consistent with the elimination of pauperism if the working class is morally enlightened. And for the reasons considered above this cannot come about by free competition in religion. Therefore it is

further necessary to go forth among the people, and there to superinduce the principles of an efficient morality ... to work for a transformation of taste and character – and there to deliver lessons ... raising the whole tone of his mind, and infusing ... the elements of duty, and of wisdom, and of self-estimation.

Moral paternalism is essential, and to be effective it must be publicly supported by a national establishment of religion (1821, 9, 7, 5, 9–10).

As late as 1844 Chalmers continued to affirm the conclusions of his argument as embodied in proposition (11). The 'spontaneous operations of Free-trade' are sufficient to regulate most economic activity, but not the supply of public goods such as 'education', 'public health' and 'public morals'. Though 'Church-extension' was a 'sacred undertaking' indeed it was also a prudent one which ought to commend itself to a government of 'calm and comprehensive and enlightened views'. For 'the Christianity of the people is the sovereign cure for all our social and our political disorders' (1844, 39). But the most exhaustive statement of his position is contained in the lectures on political economy which Chalmers delivered in Edinburgh – from the chair of Divinity – and published as *On Political Economy, in Connexion with the Moral State and Moral Prospects of Society* (1832a).

Chalmers had noted as early as 1821 that a 'merely Christian' philanthropist who knows nothing of political economy, will have 'a great initial superiority' over a 'merely civil philanthropist' versed in political economy but with no pastoral or evangelical mission. For the former, by inculcating virtue and self-restraint will actually produce the material benefits predicted by Malthusian political economy. Moreover, he will have easy access to 'nearly every household'. But a Philosophic Radical armed with neo-Malthusian pamphlets would get nowhere. 'People would laugh, or wonder, or be offended, and a sense of the utterly ridiculous, would soon attach itself to this expedition, and lead him to abandon it.' (1821, 11)

A decade later Chalmers generalized the idea. *Political Economy* was written to 'demonstrate the futility of *every* expedient, which a mere political economy may suggest for the permanent well-being of a community' (my italics). The argument of the entire volume is sustained by continual reference to a model of a national economy at or near Malthusian equilibrium set out in the first five chapters, which differs only in its slight elaboration from that originally presented in *National Resources* twenty-four years earlier. Successive chapters show that the (permanent, or equilibrium) condition of the 'Labouring Classes' is invariant with respect to foreign trade, taxation, tithes, laws of inheritance, emigration and poor laws: except insofar as the last-named may make things worse. Only a transformation of taste and character can bring about 'higher wages to the labourers and lower rents to the landlords' at equilibrium ; and do so 'not in strife and anarchy and commotion, but in showers of grace from on high upon the prayers and labours of the good' (1832a, 420, 456, 458).

This cannot be achieved by 'the mere disciples of a general literature of politics'. Only the 'parish clergyman' and his lay coadjutors, who labour to prepare the flock for immortality, may become 'the all-powerful, though perhaps the unconscious instru-

ments of those secondary, those subordinate blessings, which form
the only ones that a mere worldly philanthropist cares for'. For the
truths of religion are 'the best guarantee against the impetuous
appetency, which leads first to early marriage, and afterwards lands
in squalid destitution, the teeming families that spring from them'.
Thus a politician who recognizes this will 'uphold an ecclesiastical
establishment; but on very different grounds from those on which, in
spirit either of high state toryism, or of high church intolerance, it is
so often contended for'. For establishment is of value 'simply, as the
best machine for the extensive Christianization of the families of a
land'. Chalmers 'rejoiced more particularly, to think, that a church
may be upheld in all its endowments, without being in any right
sense of the word, an incubus upon the nation'. Indeed, the 'expense
of a well-organized and purely-administered church...would be
repaid many times over' by its effect upon the prosperity and peace
of society. Wherefore, 'whatever the coming changes in the state of
our society may be, there is none that would more fatally speed the
disorganization and downfall of this great kingdom, than if a hand
of violence were put forth on the rights and revenues of the Church
of England' (1832a, 432–4, 435, 436, 376, 330). Chalmers was, of
course, 'aware that this is not the precise and proper argument for
a religious establishment' (1832a, 376). But ecclesiology was only
one of those many complicating circumstances of the real world
which he was always so ready to amputate with Ockham's razor.

It is clear from the structure of the argument summarized in
propositions (1) to (11) that it is sufficient to subvert its conclusion
if any one causal link can be shown to be non-unique. To a very
large extent the criticism of *Political Economy* focussed on proposition
(5). If it can be established that the real wage may be permanently
increased in other ways than by the limitation of population caused
by moral restraint, then the necessary connexion is severed between
church establishment on the one hand and a reduced burden of poor
relief and the protection of property on the other. The attack on
proposition (5) was generally enveloped in a larger attack upon
Chalmers's analytical method. He assumed too readily that the
economy was always at or near to equilibrium. By ignoring
transitory effects, which might in fact persist for years or even
decades, *and which might themselves produce permanent changes in behaviour*,
he over-simplified. Even the *British Critic*, the only major periodical
to welcome his novel support of church establishment, regretted that

'in some instances' his arguments 'appear to us to have been pushed too far' (*BC* 1832, 2: 308).

No one who has read Chalmers's economic writings can fail to agree with that moderate judgement. Malthus himself had written in 1827 of *National Resources* and *Christian and Civic Economy* that 'I think in both your publications you have pushed your principle too far' (CHA 4.80.17). On receipt of *Political Economy* he wrote a long, careful response, welcoming many points of agreement but cautiously distancing himself from two of Chalmers's most unpopular pieces of reductionism: the claim that the burden of taxation fell solely on land and 'the doctrine of the non-importance of foreign commerce' (CHA 4.185.32). Hostile critics such as M'Culloch were less restrained.

M'Culloch privately regarded the book as 'a tissue of abominable absurdities' (Brown 1982, 200) and though his review for the *Edinburgh* was formally courteous he was merciless in exposing the central weakness of Chalmers's case. The crucial results 'can take place only on the supposition that the population is instantaneously, or at least very speedily, adjusted to variations in the supply of food and other accommodations'. But if the real wage were substantially increased for any reason it might take 'a period of eighteen or twenty years' before population would fully respond: and in that time workers' 'notions as to what was required for their comfortable or decent support, would consequently be raised'. Now such an increase in real wages may, and does in fact occur from 'improvements in agriculture and the arts', and from international specialization and trade. Hence the 'education of circumstances – an education that is, if possible, still more important' than the didactic education Chalmers had in mind, may produce that 'transformation of taste and character' which he correctly regarded as necessary and sufficient for a permanent improvement in living standards. To put the matter brutally – which M'Culloch himself refrained from doing – if the argument for church establishment is merely one of social expediency, then technical progress in 'agriculture and the arts' makes church establishment redundant (*ER* 1832, 56: 52–72).

Other critics identified the same weakness. Writing in the *Quarterly*, which after a brief divagation some years before (see pp. 174–5 above) had returned to its normal anti-Malthusian position, G. Poulett Scrope welcomed the 'just and sagacious general remarks of a Presbyterian bystander' in support of the Church of England, but utterly repudiated the particular argument for establishment based on political economy. Given the Malthusian axiom

and with the aid of a license not uncommon with the economists, but which none has ever carried to so unconscionable a length as Dr Chalmers – *that of assuming ultimate effects to be constantly present* (my italics)

Chalmers had constructed 'a most portentous and abominable doctrine' which 'directly discourages all attempts at the amelioration of our condition' and absolves 'the wealthy and powerful' from the duty of contributing to relieve the distresses of their poorer neighbours' (*QR* 1832, 56, 40, 69, 68, 67). The *Westminster*, whilst finding much to approve in Chalmers's model of population and rent, and admiring his inability to 'discover a shadow of an argument for the justice of forcibly preventing men from eating foreign corn', could not, of course, accept his argument for church establishment. Like the *Edinburgh* and the *Quarterly*, its reviewer found the argument to be based upon the untenable assumption of instantaneous adjustment. 'It does not follow, that because the effect of a given thing can be proved to be only temporary, it is therefore to be overlooked.' Wherefore a case for establishment based on 'the futility of every expedient which a mere political economy can suggest' for human welfare 'is exposed to the same weakness as an attempt to demonstrate the futility of a succession of good dinners' (*WR* July 1832, 24, 29, 33).

It is important to note that Chalmers was by no means ignorant of the fact that population will take time to adjust to a new level of real income. In *National Resources* he made explicit acknowledgement of this point. The equilibrium values he is interested in will appear only in 'the long run'. Moreover in disequilibrium there may be costs of adjustment. But even in that early work he allowed his intemperate haste to obtain a strong conclusion to betray him into exaggeration and self-contradiction. In the very first chapter, for example, having conceded that when tastes change and labour must be redeployed in new industries, displaced employees 'may suffer for a few months', he calmly asserts that 'the whole amount of the mischief which ensues from the annihilation of the manufacture which produces the commodity, is the loss of the enjoyment' (1808, 15, 31, 26). To a much greater extent in his later work did arrogance, refusal to hear criticism, and evangelical zeal for the 'godly commonwealth' blind him to the naivety and reductionism of his arguments. Though he knew as well as M'Culloch that tastes are learned, that they may be learned by experience, and that population adjustment may be slow enough for a 'ratchet' effect of rising living standards upon the supply price of labour, his judgement deserted him when he put pen to paper. In this he was markedly inferior to his predecessors and colleagues in Christian Political Economy, in particular to the cautious and judicious Malthus, and the powerful and omnicompetent Copleston. As the *Eclectic* put it with considerable justice,

his talents and turn of mind do not remarkably qualify him for such inquiries. He is... too sweeping a generalizer, to be correct in statements relating to complex subjects involving infinite details; too apt to suffer one great idea to fill up the whole field of his intellectual vision, to the exclusion of other objects which, by being taken in, would have corrected his false perspective. (*Eclectic Review* 1832, 2: 46)

Apart from well-nigh universal attack upon the uniqueness of the causal link in proposition (5), there were isolated criticisms of the same kind with respect to propositions (3) and (8). The first of these was raised by the *Eclectic* which pointed out that even if the real wage can be increased by a restriction of the supply of labour, there is no reason to suppose that this can only be effected through the 'moral preventive check'. For 'if the labourers come to understand that it rests with themselves to make a stand for higher wages in this way... is it not probable that they may conceive it right to combine for the same end...? Nor do we feel sure they could be wrong in so doing' (*Eclectic Review* 1832, 2: 53). Chalmers had considered this matter in some detail in volume III of *Christian and Civil Economy* during the immediate aftermath of the repeal of the Combination Acts affecting trade unions. He argued that successful unionization could only raise wages above the 'fair market price of labour' by 'excluding from the competition a certain number of their own body', who would thus become 'outcasts'. This would obviously be an unstable state of affairs. But the 'very same rise would have taken place, if, instead of that number being forced away, they had simply not been in existence'. Hence only moral restraint can effect an equilibrium increase in real wage. In 1832 he ignored the matter.

The *Quarterly* attacked the uniqueness of proposition (8). To be sure, the 'only mode of preserving the peace of society, is to afford to everyone suffering the extremity of want, some resource short of plunder and violence'. But Malthusian population control is not the only way to effect such transfers. Therefore 'the expediency of the poor law, as a mere measure of *preventive police*, may easily be demonstrated'.

Chalmers replied at length to M'Culloch in *The Supreme Importance of a Right Moral to a Right Economical State of the Community* (1832b), which Malthus told him was 'most important and completely victorious' (CHA 4.210.5). But the near unanimity of the critics and the evident cogency of their central objection had its effect. Though bishops and peers and at any rate some Oxford divines received him with enthusiasm six years later, the political economy of church establishment was a dead issue among the well-informed by the end of 1832.

THEOLOGICAL THEMES

It is evident that the political economy of church establishment implies certain theological issues, such as the nature of the Christian church, which have so far been ignored, Aside from this, Chalmers's political economy had such a large admixture of evangelical moralizing after 1808 that it raises additional questions, some of which were noted at the time and others more recently. It is necessary to consider these matters in order to appraise Chalmers's contribution to Christian Political Economy. And it is also necessary to examine his treatment of those other theological themes which his predecessors had addressed: natural theology and social ethics in relation to anti-revolutionary political apologetic.

Theological issues in Chalmers's political economy

The political economy of church establishment exposes a serious weakness in Chalmers's theology: his failure to understand the nature of the church. Secondly, his insistence on the economic benefits of 'moral and religious habits' undermines the distinction between wealth and virtue so important to ethical discourse at that time. And thirdly, his willingness to see the hand of God in day-to-day economic events has suggested to some modern commentators that he presented an 'evangelical free trade model' of the economy which was appreciably different from the model used by 'secular' or 'professional' economists. Each of these must be considered in turn.

After hearing him lecture on establishment Gladstone wrote that he did not believe Chalmers 'has ever looked in the face the real doctrine of the visible church and the apostolical succession'. Certainly Chalmers never addressed the doctrine of the church in his divinity lectures, nor is there any systematic theology of the church elsewhere in his literary works. His contempt for 'all that is transcendental or mysterious' in the church is well-documented and well-known, as is his dislike of Puseyism. He viewed the church as a 'machine' for disseminating the gospel, and the best church as simply the most efficient machine for that purpose. Voluntaryism was less efficient than establishment for the economic reasons outlined above. Hence he desired to steer a 'middle path' between the Voluntary System, or 'what has been termed the System of Free Trade in Christianity' on the one hand, and the 'corruptions' of Puseyism on the other (Sefton 1985, 166, 167).

Defective ecclesiology is connected, in Chalmers, with a vague and incomplete Christology. Though his conversion shifted the focus of his personal faith from 'the magnificence of the Godhead' to 'a total, an unreserved, and a secure dependence on Christ the Saviour', there is no detailed exposition of catholic Christology or of the doctrine of the Trinity in his work. In typically economistic fashion, Christ is regarded as 'the PRICE of our deliverance': but there is no discussion of the manner in which the atonement is realized for individual human souls by their sacramental incorporation into the body of Christ. Reviewing these facts and other evidence of his theological method a recent commentator has remarked that 'it might not be too much to say that Chalmers's conversion did not extend to certain parts of his thinking, even of his theological thinking' (Voges 1985, 158, 159 and *passim*).

It must not be supposed that Chalmers was unusual among his contemporaries in redecorating with evangelical piety a robust Scotch moderatism based upon the Common Sense philosophy of Reid and his followers. Nor was his theology very markedly inferior to that of his English associates in Christian Political Economy. But whereas the theological aspects of their programme were generally in harmony with pre-Tractarian Anglicanism, Chalmers's unique defence of the establishment cried out for a clear statement of the characteristics which ought to be possessed by any 'church' to be established. At least since Daubeny's *A Guide to the Church* (1798) there had been a growing tendency for Anglican apologists to reassert the high ecclesiology of the Caroline divines. The Tractarian movement had given marked emphasis to this direction of thought.

By the end of the 1830s Chalmers's reductionist view of the church as a 'machine' was profoundly uncongenial to the younger generation of Oxford theologians; and at least as important in discrediting his position as the deficiencies of his political economy.

As early as 1808 Chalmers had argued that 'wealth should...be made to comprise every thing that conduces to the enjoyment of man, whether that enjoyment comes to him or not through the medium of a tangible commodity' (1808, 202). The so-called 'unproductive' services of the clergy, for example, contribute to the 'wealth' of a nation. In later work he enlarged this theme in support of his case for establishment. Thus 'the people's equity and sobriety' produced by the work of 'our clergymen, subserve industry and the enjoyment of its fruits, just as any of those commodities do, which may have been accumulated for the support of future labour'. Whence

to the extent is society benefited by the church...to that extent would society be a loser should the church be overthrown...Let the immaterial products be included along with the material, as Say and others would, in the enumeration of a country's wealth; and the institution of a church may serve, not to impoverish, but to enrich a community. (1832a, 343, 351)

It is interesting to recall that Chalmers comes very near, in passages like this, to the supposed doctrines of the 'Catholic School' of political economy identified by the *Dublin Review* (1837, 176, 187-9) in its notice of Villeneuve's great work (see chapter 1 above). For according to the *Dublin* it is or ought to be a mark of Christian Political Economy to include the 'moral virtue' of a population in its national wealth.

There is no record of what Sumner, Copleston or Whately thought of this; but Malthus – who precisely because he was most sympathetic, was in some ways Chalmers's most acute critic – would have none of it. Writing in January 1827 to acknowledge receipt of *National Resources* and volume III of *Christian and Civic Economy*, he welcomed agreement on many points of economic analysis but firmly dissociated himself from Chalmers's economistic account of virtue.

...I cannot agree with you in the meaning which you seem inclined to give to wealth and productive labour. I cannot help thinking that it is more correct in regard to common usage of language, and in accordance with all our common feelings to say that security, independence, moral and religious instruction, and moral and religious habits, are very superior in importance to what we usually mean by wealth, than to say that they ought to be included in the term. It surely cannot be necessary to call independence and morals by an inferior name in order to encourage the pursuit of them. And what will be the meaning of the language of our divines and moralists who dissuade men from the eager pursuit of riches, if riches are so defined, as to include every source of human happiness [?] Surely distinctions are wanted in order to enable us to explain ourselves; and I much doubt if we can find some more natural and obvious than that which divides the gratifications derived from matter and those which are derived from other and different sources. I am quite willing to give all the importance which you can possibly desire to the labours of an enlightened legislator, but as I cannot possibly estimate the gross wealth that he produces, I think I do him much more honour, and at the same time contribute more to the precision of conclusions respecting national wealth by placing him in a separate class of labourers from a manufacturer. (CHA 4.80.19)

In his usual, bull-headed way, Chalmers completely ignored this friendly criticism and seems not to have answered the letter. Five years later he sent Malthus a copy of *Political Economy* which repeats the same questionable doctrines in virtually the same words. For Chalmers's only response to disagreement, like that of an Englishman faced with the incomprehension of foreigners, was to say it again and to say it more loudly. Malthus answered in March 1832 with that patient courtesy which all who knew him continually remarked,

You know my views respecting the definition of wealth … I consider … that it is paying morals a very bad compliment to put them in the same category with cottons, and estimate their value by the money which has been given for them. We have always been told, and most properly, to prefer virtue to wealth; but if morals be wealth, what a confusion is at once introduced into all the language of moral and religious instruction (CHA 4.185.32)

But Chalmers never desired criticism, and there was no genuine intellectual communication between him and Malthus – or with any other economist so far as can be discovered.

Every reader of Chalmers must note the obtrusively homiletic manner in which he dealt with every topic, including political economy. So marked is this that it has led some recent authorities to conclude that Chalmers – and other 'clerical' or 'christian' or 'evangelical' economists – presented a theoretical model of the economy that differed, *for theological reasons*, from that employed by 'professional economists like Ricardo'. The latter were 'optimistic about the effects of industrialization and the possibilities of sustained economic growth by means of continual technical progress. The 'christian' economists were 'pessimistic' and their model 'static (or cyclical), nationalist, retributive and purgative' (Brown 1982, 195–203; Hilton 1988, 67–9, 117–19). It is evident that this judgement, if correct, would have profound implications for the history and philosophy of economic science in general, and for the argument of my book in particular. For if economic theory be sensitive to the theological beliefs of its practitioners, then Whately's sharp distinction between 'scientific' and 'religious' knowledge is undermined. The scientific pretensions of modern economics are founded upon that supposed dichotomy. And the account I have presented in this book of an ideological alliance of Christian theology and political economy can only be coherent if the two disciplines are believed to be epistemologically distinct.

There can be no doubt that Chalmers often wrote in a way that suggested a blurring of this distinction, above all in his *Commerical Discourses* preached in Glasgow in 1817–18 and published in 1820. In these immensely popular sermons Chalmers maintained that self-love must be disciplined by Christian temperance in order to impel the market economy to an optimum pattern of production and employment.

An affection for riches, beyond what Christianity prescribes, is not essential to any extension of commerce that is at all valuable or legitimate; and...it is the excess of this spirit beyond the moderation of the New Testament, which, pressing on the natural boundaries of trade, is sure at length to visit every country, where it operates with the recoil of those calamities, which, in the shape of beggared capitalists, and unemployed operatives, and dreary intervals of bankruptcy and alarm, are observed to follow a season of overdone speculation. (Chalmers 1820, v–vi, cit. Hilton 1988, 117)

Boyd Hilton (1988) has fully documented the extent to which such ideas came to permeate the consciousness of British evangelicals in the first half of the nineteenth century. He is correct to state, moreover, that the *analytical* component of Chalmers's doctrine was a combination of the (orthodox) Malthusian conception of limits to growth imposed by natural resources, with the (heterodox) Malthusian conception of the possible recurrence of 'general gluts'. There is plenty of evidence for the view that both Malthus and Chalmers were agreed by 1827 that their particular brand of political economy was significantly different from that of the 'New School' on several important matters (e.g. CHA 4.80.19). And it is the case that in his Bridgewater Treatise Chalmers asserted that 'it should rectify certain errors which have been committed...in... political economy, if it can be demonstrated that some of the undoubted laws of human nature are traversed by them; and so, that violence is thereby done to the obvious designs of the Author of Nature' (1833, I, 55). For three reasons, however, it must be doubted whether Chalmers's political economy actually was in any fundamental sense determined by his theology.

In the first place, as I have indicated above, the hard core of Chalmers's economic analysis was defined in 1808, three years before his evangelical conversion, and very little of analytical significance was added subsequently. D. P. O'Brien (*NP*, I, 398) has gone so far as to suggest that the 'essence' even of Chalmers's work on aggregate demand is to be found in that earliest book, which 'thus precedes Malthus's own concern with aggregate demand' first manifested in the *Principles* of 1820. Secondly, the two summaries which Chalmers made of the 'chief peculiarities' of his economics – the manuscript notes of 1824–5 (CHA 6.8.5), and the Appendix to *Political Economy* (1832a, 551–66) – contain no trace of the 'evangelical free trade model' that Chalmers seems to have had in mind in his *Commercial Discourses*. The simple analytic point is made that the rates of return to labour and capital are determined by their supply in relation to (fixed) land – technical progress is ignored or treated as temporary – and that workers and capitalists may regulate this supply. But there is no mention of the effect of an inordinate 'affection for riches' in propelling the economy into a self-correcting business cycle. Thirdly, the economic analysis of Malthus and Chalmers did not differ from that of the 'New School' by as much as either they or their contemporaries supposed. It is now understood by historians of economic thought that there exists a single 'canonical classical model of political economy' as Samuelson (1978) has labelled it, and that with the sole exception of the macroeconomic issue variously alluded to as 'effectual demand', 'aggregate demand', 'Say's Law' or 'general gluts', Malthus and Chalmers were at one with Ricardo, M'Culloch and the Mills. Differences of interpretation and of policy recommendation arose not from differences over method, or even (save for the exception noted) from differences in specification of the model. The latter was crucially determined by the Malthusian conception of diminishing returns to successive inputs of labour-and-capital with scarce land, which all agreed upon and which Chalmers was among the very earliest to see clearly. Such differences proceeded rather from merely empirical assumptions about such matters as the extent to which technical progress could offset diminishing returns. Whatever may have been the case with the non-economists whose attitudes to social and economic policy are described by Hilton, Malthus and Chalmers – and for that matter Sumner, Copleston, and Whately – belonged to the same conversation as the Philosophic Radicals.

Natural theology and social apologetic

In 1830, when Chalmers was still at the height of his fame as a defender of the establishment, he was invited by the Bishop of London, Charles Blomfield, to compose the first of the Bridgewater Treatises *On the Power, Wisdom and Goodness of God as Manifested in the Creation*. He had established his credentials as a natural theologian in his *Astronomical Discourses* (1817a), regarded by some as his most important apologetic works (Cairns 1956, 410 and *passim*; Rice 1971). The St Andrews Library 'Receipt book' for 1823 to 1828 shows that he read, or at any rate borrowed, such standard works as Edwards on *Free Will*, Abraham Tucker's *Light of Nature*, Leibniz's *Theodicée*, and King's *Origin of Evil* whilst a professor. His diary records that he began to read Sumner's *Records of the Creation* in November 1827, shortly before preparing for his new appointment at Edinburgh (Hanna 1849–52, III, 209). Chalmers chose to consider the *Adaptation of External Nature to the Moral and Intellectual Constitution of Man*; and by including human society as part of 'external nature' so far as each individual 'man' is concerned, was able to deploy political economy in the service of natural theology after the manner of Sumner and Whately. For

Both in the reciprocities of domestic life, and in those wider relations, which bind large assemblies of men into political and economical systems, we shall discern the incontestable marks of divine wisdom and care; principles or laws of human nature in virtue of which the social economy moves rightly and prosperously onward... affinities between men and his fellows, that harmonize the individual with the general interest, and are obviously designed as provisions for the well-being of families and nations. (Chalmers 1833, I, 10)

In this work and in some of his other writing Chalmers addressed – amongst many things – five of the issues raised by his predecessors in Christian Political Economy: the defence of property rights and the associated economic and social inequality; the right of the poor to subsist; the 'Invisible Hand'; utilitarian social theory; and the problem of evil.

According to Hanna (1849–52, I, 11–14), Chalmers's intellectual awakening occurred during his fourteenth year, when he read Godwin's *Political Justice* at the suggestion of his Foxite mathematics tutor, James Brown. At least by 1801 he was aware of Malthus's response, and by the time of his earliest book was assured of the usefulness and the legitimacy of property rights. In the Bridgewater Treatise, Chalmers argued that a sense of property is 'germinated' in early childhood; that others respect property claims from a sense of equity which develops subsequently from perceiving that 'the fruit of each man's labour ... should legitimately belong to him'; and that Paley was wrong to say 'that property derived its constitution and being from the law of the land' (1833, I, 238, 244, 249). The function of law is to ratify the 'existent order of things' even though the present distribution of property be the result of 'fraud or force' – provided that enough time has elapsed for 'a long continued occupation' to produce 'strong and inveterate possessory feeling' in 'every heart' (1833, I, 249, 250). Property rights secure to the owner 'the fruit of all the labour he may choose to expend upon it' and cause total output to be 'incalculably greater' than otherwise would be the case. Hence the sense of property 'implanted in man from his birth' must 'bespeak the immediate hand of God' (1833, I, 252–3, 254–5). Along with a sense of property there is a sense of 'equity' which recognizes and respects the sense of property in others. Chalmers is unique among the authors considered in this book in relating the obligation this creates, in the traditional manner (e.g., *ST* II-ii, 59: 4, 66: 6), to the dominical commandment to love one's neighbour as oneself. Hence, though the actual distribution of property is accidental and unequal, a sense of equity is the 'origin and upholder of that conservative influence which binds together the rich and the poor in society' (Chalmers 1833, I, 261, 270).

Because property is antecedent to justice, the function of the latter is to legitimate existing rights, not to create new ones. Hence the poor can have no claim on property as of right: their relief must depend upon the sense of equity of the rich. In both *Political Economy* (1832a, ch. XIV) and the Bridgewater Treatise (1833, I, 229–30, 245–9; II, 7–33) Chalmers devoted much space to attacking the Poor Law, and in the latter work explicitly denied the proposition that 'every man has a *right* to the means of subsistence' (1833, II, 27).

Chalmers ignored Copleston's careful distinction between the right
to life and the right to a particular standard of living, whilst greatly
enlarging his theme that 'an action to be virtuous must be
voluntary' (pp. 193–4 above). The teleological significance was
noted in the manner of Paley. For 'if justice alone could have
ensured a right distribution for the supply of want...then would
there have been no need for another principle, which stands out most
noticeably in our nature; and compassion would have been a
superfluous part of the human constitution' (1833, II, 28–29).

As might be expected, various examples of the 'invisible hand'
theorem are pressed into the service of natural theology. In *Political
Economy* the principle is discovered in the argument for establishment.
'In the mechanism of human society, it needs not, that, to effectuate
a given result, the people, who do in fact bring it about, should be
able intelligently to view their own part in it.' Hence the clergy who
labour for the eternal welfare of their parishioners, and all Christians
indeed who work for that end in themselves or others, are the
inadvertent means of 'temporal comfort and prosperity on earth' –
and of all the social and political benefits attaching thereto (1832a,
28, 456 and *passim*). Chapter VII of the Bridgewater Treatise was
written to provide 'a lesson in sound theology' from a review of those
'evils which ensue when the law traverses any of those principles' we
may derive from 'indelible human nature'. The whole of political
economy 'is full of those exquisite adaptations to the wants and
comforts of human life, which bespeak the skill of a master hand'.
Thus

The greatest economic good is rendered to the community by each man
being left to consult and to labour for his own particular good – or,...a
more prosperous result is obtained by the spontaneous play and busy
competition of many thousand wills, each bent on the prosecution of its own
selfishness, than by the anxious superintendence of a government, vainly
attempting to medicate the fancied imperfections of nature, or to improve
on the arrangements of her previous and better mechanism.

In later editions Chalmers directed his readers to 'See further upon
this subject, Observations by Dr Whately...in his recent volume
upon Political Economy' (Chalmers 1833, II, 3, 2, 36, 34; 1853,
240).

Like Whately, Chalmers's chief contributions to Christian
Political Economy were made at a time when it was necessary to
distinguish its ethical tradition clearly from that of the Philosophic

Radicals. Therefore his argument had to include a specific disclaimer of utilitarian principles.

Man is not a utilitarian either in his propensities or in his principles... Virtue is not right, because it is useful; but God hath made it useful, because it is right... He wills the happiness of man, but wills his virtue more; and accordingly... only through the medium of virtue, can any substantial or lasting happiness be realized. The utilitarians have confounded these two elements. (1833, II, 65–6)

But though Butler was cited several times with respect (1833, I, 68, 71, 108, 109, 205; II, 17n., 79), and though Chalmers clearly believed in the reality of conscience or a moral sense (e.g., 1833, II, 16, 108), it is not clear from his text whether he fully grasped the force of Whately's radical objection to utilitarian ethics (see pp. 213–4 above).

In only one respect did Chalmers's contribution to a natural-theology social apologetic attempt to move appreciably beyond the work of his predecessors, and even there his success was questionable. For in chapter x of the Bridgewater Treatise, 'On the Capacities of the World for making a virtuous Species happy', Chalmers had to wrestle with the problem of evil: and his solution was that 'the miseries of life, in their great and general amount, are resolvable into moral causes' (1833, II, 119).

The argument begins by noting, quite correctly, that the two attributes of infinite *power* and infinite *benevolence* are incompatible with any suffering. Unlike Malthus and Abraham Tucker, however, he preferred to deal with the problem not by reducing the number of the divine attributes, but by adding to them. This is because the traditional expedient of the idea of a future state depends upon the same evidence as that of the divine benevolence, and it is precisely because of the unsatisfactory nature of that evidence that the problem exists. As in an underdetermined mathematical system, another equation (or its logical equivalent) is required to deal with the excess variable. This Chalmers supplies by asserting that 'the supremacy of conscience is a fact or phenomenon of man's moral constitution': and that conscience provides evidence of the additional attribute of *righteousness*. Because (Chalmers argues) God wills human virtue even more than human happiness, humans have been so constituted as to be miserable when wicked. Hence 'in the vast majority of cases, the deviation from happiness, can be traced to an anterior deviation from virtue; and that, apart from death and accident and unavoidable disease,...(T)hose evils which vex and agitate man emanate, in the great amount of them, from the fountain of his own heart'. The idea of a future state is therefore to be supported not by the cheerful doctrine of the divine benevolence, but by the terrifying doctrine of the divine righteousness. For it is observable that the wicked are not always as miserable in his life as they ought to be, therefore a future state must exist in which the 'accounts between God and His creatures' are finally settled (1833, II, 103, 104-5, 106, 108, 110, 120-4). Nevertheless, enough evidence exists for a correlation between wickedness and misery for the latter to be regarded, in general, as self-inflicted. In particular, of course, this may be supposed 'of the poverty which springs from indolence or dissipation' (1833, II, 111).

The level of argument is markedly inferior to that in the corresponding portions of Paley's *Natural Theology* and Sumner's *Records*, both of which Chalmers had read. By comparison with the former (see pp. 132-3 above), his use of the Butlerian conception of human misery as divine punishment is naive and superficial. By comparison with the latter (see pp. 161-5 above), his integration of Malthusian political economy into Paleyesque teleology is casual and unsystematic, and his failure to deal explicitly with the doctrine that human life is a state of trial for eternity a strange omission. Though there is a single reference to the orthodox Calvinist belief that humans are 'a depraved species' (1833, II, 113) there is no attempt to deal with the intellectual problems this creates; nor any reference to the solutions proposed in Paley's theory of 'chance', and in Sumner's ingenious supposition that an omniscient God knows that humans would 'joyfully embrace' the offer of a state of trial and is therefore exonerated from their failure.

In short, the Bridgewater Treatise, like Chalmers's writing in political economy, is crassly oblivious of the subtler difficulties of the subject and of the attempts of his predecessors and contemporaries to deal with them. As in his other work, there are many signs of insight, even of brilliance. Malthus was 'much struck' by Chalmers's 'account and illustrations of the manner in which the notions of property spring up in the breasts of children (CHA 7, vol. II, 28: Malthus to Chalmers, 23 June 1833). The teleology implied by the 'divine discontent', only hinted at towards the end of part I, chapter x (1833, I, 129-30), is powerfully suggestive. But Chalmers lacked the discipline, as he lacked the humility, to work patiently at his ideas, refining and correcting them in the light of criticism. At bottom his deficiencies as a thinker were moral rather than intellectual. He habitually gave way to the temptation of quick results and easy applause, compensating for lack of rigour and scholarship by turning up the noise-level of rhetoric to a deafening volume.

By 1833 the literary world had had enough. The *Edinburgh* and the *Westminster* simply ignored the Bridgewater Treatise: the *Quarterly* dismissed it in one-and-a-half cruel paragraphs (*QR* 1834, 4–5). The *Gentleman's Magazine* did 'not think the Doctor at all at home in the subtle investigations of metaphysical analyses' and like the *Quarterly* and the *British Critic*, loudly protested against his style:

... the very worst we ever read, devoid of grammar, of idiom, of grace, of elegance; sometimes vulgarly low, but generally inflated and pompous; full of cumbrous ornament and glitter; perfectly anti-philosophical, abounding in words we never hear this side of the Tweed, and which would be much better fitted to a Glasgow pulpit, than an academic treatise. (*GM* July 1833, 55–6)

There was qualified praise from the *Athenaeum* (1833, 396–7), which like the others rebuked Chalmers for evading his task by including human society in 'external nature'. Only Malthus's friend, John Cazenove, who had favourably noticed *Political Economy* in the *British Critic*, wrote a long and generally appreciative review of the Bridgewater Treatise for the same journal (*BC* October 1833, 239–82). Even Cazenove, however, was unable to stomach Chalmers's mindless reassertion of exploded theodicy. If poverty and disgrace spring from indolence and misconduct, why should God allow indolence and misconduct? Throughout his whole investigation, 'Dr. Chalmers is guilty of the same defective reasoning which is triumphantly exposed by Samuel Johnson, in his review of Soame Jenyns. He is constantly producing one class of evils to account for another class of evils' (*BC* 1833, 276).

It was this objection, more courteously stated, that Malthus adverted to in his last letter to Chalmers, dated 23 June 1833.

The principal difficulty in the whole work is the impossibility of preventing the constant recurrence to the mind of the ποθεν το κακον; and everything that is said in treatises on such matters always suggests to me some difficulty in creation, and in the preparation of beings for a future state of happiness, which must ultimately resolve itself into a limitation of Power. This conclusion is equally forced upon me in natural theology, and in the old and new Testament; and I cannot think it is in any degree inconsistent with the latter. In even some passages in Butler I think he had the same feeling though he does not like to dwell upon it. I hope some time or other to meet you again either in Scotland or England. (CHA 7, vol. II, 28: Malthus to Chalmers, 23 June 1833)

Malthus's hope was speedily vouchsafed, for they met one week later at the British Association meetings in Cambridge. Chalmers contrived to sit on the same table, 'within conversation of Mr Malthus' at the banquet in Trinity College. There is no record of their exchange and Chalmers was probably more interested in the 'deafening reception' of his own speech (Hanna 1849-52, III, 383). A few months later Malthus was dead and the tradition of Christian Political Economy at an end. It finished as it had begun, with Malthus willing to incur the risk of heterodoxy rather than to assent to a theodicy which failed to exonerate the deity from the charge of creating evil.

CHAPTER 7

The end of Christian Political Economy

Chalmers's Bridgewater Treatise is the *terminus ad quem* of Christian Political Economy. After 1833 he was increasingly engaged with the ecclesiastical politics, first of his campaign for church extension, and later of his unsuccessful attempt to prevent the 'intrusion' by lay patrons of unpopular clergymen into benefices of the Church of Scotland. He wrote no substantial work of any consequence for Christian Political Economy in the last fifteen years of his life. The *Sufficiency of a Parochial System* (1841) was based upon theological lectures in Edinburgh and contained nothing new. His posthumous *Institutes of Theology* (1847), composed in the form of an extended evangelical sermon, 'has been a disappointment to many of his supporters' (Brown 1982, 377).

Even before 1833 Chalmers's communication with and intellectual relation to the other authors considered in this book were slight. He seems to have met Whately only once, and though duly impressed, reported to his wife that he found the people in Oxford 'all love better to speak than to hear' (Hanna 1849–52, III, 279). There are no references to Whately in *Political Economy* and only one in the Bridgewater Treatise; and as I have suggested above, Chalmers seems not to have grasped the importance either of Whately's demarcation between 'scientific' and 'religious' knowledge, or of his objection to utilitarian ethics. Even more surprising in view of their common evangelicalism, is the seeming unimportance of Sumner and his work to Chalmers's own enterprise. Hanna reports the meeting of 23 May 1830; and the entry in Chalmers's diary of 6 November 1827 upon his beginning to read Sumner's *Records*, a copy of which is included in the catalogue of Chalmers's library. But there is no trace of any correspondence and the Bridgewater Treatise, as we have seen, was written almost as though Sumner and his *Records* had never existed. A letter of Copleston to Chalmers survives acknowledging his present of *The Sufficiency of a Parochial System* (Chalmers sent out nearly a hundred copies to leading politicians and ecclesiastics: Copleston was one of the few to answer). 'From all that I have read of your opinions on the subject of the Poor Laws', wrote Copleston diplomatically, 'I am confident that this work will in the main coincide with my own views' (CHA 4.297.48). Copleston recommended Chalmers to read Whately's (anti-Tractarian) *Kingdom of Christ*, 'a work every way worthy of his powerful, enlightened, and intrepid mind'. Two other letters from Copleston at about the same time are printed in Hanna's selection of *Correspondence* (Hanna 1853, 380–1). There was more contact with Malthus. In 1822 Chalmers visited Haileybury and four years later the two met again in St Andrews. They saw each other at least once again in 1833, as we have noted (Hanna 1849–52, ii, 358–9; James 1979, 428–9). But there is a marked contrast between the tone of the desultory Malthus–Chalmers correspondence and that of the very much larger correspondence between Malthus and Ricardo. To his 'ablest and best ally' Malthus was courteous and patient, but somewhat distant. When presented with repeated examples of Chalmers's complete inability to hear or respond to criticism it was difficult to keep up the pretence of communication. With his greatest intellectual adversary on the other hand there was continual and lively exchange in a spirit of the most cordial friendship.

After 1833, Malthus was dead and the others too heavily committed to their ecclesiastical duties to find time for extended composition. Copleston became Bishop of Llandaff in 1827, Sumner Bishop of Chester in 1828, and Whately Archbishop of Dublin in 1831. Whately maintained his interest in political economy and strongly encouraged its study in Ireland. He also enjoyed, or made for himself, more leisure for writing than Sumner or Copleston. But he added nothing of consequence to Christian Political Economy after his *Introductory Lectures*.

It is, nevertheless, difficult to imagine that three such vigorous and powerful thinkers as Copleston, Sumner, and Whately, however busy, would altogether have given up the task of relating the new science of political economy to Christian theology had they still believed there was much left to be done. They met frequently in London; Whately, through his friendship with Senior and his patronage of political economy in Dublin, was acquainted with the new generation of economists and their works; as members of the

House of Lords they took an active part in public policy debate. Their own silence, and the absence of any successor of stature, are rather to be explained first, by the fact that the ideological need their work had met was no longer present; secondly, by its decreasing relevance to the rapidly changing world of the 1830s and 1840s; and thirdly by the lasting success of its most important intellectual achievements.

The ideological purpose of Christian Political Economy was to refute Jacobinism and to justify the *ancien régime*. By the mid-1830s both Jacobinism and the *ancien régime* were dead.

So far as Britain was concerned, the former had never been much more than a hobby of Dissenting intellectuals and disaffected romantics. What Southey had mistaken in 1817 for the 'Spirit of Jacobinism' in the English 'rabble' was merely a violent protest at the dire economic hardships and political repression of the post-war years. As prosperity returned and Peel's reforms took effect the protest subsided. What remained was channelled into largely peaceable efforts for parliamentary reform and the recognition of trade unions. Though the *Anti-Jacobin* continued to publish until 1821 its targets had long since become mere Aunt Sallies. As an effective force in British political thought Jacobinism died of self-inflicted wounds during the Terror. As a coherent body of ideas worth serious attention it was deemed to have been dispatched by the first *Essay on Population*.

To the extent that an *ancien régime* existed at all in Britain after the Glorious Revolution its disappearance coincided roughly with the end of Christian Political Economy. The Test and Corporation Acts were repealed in 1828. Catholic emancipation was enacted in 1829. The first Reform Act was passed in June 1832. Though bills for admitting Dissenters to universities and for removing disabilities from Jews were defeated in the Lords in 1834 the future course of events was clear. The Irish Church Temporalities Act of 1833 was the occasion of Keble's Assize Sermon and the resulting 'Tractarian', or 'Oxford' movement. Whately, who had already parted company with Newman over the latter's campaign against Peel in 1829, voted for the measure in the House of Lords. For though a formidable ally of traditional social apologetic he could read the signs of the times. He could understand, even if he could not wholly accept, Chalmers's belated and ill-conceived defence of the establishment, the more so in the light of Chalmers's own support of catholic emancipation. But whereas the counter-revolutionary programme of Christian Political Economy was firmly based upon an Anglican mutation of the Enlightenment, that of the Oxford movement was almost immediately revealed as an attack upon the Enlightenment itself. Whether or not Whately could have entered sympathetically into such a project had he allowed himself to do so, he could see from the outset that it was politically impossible, and set his face against it. Copleston and Sumner were no less hostile. It is at least possible that the rise of the Oxford movement in the 1830s did as much as anything to reconcile the surviving authors of Christian Political Economy to the new order.

But in any case insofar as an important ingredient of Christian Political Economy was a demonstration of the Divine Wisdom in contriving the market economy, its force was weakened by circumstances of the 1830s and 1840s which produced a marked turning away from *laissez-faire*. Legislators showed themselves willing to accept piecemeal reform in practice even when it conflicted with the economic theory to which they assented; there was a growing incidence of conditions requiring such exceptional measures; and the technique of government had been revolutionized since the eighteenth century.

Ever since the campaign to abolish slavery, parliament had slowly been growing accustomed to the idea of economic reform. As early as 1788 Hanway's bill to protect chimney sweeps had been passed; Peel's bill to control conditions of work of pauper children became law in 1802. Country squires, peers and bishops – having no particular love for the new class of industrial entrepreneurs – could generally be persuaded to legislate government intervention when presented with some flagrant case of injustice or exploitation. E. R. Norman has shown that bishops such as Wilberforce, Thirlwall, and even J. B. Sumner himself, imbued as they were with the principles of political economy, supported Factory Acts and public health legislation as exceptional cases whilst continuing to profess their belief in *laissez-faire* (Norman 1976, 138–47). The necessity for such exceptions came thick and fast during the Hungry Forties. Underlying most of them was an unprecedented urbanization. The population of England grew by tens of millions in the first half of the nineteenth century, and most of the increase occurred in London and the new industrial cities. A combination of starvation wages with overcrowding, jerry-building, and a total disregard of private or public sanitation led to the cholera epidemics of the thirties and forties. The ruling class was compelled to attend. 'To maintain the traditional patterns of English life' the new cities 'must have drains, lavatories, paved roads, houses, policemen, nurses, schools, parks, cemeteries and churches' (Chadwick 1966, I, 326). A stream of legislation was generated, all of it extending the responsibility and power of government for social welfare.

Meanwhile the ability of government to meet these demands had been revolutionized by the same combination of social, cultural, technical and material factors which was transforming the private sector. There was

a revolution in organization and behaviour and in the personnel taking the effective policy decisions; it involved an increase in the scale of operations and in the division and specialization of labour; it was marked by a new readiness to experiment with techniques and to make practical use of developments in the natural sciences; and it developed a self-sustaining momentum. (Deane 1969, 214)

A quarter-century of war had fostered the power of the state. As government became a more powerful and efficient instrument for achieving social goals, more possibilities for its use naturally suggested themselves to the reformers. When in the 1830s 'reforming legislation began to include provision for inspection and enforcement by means of state officials with executive powers' a 'point of no return' had been reached (Deane 1969, 215, 216).

Though economic political changes in the 1830s and 1840s made obsolete any refutation of Jacobinism or defence of an *ancien régime*, the more-or-less coherent structure of Christian Political Economy possessed an ideological significance which long outlasted its original purpose. For its anti-revolutionary polemic had differed sharply from the high-church neo-toryism of such 'reactionary intellectuals' as Horne and Hallifax, Horsley and Pretyman (Clark 1985, 230, 216–35 *passim*), being closer in spirit to the new, 'liberal conservatism' of Canning, Huskisson and Peel. The market economy, viewed by the Philosophic Radicals (and later by Marx) as a revolutionary instrument of social progress, was never much loved either by high-church or by romantic conservatives. Malthus and his successors saw not only that the market economy (and all that that was to imply in the nineteenth century) was here to stay, but also that it was compatible with, and actually to some extent the proximate cause of, a very conservative social order.

For according to Christian Political Economy, poverty and social inequality are the inevitable outcome of scarcity: more particularly of population pressures in a world of limited resources. Because of original sin and redemption by Christ, human life on this earth is to be regarded as a state of 'discipline and trial' for eternity. Though poverty and inequality entail some genuine suffering – to be accounted for by the Fall – they may be regarded, for the most part, as a deliberate 'contrivance' by a benevolent God for bringing out the best in His children and so training them for the life to come. The social institutions of private property and marriage are economically necessary (and indeed inevitable), suited to human nature, and consistent with scriptural teaching. A combination of the institution of private property with the competition produced by scarcity results in the market economy. The efficacy of the latter in organizing human activity for the maximization of wealth is evidence of the divine wisdom and mercy in turning human frailty to social beneficent ends. The impossibility of achieving social progress by legislation is evidence both of 'design' – in the creation of the self-regulating economy – and of the moral and religious need of Christians to practise charity and compassion. True happiness in this life is largely independent of wealth and station. But in any case wealth is positively correlated with moral worth, itself the result of faithful Christianity. Universal Christian education is then of the highest practical importance, and an essential feature of the traditional union of church and state.

'By the end of the 1830s...the most influential of the church leaders were all soaked in the attitudes of Political Economy.' Throughout the century the ideas percolated throughout the population by a process of 'layered filtration' (Norman 1976, 136–7 and *passim*). They reappear from time to time in virtually their original form in the utterances of some of the most articulate Christian Conservatives of the present day (e.g. Powell 1977; Thatcher 1978).

Far more important than the ideological defence of property rights, inequality and established institutions are the permanent intellectual achievements of Christian Political Economy. It is hardly too much to suggest that an Invisible Hand is sometimes to be seen in the history of ideas itself. For, under the stimulus of political emergency, rival authors, each seeking only the advantage in debate, discover new ways of formulating human social knowledge which outlive their occasions, 'and thus, without intending it, without knowing it, advance the interest of the society'. In my opinion the permanent achievements of Christian Political Economy are first, a singling out of the concept of scarcity as the central organizing principle of all scientific accounts of social phenomena; secondly, the demarcation between scientific and theological knowledge; and thirdly, related to the second, a recognition that 'positive' explanations of social phenomena are necessary but not sufficient for 'normative' prescriptions of social policy.

The first *Essay on Population* belongs to that tiny handful of books which have brought about a decisive shift in habits of thought. As Chalmers so early saw – and as Dugald Stewart had failed to recognize – the dominance of actual or impending scarcity in human affairs profoundly modified the picture of economic activity presented in *Wealth of Nations*. The 'ratios' imply an aggregate production function with diminishing returns; the latter implies that the social surplus which supports civilization is maximized – for a particular capital intensity and state of technique – at stationary equilibrium. The so-called 'canonical classical model of political economy' emerged in the course of three or four decades as a result of the efforts of Malthus, Chalmers, Ricardo, Senior, the Mills and others to establish, explicate and criticize these and related results. The modern discipline of 'economic analysis', which it is orthodox to suppose is continuous with classical political economy (Samuelson 1978; Hollander 1987), is widely understood to be the study of rational choice in the face of scarcity. Because scarcity is the outcome of natural fecundity in a finite world the competition it produces is by no means confined to the human species. It is well known that Charles Darwin was led to formulate his theory of natural selection by reading Malthus on *Population* 'for amusement' in October, 1838 (Darwin 1958, 59; cit. Young 1969, 126; see also Bowler 1976). The eventual outcome of the inquiry thus engendered was a vindication of human rationality, if not in the short then at least in the long run. For ironically it was the theory of organic evolution, rather than Hume's philosophic scepticism of a century before, which administered the death blow to that Paleyesque teleology in light of which the theodicy of Christian Political Economy had been erected.

Whately's demarcation between 'religious' and 'scientific' knowledge, though less widely noted at the time, has intellectual consequences at least as far-reaching as those of the concept of scarcity. It was immediately employed by Senior to define the 'positive' or 'value-free' character of economic analysis which has been a criterion of orthodoxy in the social sciences ever since. It was used to exempt the new discoveries in geology and biology from a theological veto, and later to defend the Christian faith from the more alarming implications of these discoveries. When John Henry Newman observed, in his 'General Answer to Mr Kingsley', that 'experience proves surely that the Bible does not answer a purpose, for which it was never intended' he was echoing – almost directly quoting – his ancient mentor (Newman 1950, 243; cf. Whately 1831, 19–20). The most recent, post-Wittgensteinian, attempts to demonstrate the integrity of religious and ethical discourse in face of the objections raised by logical positivism have their license in Whately's demarcation. Thus the claim advanced by Leszek Kolakowski (1982, 174 and chapter 5 *passim*) 'that there is a special kind of perception characteristic of the realm of the Sacred' is part of a belated attempt to work out the implications of Whately's epistemological dualism.

At the beginning of this book I claimed five related reasons for its existence. The *fifth* of these was to show that the eventual result of the controversies carried on by the proponents of Christian Political Economy had profound and lasting significance for economics. The object of so doing was to illustrate a more general proposition: that progress in the social sciences may occur not as the fruit of disinterested inquiry but as the unintended outcome of ideological polemic. The first two of the permanent intellectual achievements of Christian Political Economy are sufficient, I believe, to meet this object.

The *fourth* purpose was to supply evidence in support of my eccentric opinion that Malthus's *Essay on Population* is largely unintelligible without an intimate awareness of the ideological warfare of which it was a part, and of the philosophical and theological discourse of which that warfare was a part. In this case, unfortunately, no summary is possible. I can only point to the unseemly proportions of chapters 2, 3 and 4, and entreat the fair-minded reader to re-read the first five editions of the *Essay* (or at least the first, second and fifth) in light of the matter contained in these chapters. At the very least I hope to have shown that the crucial concept of 'moral restraint' is essentially theological, and was introduced into the second edition partly to repair the theodicy of the first edition and partly to strengthen the defence of property rights against Godwin.

The *third* purpose was to demonstrate that Christian Political Economy discovered tenable middle ground, during the first three decades of the nineteenth century, between an ultra-tory defence of the *ancien régime* on the one hand and 'radicalism' in any of its varieties on the other. The *second* purpose was to support I. R. Christie, Jonathan Clark and others who have criticized the 'positivist' and 'reductionist' character of much recent historiography by demonstrating its inexcusable neglect of religious and theological concerns evidently at the centre of the 'traditional' or pre-industrial mode of consciousness. In these cases too, my material defies summary. Chapter 5, and in particular the 'ideological map of the 1820s' (figure 5) and the discussion of 'political economy and ideology in the 1820s', refer largely to the *third* purpose. But my entire book affords a cumulative case in support of that claim, and even more is this the case with respect to the *second* purpose.

The *first* and original purpose of this book was to disturb, and if possible to exorcise once and for all, Tawney's banefully influential view that 'the social teaching of the Church had ceased to count' in the period of which I write 'because the Church itself had ceased to think'. Here at any rate some focus, if not summary, may be afforded by a consideration of the third permanent intellectual achievement of Christian Political Economy: the explicit recognition that 'positive' explanations of social phenomena are necessary but not sufficient for 'normative' prescriptions of social policy.

This pregnant discovery had its origin, as chapter 5 explains, in the parting of Philosophic Radicalism and Christian Political Economy in the 1820s. To the latter belongs the credit for identifying and rejecting mere technocracy. No amount of information about infant mortality, drains and hours of work in factories, *by itself*, can generate legislation to improve human welfare. Yet all such information is necessary to policy formation; and it is of a kind that is accessible to all who know how to obtain it (and only to those who know how to obtain it) regardless of the individual's ethical and religious commitments. Archbishop William Temple declared in his last and most famous book that 'It is of crucial importance that the Church acting corporately should not commit itself to any particular policy... [which] always depends upon technical decisions concerning the actual relations of cause and effect in the political and

economic world: about these a Christian as such has no more
reliable judgement than an atheist.' (Temple 1976, 40). In so doing
he was resting upon a tradition of 'Christian social thought' that
began with Malthus, and ended with Whately and Chalmers. How
then could his lifelong friend and former school-fellow, R. H.
Tawney, have supposed that the church at that time had 'ceased to
think'?

The distinction between 'scientific' and 'religious' knowledge
that Whately defended against the Philosophic Radicals was
altogether absent from pre-Enlightenment social theory. We see
from this why Troeltsch described his famous history as 'The Social
Teaching (*Soziallehren*) of the Christian Churches' (Troeltsch 1931);
and also why he ended it, for all serious purposes, with the
seventeenth century. In the world of which he wrote (at any rate
after the first three or four centuries), all 'thought' was 'christian',
but none 'scientific'. The churches' 'social theory' or 'sociology',
about which there is much in Troeltsch, is ontological, not empirical:
a metaphysical or theological view of the way human society has
been constituted by God, owing little or nothing to any systematic
investigation of social phenomena. In his treatment of Calvinism, the
sole example (according to him) of pre-Enlightenment Christianity
in which it was 'possible to combine modern economic activity with
Christian thought', Troeltsch was careful to point out that the
reason for this 'does not lie in any supposed "greater insight" into
the essence of economic process' but rather from the peculiarity of
Calvinist moral theology (Troeltsch 1931, II, 647), itself the result of
circumstances in Geneva during the formative period (II, 641–3).

We may also see, therefore, why a twentieth-century observer
such as Tawney, perceiving the abandonment in the seventeenth
and eighteenth centuries of the churches' economic discipline, could
be seduced into supposing that 'the social teaching of the Church
had ceased to count, because the Church itself had ceased to think'.

For so long as 'scientific' and 'religious' knowledge are one and
the same thing it was quite in order for those in authority in the
churches to require the obedience of the faithful to their social
doctrine, even in relation to specific practices; and to punish either
in the ecclesiastical courts or by means of the secular arm those who
transgressed. Once the distinction has appeared, however, legitimate
disagreement is possible about the 'positive' or 'scientific' component of social theory, and the *magisterium* loses the moral authority

to enforce its teaching. As Tawney himself remarked, from late Elizabethan times in England,

Objective economic science was beginning its disillusioning career, in the form of discussions on the rise in prices, the mechanism of the money-market, and the balance of trade, by publicists concerned, not to point a moral, but to analyse forces so productive of profit to those interested in their operation. (Tawney 1947, 153)

Inasmuch as 'the Church', meaning by this those in a position to determine ecclesiastical policy and practice, turned a blind eye to this new learning and continued to pronounce the antique denunciations upon commercial enterprise, it may justly be accused of having 'ceased to think'. But *precisely inasmuch as 'the Church' actually began to 'think'*, taking seriously that account of the facts of the case discovered by seventeenth-century political arithmetick and subsequently explained by classical political economy, *it must inevitably have found that its 'teaching'* – at least in the strong sense as enforced by Archdeacons' Courts and the like – '*had ceased to count*'. Because of his reluctance to concede that 'Christian' and 'political economy' could validly be conjoined, Tawney failed to recognize the implications of his own argument.

Appendices
The Malthus–Chalmers model of stationary
equilibrium

I. THE ECOLOGICAL MODEL

Suppose that 'population' and 'labour inputs into food production' are always proportional, hence the same symbol, N, will stand for either. To postulate, as Malthus did, that when population grows *geometrically* food grows *arithmetically* is to imply a functional relation between labour inputs N and food, F, of logarithmic form (Stigler 1952, Lloyd 1969). Malthus acknowledged to Macvey Napier in 1822 that he would have used logarithms in his *Encyclopaedia Britannica* article had he thought the readers would understand (BL, Add. MSS 34613.f.96). Let

$$F = L \cdot \log N \qquad (1)$$

where L is a constant, the value of which depends upon the amount of land available, the intensity with which capital goods are employed in agriculture, and the state of technique. Then if N increases *geometrically* F will increase *arithmetically* provided that L remains unchanged.

Suppose that the average, per capita subsistence requirement of food is the amount s. Suppose that in 'the savage state' (as in sub-human populations) population will increase when the actual per capita food supply f (which is F divided by N) is greater than s and vice versa. Population is in equilibrium when $f = s$, or when $F/N = s$, hence we may represent the growth of population dependent upon food supply as

$$N = (1/s) \cdot F \qquad (2)$$

Equation (1) shows that food supply is a function of population which we may write simply as $F = F(N)$; equation (2) that

264

population is a function of food supply which we may write as $N = N(F)$. The two therefore constitute a 'circular causation' – or 'chicken-and-egg' – model of food and population, which may determine the equilibrium values of F and N for a given L. If an equilibrium exists, and if it is stable, population (and food supply) are determined by the environmental factors summarized under the parameter L.

The system is represented graphically in figure 6 where equation (1) is plotted as the logarithmic curve $F(N)$ and (2) as the ray $N(F)$. Actual per capita food supply at any point, for example at population N_0, is the ratio between OF_0 and ON_0, measured as the slope of the ray OA. At N^* the slope of the ray OB is equal to s, hence population will be in equilibrium. It is evident from this analysis that the equilibrium at point B is *stable*, for if population is either greater or less than N^* the laws of the system will cause N to adjust so as to restore equilibrium. If new land were discovered, or additional capital applied to agriculture, or techniques of farming improved, L would be increased and the $F(N)$ curve shifted upward and to the left. A new equilibrium would thus be determined higher up the $N(F)$ ray, and population would grow until average food per capita had again fallen to s.

It was this model that Malthus employed in the first *Essay* for the Humean 'mental experiment' he performed in order to demolish Godwin's utopia.

The implementation of Godwin's proposals would bring about an upward shift (more properly an anti-clockwise rotation) of the $F(N)$ curve in figure 6, and possibly a clockwise rotation of the $N(F)$ curve. The former would occur because equalization of land-holdings and other productive equipment, and the abolition of luxury, would divert a larger amount of land and other resources to the production of food, so increasing the parameter L. The latter would occur if the 'subsistence' requirement, s, had been socially conditioned to include an element of 'luxury' or 'preventive' abstinence from procreation now abandoned. Suppose that before these imaginary shifts, $F(N)$ and $N(F)$ had intersected vertically above N_0, determining an equilibrium of population at that level. The initial conditions of Malthus's experiment are represented by figure 6 as actually drawn, with a new equilibrium now determined at N^*, but with present disequilibrium at point A: the food per capita ratio F_0/N_0 being in excess of the zero-population-growth

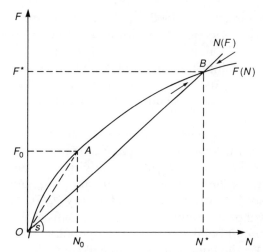

Fig. 6. The Malthusian 'ratios' and the equilibrium of population.

ratio s. Population begins to grow and the per capita food ratio, F/N, declines steadily. At some point beyond A but short of B on the $F(N)$ curve the F/N ratio will have fallen to the value at which cooperation is replaced by competition and the institutions of society reappear. When this occurs any further growth of population towards the ecological maximum, N^*, is arrested by social forces as explained in Appendix 2 below.

2. THE 'SOPHISTICATED' MODEL

We must now make explicit what was only implicit in Appendix 1: that with each additional unit of labour applied to land in the production of food there is an associated set of capital goods. Each new entrant to the work-force needs housing, clothing, furniture, horses, barns, ploughs, hand-tools and so forth with which to work. These have to be produced and maintained at efficient levels in relation to the population (work-force), hence some portion of the work-force, or some part of the working time of all workers, must be assigned to these activities. As Samuelson (1978) has argued, the variable N may be used to measure units of a 'dose' of labour-cum-capital applied to land.

Suppose that a proportion y of total agricultural labour time is employed 'directly' on the land and $(1-y)$ 'indirectly' in producing

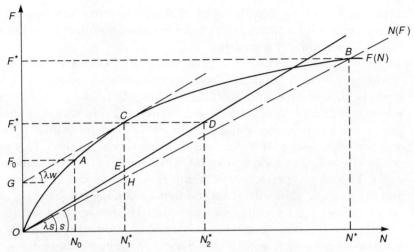

Fig 7. Population equilibrium with private property and competitive wages.

and maintaining capital goods. Production of food in relation to agricultural population now takes place according to

$$F = L.\log(yN) \tag{3}$$

Equation (3) may be plotted in a graph resembling figure 6. For any given value of y, and for given ratios of capital goods to labour inputs (e.g., one cottage per four persons and one man-year, one horse per three man-years, etc.), food production remains a logarithmic function of labour inputs. For given work-force participation, food production remains a logarithmic function of agricultural population.

In order to grasp the meaning of Malthus's 'sophisticated' model it is necessary to understand that the *slope* of the $F(N)$ curve at any point is a measure of the incremental, or 'marginal' contribution to production of labour-cum-capital employed. In figure 7 the diagrammatic representation of the Malthusian 'ratios' model (figure 6) is reproduced. As before, the point B represents equilibrium of the simple model with output F^* and population (or employment) N^*. Point A corresponds with point A in figure 6. At the point C on the $F(N)$ curve the slope of the tangent GC-extended, measured as λW in the diagram, represents the net addition to production that would result from the employment of one extra unit of labour-cum-capital when employment is already N_1^*. It is apparent to the eye that the slope of the $F(N)$ curve continuously decreases: but it is always positive, for Malthus postulated 'no limit to the productions of the earth'.

Now suppose that at some level of population between N_0 and N_1^* private property in land had been (re-)introduced, and with it a landless class of labourers working for hire. Individual employers would be willing to hire workers and capital, provided the marginal product of labour-cum-capital exceeds an amount consisting of the real (or 'corn') wage together with the rental price of those capital goods (including 'working capital') associated with unit labour input. Population pressure will create competition among workers and the desire of gain will create competition among employers. Together the two will force the real-wage-plus-return-to-capital (i.e. the payment to the 'dose' of labour-cum-capital) to equality with marginal product at each level of employment. So long as the real wage exceeds the socially-conditioned subsistence per capita income (s), population will rise. So long as the return to capital exceeds some corresponding minimum, capital stock will rise. Let the amount λs be the sum of s and the payment to that capital associated with unit labour when the return to capital is at the minimum rate. The ray OED-extended in figure 7 is drawn with a slope of λs.

Suppose that the real wage $W = s$. Then the slope of the tangent GC-extended (at C) is equal to the slope of the ray OED-extended, λs. The significance of this is that when agricultural employment/population has risen to N_1^* the marginal payment to the marginal unit of labour-cum-capital will have fallen to that level at which population and capital become stationary. The food-population pair, N_1^*, F_1^* will thus be at their equilibrium values.

At point C, however, the total share of production required to pay N_1^* workers at the going wage $W(= s)$ will be measured by the length HN_1^*. And the payment to capital will be EH. Since total production is $OF_1^*(= CN_1^*)$, this will imply a gross food surplus, measured by the length $EC(= OG)$, appropriated by the lords of the soil: Godwin's 'rent-roll of the lands of England'. It should be carefully noted that the convexity of the $F(N)$ curve – itself an implication of Malthus's famous ratios – will guarantee that at population equilibrium in the sophisticated model the food surplus is maximized.

Now 'the rich, though they think themselves of great importance, bear but a small proportion in point of numbers to the poor';

moreover, 'the quantity of food which one man [can] consume' is 'necessarily limited by the narrow capacity of the human stomach' (Malthus 1798, 289, 197). It follows that most of the surplus *EC* is available for the employment of 'unproductive' labour in personal service, 'ornamental luxuries' and the like (329–31). If we neglect as insignificant the food consumption of 'the rich', and assume that population pressures and labour market competition force wages and capital returns in the 'unproductive' sector to equality with those in the agricultural or 'productive' sector, then when capital intensity is the same in both sectors the maximum 'unproductive' population is represented in figure 7 by the length *CD* or $N_1^* N_2^*$.

It must be remembered in all this that the $F(N)$ curve represents production of food as a function of labour inputs for a given amount of available land, a given intensity of capital employed in agriculture, and a given state of agricultural technique. A change in any of these will shift the $F(N)$ curve and thereby determine different equilibrium values of agricultural and unproductive population and the gross food surplus. An increasing intensity of capital, for example, will rotate $F(N)$ anti-clockwise (implying larger food production with any labour input) and so bring about a new equilibrium with larger gross surplus and larger populations of both classes of worker. Since population must increase until the real wage is again equal to the subsistence level, the equilibrium real wage will be unaffected by any shift in the production function, however caused.

We are now in a position to summarize the analytical results of Malthus's sophisticated model.

1 If employment of labour and capital in agriculture rises with increasing population, when all other productive factors are constant, the marginal product of labour-cum-capital will fall.

2 When 'self-love' is the 'moving principle of society', the competition of landless workers for employment, and of profit-seeking employers for productive workers will drive the return to labour-cum-capital to equality with its marginal product.

3 As a consequence of (1) and (2) real wages and the return to capital will fall as population rises: when the real wage has fallen to subsistence and the rate of profit to the minimum, an equilibrium of production and population will occur.

4 When the agricultural real wage has fallen to subsistence the factor cost of production ($N_1^* E$ in figure 7) will fall short of total

product, generating a gross food surplus (EC in figure 7) which will be appropriated by 'the rich' under 'the established administration of property'.

5 This surplus will be disbursed by 'the rich' in the employment of an 'unproductive' population engaged in manufactures, commerce, public and private service, and the arts and letters.

6 In terms of figure 7, total production, at F_1^*, will fall short of F^*, which is what it would have been had the entire population been employed in agriculture, had the product been equally shared by all, and had the existing capital stock and agricultural technique obtained.

7 It would be a mistake, however, to regard F^* and N^* as the production and population which would have occured in 'the savage state'. This is because the accumulation of capital and the development of the arts are only possible where there is private property in a political society. In the 'savage state' the $F(N)$ curve would intersect the $N(F)$ ray at a point much nearer the origin.

8 Nevertheless, there is a sense in which Godwin was correct to claim that 'the established administration of property, may be considered as strangling a considerable portion of our children in their cradle'. *With existing land, capital and technique*, equilibrium population is ON_2^*, of which ON_1^* is 'productive' and $N_1^*N_2^*$ 'unproductive'. The portion of our children who are thus 'strangled' is represented by $N_2^*N^*$.

9 It is precisely because of this strangulation that population is contained at ON_2^*, thereby ensuring that a food surplus over and above the factor cost of production is available to support 'everything... that distinguishes the civilized, from the savage state'.

10 The combined operation of 'the established administration of property' (private property rights in land and capital) with 'the apparently narrow principle of self-love' (profit maximization by producers, competitive labour and other markets) ensures that the gross surplus will be maximized at equilibrium.

11 Shifts in the production function $F(N)$ caused by increased capital intensity, technical progress or land reclamation will increase production and population at equilibrium, and also the gross surplus. But the real wage of labour, though it may remain above subsistence during the transition to a new position of

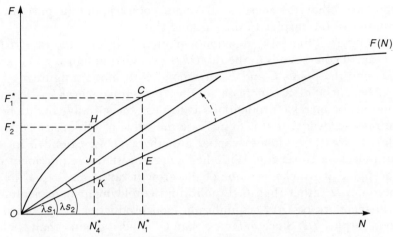

Fig. 8. The operation of the 'preventive check'.

equilibrium, will eventually fall to the subsistence level once again. The only way in which the living standards of the poor can be *permanently* improved is by an increase in the socially-conditioned subsistence wage, s. If by 'a foresight of the difficulties attending the rearing of a family' sufficiently widespread to raise s the $N(F)$ ray is rotated anti-clockwise, the ray *OED*-extended is correspondingly rotated, equilibrium production and population fall, the gross surplus declines, but the equilibrium real wage is increased. The absolute standard of living of the working class is thus improved, and also its relative share of total income, which gains at the expense of rents and profits (see Appendix 3 below).

3. THE 'PREVENTIVE CHECK'

It was remarked in Appendix 2 above, that the eleventh inference to be drawn from the 'sophisticated' Malthusian model is that living standards of the poor can only be permanently improved by an increase in the socially-conditioned subsistence wage. It was this that Chalmers seized upon and made the cornerstone of his social theory. Though Chalmers's own model was more complex than Malthus's (Waterman 1991b), the diagrammatic apparatus developed in these appendices may be adapted to illustrate this proposition and its corollary: that the increase in wages comes about in part by a transfer of the surplus to the working class.

In figure 8 the $F(N)$ function is plotted as before: the ray OKE-extended corresponds to the ray OED-extended in figure 7. N_1^* and F_1^*, and the points C and E correspond with those in figure 7.

The effect of an increase in the 'preventive check' (whether 'moral' or merely 'prudential') is to raise the socially-conditioned subsistence wage: that is to increase the value of s from s_1 to s_2 and thus to rotate the labour-capital growth ray OKE-extended in an anti-clockwise direction. With the higher subsistence requirement s_2, the point at which the slope of the growth ray is now equal to s_2 becomes H rather than C. Equilibrium employment in agriculture will therefore be ON_4^*, equilibrium food production OF_2^*, and the food surplus JH. Since JH is less than CE, and s_2 greater than s_1, the 'unproductive' or 'disposable' population will also be smaller.

Now if the subsistence wage is s_1 and production OF_1^*, the cost of production (return to capital and labour employed at the marginal-product factor price) is N_1^*E and the surplus EC. When s is increased to s_2 the surplus falls to KH as employment and production fall, and a portion JK of that surplus is transferred to capitalists and the working class. Insofar as the latter, at least, are the 'poor', some part of the power to dispose of the surplus in various 'unproductive' ways is thereby transferred from the 'rich' to the 'poor'. This is the meaning of Chalmers's proposition: 'by exalting the taste of a people, you add to the extent of the population who work for their secondary enjoyments' (1808, 258; see p. 233 above).

If the economy is growing as a result of relative capital accumulation, technical progress or land improvement, the production function $F(N)$ will be shifting continually upward and outward in anti-clockwise fashion. If s and λ remain constant the surplus available to landlords will continually increase. But if the working class can raise its expectations and control the supply of labour the labour-capital growth-ray will also rotate anti-clockwise and workers can secure to themselves all or part of the growing surplus. The issue between Chalmers and M'Culloch (pp. 237–9 above) turned upon whether the increase in s necessary to bring this about was exogenous or endogenous.

Both recognized that when population and production are in stationary equilibrium, a clockwise shift in $F(N)$, by raising the marginal product of labour-cum-capital at existing rates of employment, would cause a *temporary* increase of wages and profits above equilibrium levels. As Ricardo often did, Chalmers assumed that population and capital would increase almost instantaneously in response, hence a new position of equilibrium would quickly ensue, with wages again at subsistence. Thus for Chalmers, only an exogenous increase in s (putatively to be achieved by moral and religious instruction) could permanently raise the condition of the poor.

But M'Culloch recognized, as Malthus had even in the first *Essay* (see Waterman 1987), that the response of population to wage increase might be very sluggish. If the working class has become accustomed to above 'subsistence' wages for many years as a result of a sudden surge in economic growth, it may adjust its idea of 'subsistence' upwards. Thus s may increase endogenously if there is sustained technical progress (etc.) and Chalmers's moral and religious instruction be made otiose.

Bibliography

MANUSCRIPT MATERIAL

British Library
  Letters of T. R. Malthus, J. B. Sumner, R. Whately
Jesus College, Cambridge
  'Register of borrowers', 1783–90; 1791–1805
King's College, Cambridge
  'Accession register', vol. 1 (1741–1863)
  'King's Old Court, 1822–1825'. By a scholar of the period [W. H. Tucker]
Lambeth Palace Library
  Whately papers
National Library of Scotland
  Letter of T. Chalmers to T. R. Malthus (II: 3112.f.228)
  Undergraduate essays in political economy (P. J. Sterling, St Andrews) for T. Chalmers (X: 14273)
New College, Edinburgh
  Chalmers papers
Oriel College, Oxford
  'Books at present wanting in the library – and recommended to the librarian' (c. 1815–30)
  'Catalogue' (c. 1822)
  'Commonplace book', E. Copleston
  Letters and other papers acquired before 1932
  'Oriel college senior library catalogue' (from c. 1750)
  'Oriel college senior library handlist'
  'Register of books taken out of the library' (from c. 1750)
University of Illinois at Urbana-Champagne
  'Life of Thomas Malthus', J. Bonar
University of St Andrews
  'Catalogus librorum bibliothecae Andraeanae' (1826)
  Letters of T. Chalmers
  'Library receipt book', 1821–32, professors
  'Students' receipt book' 1791–95; 1795–1800
  'University register', 1783–1826

274

PERIODICALS

Analytical Review
Annual Review
Anti-Jacobin, or Weekly Examiner
Anti-Jacobin Review and Magazine, or Monthly Political and Literary Censor
Athenaeum
British Critic
British Review
Christian Observer
Critical Review
Dublin Review
Eclectic Review
Edinburgh Review
Farmers' Magazine
Gentleman's magazine
Guardian
Monthly Magazine and British Register
Monthly Review
New Annual Register
North British Review
Public Characters
Quarterly Review
The Times
Westminster Review

WORKS FIRST PUBLISHED BEFORE 1860

Augustine of Hippo, St, 1957. *De Civitate Dei contra Paganos*, with English translation by G. E. McCracken. London: Heinemann.

Balguy, Thomas, 1781. *Divine Benevolence Asserted*. London: Davis.

Beauchamp, Phillip. See Bentham, Jeremy.

Beeke, Henry, 1799. *Observations on the Produce of the Income Tax, and on its Proportion to the Whole Income of Great Britain*. London: Wright.

Bentham, Jeremy, 1818. *Church-of-Englandism and its Catechism examined*... London: Wilson.

[Bentham, Jeremy], 1822. *Analysis of the Influence of Nature Religion on the Temporal Happiness of Mankind. By Phillip Beauchamp*. London: Carlile.

[Bentham, Jeremy], 1823. *Not Paul, but Jesus. By Gamaliel Smith*. London: Hunt.

1838–43. *The Works of Jeremy Bentham, published under the Superintendence of his executor, John Bowring*, 11 vols. Edinburgh: Tait.

1952–4. *Manual of Political Economy* (1793–95). In *Economic Writings. Critical Edition based on his Printed Works and Unpublished MSS*, ed. W. Stark, 3 vols. London: Allen and Unwin.

Boswell, J., 1953. *Life of Johnson*, ed. R. W. Chapman. London: Oxford University Press.

Brown, Wm Laurence, 1816. *An Essay on the Evidence of a Supreme Creator, possessed of Infinite Power, Wisdom and Goodness...*, 2 vols. Aberdeen: Brown.

Burke, Edmund, 1887. *The Works of the Right Hon. Edmund Burke...*, 12 vols. London: Nimmo.

Burke, Edmund, *Speech on a Motion made in the House of Commons by the Right Hon. C. J. Fox, May 11, 1792...* in Burke (1887), VII.

Burke, Edmund, 1910. *Reflections on the Revolution in France and on the Proceedings in Certain Societies in London Relative to that Event...* London: Dent.

Burnet, Gilbert, 1819. *An Exposition of the XXXIX Articles of the Church of England.* Oxford: Clarendon.

Burney (d'Arblay), Frances, 1940. *The Diary of Fanny Burney.* London: Dent.

Butler, Joseph, 1844. *The Works of the Right Reverend Father in God, Joseph Butler...*, ed. S. Halifax, 2 vols. Oxford University Press.

   1913. *Fifteen Sermons Preached at the Rolls Chapel*, ed. J. H. Bernard. London: Macmillan.

Carus, William (ed.), 1847. *Memoirs of the Life of the Rev. Charles Simeon...* London: Hatchard.

Chalmers, Thomas, 1808. *An Enquiry into the Nature and Stability of National Resources.* Edinburgh: Moir.

   1814. *The Influence of Bible Societies on the Temporal Necessities of the Poor.* Cupar: Tullis.

   1817a. *A Series of Discourses on the Christian Revelation viewed in connection with the Modern Astronomy.* Glasgow: Smith.

   [Chalmers, Thomas], 1817b. 'On the causes and cure of pauperism', *Edinburgh Review* 28:1 ff., 29:261 ff.

   1820. *The Application of Christianity to the Commercial and Ordinary Affairs of Life...* Glasgow: Chalmers and Collins.

   1821–6. *The Christian and Civic Economy of Large Towns*, vol. I, 1821: vol. II, 1823; vol. III, 1826. Glasgow: Chalmers and Collins.

   1827. *On the Use and Abuse of Literary and Ecclesiastical Endowments.* Glasgow: Collins.

   1832a. *On Political Economy in Connexion with the Moral State and Moral Prospects of Society.* Glasgow: Collins.

   1832b. *The Supreme Importance of a Right Moral to a Right Economical State of the Community...* Glasgow: Collins.

   1833. *On the Power, Wisdom and Goodness of God, as Manifested in the Adaptation of External Nature to the Moral and Intellectual Constitution of Man* (Bridgewater Treatise I), 2 vols. London: W. Pickering.

   1838. *Lectures on the Establishment and Extension of the National Church, delivered in London...* Glasgow: Collins.

   [Chalmers, Thomas], 1844. 'The political economy of the bible', *North British Review* 2:1–52.

1847. *Institutes of Theology.* In Hanna (ed.), (1847–9), vols. VII and VIII.

1853. *On the Power, Wisdom and Goodness of God, as Manifested in the Adaptation of External Nature to the Moral and Intellectual Constitution of Man.* New edn. London: Bohn.

Cooper, Anthony Ashley. See Shaftesbury, Third Earl of.

[Copleston, Edward], 1809. *The Examiner Examined, or Logic Vindicated...* Oxford University Press.

Copleston, Edward, 1810. *A Reply to the Calumnies of the Edinburgh Review against Oxford...* Oxford University Press.

1813. *Praelectiones Academicae Oxonii habitae.* Oxford University Press.

[Copleston, Edward], 1819a. *A Letter to the Right Hon. Robert Peel, MP for the University of Oxford, on the Pernicious Effects of a Variable Standard of Value, especially as it regards the Condition of the Lower Orders and the Poor Laws...* Oxford: Murray.

[Copleston, Edward], 1819b. *A Second Letter to the Right Hon. Robert Peel, MP for the University of Oxford, on the Causes of the Increase in Pauperism, and on the Poor Laws.* Oxford: Murray.

[Copleston, Edward], 1822. 'A dissertation on the state of the currency', *Quarterly Review.* April.

[Copleston, Edward], 1830. *An Examination of the Currency Question and of the Project for Altering the Standard of Value.* London: Murray.

Copleston, W. J., 1851. *Memoir of Edward Copleston, DD, Bishop of Llandaff, with Selections from his Diary and Correspondence.* London: Parker.

[Coux, Charles de], 1837. 'Christian political economy', *Dublin Review* 3:165–98.

Daubeny, Charles, 1798. *A Guide to the Church, in Several Discourses, Addressed to William Wilberforce, Esq., MP.* London: Cadell.

Davison, John, 1817. *Considerations on the Poor Laws.* Oxford University Press.

[Davison, John], 1826. *Some Points on the Question of the Silk Trade Stated: in a letter Addressed to the Right Hon. George Canning, M.P....* London: Baynes.

Derham, William, 1713. *Physico-Theology: or, a Demonstration of the Being and Attributes of God, from His Works of Creation...* (Boyle Lectures, 1711, 1712). London: Innys.

1715. *Astro-Theology; or, a Demonstration of the Being and Attributes of God, from a Survey of the Heavens.* London: Innys.

1730. *Christo-Theology; or, a Demonstration of the Authority of the Christian Religion...* London: Innys.

Gisborne, Thomas, 1797. *An Enquiry into the Duties of Men in the Higher and Middle Classes of Society...*, 4th edn, 2 vols. London: White.

Godwin, William, 1794. *Things as they Are; or, the Adventures of Caleb Williams*, 3 vols. London: Crosby.

1796. *Enquiry Concerning Political Justice and its Influence on Morals and Happiness*, 2nd edn, 2 vols. London: Robinson.

1797. *The Enquirer. Reflections on Education, Manners and Literature in a Series of Essays.* London: Robinson.

1798a. *Enquiry Concerning Political Justice and its Influence on Morals and Happiness*, 3rd edn, 2 vols. London: Robinson. (Photographic facsimile, ed. F. E. L. Priestley, with *variora*. Toronto: University of Toronto Press, 1946. 3 vols.)

1798b. *Memoirs of the Author of a Vindication of the Rights of Woman*. London: Johnson.

1801. *Thoughts Occasioned by a Perusal of Dr Parr's Spital Sermon*. London: Johnson.

Grahame, James, 1816. *An Inquiry into the Principle of Population...* Edinburgh: Constable.

Gunning, Henry, 1854. *Reminiscences of the University, Town and County of Cambridge from the year 1780*, 2 vols. London: Bell.

Hanna, William (ed.), 1847–9. *Posthumous Works of the Rev. Thomas Chalmers...*, 9 vols. Edinburgh: Constable.

1849–52. *Memoirs of the Life and Writings of Thomas Chalmers, DD, LLD*, 4 vols. Edinburgh: Sutherland and Knox.

(ed.), 1853. *A Selection from the Correspondence of the late Thomas Chalmers, DD, LLD*. Edinburgh: Constable.

Hazlitt, William, 1881. 'William Godwin', in Cochrane (1881).

1928. *The Plain Speaker*. London: Dent. (Excerpts from *Table Talk*, 1821–2).

Hey, John, 1794. *Heads of Lectures in Divinity, delivered in the University of Cambridge*, 3rd edn. Cambridge University Press.

1796–8. *Lectures in Divinity, delivered in the University of Cambridge*, 4 vols. Cambridge University Press.

Hinds, Samuel, 1831. *An Inquiry into the Proofs, Nature and Extent of Inspiration, and into the Authority of Scripture*. Oxford: Parker.

Hobbes, Thomas, 1957. *Leviathan, or the Matter, Forme and Power of a Commonwealth Ecclesiasticall and Civil* (1651), ed. M. Oakeshott. Oxford: Blackwell.

Hooker, Richard, 1888. *The Works of that Learned and Judicious Divine, Mr Richard Hooker, with an Account of his Life and Death by Isaac Walton*, ed. J. Keble, rev. R. W. Church and F. Paget, 3 vols. Oxford: Clarendon.

Horner, L. (ed.), 1843. *Memoirs and Correspondence of Francis Horner, MP*, 2 vols. London: Murray.

Hume, David, 1778. *The History of England from the Invasion of Julius Caesar to the Revolution in 1688* ('containing the author's last corrections and improvements'), 6 vols. London: Cadell. Reprinted, Indianapolis: Liberty Press, 1983.

1788. *Essays and Treatises on Several Subjects*, 2 vols. London: Cadell. A new edn.

1962. *Enquiry into the Human Understanding* (1748) and *Enquiry Concerning the Principles of Morals* (1751), ed. L. A. Selby-Bigge as *Enquiries...*, 2nd edn. Oxford: Clarendon.

Jenyns, Soame, 1790. *A Free Inquiry into the Nature and Origin of Evil* (1757), in *The Works of Soame Jenyns, Esq., in Four Volumes*, II, London: Cadell.

Johnson, Samuel, 1755. *A Dictionary of the English Language...*, London: Knapton. Facsimile, *Times* Books, London: 1977.

   1787. *The Works of Samuel Johnson, LLD*, 11 vols. London: Buckland.

Joyce, Jeremiah, 1807. *A Full and Complete Analysis of Dr Paley's Natural Theology...*, 2nd edn. Harlow: Flower.

Keill, John, 1776. *An Introduction to the Natural Philosophy, or Lectures in Physics read in the University of Oxford in the Year MDCC*, translated from the last edition of the Latin. Glasgow: Dunlop.

King, William, 1739. *An Essay on the Origin of Evil. Translated from the Latin with large Notes...by Edmund Law MA, Fellow of Christ's College.* Cambridge: Thurlbourne.

   1821. *Discourse on Predestination by Dr King, Late Lord Archbishop of Dublin Preached at Christchurch, Dublin, before the House of Lords, May 15, 1709*, ed. R. Whately. Oxford: Murray.

Leibniz, G. W., 1951. *Theodicy. Essays on the Goodness of God, the Freedom of Man and the Origin of Evil*, transl. E. M. Huggard, ed. Austin Farrar. London: Routledge.

Lloyd, W. F., 1833. *Two Lectures on the Checks to Population, delivered before the University of Oxford, in Michaelmas Term 1832...* Oxford: Collingwood. Reprinted in *Population and Development Studies* 6: 473–96 (1980).

Locke, John, 1967. *Two Treatises of Government. A Critical Edition with an Introduction and Apparatus Criticus*, ed. P. Laslett, 2nd edn. Cambridge University Press.

M'Culloch, J. R. 1845. *The Literature of Political Economy: A Classified Catalogue.* London: Longmans.

Maclaurin, Colin, 1775. *An Account of Sir Isaac Newton's Philosophical Discoveries*, 3rd edn. London: Nourse.

Mackintosh, James, 1791. *Vindiciae Gallicae. Defence of the French Revolution and its English Admirers against the Accusations of the Right Hon. Edmund Burke...* London: Robinson.

[Malthus, T. R.], 1798. *An Essay on the Principle of Population as it Affects the Future Improvement of Society, with Remarks on the Speculations of Mr Godwin, M. Condorcet, and Other Writers.* London: Johnson.

Malthus, T. R., 1803, 1806, 1807, 1817, 1826. *An Essay on the Principle of Population, or, A View of its Past and Present Effects on Human Happiness, with an Inquiry into our Prospects Respecting the Future Removal or Mitigation of the Evils which it Occasions.* London: Johnson, 1803. Considered as 2nd edn of the above. 3rd edn, London: Johnson, 1806. 4th edn, London: Johnson, 1807. 5th edn, London: Hunter, 1817. 6th edn, London: Hunter, 1826.

[Malthus, T. R.], 1808, 1809. 'Spence on Commerce', *Edinburgh Review* 11:429–48; 14:50–60.

   1815a. *An Inquiry into the Nature and Progress of Rent, and the Principles by which it is Regulated.* London: Murray.

   1815b. *The Grounds of an Opinion on the Policy of Restricting the Importation of Foreign Corn...* London: Murray.

1830. *A Summary View of the Principle of Population.* London: Murray.

1836. *Principles of Political Economy, Considered with a View to their Practical Application,* 2nd edn. London: Pickering.

1986. *The Works of T. R. Malthus,* ed. E. A. Wrigley and D. Souden, 8 vols. London: Pickering.

[Manning, H. E. and Marriot, C.], 1839. *Catena Patrum III: Testimony of Writers in the Later English Church to the Duty of Maintaining Quod Semper, Quod Ubique, Quod ab Omnibus Traditum Est.* Tract 78 of *Tracts for the Times,* IV. London: Rivington. New edn.

Meadley, G. W., 1809. *Memoirs of William Paley, DD.* Sunderland: Graham.

Mill, James, 1808. *Commerce Defended. An Answer to the Arguments by which Mr Spence, Mr Cobbett, and others, have attempted to prove that Commerce is not a Source of National Wealth.* London: Baldwin.

1821. *Elements of Political Economy.* London: Baldwin.

Mill, J. S., 1909. *Principles of Political Economy,* ed. W. J. Ashley. London: Longmans. A new edn.

Millar, John, 1779. *The Origin of the Distinction of Ranks...* London: Murray. Considered as 3rd edn 'corrected and enlarged' of *Observations Concerning the Distinctions of Rank in Society* (1771). London: Murray.

Napier, Macvey (ed.), 1824. *Encyclopaedia Britannica. Supplement to the Fourth, Fifth and Sixth Editions.* Edinburgh: Constable.

Neale, J. M., 1859. *The Liturgies of S. Mark, S. James, S. Clement, S. Chrysostom and the Church of Malabar,* translated with introduction and appendices. London: Hayes.

Newton, Isaac, 1952. *Opticks; or, a Treatise of the Reflections, Refractions, Inflections and Colours of Light,* (1730) 4th edn. London: Innys. Reprinted, with foreword by Albert Einstein... New York: Dover.

1756. *Four Letters from Sir Isaac Newton to Dr Bentley Containing some Arguments in Proof of a Deity.* London: Dodsley.

[Otter, W.], 1836. 'Memoir of Robert Malthus', in Malthus (1836), xiii–liv

Overton, John, 1802. *The True Churchman Ascertained: or, An Apology for those of the Regular Clergy of the Establishment who are sometimes called Evangelical Ministers: Occasioned by the Publications of Drs Paley, Hey, Croft; Messrs Daubeny, Ludlam, Polwhele, Fellowes; the Reviewers, etc., etc.* York: Wilson.

Owen, Robert, 1816. *A New View of Society, or, Essays on the Formation of the Human Character Preparatory for the Developement of a Plan for Gradually Ameliorating the Condition of Mankind.* London: Longman.

Paine, Thomas, 1791–2. *The Rights of Man: being an Answer to Mr Burke's Attack on the French Revolution,* part I, 1791; part II, 1792. London: Jordan.

1887. *Theological Works.* Chicago: Belford.

Paley, William, 1808. *Sermons and Tracts by the late Rev. William Paley, DD, Archdeacon of Carlisle...,* London: Faulder. (Includes *The Clergyman's Companion in Visiting the Sick,* spur. attr.)

1825. *The Works of William Paley, DD,* ed. Edmund Paley, 7 vols. London: Rivington. A new edn.

Plato, 1953. *The Republic*, with English translation by P. Shorey. London: Heinemann.

Pope, Alexander, 1966. *Poetical Works*, ed. H. Davis. Oxford University Press.

Porteus, Beilby, 1767. *A Sermon Preached before the University of Cambridge on Commencement Sunday, July 5, 1767*. Cambridge University Press.

Pretyman (Pretyman-Tomline), George, 1812. *Elements of Christian Theology*, 9th edn, 2 vols. London: Cadell.

Price, Richard, 1790. *A Discourse on the Love of our Country, Delivered on Nov. 4, 1789, at the Meeting House in the Old Jewry, to the Society for the Commemorating the Revolution in Great Britain*. Boston, Mass.: Powars.

Priestley, Joseph, 1817–32. 'Disquisitions Relating to Matter and Spirit' (1777), in *The Theological and Miscellaneous Works of Joseph Priestly*, ed. J. T. Rutt, III. London. Printed by G. Smallfield.

Pryme, George, 1823. *An Introductory Lecture and Syllabus to a Course delivered in the University of Cambridge on the Principles of Political Economy*. Cambridge University Press.

Ray, John, 1691. *The Wisdom of God Manifested in the Works of Creation, Being the Substance of some Common Places delivered in the Chapel of Trinity-College, in Cambridge*. London: Smith.

Ricardo, David, 1810. *The High Price of Bullion, a Proof of the Depreciation of Bank Notes*. London: Murray.

  1811. *Reply to Mr Bosanquet's Practical Observations on the Report of the Bullion Committee*. London: Murray.

  1815. *An Essay on the Influence of a Low Price of Corn on the Profits of Stock...* London: Murray. Reprinted in Ricardo (1951–73, IV, 1–41).

  1817. *On the Principles of Political Economy*. London: Murray. Reprinted in Ricardo (1951–73, I).

  1951–73. *The Works and Correspondence of David Ricardo*, ed. P. Sraffa, 11 vols. Cambridge University Press.

Rousseau, J. J., 1960. *The Social Contract* (transl. G. Hopkins of *Du Contrat Social*, 1762), in Barker (1960).

Search, Edward. See Tucker, Abraham.

Senior, Nassau William, 1836. *Outline of the Science of Political Economy*. London: Clowes.

Shaftesbury, Third Earl of, 1699. *An Enquiry Concerning Virtue. In Two Discourses: viz. I. Of Virtue and the Belief of a Deity. II. Of the Obligation to Virtue...* Unauthorized edn produced by J. Toland. London: Bell.

Smith, Adam, 1910. *An Inquiry into the Nature and Causes of the Wealth of Nations* (1776), Everyman edn, 2 vols. London: Dent.

  1976. *The Theory of Moral Sentiments...* (1759) ed. D. D. Raphael and A. L. MacPhie. Oxford: Clarendon.

Smith, Gamaliel. See Bentham, Jeremy.

[Southey, Robert], 1803. 'Malthus's Essay on Population', *Annual Review* (1803), 292–301.

Spence, William, 1807. *Britain Independent of Commerce...* London: Cadell.

Stewart, Dugald, 1855. *The Collected Works of Dugald Stewart, Esq., FRSS*, ed. W. Hamilton, 11 vols. Edinburgh: Constable.

Stewart, Dugald, *Lectures in Political Economy*, in Stewart (1855), VIII and IX.

Sumner, J. B., 1802 *An Essay tending to Shew that the Prophecies, now accomplishing, are an Evidence of the Truth of the Christian Religion* (Hulsean Prize Essay, 1801). Cambridge University Press.

[Sumner, J. B.], 1814. 'On improving the condition of the poor', *Quarterly Review* (1814), 146–59.

[Sumner, J. B.], 1815. *Apostolical Preaching Considered, in an Examination of St Paul's Epistles.* London: Hatchard.

1816. *A Treatise on the Records of the Creation; with Particular Reference to the Jewish History, and the Consistency of the Principle of Population with the Wisdom and Goodness of the Deity*, 2 vols. London: Hatchard.

1824. *The Evidence of Christianity derived from its Nature and Reception.* London: Hatchard.

Thomas Aquinas, St, 1964–76. *Summa Theologiae.* Latin text and English translation (various eds. and transl.), 60 vols. London: Blackfriars.

Thornton, Henry, 1939. *An Enquiry into the Nature and Effects of the Paper Credit of Great Britain* (1802), ed. F. A. von Hayek. London: Allen and Unwin.

Tooke, Thomas, 1823. *Thoughts and Details on the High and Low Prices of the Thirty Years from 1793 to 1822*, 2 vols. London: Murray.

[Tucker, Abraham], 1763. *Freewill, Foreknowledge and Fate. A Fragment.* London: Payne.

[Tucker, Abraham], 1768. *The Light of Nature Pursued*, 2 vols. in 5. London: Payne.

Villeneuve-Bargemont, Alban de, 1834. *Economie Politique Chrétienne, ou Recherches sur la Nature et les Causes du Paupérisme, en France et en Europe, et sur les Moyens de le soulager et de le prévenir*, 3 vols. Paris: Paulin.

Wakefield, Gilbert. 1792. *Memoirs of the Life of G. W., BA, Written by Himself.* London: Hodson.

Wallace, Robert, 1761. *Various Prospects of Mankind, Nature and Providence.* Edinburgh: Millar.

Watson, Richard, 1776. *An Apology for Christianity, in a Series of Letters Addressed to Edward Gibbon, Esq....* Cambridge University Press.

1785. *A Collection of Theological Tracts*, 6 vols. Cambridge University Press.

Watson, Richard, 1818. *Anecdotes of the Life of Richard Watson, Bishop of Llandaff...Published by his son, Richard Watson, LLB, Prebendary of Llandaff and Wells.* Philadelphia: Small.

[West, Edward], 1815. *Essay on the Application of Capital to Land...by a Fellow of University College, Oxford.* London: Underwood.

[Weyland, John], 1807. *A Short Inquiry into the Policy, Humanity, and Past Effects of the Poor Laws...* London: Hatchard.

Weyland, John, 1816. *The Principles of Population and Production, as they are affected by the Progress of Society; with a View to Moral and Political Consequences.* London: Baldwin.

[Whateley, Richard], 1855. *Historic Doubts Relative to ·Napoleon Buonaparte* (1819). London: Parker.

Whately, Richard (ed.), 1821. *King on Predestination.* See King (1821).

　　1822. *The Use and Abuse of Party Feeling in Matters of Religion...* (Bampton Lectures, 1822). Oxford University Press.

　　1823. *Five Sermons on Several Occasions preached before the University of Oxford.* Oxford University Press.

　　1826a. *Elements of Logic, Comprising the Substance of the article in the Encyclopaedia Metropolitana...* London: Mawman.

[Whately, Richard], 1826b. *Letters on the Church. By An Episcopalian.* London.

　　1828a. *Elements of Rhetoric, Comprising the Substance of the Article in the Encyclopaedia Metropolitana...* London: Murray.

　　1828b. *Essays on Some of the Difficulties in the Writings of St Paul, and in other parts of the New Testament.* London: Fellowes.

[Whately, Richard], 1828c. 'Oxford lectures on political economy', *Edinburgh Review* (1828), 170–84.

[Whately, Richard], 1829. *A View of Scripture Revelations concerning a Future State: laid before his Parishioners by a Country Pastor.* London: Fellowes.

　　1831. *Introductory Lectures in Political Economy.* London: Fellowes.

　　1832. *Introductory Lectures in Political Economy,* 2nd edn, including lecture IX and other additions. London: Fellowes (Reprint, Kelly: New York, 1966).

　　(ed.), 1854. *Remains of the Late Edward Copleston, DD, Bishop of Llandaff, with an Introduction containing some Reminiscences of his Life.* London: Parker.

　　1855. *Introductory Lectures in Political Economy,* 4th edn, 'Revised and Enlarged'. London: Parker.

　　1859a. *Dr Paley's Works: a Lecture.* London: Parker.

　　(ed.), 1859b. *Paley's Moral Philosophy: with Annotations.* London: Parker.

Wilberforce, William, 1797. *A Practical View of the Prevailing Religious System of Professed Christians, in the Higher and Middle Classes of this Country, contrasted with Real Christianity.* London: Cadell.

Wollstonecraft, Mary, 1790. *A Vindication of the Rights of Men, in a Letter to the Right Honourable Edmund Burke; occasioned by his Reflections on the Revolution in France,* 2nd edn. London: Johnson.

Wordsworth, William, 1950. *Poetical Works,* ed. T. Hutchinson; new edn rev. E. de Selincourt). Oxford University Press.

　　1974. *The Prose Works of William Wordsworth* (eds. W. J. B. Owen and J. W. Smyser), 3 vols. Oxford: Clarendon.

WORKS FIRST APPEARING FROM 1860

Addinall, Peter, 1986. 'Hume's challenge and Paley's response', *Expository Times* 97:232–6.

Ajello, R., Firpo, M., Guerci, L. and Ricuperati, G. (eds.), 1985. *L'Eta dei*

Lumi: Studi Storici sul Settecento Europeo in Onore di Franco Venturi, 2 vols. Naples: Jovene.

Anderson, Gary M., 1988. 'Mr Smith and the Preachers: the economics of religion in the *Wealth of Nations*', *Journal of Political Economy* 96:1066–88.

Annan, Noel, 1984. *Leslie Stephen, the Godless Victorian*. London: Weidenfeld and Nicolson.

Bagehot, Walter, 1889. *Works*, ed. F. Morgan, 5 vols. Hartford, Conn.: Travellers Insurance Company.

Barker, Ernest (ed.), 1960. *Social Contract: Essays by Locke, Hume and Rousseau, with an Introduction by Sir Ernest Barker*. Oxford University Press.

Blaikie, W. G., 1896. *Thomas Chalmers* (Famous Scots series.) Edinburgh: Oliphant.

Blaug, Mark, 1978. *Economic Theory in Retrospect*, 3rd edn. Cambridge University Press.

Bonar, James, 1885. *Malthus and his Work*. London: Allen and Unwin.
   1894. 'Copleston', in Palgrave (1894).
   1924. *Malthus and his Work*, 2nd edn with notes and expanded biography. London: Allen and Unwin.

Bowler, P. J., 1976. 'Malthus, Darwin and the concept of struggle', *Journal of the History of Ideas* 37:631–50.

Brown, Stewart J., 1982. *Thomas Chalmers and the Godly Commonwealth in Scotland*. Oxford University Press.

Bullard, J. V. (ed.), 1934. *Constitutions and Canons Ecclesiastical 1604, Latin and English*. London: Faith.

Bullock, F. W. B., 1955. *A History of the Training for the Ministry of the Church of England and Wales from 1800 to 1874*. St Leonards-on-Sea: Budd and Gillatt.

Butler, Marilyn, 1975. *Jane Austen and the War of Ideas*. Oxford: Clarendon.

Butt, Margot, 1985. 'The Chalmers papers', in Cheyne (1985).

Cage, R. A. and Checkland, E. O. A., 1976. 'Thomas Chalmers and urban poverty: the St John's parish experiment in Glasgow, 1819–1837', *Philosophical Journal* 13:37–56.

Cairns, David, 1956. 'Thomas Chalmers' Astronomical Discourses: a study in natural theology?' *Scottish Journal of Theology* 9: 410–21.

Carter, K. C. (ed.), 1971. *Enquiry Concerning Political Justice by William Godwin, with Selections from Godwin's other Writings, Abridged and Edited*. Oxford: Clarendon.

Cassirer, Ernst von, 1955. *The Philosophy of the Enlightenment* (transl. F. C. A. Koelln and J. P. Pettegrove). Boston Mass.: Beacon.

Catholic Encyclopedia 1909. 15 vols. New York: Appleton.

Chadwick, W. O., 1966. *An Ecclesiastical History of England* (gen. ed. J. C. Dickinson), vol. VII: *The Victorian Church*, part 1. London: Black.
   1975. *The Secularization of the European Mind in the Nineteenth Century*. Cambridge University Press.
   1985. 'Chalmers and the state', in Cheyne (1985).

Checkland, S. G., 1951. 'The advent of academic economics in England', *Manchester School of Economic and Social Studies* 19:43–70.

Cheyne, A. C. (ed.), 1985. *The Practical and the Pious: Essays on Thomas Chalmers (1780–1847)* Edinburgh: St Andrew.

Christie, Ian R., 1984. *Stress and Stability in Late Eighteenth Century Britain: Reflections on the British Avoidance of Revolution* (Ford lectures, 1983–4). Oxford: Clarendon.

Claeys, Gregory, 1984. 'The effects of property on Godwin's theory of justice'. *Journal of the History of Philosophy* 22:81–101.

Clark, J. C. D., 1985. *English Society, 1688–1832: Ideology, Social Structure and Political Practice during the Ancien Régime.* Cambridge University Press.

Clarke, M. L., 1974. *Paley: Evidences for the Man.* London: SPCK.

Cochrane, R. (ed.), 1881. *Treasury of Modern Biography.* Edinburgh: Nimmo.

Cohen, Albert K., 1974. *The Elasticity of Evil: Changes in the Social Definition of Deviance.* Oxford: Blackwell.

Cone, Carl B., 1968. *The English Jacobins: Reformers in late Eighteenth-Century England.* New York: Scribner.

Corsi, Pietro, 1980. 'Natural theology, the methodology of science, and the question of species in the works of the Reverend Baden Powell'. D.Phil. thesis, Oxford.

Cowherd, Raymond G., 1977. *Political Economists and the English Poor Law.* Athens, Ohio: Ohio University Press, 1977.

Crimmins, James E., 1983. 'John Brown and the theological tradition of utilitarian ethics', *History of Political Thought* 4:523–50.

1986. 'Bentham on religion: atheism and the secular society', *Journal of the History of Ideas* 47:95–110.

1989a. 'Religion, utility and politics in the thought of Bentham and Paley', in Crimmins (1989b).

(ed.), 1989b. *Religion and the Development of Political Thought: Thomas Hobbes to J. S. Mill.* London: Routledge.

Darwin, Charles, 1958. *Autobiography: or, The Autobiography of Charles Darwin 1809–1882, with Original Omissions Restored,* ed. N. Barlow. London: Collins.

Davies, H. S. and Watson, G. (eds.), 1964. *The English Mind, Studies in the English Moralists presented to Basil Willey.* Cambridge University Press.

Deane, Phyllis, 1969. *The First Industrial Revolution.* Cambridge University Press.

Dickinson, H. T., 1977. *Liberty and Property, Political Ideology in Eighteenth Century Britain.* New York: Holmes and Meier.

Dictionary of National Biography, 1975. Compact edn, 2 vols. Oxford: Oxford University Press.

Dodds, J., 1870. *Thomas Chalmers: a Biographical Study.* Edinburgh: Oliphant.

Dunn, John, 1983. 'From applied theology to social analysis: the break between John Locke and the Scottish enlightenment', in Hont and Ignatieff (1983).

Dupâquier, J., Fauve-Chamoux, A. and Grebenik, E. (eds.), 1983. *Malthus: Past and Present*. London: Academic Press.

Durkheim, Emile, 1938. *The Rules of Sociological Method*. Chicago: University of Chicago Press.

Eatwell, J., Milgate, M. and Newman, P. (eds.) 1987. *The New Palgrave: A Dictionary of Economics*, 4 vols. London: Macmillan.

Edwards, Paul (ed.), 1967. *The Encyclopedia of Philosophy*, 8 vols. London: Collier-Macmillan.

Ehrman, John, 1983. *The Younger Pitt: The Reluctant Transition*. London: Constable.

Eltis, Walter, 1984. *The Classical Theory of Economic Growth*. New York: St Martin's.

Evans, Robert F., 1968. *Pelagius: Inquiries and Reappraisals*. London: Black.

Fitzpatrick, W. J., 1864. *Memoirs of Richard Whately, Archbishop of Dublin, with a Glance at his Contemporaries and Times*, 2 vols. London: Bentley.

Flew, Antony, 1957. 'The structure of Malthus' population theory', *Australasian Journal of Philosophy* 35: 1–20.

Flew, Antony (ed.), 1970. *Malthus, T. R., An Essay on the Principle of Population and a Summary view of the Principle of Population*. Baltimore: Penguin.

Floud, R. and McCloskey, D. (eds.), 1981. *The Economic History of Britain since 1700*, vol. 1: 1700–1860. Cambridge University Press.

Fontana, Biancamaria, 1985. *Rethinking the Politics of Commercial Society: the Edinburgh Review, 1802–1832*. Cambridge University Press.

Fraser, Donald, 1881. *Thomas Chalmers DD LLD*. London: Hodder and Stoughton.

Freeman, Michael, 1980. *Edmund Burke and the Critique of Political Radicalism*. Oxford: Blackwell.

Furgol, Mary T., 1985. 'Thomas Chalmers and poor relief: an incidental sideline?' in Cheyne (1985).

Gascoigne, John, 1984. 'Politics, patronage and Newtonianism: the Cambridge example', *Historical Journal* 27: 1–24.

1989. *Cambridge in the Age of the Enlightenment*. Cambridge University Press.

Gordon, Barry, 1976. *Political Economy in Parliament, 1819–1823*. London: Macmillan.

1979. *Economic Doctrine and Tory Liberalism, 1824–1830*. London: Macmillan.

Halévy, Elie, 1928. *The Growth of Philosophic Radicalism*, transl. M. Morris. London: Faber, 1928.

1949. *A History of the English People in the Nineteenth Century*, vol. II: *The Liberal Awakening* (transl. E. I. Watkin), 2nd edn. London, Benn.

1952. *The Growth of Philosophic Radicalism*, transl. M. Morris, new edn, reprinted with corrections. London: Faber.

Harper, J. Wilson, 1910. *The Social Ideal and Dr Chalmers' Contribution to Christian Economics* (The Chalmers Lectures, Eighth Series). Edinburgh: MacNiven and Wallace.

Hartwick, John M., 1988. 'Robert Wallace and Malthus and the ratios', *History of Political Economy* 20:357–79.

Harvey-Phillips, M. B., 1984. 'Malthus' theodicy: the intellectual background of his contribution to political economy', *History of Political Economy* 16:591–608.

Haslehurst, R. S. T. (ed. and transl.), 1927. *The Works of Fastidius*. London: Society of SS. Peter and Paul.

Heimann, P. M., 1978. 'Voluntarism and immanence: conceptions of nature in eighteenth century thought', *Journal of the History of Ideas* 39:271–84.

Hilton, Boyd, 1977. *Corn, Cash and Commerce: The Economic Policies of the Tory Governments, 1815–1830*. Oxford University Press.

1985. 'Chalmers as political economist', in Cheyne (1985).

1988. *The Age of Atonement: the Influence of Evangelicalism on Social and Economic Thought, 1785–1865*. Oxford: Clarendon.

Himmelfarb, Gertrude, 1968. *Victorian Minds*. New York: Knopf.

1984. *The Idea of Poverty: England in the Early Industrial Age*. New York: Knopf.

Hole, Robert, 1989. *Pulpits, Politics and Public Order in England, 1760–1832*. Cambridge University Press.

Hollander, J. H. (ed.), 1932. *Minor Papers on the Currency Question, 1809–1823 by David Ricardo*. Baltimore, Johns Hopkins Press.

Hollander, Samuel, 1986. 'On Malthus's population principle and social reform', *History of Political Economy* 18:187–235.

1987. *Classical Economics*. Oxford: Blackwell.

Hont, I. and Ignatieff, M. (eds.), 1983. *Wealth and Virtue: the Shaping of Political Economy in the Scottish Enlightenment*. Cambridge University Press.

Hont, I., Ignatieff, M. and Fontana, B., 1980. 'The politics of Malthus' first Essay and the Scottish tradition'. Unpublished paper delivered at Congrès Malthus, Paris, May 1980.

Horne, Thomas A., 1985. '"The poor have a claim founded in the law of nature": William Paley and the rights of the poor', *Journal of the History of Philosophy* 23:51–70.

Huntley, F. L., 1970. *Jeremy Taylor and the Great Rebellion: A Study of his Mind and Temper in Controversy*. Ann Arbor: University of Michigan Press.

Jacob, Margaret C., 1976. *The Newtonians and the English Revolution, 1689–1720*. Ithaca, N.Y.: Cornell University Press.

1981. *The Radical Enlightenment: Pantheists, Freemasons and Republicans*. London: Allen and Unwin.

James, Patricia, 1979. *Population Malthus: his Life and Times*. London: Routledge.

4

288 *Bibliography*

Kanth, R. K., 1986. *Political Economy and Laissez-Faire: Economics and Ideology in the Ricardian Era.* Totowa, N.J.: Rowman and Littlefield.

Keynes, J. M., 1936. *The General Theory of Employment, Interest and Money.* London: Macmillan.

1971–82. *The Collected Writings of John Maynard Keynes*, eds. E. Johnson and D. Moggridge, 29 vols. London: Macmillan.

1971. *A Tract on Monetary Reform*, in Keynes (1971–82, IV).

1972. *Essays in Biography*, in Keynes (1971–82, X).

Kinnaird, John, 1978. *William Hazlitt, Critic of Power.* New York: Columbia University Press.

Knight, Freda, 1971. *University Rebel: the Life of William Frend, 1757–1841.* London: Gollancz.

Kolakowski, Leszek, 1982. *Religion.* Oxford University Press.

Lakatos, Imre, 1970. 'Falsificationism and the methodology of scientific research programmes', in Lakatos and Musgrave (1970).

Lakatos, Imre and Musgrave, Alan (eds.), 1970. *Criticism and the Growth of Knowledge.* Cambridge University Press.

Le Mahieu, D. L., 1976. *The Mind of William Paley: a Philosopher of his Age.* Lincoln, Nebr.: University of Nebraska Press.

1979. 'Malthus and the theology of scarcity', *Journal of the History of Ideas* 40:467–74.

Levin, Samuel M., 1966. 'Malthus and the idea of progress', *Journal of the History of Ideas* 27:92–108.

Levy, David, 1978. 'Some normative aspects of the Malthusian controversy', *History of Political Economy* 10:271–85.

Lewis, C. S., 1969. *Selected Literary Essays*, ed. W. Hooper. Cambridge University Press.

Lincoln, Anthony, 1938. *Some Political and Social Ideas of English Dissent, 1763–1800.* Cambridge University Press.

Lloyd, Peter J., 1969. 'Elementary geometric/arithmetic series and early production theory', *Journal of Political Economy* 77:21–34.

Locke, Don, 1980. *A Fantasy of Reason: The Life and Thought of William Godwin.* London: Routledge.

Lovejoy, A. O., 1936. *The Great Chain of Being: A Study of the History of an Idea* (William James Lectures, 1933). Cambridge, Mass.: Harvard University Press.

1941. 'The meaning of romanticism in the history of ideas', *Journal of the History of Ideas* 2:257–78.

MacPherson, C. B., 1962. *The Political Theory of Possessive Individualism: Hobbes to Locke.* Oxford: Clarendon.

Marx, Karl, 1954–9. *Capital: A Critique of Political Economy*, transl. from 3rd German edn. S. Moore and E. Aveling, ed. F. Engels, 3 vols. Moscow: Progress.

McCaffrey, John F., 1981. 'Thomas Chalmers and social change', *Scottish Historical Review* 60:32–60.

1985. 'The life of Thomas Chalmers', in Cheyne (1985).

McCleary, G. F., 1953. *The Malthusian Population Theory.* London: Faber.

Mechie, Stewart, 1960. *The Church and Scottish Social Development, 1780–1870*. Oxford University Press.

Mill, J. S., 1865. *An Examination of Sir William Hamilton's Philosophy and the Philosophical Questions discussed in his Writings*. London: Longmans.

Mitchell, B. R. and Deane, Phyllis, 1962. *Abstract of British Historical Statistics*. Cambridge University Press.

Mitchell, Leslie, 1980. *Holland House*. London: Duckworth.

More, P. E. and Cross, F. L., 1935. *Anglicanism*. London: SPCK.

Morris, John, 1965. 'Pelagian literature', *Journal of Theological Studies* NS 16:26–60.

Mozley, T., 1882. *Reminiscences, Chiefly of Oriel College and the Oxford Movement*. London: Longmans.

Newman, J. H., 1950. *Apologia pro Vita Sua* (original 1864 text). New York: Modern Library.

Nisbet, J. W., 1964. 'Thomas Chalmers and the economic order', *Scottish Journal of Political Economy* 11:151–7.

Norman, E. R., 1976. *Church and Society in England, 1770–1970*. Oxford: Clarendon.

   1979. *Christianity and the World Order* (BBC Reith Lectures, 1978). Oxford University Press.

O'Brien, D. P., 1987. 'Thomas Chalmers (1780–1847)', in Eatwell, Milgate and Newman (1987, vol. 1).

O'Brien, P. K. and Engerman, S. L., 1981. 'Changes in income and its distribution during the industrial revolution', in Floud and McCloskey (1981).

Oliphant, Margaret, 1893. *Thomas Chalmers, Preacher, Philosopher and Statesman*. London: Methuen.

Palgrave, R. H. I. (ed.), 1894. *Dictionary of Political Economy*. London: Macmillan.

Patinkin, D., 1956. *Money, Interest and Prices: An Integration of Monetary and Value Theory*. Evanston, Ill.: Row, Peterson.

Pears, D. F. (ed.), 1966. *David Hume: a Symposium*. London: Macmillan.

Petersen, William, 1979. *Malthus*. Cambridge, Mass.: Harvard University Press.

Pocock, J. G. A., 1985a. *Virtue, Commerce and History: Essays in Political Thought and History, chiefly in the Eighteenth Century*. Cambridge University Press.

   1985b. 'Clergy and commerce. The conservative enlightenment in England', in Ajello *et al.* (1985, vol. 1).

Pollard, A. and Hennell, M., 1959. *Charles Simeon, 1759–1836*. London: SPCK.

Powell, Enoch, 1977. *Wrestling with the Angel*. London: Sheldon.

Preston, R. H., 1979. *Religion and the Persistence of Capitalism*. London: SCM.

Prior, Mary, 1967. 'Whately, Richard (1787–1863)', in Edwards (1967, vol. VIII).

Pryme, George, 1870. *Autobiographical Recollection of George Pryme, Esq., MA, edited by his Daughter*. Cambridge: Deighton and Bell.

Pullen, J. M., 1981. 'Malthus' theological ideas and their influence on his principle of population', *History of Political Economy* 13:39–54.

   1986. 'Correspondence between Malthus and his parents', *History of Political Economy* 18:133–54.

   1987. 'Some new information on the Rev. T. R. Malthus', *History of Political Economy* 19:127–40.

Quasten, Johannes, 1950–60. *Patrology*, 3 vols. Utrecht: Spectrum.

Rashid, Salim, 1977. 'Richard Whately and christian political economy at Oxford and Dublin', *Journal of the History of Ideas* 38:147–55.

Rice, Daniel F., 1971. 'Natural theology and the Scottish philosophy in the thought of Thomas Chalmers', *Scottish Journal of Theology* 24:23–46.

   1979. 'An attempt at systematic reconstruction in the theology of Thomas Chalmers', *Church History* 48;174–88.

Ring, Sr Mary Ignatius, SND, 1935. *Villeneuve-Bargemont: Precursor of Modern Social Catholicism, 1784–1850*. Milwaukee: Bruce.

Robbins, Caroline, 1961. *The Eighteenth Century Commonwealthman. Studies in the Transmission, Development and Circumstances of English Liberal Thought from the Restoration of Charles II until the War with the Thirteen Colonies*. Cambridge, Mass.: Harvard University Press.

Rose, M. E., 1981. 'Social change in the industrial revolution', in Floud and McCloskey (1981).

Russell, Bertrand, 1945. *A History of Western Philosophy*. New York: Simon and Schuster.

Samuelson, P. A., 1958. *Economics: an Introductory Analysis*, 4th edn. New York: McGraw-Hill.

   1978. 'The canonical classical model of political economy', *Journal of Economic Literature* 16:1415–34.

Sanders, Lloyd, 1908. *The Holland House Circle*. London: Methuen.

Santurri, E. N., 1982. 'Theodicy and social policy in Malthus' thought'. *Journal of the History of Ideas* 43:315–20.

Schofield, Thomas Philip, 1986. 'Conservative political thought in Britain in response to the French revolution', *Historical Journal* 29:601–22.

Schumpeter, Joseph, A., 1954. *History of Economic Analysis*. London: Allen and Unwin.

Sefton, Henry R., 1985. 'Chalmers and the church: theology and missions', in Cheyne (1985).

Shelton, George, 1981. *Dean Tucker and Eighteenth-Century Economic and Political Thought*. London: Macmillan.

Skinner, Quentin, 1969. 'Meaning and understanding in the history of ideas', *History and Theory* 8:3–33.

Smith, Kenneth, 1951. *The Malthusian Controversy*. London: Routledge.

Soloway, R. A., 1969. *Prelates and People: Ecclesiastical Social Thought in England, 1783–1852*. London: Routledge.

Stanley, A. P., 1881. *The Life and Correspondence of Thomas Arnold, DD*, 12th edn, 2 vols. London: Murray.

Stephen, Leslie, 1876. *History of English Thought in the Eighteenth Century*, 2 vols. London: Smith, Elder. 2nd edn, 1881.

Stigler, George, 1952. 'The Ricardian theory of value and distribution', *Journal of Political Economy* 60: 187–207.

Sutherland, L. S. and Mitchell, L. G. (eds.), 1986. *The History of Oxford University*, vol. v. *The Eighteenth Century*. Oxford: Clarendon.

Sykes, Norman, 1934. *Church and State in England in the XVIIIth Century*. Cambridge University Press.

Tasker, R. V. G. (ed.), 1945. *Saint Augustine, The City of God. John Healey's Translation, with a Selection from Vives' Commentaries*, 2 vols. London: Dent.

Tawney, R. H., 1947. *Religion and the Rise of Capitalism: a Historical Study*. New York: Mentor.

Taylor, Stephen, 1988. 'Church and Society after the Glorious Revolution', *Historical Journal* 31: 973–87.

Temple, William, 1976. *Christianity and Social Order*. London: SPCK.

The Malthus Library Catalogue. The Personal Collection of Thomas Robert Malthus at Jesus College, Cambridge. New York: Pergamon, 1983.

Thatcher, Margaret, 1978. '"I believe": a speech on Christianity and politics at St Lawrence Jewry, next Guildhall, London, Thursday 30 March, 1978'. Conservative Central Office Press Release 442/78, London.

Thomas, Wilson, 1979. *The Philosophic Radicals: Nine Studies in Theory and Practice, 1817–1841*. Oxford: Clarendon.

Thompson, E. P., 1968. *The Making of the English Working Class*. London: Pelican.

Trevelyan, G. M., 1929. *Lord Grey of the Reform Bill: the Life of Charles, second Earl Grey*, 2nd edn. London: Longmans.

Troeltsch, Ernst, 1931. *The Social Teaching of the Christian Churches*, transl. O. Wyon, 2 vols. London: Allen and Unwin.

Tuckwell, W., 1909. *Pre-Tractarian Oxford: A Reminiscence of the Oriel 'Noetics'*. London: Smith, Elder.

Tunzelmann, G. N. von, 1981. 'Technical progress during the industrial revolution', in Floud and McCloskey (1981).

Venn, John and J. A., 1922–54. *Alumni Cantabrigiensis: a Biographical List of all known Students, Graduates and Holders of Office at the University of Cambridge, from the Earliest Times to 1900*, 10 vols. Cambridge University Press.

Viner, Jacob, 1972. *The Role of Providence in the Social Order: An Essay in Intellectual History* (Jayne Lectures, 1966). Philadelphia: American Philosophical Society.

   1978. *Religious Thought and Economic Society: Four Chapters of an Unfinished Work*, ed. J. Melitz and D. N. Winch. Durham, N.C.: Duke University Press.

Voges, Friedhelm, 1985. 'Chalmers' thinking habits: some lessons from his theology', in Cheyne (1985).

Walker, N. M. L., 1880. *Thomas Chalmers, his Life and its Lessons*. London: Nelson.

Waterman, A. M. C., 1983a. 'The ideological alliance of political economy

and christian theology, 1798–1833', *Journal of Ecclesiastical History*
34:231–44.

1983b. 'Malthus as a theologian: the "First Essay" and the relation
between political economy and christian theology', in Dupâquier,
Fauve-Chamoux and Grebenik (1983).

1987. 'On the Malthusian theory of long swings', *Canadian Journal of
Economics* 20:257–70.

1988. 'Hume, Malthus and the stability of equilibrium', *History of
Political Economy* 20:85–94.

1991a. 'A Cambridge *via media* in late Georgian Anglicanism', *Journal of
Ecclesiastical History* 42 (forthcoming).

1991b. 'The "canonical classical model" in 1808 as viewed from 1825:
Thomas Chalmers on the national resources', *History of Political
Economy* 23 (forthcoming).

Watson, George, 1964. 'Joseph Butler' in Davies and Watson (1964).

Watson, J. S., 1960. *The Oxford History of England*, vol. XII: *The Reign of
George III, 1760–1815*. Oxford: Clarendon.

Watt, Hugh, 1943a. *The Published Writings of Dr Thomas Chalmers
(1780–1847). A Descriptive List.* Privately printed.

1943b. *Thomas Chalmers and the Disruption.* Edinburgh: Nelson.

Whately, E. Jane, 1875. *Life and Correspondence of Richard Whately, DD, late
Archbishop of Dublin*, new edn. London: Longmans.

Willey, Basil, 1940. *The Eighteenth Century Background: Studies on the Idea of
Nature in the Thought of the Period*. London: Chatto and Windus.

Williams, B. A. O., 1966. 'Hume on religion', in Pears (1966).

Williams, N. P., 1927. *The Idea of the Fall and of Original Sin* (Bampton
Lectures, 1924). London: Longmans.

Winstanley, D. A. 1935. *Unreformed Cambridge: A Study of Certain Aspects of
its Development in the Eighteenth Century*. Cambridge University Press.

Wood, Grace Chalmers (ed.), 1912. *The Opinions of Dr Chalmers concerning
Political Economy and Social Reform, compiled from his Writings by Miss Grace
Chalmers Wood*. Edinburgh: Douglas.

Young, Robert M., 1969. 'Malthus and the Evolutionists: the common
context of biological and social theory', *Past and Present* 43:109–41.

Index

Aberdeen, George Hamilton-Gordon, 4th
    Earl of, 218
Addinall, Peter, 123, 283
Ajello, R., 283
Alexander the Great, 30
Ambrose of Milan, St, 118
Amiens, Peace of, 160
Analytical Review, 17, 19, 26, 111
ancien régime, 134, 257
    British, 4, 6, 10, 216, 255, 261
    church establishment in Britain, 217,
        222, 255
    European, 4, 9, 10, 11
    unity of church and state in, 9, 196, 258
Anderson, Gary M., 232, 284
animals
    predacity of, 135
    suffering of, 125
Annan, Noel, 119, 284
Annual Review, 135, 146
Anti-Jacobin Review, 18–20, 26, 45, 53, 111,
    114, 117, 255
anti-Jacobin theory, 5, 6, 7, 26, 56, 57, 121,
    139–43, 145, 150, 171
    Malthusian, 16, 37–57, 98–101, 139–44
Anti-Jacobin Weekly, 25
Aristotle, 62
Arminius, Jacobus, 157
Arnold, Thomas, 183, 184
Athenaeum, 251
Athanasius, St, 62
    Creed of, 111
atonement, doctrine of, 124–5, 125, 159,
    167
    Adam Smith on, 159
    Chalmers on, 241
Augustine of Canterbury, St, throne of,
    152
Augustine of Hippo, St, 58, 63, 65, 76, 95,
    126
    Civitate Dei, 76, 79–80, 275

doctrine of the Fall, 65–6, 99, 105, 134
political theory, 76–7, 118
state as *remedium peccatorum*, 76–7
on war and peace, 79–80
Austen, Jane
    the age of, 61
    Persuasion, 61
    Pride and Prejudice, 173
    Whately's review of, 205

Bacon, Sir Francis, 1st Viscount St Albans,
    92
Bagehot, Walter, 7, 140, 284
Balguy, Thomas, 127, 166
    Divine Benevolence Asserted (1781), 126, 275
Bank of England, 178
    inconvertible paper currency of, 178,
        185; as cause of inflation, 187
Baring, Francis Thornhill, Baron
    Northbrook, 181
Barker, Sir Ernest, 281, 284
Barrow, Isaac, 90
Barruel, Augustin de, 19
Beadon, Richard, 116
    Master of Jesus College, 83, 116
Beauchamp, Phillip, *see* Bentham, Jeremy
Beaufort, Charles Noel Somerset, 4th Duke
    of, 181
Beccaria, Cesare Bonesana, Marchese di,
    35, 200
Bedford, John Russell, 6th Duke of, 19
Beeke, Henry, 191, 204
    Observations on the Income Tax (1789), 184,
        275
benevolence, concept of, 29, 32, 34, 35, 40,
    41, 42, 56, 133, 142, 162, 215, 221
Benson, George, 90
    On the Man of Sin, 93
Bentham, Jeremy, 10, 57, 60, 196, 199,
    202, 214
    Fragment on Government (1776), 115

encourages Buonaparte to invade Britain, 20

Rights of Man (1791, 1792), 22, 23, 129, 280

Age of Reason (1795), 20, 25

Paley, 'school of', 133, 183

Paley, William, Archdeacon (later Chancellor) of Carlisle, 2, 11, 24, 61, 63, 67, 76, 81, 88, 89, 93, 99, 108, 112, 145, 147, 151, 153, 155, 156, 157, 160, 165, 166, 167, 190, 191, 192, 205, 213, 214, 216, 217, 247

Christian Political Economy, contribution to, 133–5

influence upon Malthus, 119–23, 144–50

life and work, 114–35, 218

parable of the pigeons, 117, 118, 155

his political economy, 117, 120–1, 135

his theology, 119, 123–33

Moral and Political Philosophy (1785), 113, 117, 118, 119, 120, 121, 122, 123, 128, 135, 156, 183

Evidences (1794), 70, 119, 123, 156, 161, 183

Reasons for Contentment (1794), 129, 145, 163

Horae Paulinae (1795), 119, 123, 156, 183

Sermons, 156, 280

Natural Theology (1802), 12, 70, 113, 122–3, 123, 125, 126–33, 134, 135, 147, 151, 156, 160, 172, 183, 194, 206, 212, 250

Palgrave, R. H. I., 289

Pascal, Blaise, 65

passion(s), concept of, 32, 145, 147–8, 148 'passion between the sexes', 38, 43, 55, 141, 148, 164, 165

restraint of passions, socially necessary, 145, 147, 163, 229, 230, 235

passive obedience, doctrine of, 197

paternalism, moral, 222, 234

Patinkin, Don, 192, 289

Paul, St, 65, 149

Pauline theology, 65, 131

pauperism, 186, 230

Chalmers on, 224

Pearce, Zachary, British of Rochester, *Sermons*, 90

Pears, D. F., 289

Pearson, John, Bishop of Chester, 90

Peel, Sir Robert, 6, 177, 181, 203, 218, 255, 256, 257

'Peterloo', massacre of, 177

Petersen, William, 82, 289

Petty, Sir William, 38

Political Arithmetick (1676–90), 12

Pitt, William (the younger), 21, 25, 61, 112, 122, 184

Place, Francis, 202

Plato, *Republic*, 38, 281

Playfair, John, 181

Plotinus, 62

Pocock, J. G. A., 5, 33, 75, 115, 289

polemic, concept of, 8

as competitive sport, 8

defined, 8

ideological, 8, 9

political arithmetick, 263

political economists, intellectual sovereignty of, 210

political economy, 3, 4, 5, 6, 10, 58, 183, 196, 197, 198, 203; autonomous with respect to theology, 11, 207–8, 244, 259–60; 'canonical classical model of', 6, 12, 226, 245, 259; *économie politique chrétienne*, 12; French 'Catholic' school of, 12–14, 242; 'French OEconomists' ('Physiocrats'), 199, 225, 226; as 'hostile to religion', 10, 200, 203, 206, 207, 208; and ideology in the 1820s, 196–204, 261; Malthusian, 222, 223, 235, 244; Ricardian, 199, 202, 210

classical, 6, 11, 12, 17, 18, 135, 168, 263; capital, concept of, 169; division of labour, 165, 226; 'free-rider' problem in Malthus, 142, 143; 'surplus', concept of, 42, 47, 49, 52, 53, 137, 168, 170, 225–6, 227, 230, 259, 268, 269, 269–70; wage theory, 52, 54, 230, 233, 239, 268, 269–71

see also Christian Political Economy; economic analysis; inflation; international trade; rent; wage labour

Political Economy Club, 154, 200

Pollard, A., 154, 289

Poor Law Commissioners, Minority Report for Scotland (1910), 220

Poor Laws, English, 57, 108, 122, 143, 144, 171, 185, 186, 187, 188, 215, 230, 235, 240, 247, 254

Copleston on, 186–90

'create the poor they maintain', 122, 143, 169

Malthus on, 108, 122, 143–4, 190

Sumner on, 158, 179

Poor Laws, Irish, 231

Poor Rate, English, 178–9, 190, 230

poor, the

have no rights as a class, 193, 247

improvement of, 190, 222, 233, 234, 272

target real wage, 141, 169, 190, 233, 235

DATE DUE

MAY 1 8 2005			